BEYOND THE
BIG BANG

BEYOND THE BIG BANG

Quantum Cosmologies and God

Willem B. Drees

OPEN ❀ COURT

La Salle, Illinois

OPEN COURT and the above logo are registered in the
U.S. Patent and Trademark Office.

© 1990 by Open Court Publishing Company

First printing 1990

Printed and bound in the United States of America.

Library of Congress Cataloging-in-Publication Data

Drees, Willem B., 1954-
    Beyond the big bang : quantum cosmologies and God / Willem B.
Drees.
        p.   cm.
    Originally presented as the author's thesis (doctoral—University
of Groningen).
    Includes bibliographical references and index.
    ISBN 0-8126-9117-2. — ISBN 0-8126-9118-0 (pbk.)
    1. Creation. 2. Cosmogony. 3. Cosmology. 4. Quantum theory.
5. Religion and science—1946- I. Title.
BS651.D74 1990
231.7'65—dc20   90-38498
                                                              CIP

To my father
WILLEM DREES
and to the memory of my mother
ANNA ERICA DREES-GESCHER

CONTENTS

PREFACE

Is it possible to take religion seriously in an age of science? I intend to do so, especially by affirming humbly that "we are given to understand little and only within a conceptual model accessible solely to our culture" (Heller 1986b, 36). Many popular books on the Universe combine science with opinions on religious issues. This book criticizes religious abuse of science; it also criticizes the simple dismissal of religious questions, as if science would unambiguously supply all the answers. I hope to convey something of the meaningfulness and fun of religious and philosophical questions.

This study continues discussions exemplified by the European conferences on Science and Religion (Andersen and Peacocke 1987; Fennema and Paul 1990), some exchanges in the United States (for example, in *Zygon*), and at the Vatican (Russell, Stoeger, and Coyne 1988). But I consider some of the assumptions underlying many of these contributions dubious. Authors as different as Pannenberg, Torrance, and Peacocke, including many in the New Age movement, seem to argue for methodological parallels between science and theology or to look for harmony between theology and the results of science. Examples of such a descriptive consonance, for example between the Big Bang as a beginning and *creatio ex nihilo*, I find inadequate. More importantly, the assumption of harmony might easily lead to a theology which neglects the critical distance between theology and science.

I therefore develop an outline of a theology which takes science seriously, but does not restrict itself to the quest for a fit with the results of science. I hold that an adequate theology should deal with experiences of imperfection and injustice, and hence has to maintain a 'prophetic' dimension, a judgment of disparity between the way things are and the way they should be. This brings me closer to the dominant position among Protestant theologians on the European continent. In accepting a distance from realism in theology I side with those who defend the impossibility of a doctrine of God based upon natural knowledge. The emphasis on the critical distance is intended to avoid the conservative implications of a natural theology which takes the actual state of affairs as normative. However, theologies which retreat to a separate domain are in danger of becoming unintelligible and irrelevant. I seek a theological position in critical coherence with science.

The book is aimed at theologians and scientists, as well as others with sufficient endurance and interest. No knowledge of theology or theories about the Universe is assumed, nor any mathematical skills. Numbers have been written occasionally as powers of ten; these numbers can be regarded as 'very large' (or, if the exponent—the superscript—is negative, 'very small'). A 'billion' is used, according to American custom, to mean one thousand million.

Many persons contributed to the ideas presented here. The notes and references show some of my debts. A few deserve more credit than thereby provided.

Rob Hensen contributed much to the development from an incoherent collection of commonsense comments to a theological position. He combines an extremely rich and diverse knowledge with persistent questioning, always allowing for a grain of truth in the opposite position. Any remaining immaturity is entirely my own.

The astronomer Hugo van Woerden contributed significantly to the readability of the book, as well as to the careful treatment of the science involved. Working with him gave me a glimpse of the potential personal importance of such studies for religiously interested scientists.

The philosopher of religion H. G. Hubbeling provided, by the broad scope of his interest, the environment in which I dared to embark on studies in science and religion. His death in October 1986 took away a mentor whose comments would have enhanced the clarity and cogency of this study. I also extend my thanks to colleagues and staff of the Department of Theology at the University of Groningen.

Robert J. Russell, the founder and director of The Center for Theology and the Natural Sciences (Graduate Theological Union, Berkeley) asked many penetrating questions during the fall of 1987. It was very encouraging to discover that he, with his sharp mind and detailed knowledge of physics, was working along so many similar lines. Conversations and classes with Ted Peters and Nancey Murphy have provided valuable additional stimuli. Phil Hefner of the Chicago Center for Religion and Science (Lutheran School of Theology at Chicago) offered hospitality and raised thought-provoking questions about the theological core of my writing during the winter and spring of 1988. My gratitude also extends to many other contacts in the Chicago area, especially to those who participated in the LSTC course which I used as a 'try out' for my ideas.

Encouraging letters from the cosmologists Don Page and, especially, Chris Isham, and conversations and correspondence with Frank Tipler, have contributed significantly to my understanding of the science involved. Any remaining errors are entirely mine. I also want to thank the cosmologist and priest Michael Heller for his supportive interest and for the example set by his treatment of theology and cosmology (especially his *The World and the Word,* 1986).

The Dutch working group on theology and science, Atomium, provided a valuable forum in which I could present subsequent stages of the project. Especially memorable is the way Henk Plomp supported my work by linking it to the freedom one could imagine Adam to have possessed, in conferring names upon things.

The investigations were financially supported by the Foundation for Research in the field of Theology and the Science of Religions in the Netherlands (STEGON), which is subsidized by the Netherlands Organization for the Advancement of Research (NWO). A Fulbright grant and additional support from a number of Dutch foundations (de Haak Bastiaanse Kuneman Stichting, het Hendrik Muller's Vaderlandsch Fonds, de Groningse Vereniging van Vrijzinnig Hervormden, het Genootschap Noorthey, het Fonds 'Aanpakken', het Groninger Universiteits Fonds) made it possible for me to spend a year in Berkeley and Chicago.

Finally, I am grateful for the way Open Court Publishing Company, and especially its editor David Ramsay Steele, have taken care of the book.

The book is dedicated to my father and the memory of my mother. My father instilled in me the desire for rational argument and for knowledge, as well as the desire for a better world. To my mother I owe my 'will to believe'. The present book may well be understood as an attempt to integrate both influences.

INTRODUCTION

0.1. RELIGIOUS QUESTIONS AND SCIENTIFIC ANSWERS

> It may seem bizarre, but in my opinion science offers a surer path to God than religion. (Paul Davies 1983a, ix)

> I can live with doubt and uncertainty. . . . I don't feel frightened by not knowing things, by being lost in a mysterious universe without any purpose, which is the way it really is, so far as I can tell. (Richard Feynman 1981, quoted in Pagels 1985a, 368f)

Humans usually prefer certainty, and demand it from preachers, doctors, and scientists. Science as "a surer path to God" suggests that perhaps science gives answers which should be used for the purification of religious views.

But science is not only a body of answers, given in textbooks. Science is also an activity, a way of persistent questioning, doing research. Its answers are revisable, not final. Seen this way, science seems to support a more open and playful attitude, in combination with an awareness of uncertainties and ambiguities. We will find reasons in the course of this book to come back to the nature of the certainties and uncertainties we are dealing with. But we will start with the answers which science apparently offers, and see whether they suppport theology or rule it out.

Many popular books on science relate the results of science to religious ideas. The astronomer Robert Jastrow ends his book *God and the Astronomers* on this confident note:

> For the scientist who has lived by his faith in the power of reason, the story ends like a bad dream. He has scaled the mountains of ignorance; he is about to conquer the highest peak; as he pulls himself over the final rock, he is greeted by a band of theologians who have been sitting there for centuries. (Jastrow 1980, 125)

By contrast Carl Sagan concludes his introduction to a book by the cosmologist Stephen Hawking with:

> Hawking is attempting, as he explicitly states, to understand the mind of God. And this makes all the more unexpected the conclusion of the effort, at least so far: a universe with no edge in space, no beginning or end in time, and nothing for a Creator to do. (Sagan 1988, x)

Jastrow understands the Big Bang theory as describing a radical beginning, an edge best understood by involving the idea of a creator. Sagan argues that more recent developments have done away with that edge and thereby have made a creator superfluous. The first part of this book will pursue such issues further. It deals mainly with topics which have been used in arguments for or against the existence of God: an absolute beginning, the contingency of the Universe, and the claim that science might offer a complete explanation.

An even stronger claim has been made by John Gribbin. He interprets Hawking's cosmological ideas, first proposed at a conference at the Vatican, to imply an end to metaphysics.

> As of the Vatican conference of 1981, it is the metaphysicians who are out of a job. Everything else skrinks into insignificance alongside such a claim, and the end of the road for metaphysics certainly seems a good place to end this book. (Gribbin 1986, 392)

Gribbin's 'end of the road' might also be a good place to *start* another book—the present work. A confrontation of theological and scientific ideas needs a mediation between the categories specific to theology and those specific to science. What else is such a mediation but metaphysics? Metaphysical issues will be pointed out within research at the frontiers of cosmology. Such elements are, of course, present in theology as well. The second half of this book will develop a proposal for a theological position which takes scientific cosmology seriously.

Identifications (like Jastrow's), contrasts (like Sagan's and Gribbin's), or other implications of recent cosmology for theology and metaphysics can be found in abundance, especially on the last pages of popularizations of science. Such statements are not as sophisticated as the science that has been drawn upon in the preceding pages. These glib statements express much too simple views of how science and theology interact. They are unsatisfactory for all the fields involved: philosophy, theology, and science. Such statements are often philosophically naive, as they neglect the methodological problems arising in the transfer of ideas from one more or less coherent system of language and thought to another. Theology and metaphysics are misunderstood as pre-scientific answers to questions now better answered by science—and therefore to be abandoned. This view of theology as an unsuccessful attempt at explanation is, however, not in line with theology's present-day conception of its own task. For example, 'creation' is in most theological systems not a term referring simply to an event in the beginning. The Big Bang theory is an excellent scientific theory within its proper domain. However, the apparent 't = 0' moment is not part of that domain. The Big Bang theory is not science's definitive answer. There is a variety of recent developments with wider explanatory scope, the quantum cosmologies. This variety is partly due to different metaphysical assumptions—different views of the world and of the nature of knowledge. Issues that seemed settled with the Big Bang theory, for instance that the Universe had a 't = 0' moment a finite time ago, turn out to be disputed again in contemporary research.

In short: in order to improve the level of intellectual discussion a more critical reflection on possible relations between cosmological and theological thinking is required.

There is also an anthropological reason for a study like the one presented here. Many humans, at least in the European cultural traditions, have a thirst for understanding and integration of the diverse aspects of knowledge and life. Such an integration implies that one considers the relations between different aspects (such as science, morality, esthetic judgements, religious beliefs); that one intends to provide grounds for one's fundamental assumptions and principles; and that one aims at a coherent and consistent presentation of one's beliefs. The second implication, providing grounds as far as possible, assumes the possibility of argument across the boundaries of specific moral and religious views, and hence a meta-level of honest intellectual discourse.[1] An integration is not only intellectually satisfactory and, perhaps, desirable. Integration might also affect one's values and actions. And the need for integration might well arise out of the actual lives we live, to clarify our present situation and to guide our present actions.

The next section (0.2) presents an outline of the approach followed in this study. It introduces the distinction between two theoretical models of belief systems, which is important for the relation between the first and second parts of this book. The section also includes provisional definitions of major terms and observations on approaches which I have decided not to follow. The third section (0.3) previews the book chapter by chapter.

0.2   APPROACH: DEFINITIONS AND DECISIONS

John Gribbin suggests that the end of metaphysics has arrived (see 0.1). I do not assume a single well-developed metaphysical scheme, like that which process theologians have adopted from the philosopher Alfred North Whitehead. Rather, the presence of metaphysical issues, ideas about 'the way the world is', is shown in the description of specific scientific research programs and assumed principles. These metaphysical elements are necessary, if considered from within a specific approach. They become visible through a comparison of different positions, and have to prove their viability in such a competition.

Within religious traditions humans have stories and myths which shape and articulate their lives. However, religious views are no longer elaborate systems of myths with which one can argue, 'mythologies'. Rather, there are at a more conceptual level systems of beliefs, open to more or less strict argument. Such beliefs relate to ideas about 'the way the world is'. Metaphysical elements mediate between the myths and the ontological and referential claims involved in the belief systems.

It may be useful to give provisional definitions of some major terms.

Metaphysics is used for the discourse which relates specific categories of different disciplines, and hence a discourse which is necessary to any integration of and mediation between theology and science. *Ontology* is the term used for the most fundamental ideas about 'the way the world is'. However, often ontological notions will be included under 'metaphysics'. Any specific ontology or metaphysics is related to other fields, especially to scientific and religious beliefs. They are not beyond dispute, nor unchanging, nor given, but are aspects of one's whole system of thought which may change as other aspects change. Awareness of the problematic nature of many underlying assumptions, for example about the nature of time, intelligibility, and facts, implies that one works with tentative proposals.

Cosmology is one of those words with a variety of meanings, ranging from a comprehensive metaphysical system to a branch of astrophysics. The latter usage is followed in this study. *Astrophysical cosmology* is the study of the Universe (capitalized as a name) including ideas about 'the Very Early Universe', even its 'beginning', and about its far future. 'Cosmology' in this work is restricted to cosmology as developed after the achievement of broad consensus on the Big Bang theory due to the discovery of the cosmic background radiation in 1965. A major part of this study focusses on even more recent developments which go beyond the Big Bang theory.

Theology is used for systematic reflection on Christian faith; theologies are more or less coherent collections of ideas about what the nature and content of the Christian faith is or should be. This work confines itself to Western Christian theology and its critics.[2] 'God' is used with two fundamental connotations: perfection (in justice, and so on) and being beyond our grasp, elusive.

Two different theoretical models of belief systems will be used in this study. To characterize them briefly, they differ as to whether God is thought of, primarily, as present in or as absent from the world. Does the world show some of God's perfection, the goodness of God's creative work, or should one rather emphasize the world's imperfection, and hence God's absence or the world's fall away from God, correlated with a cry for God to become present? The possibility of absence expresses in 'person' language the unattainability of God. Such a notion of absence assumes, of course, the possibility of presence, and is therefore something quite different from an atheistic denial of the existence of God or of the meaningfulness of the notion 'God'. Both models can be found, with many nuances, of course, in the Christian tradition.

First, belief could be understood as, primarily, being about God's presence. The ontology could include, aside from ordinary reality, a hidden 'dimension' of reality or a separate spiritual or even divine realm. God's presence implies an ontological harmony and unity between these realms. In that case, theology becomes primarily metaphysical reflection upon the nature of this dual reality and the relations between the two realms. The assumption of harmony gives an *a priori* reason, theologically, to expect *consonance* between our theological thinking on the God-world relation and our scientific knowledge about that world. In this context, apologetic studies relating science and theology try to make credible the existence of such a God, or such a hidden realm of reality. Consonance is expected to be there, descriptively.

In the first part of this study many aspects of possible arguments for such consonance, or even for the existence of God, will be discussed. My conclusion will be that this project fails. Scientific cosmology does not support belief in God, though it does not exclude it either (3.6, 6.1.1).

The absence of descriptive consonance might be understood as a reflection of the limitations of our knowledge. To make again the point about metaphysical assumptions involved in many branches of thinking, the quest for descriptive consonance is closely connected to a realistic-referential view of knowledge. The position defended here will be that knowledge is a product, a construction made by humans—with their conceptual apparatus, in their mathematical and natural languages—in their encounter with reality. Hence, any consonance is also a construction and not a discovery of a pre-established harmony found in reality. One can construct notions of God which are consonant with the different cosmologies. The meanings of theological notions become related to a scientific view of the Universe. A more explicit theological conclusion will also be drawn. The expectation of consonance as a feature present in reality was based upon the assumption of God's presence in this world, 'God showing through'. If consonance is not found one might question that presence.

A second type of belief emphasizes the apparent absence of God as an interpretation of experiences with unjust suffering and other forms of evil, finitude, and imperfection. Theology reflects primarily upon (in)justice in this world, upon values, upon activities against injustice, and upon ways to live with failures and losses. The confrontation with the natural sciences seems less relevant for such theology, with its human-centered, and perhaps even political, emphasis. However, such theologies too assume metaphysical views. The duality of the previous type might return as the locus of justice and perfection, for instance in a heavenly or future Kingdom.

I assume that the task of theology is primarily of this second type, facing irrationality and injustice as apparently suggesting the absence of God. Any metaphysical scheme, perhaps with a 'hidden realm', should be evaluated by the way it allows articulation of the concern for justice and love, evocation in the face of injustice, and consolation in the face of losses. My preference for such an understanding of the task of theology will become more explicit in the second part of this study.

If evil is really evil and injustice in this world is not illusory, any proposal for meaning is just that: a proposal, an orientation intended to guide action towards a better world, 'dreaming of peace'. The constructive nature of theology is not only a limitation of our knowledge; it reflects the nature of the theological enterprise.

The constructive quest for consonance between our knowledge of the world through the natural sciences and an adequate theology suggests, as a label for the method of this study, *constructive consonance*. Assuming consonance between a theological idea and a scientific theory implies that we search for a suitable interpretation of the concepts involved. This probably implies that we place both in a (not necessarily complete) metaphysical perspective. By doing so the terms at all three levels—theology, metaphysics, and science— might change meaning.

What exactly gives way and what remains unchanged depends on the relative importance of the elements and their reliability. In general, scientific knowledge is considered to be the most reliable. However, sometimes science itself allows for different interpretations—as in contemporary quantum theories. And science is changing. At the frontier, where science is dealing with unsolved problems, there is a variety of avenues to pursue—as we will see for the case of quantum cosmology. In such cases a metaphysics informed by a religious perspective might determine the criteria for theory development and appraisal. There is a similarity between my 'constructive consonance' and an interanimation theory of metaphors (Soskice 1985), and even more with an understanding of scientific and religious research as a metaphoric process (Gerhart and Russell 1984). Interesting metaphors are not merely substitutions of one term for another, nor direct comparisons. Constructing consonance is neither a substitution of scientific terms for theological ones nor a direct comparison. It changes the interpretations of the concepts used. It implies that one constructs a new understanding of reality (see Chapter 5).

A brief aside on 'natural theology' seems useful here. Natural theology has been rejected, or at least considered with mistrust, by many in twentieth-century European Protestantism. However, 'natural' should not be misunderstood as referring merely to nature. Natural theology refers to efforts to construct a theology on the basis of reason and experience without appeal to faith or special revelation, and stands therefore in constrast with theology based on God's self-revelation in history.[3]

The second model described above, that of a theology which considers imperfection and injustice as signals of God's absence, might be able to incorporate two of the legitimate epistemological and political concerns of the 'anti-natural theology' approaches. The methodological impossibility of a doctrine of God based upon natural knowledge parallels my criticism of cosmological arguments for the existence of God (3.6, 6.1.1). The chapter on eschatology (4) and the resulting doctrine of God (6.2) are explicitly intended to avoid the conservative implications of a natural theology which suggests too much perfection in the actual state of affairs and thereby comes close to an identification of the *status quo* with the way the world should be. The method proposed (5) leaves room for a theological understanding built upon the particular experiences related to Israel and Jesus. As the terms have been defined by Hendry (1980, 14), this study results in a theology of nature, 'a knowledge of nature in the light of God', rather than in a natural theology, 'a knowledge of God in the light of nature'. However, the distinction is not as absolute as has been suggested. An interesting theology of nature might function as a way to the underlying theological perspective for someone who recognizes the description of nature as credible. And a theology of nature which opens itself to non-theological knowledge runs the (positive) risk of changes in its theology.

This work is minimalistic with respect to the Biblical tradition. It does not defend a Biblical worldview or engage in a discussion on the meaningfulness of such a notion. Nor do I draw on the richness of the Biblical and theological traditions. I argue here only for the meaningfulness of a few central notions, without developing these notions in an elaborate theological system.

This book is also minimalistic on the metaphysical side. A more elaborate theology requires a more extensive metaphysical scheme, for instance that of Thomism, Whiteheadian process thought, or the 'axiological cosmology' proposed by Robert Neville. In this work I do not presuppose a specific developed metaphysics. Instead, I introduce metaphysical notions whenever they appear to be useful. As for the theology, I argue for the meaningfulness of certain metaphysical problems without offering a detailed or comprehensive system.

The text is also very restricted in its use of the theological and philosophical literature. Ideas of other authors are discussed only insofar as they seem relevant to the argument developed here, and not according to their function and meaning within the philosophical or theological conceptions of their authors.

My approach in this work is 'from below'. There is no specific source of information about God. Theological concepts are, as far as I was aware of them, explicitly introduced as assumptions. These notions do come out of a tradition, but in this study their origin—

in Scripture, revelation, or whatever—is not used as an argument. That limits what can be said, but, hopefully, makes the argument more interesting in a culture with religious and non-religious diversity. I aim to construct a position which is adequate with respect both to the theological assumptions and to the natural sciences.

My aim here is not to prove the truth of a specific theological view on the basis of the truth of scientific findings. But my aim is apologetic in a weaker sense. I want to show the possibility of theological and metaphysical language as language which remains meaningful if cosmology is taken seriously. Theology need not be discarded as a pre-scientific attempt at explanation which has lost out to science, nor does theology need to retreat completely to an existential realm apparently beyond the reach of science. Rather, theology can take up the language of science to express and develop the meaning of theological concepts. This helps communication about those concepts with people who feel at home in the scientific language. But it is not only a matter of language, of semantics. As one can speak of 'guilt by association', there is also something like 'truth by association'. If ideas about God can be successfully embedded in a network of concepts, the ideas about God receive some credibility from the overall credibility of the network. If we can incorporate the best of contemporary cosmology, and thus much of physics and astronomy, the whole network then deserves to be taken seriously—if the network is also internally coherent. This justification of credibility by coherence is also present in theoretical science, and certainly in cosmology. It does not justify a strong claim on truth as correspondence between concepts and reality, at least not for those elements at a distance from the most empirical elements, but it suggests that through those concepts we might be in touch with something 'out there'.

0.3 PREVIEW

The first part of this book deals with arguments which relate to God's presence in the world, as they may be based upon cosmology, especially in relation to the apparent 'beginning' of the Universe and to its contingency. Arguments against such an understanding of the world, and hence against a God thus understood, are included as well. The second part develops a different view of the task of theology (in the chapter on eschatology). This results in a proposal for a method in relating theology to science and a tentative understanding of God.

Outline of Part I

In Chapter 1 I critically discuss some suggested relations between theology and the Big Bang theory. The chapter begins with a very brief sketch of this theory. Some have used it as support for Christianity, others as grounds for rejecting Christianity. Some reject the theory because it conflicts with their understanding of Christianity. Yet others argue for a separation, while some defend a position close to my own: 'consonance'. I argue that there are at least three *inadequate* ways of relating the Big Bang theory to Christianity: through cosmological arguments for the existence of God; by claiming parallels with the Biblical creation stories; and by claiming parallels with the doctrine of *creatio ex nihilo*.

Many interesting issues are just beyond the scope of the Big Bang theory. My subsequent chapters deal with some recent developments, the so-called quantum cosmologies.

Chapter 2 gives a brief presentation of the limits of the Big Bang theory and of developments beyond that theory, outlining different assumptions and worldviews behind three examples of current research. Andrej Linde's cosmology is eternal and chaotic. Stephen Hawking's cosmology is without edges, but in a sense also timeless. Roger Penrose's cosmology is realistic about both time and time-asymmetry, emphasizing the specialness of the beginning. The variety of approaches in scientific research is related to the influence of metaphysical convictions within that research. This raises methodological issues for dialogues between theology and science. I discuss the issue of the 'beginning' with special reference to Hawking's cosmology, a cosmology which does not fit with a deistic notion of God. But one might understand God as sustaining the world at every moment. Any transcendence beyond the Universe must be understood as related to all moments, and not as especially related to an initial moment.

In Chapter 3, I scrutinize the 'anthropic principles', which relate the existence and features of the Universe to our own existene. They have been used in arguments both for and against the existence of God. However, these principles are not results from science, unlike the coincidences on which they are based. Rather, they are metaphysical ideas expressed in scientific language. Contingency and necessity are both outside the realm of science. Cosmology, therefore, does not support a design argument for the existence of God.

It has been claimed that recent developments in quantum cosmology open the possibility of a complete explanation of the Universe. I argue that the completeness and unity are partly due to a process of abstraction from the diversity of particulars. The issue of unified and complete explanations touches on the traditional tension between the One and the Many. Trinity (unity and diversity in God), christology (a particular person of universal significance), and creation (unity in God, diversity in the world) are different ways of dealing with this tension in theology.

The contingency of existence — why is there anything at all? — is not threatened by science, irrespective of the level of completeness of its theories. Hence, one can interpret the Universe as the free gift of an ontologically transcendent Creator, or as something that just happens to be. Because all cosmological theories are conceptually bounded one can also think of transcendence with respect to a conceptual space. Such an epistemological understanding of transcendence implies also a scientific agnosticism with respect to that transcendence.

Chapter 3 concludes with a section which recapitulates the results of these three chapters in relation to arguments for the existence of God. The more general argument about the intelligibility of the Universe is considered as well. All arguments are found wanting, though they suggest ways of formulating aspects of one's understanding of God.

Outline of Part II and Appendixes

In Chapter 4 eschatology is understood as reflecting the interest in perfection and justice as the overcoming of, or coping with, finiteness and evil. Perfection may be located in another place, like Heaven, or another time, say a future Kingdom. That raises the questions about the relation between that other place and time and cosmological ideas about the far future. Cosmology seems in the long run pessimistic, predicting either freezing in an ever-expanding universe or frying in a Big Crunch. A few, recently the scientists Freeman Dyson and Frank Tipler, have presented more optimistic visions, relating them to ideas about an evolving God. I present a view of eschatology which has no need for the speculative visions of Dyson and Tipler, because it emphasizes the present instead of the future. In this context, two ways of describing systems in physical terms are presented. Quite apart from the description of systems as evolving in time, it is possible to use whole histories as the basic entities. There is a view from within time as well as a view *sub specie aeternitatis*.

In Chapter 5 I consider some recent discussions about methodological issues related to theology and science. One approach emphasizes that both science and theology aim at depicting realities, although they do so only approximately and tentatively. This 'critical realism' corresponds to an understanding of the world as showing God's perfection shining through. Others emphasize the interpretative process in science and theology. Both approaches, especially the 'critical realistic' one, are primarily arguments for the rationality, or at least respectability, of theology, by pointing out its similarities with science. They apparently accept implicitly that science provides the norm for theology. A more continental-European type of theology, with an emphasis on the distinctiveness of theology, is also considered. Its underlining of the difference between theology and science is important. However, even though arguments for a similarity between theology and science become superfluous, the need persists for mutual consistency between the results of science and the existential and metaphysical claims of theology. Constructive consonance takes up elements of the different approaches described, but is presented as a model for adequately relating the contents of theology and science.

In Chapter 6 I argue that there is no cognitive need for the hypothesis 'God' in the light of the sciences, although they allow the possibility of such a hypothesis. Some deny the reality of injustice by reference to the existence of perfection in the world or in a more or less accessible hidden world. Others accept imperfection, or chaos, or pointlessness. If one rejects such options, the conjecture of perfection, the God hypothesis, arises as a regulative transcendental idea out of the apparent absence of God.

The meaning of 'God' is formulated by recapitulating themes from the previous chapters: God as Creator at all moments, the tension between emphasis on unity and the diversity of particulars, the relation between eternity and present, and the realm of possibilities present in each moment.

The final section returns from the theological discussion to the world, especially by contrasting the theological position developed here with the way the Integrity of Creation theme has been developed in some recent documents of the World Council of Churches.

The appendixes give additional information about cosmology, creation stories, and the history of the doctrine of *creatio ex nihilo*. However, the main text should be readable without the appendixes, and also without prior specialized knowledge of either cosmology or theology.

More references to the literature have been included than necessary for the argument and credit to others. Hopefully, these references in the text and notes will help to make the full range of opinions on these issues more widely known.

PART ONE

A Common Quest for Understanding?*

*This title is an allusion to *Physics, Philosophy, and Theology: a Common Quest for Understanding*, edited by R. J. Russell, W. R. Stoeger, and G. V. Coyne (1988), the fruit of a very interesting conference at the Vatican.

THEOLOGY AND THE BIG BANG THEORY

1.1. INTRODUCTION

The standard Big Bang theory represents the scientific consensus since the mid-1960s. It describes the Universe as if it began a finite time ago. The theory is a combination of general relativity (a well-confirmed theory about gravity, space and time) and particle physics as tested on Earth. It explains observed features of the Universe such as the isotropic background radiation, the relative abundances of helium and other light elements, and the velocities of galaxies. These velocities are best interpreted as correlates of a continuous increase in the average distance between cosmological objects, the expansion of the Universe.

The Big Bang model for the Universe has an edge in the past, an initial moment of infinite density and temperature, which is called 'the Singularity'. However, the standard theory is only valid after the temperature and density have dropped sufficiently, less than a second after the Singularity. It would be appropriate to call this moment, slightly later than the Singularity, 'the Big Bang'. But the term is also used for the Singularity and even for the first few hundred thousand years (Pagels 1985a, 256). It is important for the arguments in this study to emphasize the distinction between: 1. the beginning of the domain where the theory can be trusted, and 2. the extrapolated 't = 0' moment. The Big Bang theory, and scientific cosmology in general, is a theory about the subsequent evolution of the Universe rather than about its origination—the topic which has been picked up in many philosophical and religious responses. The 'instant of creation' has however increasingly become an object of scientific speculation in more recent developments, as discussed in Chapter 2.

The Big Bang theory assumes initial conditions, like that of similarity in different directions. This isotropy is amazing since there cannot have been any causal contact between such regions of the Universe, at least according to the standard Big Bang theory.

More information on the astronomical Universe and the Big Bang theory is supplied in Appendix 1. For this chapter it is enough for the reader to know: 1. the basic idea of a universe expanding from a hot and dense initial state, and 2. the distinction between the apparent 'beginning of the Universe' and the beginning of the domain of the Big Bang model.

There have been widely different theological responses to the Big Bang theory. It has been hailed as support for the Christian idea of creation. But it has also been rejected, either because it conflicts with the idea of a creation a few thousand years ago, or because it looks too much like a creation. Others have defended a mutual neutrality, which has been developed by some writers in terms of consonance. The next section discusses a few of these diverse views.

More specifically, three kinds of arguments have been employed to make the Big Bang theory favor theology: 1. the theory provides the material premiss for a cosmological argument for the existence of a Creator; 2. there are parallels with Biblical creation stories; and 3. there are parallels with the doctrine of *creatio ex nihilo*.

These claims will be examined and rejected in the remaining sections of this chapter.

1.2. A VARIETY OF OPINIONS ON BIG BANG AND CREATION

1.2.1. *Big Bang Supports the Idea of Creation*

The singularity of the universe is a gigantic springboard which can propel upward anyone ready to exploit its metaphysical resilience and catch thereby a glimpse of the absolute. (Jaki 1978, 278)

As we have seen, the astronomer Jastrow describes the scientific discoveries which led to the Big Bang theory as climbing the same peak as theology, the theologians having reached the summit first. A major question is, of course, whether scientists and theologians are climbing the same peak.

The priest and historian of science Stanley Jaki similarly defends a positive relation between the findings of contemporary science and a Christian concept of God. Apart from occasionally incorrect and unfair polemics against others,[1] Jaki appeals to the limits of scientific explanation as far as the beginning and the contingency of the Universe are concerned, and to the role of time in contemporary cosmology.

1. Cosmology always raises further questions, "showing thereby the built-in inadequacy of scientific answers" (Jaki 1978, 277). The Universe is *contingent:* it could have been different. Its contingency "is intimated in the scientific portrayal of the specificity of the universe. A universe which is contingent is the very opposite of cosmic necessitarianism, the age-old refuge of materialists, pantheists and atheists" (Jaki 1982, 258). All specific entities— specificity being a sign of limitation—find their explanation in the Creator, who is the totality of perfections (Jaki 1978, 273). Without this metaphysical assumption, scientists cannot give a final explanation, but commit "the fallacy of infinite regress".

2. Scientific cosmology never excludes hypothetical previous stages, but it shows that the "universe carries on itself the stamp of time" (Jaki 1982, 260). And creation in time is "the theme or dogma which supports all other Christian themes and dogmas" (Jaki 1982, 259).

Jaki clearly uses cosmology to argue for the existence of God. I return to many of these issues later. My conclusion will be that this way of presenting the case for God does not work. Cosmology is more ambivalent about the beginning, contingency, and time than Jaki claims. Jaki uses God where the scientific explanation stumbles upon something apparently unexplainable. As such it is a kind of 'God of the gaps' approach, introducing God at the boundary formed by our present scientific ignorance. This is both vulnerable to future developments and an unsatisfactory view of God. It easily leads to 'deism': God made the firecracker and lit the fuse, but is irrelevant to the present processes within it. In 1.2.5 we will see that the 'consonance' school aims at the opposite: connecting our religious and our scientific understandings of the world.

Others point to similarities between the picture presented by science and that offered by religion.[2] One peculiar example: Astronomy and geology confirm, according to Peter Stoner, all the verses of Genesis 1. The second verse, about the Earth being without form and void and about the darkness upon the face of the deep, "refers to a dark nebula", which is the origin of our solar system. "The second verse now becomes very remarkable. How did Moses know that a dark nebula existed thousands of years before science discovered the first one? And how did he know that the earth came from one?" (Stoner 1958, 141). Similar parallels are described for the other verses, proving the authenticity of the Scripture as coming from God, for Moses or any other mere man could not have gotten the details correct.

1.2.2. *The Big Bang Theory is Wrong: Recent Creation*

There is a branch of Christianity which defends the literal truth of the Bible, and hence a creation a few thousand years ago. Because not all who believe in creation believe in such a recent creation, I refer to those who defend such a recent creation as 'creationists' (in quotation marks).

Either God or Evolution

According to 'creationists', one must believe either in God or in evolution and the Big Bang theory, or, as Duane Gish puts it, "In the Beginning, God"—or ". . . , Hydrogen" (Gish 1982). This is a consequence of the way evolution is defined as a process of self-transformation (Slusher 1977, 41), "without the intervention of any outside agency" (Gish 1982, 28).

In my opinion, defining evolution as mechanistic self-causation excluding external intervention makes the either/or dichotomy trivial, unless one takes God to be completely inside the world. Others interpret the evolutionary process in a different way, not excluding an intimate relatedness with God. One example: Howard Van Till (1986a) interprets natural laws as descriptions of the behavior of natural entities, not as prescriptions or ultimate causes. The laws reflect the orderly and coherent character of God's governing. There are many other religious ways of understanding the origin of the world aside from sudden creation, for example as a struggle between chaos and order, or emerging by birth (Long 1963 and 1987; Sproul 1979).

The 'either God or evolution' position assumes that they are conflicting answers to the same question. Other theists defend some separation, like "categorical complementarity" (Van Till 1986a): evolution and creation are answers to different questions. A trivial example: an answer to a question about the shape of an object never conflicts with an answer to a question about its color; such questions deal with different aspects.

God as Creator of a Developed Universe

According to 'creationists' a Christian believing in creation must accept that some apparently preceding state is not real, but "the fantasy of false (because atheistic) method" (Cameron 1983, 93). Identifying the creation with the Big Bang is methodologically the same as drawing the line at any other moment. It is easily possible to assume that God created an apparently 'developed' universe.[3]

I think that belief in God as deserving worship is inconsistent with the idea that God fools us by creating a 'developed' universe which is deliberately faked to appear older than it really is. However, if one sees God as the great magician, without qualifying this with such moral categories as trustworthiness, the position that God created an apparently old universe is irrefutable. But it has its price: light from beyond a few thousand light years—a limit well within our Galaxy—is not produced by its apparent sources, stars and galaxies, but was created 'on its way'. Most apparent objects within, and all beyond, our Galaxy would be mere illusions caused by God. "The idea raises the question . . . whether scientific research is a worthwhile occupation, if it is reduced to revealing the extent of a deception that has been practised upon us" (Batten 1984, 35).

Whether 'creationists' are satisfied by the argument that they are free to draw the line somewhere might be doubted, if judged by their strenuous efforts to show that the evidence we have points to a young Universe.

The Second Law: Creation and Fall

'Creationists' often state that the Second Law of Thermodynamics (see Appendix 2) implies a beginning in a very ordered state and subsequent drift towards less order. This would concur with 'creation and fall'. Evolution, growth of ever more complex systems, is the opposite. Therefore, according to 'creationists', evolution is in deep trouble.

Their use of the Second Law in this cosmological context is wrong. The expansion which is part of the standard Big Bang model implies the disequilibrium which is needed to explain the formation of structure in the Universe (for example Frautschi 1982). For chemical and biological evolution, the work of Prigogine and others on systems far from equilibrium provides a scientifically sound harmony between evolution and thermodynamics. Penrose's proposal for gravitational entropy would also solve this apparent contradiction between evolution and thermodynamics.

Arguments for a Young Universe

Besides believing in a supernatural origin, which could be reconciled with the Big Bang theory, 'creationists' have a strong interest in a literal interpretation of the Bible. Therefore, the age of the Universe must be a few thousand years. Arguments are based on apparent difficulties within the standard theory.[4] A good account of discussions about the age of the Universe and the Earth by an evangelical Christian has been given by D. A. Young (1982, also Brugger 1982). Although 'creationists' claim to be scientific, even more scientific than their opponents, the arguments for a recent creation (a few thousand years) are based on distortions of scientific facts and theories. They use details to question models, but neglect the overall coherence of the models. Falsification of some details of the models is not enough to discard the line of thought behind them. A few problems in combination with many confirming experiences is a challenge, not a refutation.

Many books on 'creationism' have been written in the last few years.[5] To them I leave the debate on the scientific, antiscientific, or extrascientific value of 'creationism'. 'Creationism' is not just a continuation of religion from a pre-scientific age. Rather, as forcefully argued by Langdon Gilkey (1985), it appears as an offspring of our scientific culture. In a trial on equal time for 'creation science' in science classes, scientists appeared as witnesses on both sides. The issue is not only the facts, although 'creationists' do object to these as well, but also the nature of science and of religion. 'Creationists' do not seem to be motivated by a serious analysis and criticism of scientific ideas about the world, but by the fear that one loses God and morality if one does not hold to the literal truth of the Bible: "there is no God, no one to whom they are responsible" (Gish 1982, 29).

1.2.3. *No Big Bang, because of its Theistic Implications*

Some scientists advocate alternatives to the Big Bang theory, because to them it looks too much like creation. Hannes Alfvén and Fred Hoyle are major representatives of this view.[6]

'Beginning' is Metaphysics, Not Science

The abrupt beginning in the Big Bang theory is a repugnant metaphysical idea and an intrusion of religion into science. According to Alfvén a scientific theory must not contain any elements of metaphysics or mythology. An attempted picture of the universe should embrace a logical synthesis of the observations, with all guesswork left out. . . . This 'watchdog' duty is no less imperative today, especially since our contemporary myths like to garb themselves in scientific dress in pretense of great respectability. (Alfvén 1966, 3)

The Big Bang theory is, according to Alfvén, unscientific in this sense since it presupposes a divine creation. He thinks that this was very attractive to Abbé Lemaitre, the Belgian astronomer and priest who was one of the original proponents of the model "because it gave a justification to the creation *ex nihilo,* which St Thomas had helped establish as a credo" (Alfvén 1977, 7).

This statement about Lemaitre's motive is historically false. He was very unhappy with the way Pope Pius XII, in 1951, used the Big Bang theory as a physical proof of creation (McMullin 1981, 53; Deprit 1984, 387; Godart and Heller 1985; Kragh 1987).

Hoyle too accuses proponents of the Big Bang theory of hidden theological motives. "Unlike the modern school of cosmologists, who in conformity with Judaeo-Christian theologians believe the whole universe to have been created out of nothing, my beliefs accord with those of Democritus who remarked that 'Nothing is created out of nothing' " (Hoyle 1982, 2f).

The Lack of Scientific Success of the Big Bang Theory

The Big Bang theory has not been successful, according to Hoyle and Alfvén. The Big Bang theory does not account for the elements heavier than helium. The theory was wrong in predictions of the density of the Universe (only 1% of the observed density). Predictions for the temperature of the cosmic background radiation were "minimally wrong by about 1,000 percent and maximally wrong by about 100,000 percent" (Hoyle 1982, 8). The model can only be saved by *ad hoc* hypotheses, similar to the way in which the Ptolemaic system was saved by adding more and more epicycles (Alfvén 1977, 10).

In my judgement these objections are not well-founded. An explanation of all the elements having originated in the early Universe has been tried, but as early as the 1950s the heavier elements were supposed to have been produced during stellar evolution. And that was part of the standard model in 1973, when Alfvén's article (1977) was presented at a conference. The standard model does not predict a density of the Universe, but takes that density as one of its data to decide in what type of Universe we happen to live. The first prediction, in 1948, of a temperature was a bit too high (5K instead of 3K, Alpher, Herman 1948). Generally this is seen as a good prediction, given the limitations of the data available. Hoyle's "1,000 to 100,000 percent" seems strange, since he has just stated that 5K was predicted and 3K (actually 2.7) is measured. However, the figures are consistent; it is purely a matter of presentation.[7]

So much on some scientists who hold that the Big Bang model is a religious intrusion into the domain of science. Their alternatives have not been successful, but their questions remain interesting. The arguments are not as bad, scientifically, as the arguments used by the 'creationists', but they have a similar flavor: scratching together what seems to confirm a preconceived opinion and throwing doubt on the current alternative. Modification of theories is common in science. Alfvén and Hoyle are expressing their own convictions, while objecting to metaphysics in science. Hoyle uses religious terms to describe his "Greek attitude" to a universe which carries "its own divinity". As so often, as also among Christians, the appeal to an old and respectable tradition ascribes to the tradition a unity and similarity to the position being defended which do not stand up to historical research. But the weakness of the appeal does not diminish the worth of Hoyle's metaphysical position as an alternative to Christian positions.

1.2.4. *The Big Bang Theory is Religiously Neutral*

There are different arguments for the religious neutrality of the Big Bang cosmology.

The 'Beginning' Might Have Been an Infinite Time Ago

The Singularity might have been an infinite 'time' ago if a different definition of time is used. As the physicist Charles Misner argued, defining time on the basis of clocks does not work for the very beginning, for there is no single clock imaginable which would work all the way back to the moment of infinite density and temperature. "One should ignore as a mathematical abstraction the finite sum of the proper-time series for the age of the universe, if it can be proved that there must be an infinite number of discrete acts played out during its past history" (Misner et al. 1973, 814). Thus, "the usual statement, that the Universe is ten or twenty billion years old, is not accurate for philosophical or theological discussions" (Misner 1977, 92), although there is a technical sense in which the statement is correct. His comments are part of a wider expectation: "that as we understand better and better the very early Universe, we may learn that complexities are to be found at every smaller and smaller level in the remote past", so "infinite regress should be part of our picture of the cosmological singularity" (Misner 1977, 91).

'Beginning' is Theory-Dependent

Milton Munitz defends the view that "science is grounded in the Principle of Sufficient Reason and, therefore, always leaves open the possibility of finding the explanation of *any* event. To say there is some unique event, marking the beginning of the universe for which no explanation *can* be given, is to say something contrary to the method of science" (Munitz 1974, 139). 'The origin of the Universe' is in cosmology an expression for the conceptual limit of a certain theory, and not a description of a state of affairs (Munitz 1981, 171f.).

Ideas and Existence

"God blessed one formula in some creative act" (Misner 1977, 96). Even if we would have a complete theory, we would not be able to bring into existence other universes. "Saying that God created the Universe does not explain either God or the Universe, but it keeps our consciousness alive to mysteries of awesome majesty that we might otherwise ignore" (Misner 1977, 96). I will return to this 'mystery of existence' (3.4.3).

'How' and 'Why', Facts and Symbols

The 'how' of creation might be seen as open to scientific investigation, while the 'who' and 'why' remain invisible behind the actual process used (Berry 1983, 48; Gingerich 1983, 129). Similar distinctions are those between prediction and control as the domain of science and between values and meaning as the domain of religion (Hesse 1975; Küng 1978), or more generally, between the nature of science and the nature of religion. Langdon Gilkey distinguishes between the factual meaning of Genesis as a proto-scientific account and its religious meanings. The religious meanings of the symbol of creation, like God's sovereignty and the goodness and dependency of creation, are persistent throughout the tradition, even though thought of in different ways (Gilkey 1959; 1985, 224–231). Religious symbols are not scientific facts or explanations; rather, they "interpret, illumine, and clarify the basic nature of our human existence and history" (Gilkey 1979, 8).

According to John Hick any scientific theory without reference to God "is compatible with the belief that God has deliberately created a universe in which he is not compulsorily evident but can be known only by a free personal response of faith" (Hick 1968, 96). As has been argued by many (for instance Mascall 1956, 161f; Brown 1987, 46), both the Big Bang theory and the Steady State theory can be interpreted in terms of the world's utter dependence upon God, though they can be interpreted atheistically as well. "If the scientific picture should change in the future (as it most certainly will) each new version will be equally amenable to a religious interpretation" (Hick 1989, 86), but also to an atheistic interpretation. The Universe is, upon such a view, religiously ambivalent.

A separation which links theology to metaphysics has been proposed by the Catholic theologian Karl Rahner. The sciences investigate a *posteriori* the plurality of individual phenomena. Theology poses the *a priori* question about the whole of reality and its ground. Theology faces the enormous question of whether one can conceive of such a fundamental unity beyond the plurality, and the related question whether humans, as part of the plurality, can have a real relation with that unity (Rawer and Rahner 1981, 39).[8] The sciences, based upon individual phenomena, are in principle unable to incorporate the unity of the whole; they are and should be methodologically atheistic.

As Pope John Paul II (1982, 48), implicitly following Galilei,[9] stated, the Bible "ne veut pas enseigner comment a été fait le ciel, mais comment on va au ciel"; it is not about the making of the physical heavens, but about the proper way to heaven. And: given "the time and person with whom God was communicating, the account of creation had to be simple, much simpler than the actual process God chose" (Berry 1983, 54f).

1.2.5. *Consonance*

An interesting modification of the 'neutrality' position has been formulated by the philosopher Ernan McMullin. He does not believe in 'support' from the Christian doctrine of creation for the Big Bang model, or the other way round. But the Christian "*must* strive to make his theology and his [scientific] cosmology consonant in the contributions they make to this world-view" (McMullin 1981, 52). This consonance is "in constant slight shift".

Ian Barbour, professor of physics and of religion, seems to be searching for a similar combination of independence and harmony with a rejection of a commitment to certain scientific theories. He is cautious about relating the 't = 0' to God. It would seem too much like a God of the gaps: bringing God in to explain gaps in the scientific account of the day. Besides, the Big Bang scenario might be embedded in a theory of an oscillating universe, which perhaps could have an infinite past. Both a beginning of time and an infinite span of time are unimaginable, unlike our experience, and start from an unexplained Universe. The choice of theories is to be made on scientific grounds. The difference between them "is only of secondary importance religiously" (Barbour 1989). However, that is not the end of his discussion. Cosmological models have relevance for theological models of creation—for instance, for our understanding of contingency.

The theologian Ted Peters calls his methodology "hypothetical consonance between theology and the sciences". Their separation was useful to avoid conflicts, but "we must now ask for more than simple avoidance of cognitive dissonance. I believe we should seek for cognitive consonance" (T. Peters 1988, 275.) Fruitful results of a conversation between scientists and theologians are hoped for, even expected, because both groups are seeking to understand the same reality. This is an explicitly methodological commitment—keep looking—based on the realism of future scientific and theological descriptions. It allows for dissonances at any moment. Peters wants to avoid a premature "single worldview".

Looking for consonance, he discerns it between the doctrine of *creatio ex nihilo* and the Big Bang theory. Drawing upon ideas about evolution in the Universe, "we may speak intelligibly of *both* a beginning creation and a continuing creation" (T. Peters 1988, 284). In an earlier article Peters endorses a policy of caution with respect to correlations between the Big Bang theory and the doctrine of *creatio ex nihilo*, because the first might represent a methodological frontier and not the ontological affirmation made by Christian theology. "This is just a caution, however; it is not a hands-off policy. Theology may begin with an experience with the Beyond, but it does not end there. It seeks to explicate this experience in terms of the scientific knowledge available" (T. Peters 1984, 388). Thus:

> The awareness of the Beyond is a matter of faith. Thinking about the Beyond is an intellectual activity, the structure of which we share with all other thinking activities. The Christian doctrine of creation, as we have it, then, is the product of both revelation and reason, of both faith and science. It is the result of *evangelical explication.* (Peters 1984, 390)

Robert Russell, physicist and theologian, adds to "the gleaming goal of consonance" the "dusty reality of dissonance" (Russell 1989). An example is his analysis of "finitude" as a form of contingency. Aside from the 't = 0' issue of a finite past, Russell's approach incorporates finiteness with respect to the future and in spatial dimensions. His conclusion is that finitude in all respects holds for only one out of seven models.[10] According to Russell, "the particular elements of contingency in a given cosmological model both interpret and limit the theological claim that creation is contingent" (Russell 1989). He considers this beneficial. The presence of an 'is not' component in a religious metaphor provides the distinction between our knowledge of God and God. Otherwise, our idea of God would replace God.

I feel uneasy about the need for dissonance to avoid idolatry. Wouldn't we be happy with complete consonance between our scientific and theological descriptions, while still acknowledging that neither description (nor both together) completely covered God's being and activities? Is this beneficial role of dissonance not dependent upon a realistic understanding of scientific and theological knowledge, and thereby upon a correspondence view of truth? His other thesis, that the particular aspects of contingency in a specific theory interpret a theological claim, seems to keep more distance from such realism about science and theology.

The search for 'consonance' is based on assumptions about the nature of science and religion in their relation to the world. The hypotheses involved might be formulated as follows:

1. Science and religion make, independently, statements about the same world.

2. Some aspects of the world, like its order, its dynamic character, and its origin or ground, are subject to both scientific and theological description.

3. Correct descriptions must fit together without contradictions.

A major advantage of 'consonance' over the position advocated by Jaki and others is that 'consonance' does not relate the religious to the *ignorance* of science but to its successes. The 'creationists' and Hoyle and Alfvén might be understood to share the three hypotheses. The first group rejects consonance with the Big Bang, since it does not fit their religious view. And in that case, they hold that science is the one to give way. For Hoyle and Alfvén, it is fundamentally the same: science has to change because the Big Bang meshes too easily with a religious view which they reject.

'Consonance' suggests a pre-established harmony. An outsider listens to two independent contributions, and recognizes consonance or its absence. Belief in the independence of theology and science is combined with the conviction that both result in similar descriptions of the same reality. 'Realism' in science and in theology is much disputed. I want to keep some distance from such a realistic interpretation of consonance, which might be labelled 'descriptive consonance'. Consonance is not something found by an objective outsider. Rather, consonance is an assumption in the construction of a worldview in which theology and science come together. This notion of *constructive consonance,* and its relation to 'realism', will be further developed in 5.5.

1.3.   COSMOLOGICAL ARGUMENTS FOR THE EXISTENCE OF GOD

An issue in philosophy of religion, related to cosmology, is the philosophical cosmological argument. (I drop the 'philosophical' for brevity.) Though there are many cosmological arguments, I employ the singular here because they all present the existence of the world as the basic fact which is in need of explanation and which cannot find its explanation within itself. In the following the focus is on connections with science. I will look at two modern versions of the argument, one by Craig, referring to a beginning in time, the other by Swinburne, based on contingency.

1.3.1. *The Argument from a Beginning in Time*

The argument has a simple logical structure of two premises and a conclusion, at least in Craig's version (1979, 63):

1. Everything that begins to exist has a cause of its existence.
2. The universe began to exist.
3. Therefore the universe has a cause of its existence.

The *first premiss*

is so intuitively obvious that no one in his right mind *really* believes it to be false. . . . Indeed the idea that anything, especially the whole universe, could pop into existence uncaused is so repugnant that

> most thinkers intuitively recognise that the universe's beginning to
> exist entirely uncaused out of nothing is incapable of sincere af-
> firmation. (Craig 1979, 141)

This premiss—nothing from nothing, everything has a cause—is a
metaphysical assumption. Hoyle employed it against the Big Bang
model with a finite past; others such as Craig use it to argue for the
existence of something 'beyond' the Universe. I shall concentrate on
the use of science as support for this premiss.

'Nothing from nothing', understood as the requirement of previous material, appears similar to science's conservation laws. So this
rule seems supported by the scientific evidence for the conservation
of energy, momentum, charge, and the like. However, as we will see
in more detail in the next chapter, those conservation laws believed
to be valid for the Universe as a whole conserve a total quantity
which is zero, as holds for the total charge. Other conservation laws,
like, perhaps, conservation of mass and energy, are not applicable
to the Universe as a whole and don't call for a zero total. As far as
the scientific conservation laws are concerned, the Universe might
indeed come from a 'nothing'. If one objects to this on the basis of
ex nihilo nihil fit, one is using a metaphysical principle, something
like 'conservation of actuality', which is not equivalent with or justified by the scientific conservation laws.

'Nothing from nothing' as a requirement of a preceding cause
also seems similar to the *methodological* principle of sufficient reason:
one should always seek reasons. Science "could not abandon the
presupposition that reasons can be given for the properties or pat-
terns things are found to have, without surrendering its very character as a continuing and endless quest for such reasons, and for
continually better ways of expressing these reasons" (Munitz 1974,
105). However, as emphasized by Munitz, this methodological rule
should be distinguished from the *metaphysical* principle of sufficient
reason, which states that there must be such reasons, whether we
can find them or not. This latter principle is outside science, although
it is supported by those instances where, in searching for reasons,
science has been successful. Quantum theory might be interpreted
as a case where the metaphysical principle is not valid. The evolution
according to the Schrödinger equation is determinate, but the 'reduction' to one of the possible states appears to be indeterminate,
unpredictable, and 'without cause'.

The *second premiss* has been defended on philosophical grounds,
especially by an argument for the impossibility of the existence of

an actual infinite set. Although I have doubts about this reasoning, I leave that aside to focus on the appeals which have been made to natural science.[11] Craig claims empirical confirmation for this premiss. The empirical confirmation is there to convince people who "distrust metaphysical arguments" (Craig 1979, 110).

Craig makes two claims: 1. that the Big Bang theory shows that there was a 'beginning' (The Steady State theory is observationally ruled out, while the oscillating model is incorrect since our Universe is ever-expanding); 2. that the entropy (disorder) of the Universe is increasing, because "by definition the universe is a closed system, since it is all there is" (Craig 1979, 131). An eternal universe would have reached its state of maximal entropy and be in total equilibrium. Thus it follows that our Universe must have had a beginning. The idea, originally due to Boltzmann, that a universe at low entropy might be a gigantic fluctuation in a universe in equilibrium, is rejected since the fluctuation would have to be so big, and hence so improbable, as to be ruled out.

Quantum effects are completely absent in these two empirical arguments for the second premiss, a serious omission since they bear on entropy, on the possibility of an oscillating universe, and on a 'universe arising from nothing'.

Although there were in 1979 almost no results in quantum cosmology, there was consensus among cosmologists that a complete theory needed a quantum theory of gravity. A philosopher could (and should) have known that there was a limit to the validity of the standard Big Bang theory. The consensus, which perhaps existed a decade ago, about the Universe having had an absolute beginning some ten to twenty billion years ago, has disappeared. In current cosmological research (see the next chapter) there are several different approaches to the period before the standard model, and these different approaches have different implications for the cosmological argument. Some are eternal, without a 'beginning', others have an uncaused 'appearance out of nothing'—which challenges the first premiss. I will argue that some scientists claim too much. The 'nothing' is like a physical vacuum, existing, not a philosophical nothing. But still, to reach Craig's conclusion, one needs to explain why only those programs which work with a 'beginning' are correct science. As things stand today there is no such criterion for what counts as good science—at least not one used by the scientific community in selecting articles for inclusion in their journals.

I also have doubts about Craig's use of thermodynamics. There are three meanings of 'open' involved here: 1. 'open' as forever expanding with diminishing density (In this sense, the Universe might be open according to Big Bang cosmology); 2. 'open' as having interaction with an environment; 3. 'open' as regarding the applicability of the Second Law of Thermodynamics. Craig and others mix these meanings by saying that the Universe is by definition closed (having no environment, referring to 2.), so the Second Law is applicable (referring to 3.). However, that is not correct for an expanding Universe. Entropy "is carried away into the expanding space" by the background radiation. The expansion works as if there is an environment, although there is none.[12] Meanings 2. and 3. are equivalent if the notion 'environment' is unproblematic, but not for expanding universes.

Furthermore the absence of a clear concept of entropy in relation to gravity makes the application of the concept of entropy to the whole Universe disputable. And the statistical character of the Second Law might allow for the occasional occurrence of states of low entropy in an otherwise eternal universe in equilibrium. In combination with the inflationary scenario (see the next chapter) the fluctuation does not need to be big, nor is it obvious that a much smaller universe with observers like ourselves would be more probable. In Craig's book the belief in the unrestricted validity of laws like the Second Law is too strong. I am not defending the skeptical view that we cannot know anything about the very early universe, but I call for caution in the extended use of commonsense notions or laws known to be valid under 'ordinary' circumstances.

My conclusion is that a cosmological argument for the existence of God, derived from the 'beginning' of the Universe, does not work, and certainly not on the basis of the Big Bang theory, which has a limited domain of validity. An argument for a beginning of the Universe or for *ex nihilo nihil fit* must be metaphysical rather than empirical.

1.3.2. *The Non-Temporal Cosmological Argument*

The philosopher of religion Richard Swinburne thinks that, in descriptions of the evolution of the Universe, God might appear as either responsible for the first state, as considered above, or as responsible for natural laws. Each state of the Universe will have a full explanation in terms of a prior state and the natural laws. The most fundamental law is scientifically inexplicable. It must either be completely inexplicable, or have a non-scientific explanation, a God who brings it about that this law operates. "The choice is between the universe as stopping-point and God as stopping-point" (Swinburne 1979, 127).

According to Swinburne, a universe is much more complex than God, so the latter stopping-point is preferable. The supposition that there is a God is an extremely simple supposition. A God of infinite power, knowledge, and freedom is the simplest kind of person there could be, since the idea has no limitations requiring explanation. The Universe, on the other hand, has a complexity, particularity, and finitude which cry out for explanation (Swinburne 1979, 130).

There is no explicit use of science in this argument. It might be rational and valid, but that is to be debated at the level of philosophical reasoning without support from science.[13] The scientific contribution lies in the description of the Universe.

However, if the choice between accepting the Universe as a brute fact or as needing an explanation of a different kind is justified by comparing the simplicity of the two hypotheses (as Swinburne does), it is a matter of the utmost importance to understand how complex or simple the two alternatives are. Many cosmologists believe that their theories are of an impressive simplicity and elegance in structure and assumptions, even if the mathematics is difficult. Whether this makes it more or less reasonable to regard the Universe as a 'creation' is not clear (why could one not believe that God made a universe with a simple structure?), but it does undermine Swinburne's argument based on simplicity.

1.4. PARALLELS WITH GENESIS

In the beginning God created the heavens and the earth. The earth was without form and void, and darkness was upon the face of the deep; and the Spirit of God was moving over the face of the waters. (Genesis 1:1–2)

Before evaluating the nature of apparent parallels between biblical references to creation and the Big Bang theory (1.4.2) I will first briefly present the way in which some contemporary biblical scholars understand the biblical narratives (I give more details in Appendix 7).

1.4.1. *The Bible and Creation*

Cosmogonic[14] legends serve a variety of functions. Besides explaining the actual world with its tragic elements like death and decay, they legitimize social or religious structures and traditions, present an ideal against which actual practices are measured, provide a background to the ethics of a culture, and so on. Myths of beginnings are "not so much a question of knowing how the world began as ensuring its existence and permanence" (Pettazzoni 1954, 29).

In the Bible the world is seen as created. But the Bible does not present just one view of 'how God did it'. Dominant is the emphasis on 'who created', the one God of Israel. Monotheism is not primarily a philosophical statement. It expresses an existential interest: one God implies that the enemies don't have a God as powerful as Israel's God. The same God who is present in the life and history of Israel is also the One who was at the beginning, and who has the power to change or create whatever is necessary to his people. The genealogy of heaven and earth is part of the genealogy of Israel. The world is, according to the biblical narratives, real (not an illusion), and it has been good. The world itself is not divine; there is a qualitative difference between God and his creatures.

Genesis 1, the well-known story of the creation in seven days, is not the major, and certainly not the only, text where reflections on God as the Creator can be found. The first few chapters of Genesis have been overemphasized as the stories about creation and fall, the sources for cosmogony and anthropology. Such an emphasis neglects the variety of Biblical images concerning creation. It also tends to misinterpret Genesis as if it were an answer to our cosmological questions. From the second verse on, the story of Genesis 1 concentrates on 'the Earth' as the context of life. This includes a vision of social life, especially through its emphasis on the Sabbath, the seventh day, which is a major element in the identity of the people of Israel.

Creatio ex nihilo has often been read into Genesis 1:1–2 (references can be found in Westermann 1974, 150ff [1984, 108ff]), for example "the Creator first prepared for himself the raw material of the universe with a view to giving it afterwards order and life" (Cassuto 1961, 23). But for the author of Genesis 1:1, the Earth is either creation or desolate and threatening, 'tohu and bohu'. The latter is not just 'raw material' created by God first. And the verb used for 'to create' does not imply *ex nihilo*. However, the alternative, pre-existent formless matter used by God, is also disputable. Our neutral and abstract concept of matter does not fit. We might wish that the text gave an answer to our questions, but that is not within its scope. In the Bible there is no statement about the absence of anything. *Creatio ex nihilo* arose, in confrontations with other philosophical currents, as a natural explication of the biblical ideas (see Appendix 8).

1.4.2. *Problems with Parallels between Big Bang and Bible*

> Is modern science, with all its sophisticated machinery, merely rediscovering ancient wisdom, known to the Eastern sages for thousands of years? (Fritjof Capra 1984, 297)

Both the Big Bang idea and the biblical narratives evoke the image of a sudden appearance of the world. A similarity of such a general nature is not very surprising; there are at that level only two possibilities: either the Universe had an abrupt beginning or it had no such beginning. In many cultures there have been narratives recounting a sudden beginning of the world.

Parallels with greater informative content fail upon closer inspection. For instance, the supposed coincidence that both the Big Bang idea and Genesis describe a sudden appearance out of nothing is not based on a reading of Genesis 1 in its context. Genesis 1 does not answer questions about the existence or non-existence of primordial matter. The same goes for other biblical references to 'creation'. Statements that appear to say something about the 'out of nothing' have a different function, mostly to express a certain view of God, God's power and God's relation to mankind, especially the people of Israel. Besides, there is not one single coherent biblical concept of the creation process. Several images are used, some more in line with *ex nihilo*, like God ordering as a king that there must be light, others more at odds with it, like God working as a potter.

The contention of Stoner (see 1.2.1) that Moses, the supposed author of Genesis, must have been inspired by God since he wrote down the way God created the Universe a few millennia before mankind actually discovered the relevant physical processes, is based on a complete misunderstanding of the narrative of Genesis 1.

In general, claiming such parallels is only possible if the text or idea is taken out of its context. The content is read, in a certain way, but its function is neglected. Sal Restivo (1984) has analyzed the alleged parallelism between physics and Eastern mysticism. Parallels can only be established if there is something to be compared, namely: statements in a common language. I agree with Restivo about the following major problems with such a procedure:

1. *Translations*. Both statements are translations, both in the lin-

guistic sense (from Hebrew and from mathematics) and in the cultural sense (a culture of a far past and the scientific, theoretical culture).

2. *Representativity.* If two statements are used to argue for a parallel between two conceptual structures (modern scientific and biblical world view), the question arises whether the statements are representative for the whole. Genesis 1 is not representative for the whole Bible, or even the Old Testament, which is mostly about the history of Israel. A parallel between Genesis 1 and the Big Bang idea would not imply that the Big Bang theory confirmed a religion based on the Old Testament, since the most important aspect from the biblical point of view, God's presence throughout history, is missing. The same can be said for the scientific side, since the Big Bang theory describes the evolution of the Universe after the first fraction of a second, and not the beginning, which is beyond the limits of its applicability.

3. *The different functions of language.* In science the main function of language is communication among scientists about observations, experiments and theories. Conceptual clarity and logical consistency are important for such a purpose. Religious language serves other functions, like reassuring and comforting people and evoking moral attitudes. Whether there is some common aspect of language is something I will discuss later, but there is surely much divergence. It is hardly convincing to claim parallels without paying attention to the differing functions of language.

4. *Misleading transpositions of terms.* Words used in one context get used, with another meaning, in a different context. Parallels based on the use of the same word might be a consequence of such 'corruption of languages'. Notoriously risky are words like 'energy', 'order', 'nothing', and 'creation'. The use of the *creatio ex nihilo* formula in articles treating the beginning of the Universe as a quantum event (see 2.1.3) might be of such a nature.

1.5.   *CREATIO EX NIHILO* AND THE BIG BANG

1.5.1. *The Historical Background of* Creatio ex Nihilo

Creatio ex nihilo as a philosophical statement expressing the Christian view of creation arose in the second century A.D. As with other parts of Christian thought, the doctrine of creation became what it now is through the acceptance and rejection of elements of other religious and philosophical ideas, especially in confrontation with Gnosticism, Marcionitism, and Platonism. Details are given in Appendix 8.

Gnosticism and Marcionitism influenced decisions about the canon (retaining the Old Testament) and the formulations of confessions ('I believe in God, the Creator of the Heavens and the Earth'), which are the basis of all subsequent theological thinking about creation. For the gnostics and for Marcion the origin of evil and the origin of the material world go together. Therefore the world cannot be the intended product of the good God who is the father of Jesus Christ. It must have been made by a different God. According to Christian theologians, the whole creation (material and spiritual) is distinct from God, but made by the same God who is present in Israel and Jesus, and so the creation is not the product of a lesser or other God. Being distinct from God is included in *creatio*, while being made by no one else but the God of Israel and Jesus is part of *ex nihilo*.

Platonism had a cosmogony which assumed a few eternal principles: the Demiurge who made the world, the Ideas, and Matter. *Creatio ex nihilo* expresses objections against independent eternal principles aside from God. The Ideas are interpreted as God's thoughts, and the existence of eternal, ungenerated matter is denied.

Historical necessity is disputable, but I agree with May (1978, 153) that, given the philosophical context in the second century of Christianity, *creatio ex nihilo* as an ontological statement was to be expected as a necessary consequence of biblical traditions in a critical confrontation with philosophical ideas about 'principles'.

1.5.2. *The Doctrine of Creation in Our Time*

The majority of theologians in the twentieth century have taken the doctrine of creation as unrelated to the natural sciences. Many deny the significance of metaphysics or cosmology, philosophical as well as scientific, for faith and theology. Separation has been based on dichotomies between God's self-revelation in Christ and man's discovery (Barth, neo-orthodoxy), or between subjective involvement and objective detachment (existentialism, Bultmann), or on an analysis of the different functions of language.[15] In the neo-orthodox approach, creation is interpreted from the perspective of salvation (Barth 1945). In the existentialist approach, belief in God as the

Creator is an expression of a new understanding of one's own life (Bultmann 1958). In the linguistic approach, saying that the world has been created is not a factual statement, but an expression of a way of looking at the world, having a certain attitude with respect to the world (Evans 1963; see Kelsey below).

Among those who pay attention to science and to philosophical issues related to science, many (such as Peacocke, Moltmann) have paid much attention to the theory of evolution in relation to the emergence of new levels of being (life, consciousness). Theologically, this implies emphasis on *creatio continua* instead of *creatio originalis*. Arthur Peacocke interprets *creatio ex nihilo* as a term for a present and timeless relation of absolute dependence of the cosmos on God (Peacocke 1979, 43f). To call God creator is to postulate a perennial, eternal, and timeless relation between God and the world (Peacocke 1987b, 45). Scientific cosmology "cannot, in principle, be doing anything which can contradict such a concept of creation" (Peacocke 1979, 79).

The concept of *creatio ex nihilo* is, even if important, used in many ways. Eberhard Wölfel (1981) warns against substantiating the *nihil*. In the context of *creatio ex nihilo* the *nihil* expresses that God was alone and that the act of creation is a self-limitation of God. God, the necessary existent, is the ontological *principium ex quo*, from which all contingencies result. As a result, the *creatio ex nihilo* is not really *ex nihilo*, but out of the fullness of God. This is neither substantial nor causal, but 'mystical'. As such, there is no conflict with the philosophical principle *ex nihilo nihil fit*.

David Kelsey (1985) explains the doctrine as a combination of claims and attitudes. The claims are about the relation between God and the world (dependence and so forth), and about the existence of a first event. Following Evans (1963) Kelsey interprets the doctrine of creation as a 'parabolic onlook', similar to 'I look on Harry as my brother', which implies a similarity of attitude (feeling about Harry as such and treating Harry as such) and a similarity of fact, which makes the similarity of attitude appropriate. The 'brother' is the parable, the analogue, for the attitude. The historical claim that the world originated in a singular event in the past does not introduce a new parable for 'looking on' the world, which is not already present in the metaphysical claim about the world's dependency on God. We can drop the historical claim without loss.

Kelsey's stress on the self-involving character of the affirmation for the doctrine of creation is very relevant, and should not be forgotten while focussing on the dialogue with the natural sciences. The claim that a beginning does not introduce a new 'parable' seems correct. But it might be, and is for some, the only interpretation of other, metaphysical claims, especially about God actualizing the world. To take the metaphysical claims as independent, and subsequently conclude that the historical claim does not add anything, begs the question whether one can understand and believe the doctrine of creation without taking it to imply an absolute origination— the historical claim. The task becomes to find another interpretation of the metaphysical claims, an interpretation in relation to the scientific understanding of the world. I will make proposals in the next two chapters. They align with Wölfel's understanding of *creatio ex nihilo* as a modal (and not causal) notion expressing a form of contingency of the world.

Process philosophers and theologians defend a view for which the word 'pan-en-theism' has been coined as an intermediate term between theism—God transcending the world—and pantheism— God totally immanent in the world. God, according to process theologians, is not the cosmic moralist, nor the unchanging and passionless absolute, nor the controlling power, nor the sanctioner of the status quo (Cobb and Griffin 1976, 8f). God and world are co-operating, God luring the world into novelty, to greater complexity, harmony and order, while being influenced by experiences with the world. There is freedom in all entities. God influences and tries to persuade, but God does not coerce. "Process theology rejects the notion of *creatio ex nihilo*, if that means creation out of *absolute* nothingness. That doctrine is part and parcel of the doctrine of God as absolute controller. Process theology affirms instead a doctrine of creation out of chaos" (Cobb and Griffin 1976, 65).

Defending this position, Charles Hartshorne (1948, 30) insists that divine creativity is nonetheless different from human creativity.

> What does distinguish God is that the preceding phase was itself created by God, so that he, unlike us, is never confronted by a world whose coming to be antedates his own entire existence. There is no presupposed 'stuff' alien to God's creative work; but rather everything that influences God has already been influenced by him, whereas we are influenced by events of the past with which we had nothing to do. This is one of the ways in which eminence is to be preserved without falling into the negations of classical theology.

The Universe is co-eternal with God, but there are no enduring things within that Universe, thus preserving God's uniqueness.

Throughout the next three thematic chapters, and in the final chapter on the doctrine of God, I will quarrel with a number of different elements of process theological thinking, especially about transcendence and time. I intend to present an alternative in defense of the significance of *creatio ex nihilo* as an expression of the Universe's dependence upon a God who is transcendent.

1.5.3. *Is There a Parallel?*

I have already taken a dim view (1.4.2) of attempts to establish parallels between the Biblical narratives and the Big Bang. Turning to the theological doctrine of *creatio ex nihilo*, we find a stronger argument for such a parallel. Unlike the narratives, the doctrine is supposed to be a product of coherent, systematic reflection. Some functions of the narratives, like comforting people or evoking certain attitudes, have moved to the background. However, even if there is a parallel in content between the *ex nihilo* formula and current scientific cosmology, the religious doctrine still serves other functions besides the cognitive one, functions which are not part of the scientific theory.

There is a variety of views within Christianity. A beginning of the Universe seems similar to *creatio ex nihilo,* but for many theistic theologians today an eternal Universe is also acceptable. It would, in their opinion, still need a ground (not a temporal cause) for its existence. Process theologians think that only an eternal Universe is compatible with their ideas. They defend an analogy between divine and human activity, each using other entities. This analogy is also present in the linguistic structure of the theistic formula 'God creates *ex nihilo*'. But any such analogy is so strongly qualified by the *nihil* that a fundamental difference between God's creativity and that of humans is retained.

QUANTUM COSMOLOGIES AND 'THE BEGINNING'

2.1. INTRODUCTION

Carl Sagan interprets the cosmology developed by Stephen Hawking as support for an atheistic stance: "a universe with no edge in space, no beginning or end in time, and nothing for a Creator to do" (Sagan 1988, x).

In this chapter I concentrate on cosmological issues which seem to be connected especially closely with the very early universe: its initial conditions and the nature of the origination event (if any). I also discuss the nature of scientific research at the frontier of cosmology, and suggest a number of methodological implications for the way theology deals with science, if one takes seriously the absence of consensus in contemporary cosmological research.

Naturally, my discussion of recent scientific developments can only be very incomplete. Additional information can be found in the appendixes on inflation (Appendix 3) and on Hawking's cosmology (Appendix 4), as well as in popular and scientific literature.[1]

2.2. THE LIMITS OF THE BIG BANG THEORY

2.2.1. *Big Bang, Planck Time, and Singularity*

The Big Bang theory is the accepted theory about the evolution of the Universe over billions of years. However, the theory is often misunderstood as dealing with an initial explosion. Judging by the title of Steven Weinberg's popular exposition, *The First Three Minutes,* it seems as if the Universe has a beginning and as if we can describe processes right from the very first instant.

The Big Bang theory is a combination of two theoretical systems describing the processes happening to the contents of the Universe: general relativity for spacetime and quantum theory for matter. This implies three limits to the Big Bang theory (see Figure 1):

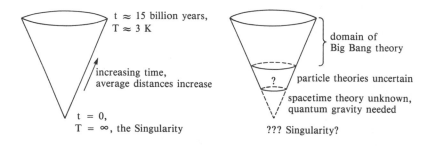

FIGURE 1. On the left the Big Bang model is depicted as a cone, with each horizontal slice representing the three-dimensional universe at a given moment of time. On the right the major uncertainties are stressed.

1. Current theories about matter valid only up to a finite temperature, and hence valid only *after* the first fraction of a second following the Singularity, the initial moment entailed by general relativity. This implies a, perhaps temporary, epistemological boundary to the domain where the Big Bang theory can be trusted. Further speculations have to deal with temperatures and densities for which particle physics is not yet well established.

2. Closer to the Singularity there comes a moment, presumably the 'Planck Time'—a number constructed from the fundamental constants of quantum theory and gravity, about 10^{-43} seconds after the initial Singularity—when general relativity must be replaced by a quantum theory of gravity. Theories of space and time applicable before the Planck Time are not known; even the meaningfulness of 'space' and 'time' is uncertain. (Which is troublesome; once time is no longer meaningful, it becomes unclear what can be meant by 'before'.)

3. The initial Singularity itself is a third limit, at least if there is such an initial Singularity. The Big Bang theory results in unrealistic numbers, like infinite density and so on. For some time it was as-

sumed that the unrealistic breakdown of the solutions was a feature of idealizations made in the calculations, for instance the assumption of perfect homogeneity. However, it has since been shown that such peculiarities are unavoidable in general relativity, once certain very general assumptions are made, like causality and a positive energy density (Hawking and Penrose 1970). On the other hand, general relativity itself is probably invalid in the moments before the Planck Time. Whether there is such a singular moment in a theory of quantum gravity which is to supersede general relativity cannot be decided *a priori,* before such a theory of quantum gravity has been proposed.

The first and second limit are clearly limits to our present knowledge, the third, the Singularity, seems to be an edge of reality, but is hidden behind the other two.

To describe our Universe with the Big Bang theory we need, in addition to the laws, some initial conditions, numbers which are not explained by the theory but assumed. Among them is large-scale homogeneity peppered with just the right amount of inhomogeneities to produce galaxies. The density turns out to be very close to the critical density, which is the boundary between an infinitely expanding (open) and a recollapsing (closed) universe. This leads to a question known as the flatness problem: why is the density of our Universe so close to that density which corresponds to a 'flat universe'? Particle theories predict the existence of other particles, like magnetic monopoles. Since these have not been detected, their abundance has to be below the present observational limits. This restricts the range of possible theories. Particle theories at first predicted a monopole mass density much larger than the total mass density of the Universe.

Some of these initial conditions are even more peculiar than they seem as a consequence of the horizon problem: regions which we observe in different directions have not been in causal contact during the whole past of the Universe, according to the Big Bang theory, and yet they look very similar, that is, they have the same density.

A description of an actual collision of billiard balls needs, in addition to the theory, the initial positions and velocities. If a calculation backwards shows that the balls were at some arbitrary position on the cloth, nobody would ask for an explanation. But if they appeared to be in some special arrangement, one would start asking for an explanation. This is the case for the Big Bang model. The need for initial conditions is nothing to worry too much about. But some of them appear to be rather peculiar, for instance the fact that, despite the horizon problem, the homogeneity (with inhomogeneities) is about the same in all directions.

Besides those initial conditions the Big Bang theory also assumes certain general features of the Universe: the laws of physics, the three spatial dimensions and the one dimension of time, as well as the Universe's existence.

Developments beyond the Big Bang theory do not mean that there is anything wrong with the theory. "In sum, all the available evidence indicates that the standard cosmology provides an accurate accounting of the evolution of the Universe from 0.01 sec after the bang [Singularity] until today, some 15 or so Byr [Billion years] later—quite a remarkable achievement!" (Turner 1985, 271). None of the scientists to be discussed below objects to the theory within its limits. Each of the problems and assumed initial conditions is "not an inconsistency in the standard model, but represents a lack of explanatory power" (Blau and Guth 1987, 535). The challenge for physicists has been to explain the assumptions (laws, initial conditions) and to extend the domain of validity of the theories.

2.2.2. Beyond the Big Bang Theory

Initial Conditions

Some defend a chaotic cosmology. The initial conditions of the Big Bang theory might be irrelevant. Almost anything goes, as with a beach of sand, where almost any initial condition—from a dozen sandcastles to a smooth beach—results in a similar, almost smooth beach after some time. In its most recent form this approach is based on inflationary scenarios (Appendix 3). For Andrej Linde this is combined with the idea that the Universe continuously forms bubbles or domains which, due to quantum effects, have different initial conditions and even different physics (kinds of particles and interactions, perhaps even dimensionalities). One could say that all possibilities are realized. Those bubbles that have an inflationary phase, like ours had, are the ones that become significant. One might interpret this as a Darwinian cosmology, a survival of the fittest, although not through competition (2.3.1).

No boundary conditions, and hence the absence of choice, is the proposal of Stephen Hawking. "It would mean that we could describe the universe by a mathematical model which was determined by the laws of physics alone" (Hawking 1984a, 358f). According to him, physics is fundamentally time-symmetric. Hawking accepts the Many Worlds Interpretation of quantum physics, and therefore there is no choice left once a probability distribution is given: all possibilities are actual (2.3.2.).

The initial conditions were special, according to Roger Penrose. Our kind of universe is very rare among the set of all initial conditions, within the context of physics as known today. Penrose argues for a new law, which would restrict the set of possible initial conditions, and thereby remove the specialness of our Universe within the set of possible universes. This new law would introduce time-asymmetry in the fundamental laws of physics, while it is also related to the interpretation of quantum mechanics, bringing it closer to a notion of 'objective reality' (2.3.3).

The Origination Event

Current discussions of the 'origination event' use the recent conjecture that the Universe might be equivalent to a vacuum.[2] There are no conserved physical quantities which have a non-zero sum over the whole Universe. Either the sum is zero (for example electrical charge) or the quantity is not conserved (for example baryon number, which makes the distinction between protons and anti-protons). Even total energy is zero, or not conserved, or not a meaningful concept.

Discussions of the origination event have to go beyond the first two limits of the Big Bang theory—the limit of our knowledge of particle theories and the limit of the quantum theory which is to replace the theory of general relativity. Most proposals are not too dependent on the details: they are more like visions which guide subsequent research.

The idea still survives of an eternally oscillating universe. According to the Russian cosmologist Markov, the Universe would transform into a vacuum when it comes close to the apparent Singularity. It would therefore behave according to the De Sitter solution which has no initial Singularity (see Appendix 1). As there would be no particles, entropy would not be definable. Each cycle would start afresh. He claims as its major advantage that this model has "no problem of origination of the world" (Markov 1983a, 353).

Rozental, another Russian cosmologist, maintains in his book *Big Bang Big Bounce* that the origin of the observable Universe out of nothing is nonsense. According to him this was "always the opinion of the great philosophers and physicists" (Rozental 1988, 112). Spinoza, whom he holds to have been excommunicated for this reason, and Einstein are his major examples. However, Rozental is less explicit on the idea of a 'bounce', as if the Universe were a single entity which would be traceable through successive cycles. Rather, he defends the notion of "coming out of" and "merging into" the vacuum, which makes him belong to the next group concerning ideas about beginnings. "The Universe—eternal and infinite—lives a stormy life reminiscent (metaphorically, of course) of a pot of boiling liquid" (Rozental 1988, 124).

The Singularity might be like conception or birth, being the beginning of time from the perspective of the child, but an event in time as seen by the mother (see Figure 2). Linde's approach, to be discussed in more detail below, is an example. At 'conception' the universe is like a bubble within an embedding spacetime (Brout *et al.* 1980; Gott 1982 and 1986; Atkatz and Pagels 1982; Moss and Wright 1984; Guth and Steinhardt 1984; Narlikar 1988). However, children tend to fill (and thereby kill) their mothers, since this conception of bubbles within the maternal womb is assumed to have happened for an infinitely long time (Linde 1983b). 'Birth' fares better: a mini-universe appears as a bubble on the "surface" of the mother. After evaporation of the connection it becomes spatially disconnected (Sato *et al.* 1982).

Such ideas might be formulated in terms of vacuum fluctuations, similar to the sudden appearance for a short time of an electron, an anti-electron, and a photon. As creation theories they are 'incomplete', since they assume the pre-existing spacetime framework. Some thinkers attempt to evade the assumption of a spacetime, basically by taking up the idea that 'time' is part of the created order, not prior to it.

Appearance out of nothing has been under discussion during the last few years (Vilenkin, Grishchuk, Zeldovich, and Starobinsky). I will pay attention to the proposal of Hartle and Hawking (2.3.2 and Appendix 4). Even if one does not agree with a complete philosophical *ex nihilo* interpretation of such theories (see 2.5), they do relate to traditional metaphysical questions, like 'why the Universe is as it is'.

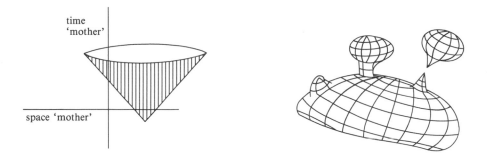

FIGURE 2. On the left, a 'child' universe appears within the 'mother' spacetime. On the right, the 'child' is 'born', external to the 'mother', with a separate space and time.

The variety of positions has implications, apart from the specific implications of any particular view. Do these different options deserve serious consideration? Are they still science? They are not yet established, like the theories in textbooks, but they are topics of current research. Shipman (1986, 6f) suggests, in a similar context, the distinction between concrete theories, working models, and speculative scenarios. Concrete theories are backed up with many data which have been interpreted according to well-established physical laws and models. These theories are the most stable part. The details of working models are still subjects of active research, but the picture is already sufficiently clear to allow for specific calculations and comparisons with observations. Scenarios are much more sketchy, typical of first explorations of phenomena. The Big Bang theory can be seen as an example of concrete theory within its domain, starting a fraction of a second after the apparent 'beginning'. There are still some disputes, both about details and substantial issues, but the theory seems to be well-established. Ideas which go beyond the Big Bang theory, extending the domain to earlier times and the explanatory scope to parameters assumed as inital conditions in the Big Bang theory, are much more sketchy. Perhaps 'inflation' could be considered a contemporary working model. Theories about many bubbles (mini-universes) are, at the moment, speculative scenarios, especially since we lack a definite theory which integrates quantum physics and theories about space and time. However, the speculative scenarios deserve interest, since they are related to different interpretations of the concrete theory, the Big Bang theory.

2.3. PHILOSOPHICAL ELEMENTS IN THREE RESEARCH PROGRAMS

Three different approaches will be described each by referring to the work of one major cosmologist, Andrej Linde, Stephen Hawking, and Roger Penrose.

2.3.1. *Andrej Linde: Eternal Chaotic Cosmology*

> the performance is still going on, and it will continue eternally. In different parts of the universe different observers see its endless variations. (Andrej 1987b, 68)

Andrej Linde is one of the cosmologists who developed the idea that the Universe underwent a period of rapid expansion—so called inflation (see Appendix 3). His version is called chaotic inflation, which leads to his view of a universe consisting of many smaller 'universes'.

The original proposals for inflation needed the initial conditions, or rather the shape of the potential, to be just right, like starting with a ball right on top of a hill. Linde has argued that this is unnecessary; the ball might be somewhere along the slope. That is, according to him, much more reasonable, as quantum effects make a precisely localized initial condition rather improbable. Inflation is understood as "a natural and maybe even inevitable consequence of the chaotic initial conditions in the very early universe" (Linde 1983b, 180—to my knowledge the first article on this scenario).

Because of this, I consider the inflationary scenario together with the basic idea of chaotic cosmology, although inflation might also be part of other cosmological complexes of ideas. Chaotic cosmologies try to explain features like homogeneity, which we find special about our Universe, as the consequence of natural processes without requiring any special initial conditions. If one has the set of all possible initial conditions, the subset of initial conditions which are compatible with the kind of Universe we see is dominant, or at least very large.

Earlier versions of chaotic cosmology emphasized the role of dissipative processes, which would smear out imhomogeneities and produce after billions of years a universe which looks as homogeneous as the Universe we observe. Imagine a beach where children have built castles from sand and another beach which has remained untouched. After a few days of wind and tides, the beaches will look similar. Almost all initial conditions produce similar results if dissipative processes are sufficiently effective.

Linde does not emphasize dissipative processes. Rather, he proposes that the conditions for inflation might have been satisfied in some regions (domains) of the Universe while not, or only later, in other domains. Some domains would inflate. They form very large bubbles. Sometimes these are called 'mini-universes', but 'mini' should not be misunderstood; they are each supposed to be much larger than the observable Universe. Each mini-universe would resemble a Big Bang universe, quite homogeneous and of the right density. However, the universe at large would not be homogeneous, but a cluster of bubbles, mini-universes, attached to each other.

Bubble universes need not all have the same properties. As an analogy, the physics used to describe water and that used to describe ice are quite different, although the fundamental underlying theory is the same. Solid state physics describing ice is, in this example, the low-energy physics. Something similar happens in the theories which describe the particles and geometry in bubble universes, with one complication: there is not just one low-energy state (ice) with one low-energy physics, but there appear to be many different possible low-energy states, each with other physical properties and therefore described by different physical laws, even though all the laws are consequences of the same fundamental theory.

One idea, formulated in Kaluza-Klein theories, is that the underlying theory is not based upon three spatial dimensions and one dimension of time. It might be ten- or eleven-dimensional. Some of those dimensions compactify—they become very small. We observe the four 'large' dimensions, while the others are unobservable as spatial dimensions, although their presence might influence the physics. The small dimensions are closely related to the interactions (forces) that are observed in the world as described in terms of the large dimensions. There appears to be more than one way in which the higher-dimensional underlying structure might compactify, and hence there are more possible low-energy states with apparently different physics (dimensionality and/or interactions and kinds of particles). Linde considers it likely that "the universe is an eternally existing, self-producing entity, that is divided into many mini-universes much larger than our observable portion, and that the laws of low-energy physics and even the dimensionality of space-time may be different in each of these mini-universes" (Linde 1987b, 68).

There is no problem with energy. Binding energy, as provided by the attractive force of gravity, is negative—it costs energy to free the constituents. Inflation implies that this gravitational energy becomes more negative, a loss which provides the energy for the production of inflating domains. When the inflationary process ends, the energy which was in the field which drove the expansion is converted into radiation and particles.

Time: End, Beginning, and Evolution

Bubble formation goes on; the universe "unceasingly reproduces itself and becomes immortal" (Linde 1987b, 66). People and mini-universes die, but the show goes on. It "no longer seems necessary to assume that there actually was some *first* mini-universe appearing from nothing or from an initial singularity at some moment t = 0 before which there was no space-time at all' " (Linde 1987b, 66). This solves "the singularity problem. The problem is not the existence of singularities in the universe, but the statement (or common belief) that the universe does not exist eternally and that there exists 'some time at which there is no spacetime at all' " (Linde 1987a, 606).[3]

Although Linde's approach is mostly formulated in evolutionary language, for instance 'inflation' as spatial expansion in time, he also holds that there is no evolution in time for the universe as a whole. "What we measure is phenomenological time, which can be introduced by a local observer inside a long-living virtual mini-universe. . . . An eastern philosopher would say that the absolute does not evolve in time, but the virtual apparent world is observed as being time-dependent" (Linde 1985b, 289; see also Linde 1989, 355; we return to such notions of time and timelessness in section 4.4).

However, Linde's argument is not completely clear. Time is not strictly restricted to a phenomenon inside the bubbles. "Any two points of such a universe in a sufficiently distant past could be causally connected and corresponding observers could synchronise their clocks even though later they may live in mini-universes which have become causally disconnected due to the exponential expansion of the universe" (Linde 1987a, 620).

The conditions for different universes appear by chance. Some of the domains inflate to a more significant long-lived status. This gives, as acknowledged by Linde (1987b, 66), a Darwinian flavor to his cosmology. There are even mutations, as subsequent bubbles may differ from their 'mother', for instance in dimensionality. Selection finds its parallel in inflation, which gives a long life to a bubble. Linde combines the idea of selection operating on chance mutations with another, rather different but in my opinion more fundamental, philosophical idea, the realization of all possibilities. For instance, all possible dimensionalities and phenomenological laws of physics "should exist in different domains of the universe" (Linde 1987a, 623). "One may say therefore that not only could God create the universe differently, but in His wisdom He created a universe which has been unceasingly producing different universes of all possible types" (Linde 1987a, 607).

There is a danger of terminological confusion when for instance Linde writes that "our universe actually consists of many universes of all possible types" (Linde 1987a, 627). I prefer to follow Munitz (1986, 55), who restricts the use of the word 'universe' for the most inclusive system of a particular theory.[4] During the history of cosmology different systems have been called 'universes'. Galaxies, for example, were once described as 'island universes'. However, the present description places those objects within a larger system, and this deserves the name 'the observable Universe'. Linde's approach suggests that our observable Universe, and even the larger system which is 'the Universe' in the context of the Big Bang theory, is only part of the whole Universe conceived on the largest scale. The bubbles, which have also been called mini-universes, could best be considered, like the galaxies, to be embedded in the Universe, in discussions of Linde's cosmology.

I will return to 'uniqueness' in the next chapter. For the moment, let me point out that Linde's answer is not a definite one. Even though all possible bubbles in his cosmology become actual in the eternity of time available, this is only what is possible *within* his cosmology. Whether God has any options aside from this eternal chaotic universe with all its bubbles—that is the form the uniqueness question takes at this level. It is not settled by saying that all possibilities within Linde's theory are realized: we need to know whether other theories are possible. Let us therefore look at other proposals beginning with the quantum cosmology of Hawking.

2.3.2. *Stephen Hawking: Timeless Quantum Cosmology*

Stephen Hawking, a famous cosmologist, titles his 1980 inaugural lecture for the Lucassian chair (Newton's Chair) in Cambridge *Is the End in Sight for Theoretical Physics?*

> I think that the initial conditions are as suitable a subject for sci-
> entific investigation as are the local physical laws. We shall not have
> a complete theory until we can do more than merely say that "things
> are as they are because they were as they were". (Hawking 1980
> [Boslaugh 1985, 133])"

According to Hawking, physics is about to discover and explain the
most fundamental laws as well as to explain the ultimate boundary
conditions of the Universe. This goes against the standard view,
which sees initial (or boundary) conditions as given: the way a situation has been set up. Ordinary physics explains a collision of billiard balls, *given* their initial positions and velocities. Hawking holds
that physics can, when considering the whole Universe, do without
such an unexplainable "given". He proposed in 1984, in collabora-
tion with J. B. Hartle, a quantum cosmology which seems to do
without initial conditions. I now summarize his proposal; more details are given in Appendix 4.

The Hartle-Hawking Proposal

In classical physics the physical state of a system at a certain
moment, for example the positions and velocities of billiard balls,
can be calculated when the state of another moment and the laws
which describe the evolution from one state to another are known.
In the Big Bang theory the state of a universe at one time can
similarly be calculated by using the equations and, as a boundary
condition, the state at another time. In that sense one could say that
one state 'arises out of' another state. One could visualize this as a
pancake, a slice of time with two surfaces representing the initial
and the final state considered in the calculation. (Each surface in
this image stands for a three-dimensional space with material content; the pancake is supposed to be a four-dimensional 'volume'.)

The major achievement of the Hartle-Hawking proposal is that
it does without such an initial state. We calculate the probability of
one state while using that state as the only boundary. (We have to
deal with probability, since the proposal is in the context of quantum
physics.) Instead of a pancake, a slice of time with two surfaces
representing the initial and the final states as suggested for the standard view, one could think of a single closed surface, like a sphere,
representing only the final state. We calculate the probabilities for
a certain configuration, a three-dimensional curved space with fields
representing the material content, without referring to other states
or to evolution from such other states. As Hawking puts it, the
boundary condition for the Universe is that it has no boundary.

Requiring compactness, and hence the absence of a boundary, is in a sense a boundary condition—although not of properties of fields on the boundary but rather of the properties of the boundary itself. Hawking's proposal is certainly attractively simple. But other metaphysical views might lead to other proposals for the boundary condition. For example, Frank Tipler proposes the 'Teilhard Boundary Condition', essentially a condition of the future boundary (Tipler 1989; see 4.3 below). And Alexander Vilenkin (1986, 3568) advances a boundary condition based on causality, an idea which seems similar in spirit to the cosmology of Roger Penrose, who assumes a fundamental difference between initial and final singularities (see below, 2.3.3).

Hawking's ploy is not without its repercussions. Ordinary time with its notion of 'becoming' disappears. One could still see a trace of the original time variable in the internal four-dimensional space which fits at the three-dimensional boundary, but it is an imaginary time variable, and thereby the 'time' dimension is completely on a par with the spatial dimensions. ('Imaginary' is not to be understood as 'fantastic'. It refers to a mathematically well-defined type of numbers with certain properties.) There is no reason to call the fourth dimension a time variable at this level.[5] But we can still reconstruct the notion of time by changing to another description, as we will see below.

The calculations are complicated, and certainly so if one includes all fields that should be part of a realistic theory. No model describing our Universe yet exists. But there are some results, indicating that the density should—at least in a simplified model—be close to the critical density (Hawking and Page 1986) and that most universes of this type have an inflationary phase (Gibbons, Hawking, and Stewart 1987).

The Primacy of the Timeless Description

The Hartle-Hawking cosmology has two levels of calculation. One can consider two states at different moments. This is a description from within time. The other approach, described above, is the unique feature of this proposal. It doesn't require reference to any other state in calculating the probability of one state. In that sense the theory is a timeless description of the states of the Universe.

From the timeless perspective we can reconstruct the other description. First, the notion of time has to be introduced and then the three-dimensional spaces have to be ordered in a time-sequence. Time can be defined on the basis of the fields and the geometry of the states. In that sense time is a phenomenological construct. (Something similar is possible in a Big Bang universe, where time can be defined on the basis of the temperature of the background radiation or of the curvature.)

In the timeless approach we can calculate the probabilities of all the three-dimensional spaces and then line them up in stacks which resemble four-dimensional spacetimes like our Big Bang universe. It turns out that those sequences behave according to an equation which describes their evolution—if the system is described from within time.

Compared with the Big Bang theory there are two important qualifications:

1. This theory does not produce one stack, one Big Bang universe. The three-dimensional spaces form a whole variety of such stacks, each stack corresponding to one particular possible evolutionary sequence of three-dimensional geometry and matter configurations in a universe.

2. Not all spaces fit in a stack, and hence not all can be interpreted as being part of an evolutionary sequence. It works well for the states which reproduce the classical theory. "But the more 'quantum mechanical' is the state, the harder it becomes to sustain an interpretation of anything 'evolving' in time. In effect, the concept of 'space-time' only has an unambiguous meaning within the framework of non-quantum physics, whereas the idea of three-dimensional 'space' can be applied to both the quantum and the classical theories" (Isham 1988, 397).

To sum up, the timeless level of description in this theory is more fundamental than the description from within time.

The Beginning of Time

What about the 'beginning', the 't = 0'? There are two alternative ways to explain how this theory avoids the problem of an initial Singularity as present in the Big Bang theory.

First, time near the Singularity might be very unlike our ordinary time. If one uses the Hartle-Hawking scheme for spaces which are close to the 'beginning' of the Big Bang Universe (small spaces) one would expect to approach the interesting 't = 0' moment. However, "the phenomenological time begins to pick up something like an imaginary part with its associated non-physical features. By this means, the problem of the 'beginning of time' is adroitly averted" (Isham 1988, 400). In this sense, the theory has no initial singularity where the theory breaks down. Only our interpretation in terms of our usual notion of time breaks down.

The second way to present it, often used by Hawking, is easier to visualize: there is a beginning of the co-ordinate but no edge—as the North Pole is an extreme of our co-ordinates based on degrees of latitude, but not an edge of the globe. "Time ceases to be well defined in the very early universe just as the direction 'north' ceases to be well defined at the North Pole of the Earth. . . . The quantity that we measure as time had a beginning, but that does not mean spacetime has an edge, just as the surface of the Earth does not have an edge at the North Pole" (Hawking 1984c, 358; 1984d, 14). As spacetime is compact, according to his proposal, a past or future infinity is impossible. "Thus, in this sense, the universe will have a beginning and an end" (Hawking 1987, 650). However that need not be a singularity in the sense of a breakdown of the laws of physics.

Hawking points to the similarity between his view and the one of Augustine,[6] who introduced into the Christian tradition the notion of creation with time, time being part of the created order. This notion had a few centuries earlier already been expressed by Philo of Alexandria, who thought that time might even start after the creation of the material world, when movement would start.[7] According to Hawking, 'creation from nothing' requires time to exist prior to the Universe.

> But time is defined only within the universe, and does not exist outside it, as was pointed out by Saint Augustine (400): "What did God do before He made Heaven and Earth? I do not answer as one did merrily: He was preparing Hell for those that ask such questions. For at no time had God not made anything because time itself was made by God."
>
> The modern view is very similar. In general relativity, time is just a co-ordinate that labels events in the universe. It does not have any meaning outside the spacetime manifold. To ask what happened before the universe began is like asking for a point on Earth at 91° north latitude; it just is not defined. Instead of talking about the universe being created, and maybe coming to an end, one should just say: the universe is. (Hawking 1987, 651)

There is, of course, also a very important difference between Augustine and Hawking. Augustine probably understood the beginning of time with the creation as an event outside the scope of natural knowledge. But Hawking holds it to be only the beginning of a co-ordinate without reference to any special event, and without a breakdown of physical describability. This has, for Hawking, theological implications. "So long as the universe had a beginning, we could suppose it had a creator. But if the universe is really completely self-contained, having no boundary or edge, it would have neither beginning nor end: it would simply be. What place, then for a creator?" (Hawking 1988, 141). We will return to timelessness in 4.4 and to edges and *creatio ex nihilo* below (2.5). For the moment, it suffices to emphasize that the role of a beginning is much less important in the Hawking proposal than in the Big Bang theory, at least as it is generally understood.

The Arrow of Time

In common experience there is a clear sense of the difference between looking at the past and looking towards the future. The past is fixed, and we have memories of it. The future is not yet there, we make plans and try to influence the events to come. This asymmetry between the past and future is called the arrow of time. In physics there are a number of ways to formulate such an arrow, as we will see when we discuss Penrose's approach. The two most obvious, in the cosmological context, are the arrow based on the expansion of the Universe (and hence on the decrease in temperature of the background radiation) and the thermodynamic arrow, based on the evening-out of temperature differences, or more generally the decrease in usable (free) energy—for instance through the burning of stars.

The most fundamental theories in physics (classical mechanics, quantum mechanics, general relativity) are in general understood as being time-symmetric. Time asymmetry is then seen as due to improbable initial conditions and statistical effects of large numbers. If one were shown a film of billiard balls colliding (without any friction), it would be impossible to tell whether the film was run in the ordinary direction or in reverse. Both sequences of events would be in accordance with the fundamental laws of physics. Of course, friction makes a difference: a slowing down is observed when the film runs according to the ordinary time direction. But that too is somewhat anomalous. At the level of molecules, atoms, and electrons there is no sense of direction. Friction is the result of many different interactions which are each individually perfectly time-symmetric. Time asymmetry arises as an effect of the presence of many interacting particles, not as the result of some fundamental law.

Hawking commences an article on time asymmetry in the context of his quantum cosmology with the statement that physics is time-symmetric. The total wave function of the Universe can be shown to be time-symmetric (within his cosmology). However, "the Universe that we live in certainly does not appear time symmetric" (Hawking 1985, 2489). The illusion of time asymmetry is what needs an explanation.

At first Hawking had considered it purely a matter of definition. He thought he could show that the thermodynamic arrow, which underlies all life processes, and the cosmological arrow of expansion always coincide. Hence if the Universe came into a contracting phase, the thermodynamic arrow would reverse. Those living in such a phase would define the direction of time according to the thermodynamic arrow, and hence opposite to our definition. They too, using their definition of time, would see an expanding universe.

In a "Note added in proof" Hawking agrees with the conclusion reached by Page (1985) that, still in the context of Hawking's theory, it is not necessary that the thermodynamic and the cosmological arrow coincide. Although Hawking maintains that the total wave function must be time-symmetric, it might be that individual solutions (stacks which resemble the classical solutions: Big Bang type universes) are individually not time-symmetric. Within such a classical solution living beings would define their arrow of time on their biological processes, hence according to the thermodynamic arrow. An explanation for the fact that we happen to be in an expanding phase cannot be based on a necessary parallelism of the two arrows. Hawking and Page (1986) have proposed an explanation based on a weak anthropic argument (see 3.2 below): if the expanding phase is sufficiently long, as it is in universes which have an inflationary phase, stars will burn out during that phase. Life depending on stars (sunlight) would only exist during the expanding phase.

2.3.3. *Roger Penrose: Time-Asymmetric Realist Cosmology*

> But by then [1976], there had begun to emerge a certain divergence of opinion between Hawking and myself—something which we still have not found ourselves able to resolve. . . . this conflict has proved immensely stimulating to us both. My own line of argument has been driven, in part under the sting of Hawking's penetrating criticism, into some dangerous but fascinating territory. (Roger Penrose 1981a, 244)

Roger Penrose is an Oxford mathematician and cosmologist. In the late 1960s, together with Hawking, he proved theorems about the presence of singularities in wide classes of physically reasonable solutions of the equations of general relativity (Hawking and Penrose 1970). However, he has diverged from Hawking with respect to time, the nature of quantum reality, and the specialness of the Universe. Those issues form the heart of the "dangerous, but fascinating territory".[8]

The Specialness of the Initial State

According to Hawking the initial conditions of the Universe are the only ones possible—he does not allow any variety. Linde argues that all possibilities happen from time to time. Penrose argues that the initial state was very special. His argument is based on entropy. The observed entropy per baryon (proton, neutron) is about 10^8. There are about 10^{80} baryons in the observable Universe. Hence the total entropy of the observable Universe is 10^{88}. This seems enormous but is, according to Penrose, incredibly low. If all the mass had been clustered in solar-size black holes, the entropy per 'baryon' would have been 10^{20}. If the whole observable Universe had consisted of only one black hole, its entropy would be 10^{123}. "This provides us with a measure of the degree to which the initial state was special" (Penrose 1981a, 248). Entropy is logarithmically related to the volume in phase space, the mathematical space of all configurations (one point representing one possible universe). Imagine such a space W,

> whose points represent the various initial configuration of the universe. Imagine the Creator armed with a pin which is to be placed at one spot in W thereby determining the state of our actual universe. . . . we are led to the estimate that the accuracy of the Creator's aim must have been at least of the order of . . . one part in
>
> $$10^{(10^{123} - 10^{88})} = 10^{10^{123}}$$
>
> . . . Without wishing to denigrate the Creator's abilities in this respect, I would insist that it is one of the duties of scientists to search for physical laws which explain, or at least describe in some coherent way, the nature of the phenomenal accuracy that we so often observe in the workings of the natural world. Moreover, I cannot even recall anything else in physics whose accuracy is known to approach, even remotely, a figure like . . . [this]. So we need *a new law of physics* to explain the specialness of the initial state! (Penrose 1981a, 248–249)

Penrose considers an anthropic explanation (see below, 3.2); could the observed (or inferred) low entropy be explained as a requirement for life and consciousness? Such an explanation fails. A universe with entropy of 10^{115} would have fitted as well, and it would have been "a vastly 'cheaper' method than the one which appears actually to have been used" (Penrose 1981a, 254). "Indeed, it would appear from this that the Creator was not particularly 'concerned' about our existence, but was constrained in some very precise time-symmetric way for some quite other reason. From this point of view, our present existence would arise merely as a byproduct!" (Penrose 1981a, 255).

Time Asymmetry

If time were reversible the beginning of the Universe would have to be like its end. In Penrose's view time is asymmetric, which is in accordance with his emphasis on the specialness of the initial conditions. Penrose accepts that all the laws of ordinary physics are time-symmetric. The standard explanation that the asymmetry we observe is an effect of the low entropy of the initial conditions is also accepted. But that leaves us with the question why those initial conditions were so special. Penrose defends the idea that there must be a new law which severely restricts initial singularities. He conjectures that the law implies the absence of gravitational clumping in initial states. Although it looks like an initial condition, he presents it as a new law, which should hold for all initial singularities.

The asymmetry of time is for Penrose not only manifest in the initial conditions. He lists seven arrows of time, of which most can be traced back to the specialness of the initial conditions. For Hawking the time symmetry of the theory is beyond doubt, and the time asymmetry of the observations needs to be explained away. For Penrose it is the opposite: the experience of time asymmetry is taken beyond doubt, and hence the theory should be changed to incorporate time asymmetry.

> Some readers might feel let down by this. Rather than finding some subtle way that a universe based on time-symmetric laws might nevertheless exhibit gross time-asymmetry, I have merely asserted that certain of the laws are not time-symmetric—and worse than this, that these asymmetric laws are yet unknown!
>
> It is, to me, inconceivable that this asymmetry can be present without tangible cause. . . . In my own judgement, there remains the *one* ('obvious') explanation that the precise physical laws are actually *not* all time-symmetric! The puzzle then becomes: why does Nature choose to hide this time-asymmetry so effectively? (Penrose 1979, 635, 637–38)

Another hidden asymmetry can be found in biology. Almost all animals on Earth are externally symmetric with respect to left and right. However, the DNA molecules in the cells, which guide the growth of these symmetric beings, are all asymmetric, and even all in the same way (Penrose 1979, 638).

Quantum Reality

Quantum theories are very successful, but their interpretation is still subject to discussion. The state vector (or equivalently the wave function) might describe the system as being in a combination of a plurality of states, say an electron with spin up or down, or a particle going through gate A or gate B. This is called a linear superposition, as the different possibilities are added in the state vector. Some have tried to escape this view of reality by claiming that the superposition merely reflects our ignorance ('hidden variables'). This has been shown to imply that one must give up on physics as describing local interactions which do not immediately affect the state of the system at other places.

One could perhaps live with the superposition as real at the submicroscopic, quantum level. But it appears to carry over to macroscopic objects. There is a famous thought experiment leading to Schrödinger's cat in a superposition of being dead and being alive. Penrose rejects this. "Surely, at that level the cat *is* either dead or alive" (Penrose 1987a, 32).

The tension between many possibilities and the (apparently) one actuality lends itself to a variety of interpretations of the quantum formalism.

The 'Many Worlds Interpretation', first proposed by Everett (1957; see DeWitt, Graham, eds. 1973), maintains the superposition throughout. All possible outcomes of measurements are actual outcomes. This might be interpreted as a branching of the world into many 'worlds' with slight differences, say some with the spin of an electron along a vertical axis and others with the spin along a horizontal axis. Since any process with different possible outcomes implies splitting, this view seems to lead to an enormous number of 'universes', co-existing without interacting. However, Tipler has argued forcefully that 'everything else' need not split with the property considered; quantum transitions on distant stars do not induce splits in human beings.[9] It could also be interpreted as the splitting of the measurement apparatus, or, extrapolating, the splitting of consciousness. Each part of the consciousness would perceive one of the states without being aware of the other parts of the consciousness which perceive other states. In any case the Many Worlds idea eliminates the tension between potentiality and actuality by equating them.

The presence of superposition at macroscopic levels has been heavily criticized (Bell 1981, Stein 1984, Healey 1984, Shimony 1986). Penrose assumes that there is no superposition for macroscopic bodies, although the principle is valid at the quantum level. Rejecting the transfer of superpositions from the quantum level to the macroscopic level implies that there has to be a reduction of the many possible states to one state. It has been related to measurements (the Copenhagen interpretation) or the involvement of consciousness—which is in itself not well understood. Besides, according to Penrose, "the view seems to assign a privileged role to those corners of the universe where consciousness resides—and they may be very rare indeed" (Penrose 1987a, 33).

Penrose thinks that quantum mechanics with its linear superposition has to be replaced by a non-linear theory, which would not have these problems. This would be similar to the transition from Newton's theory of gravitation (which has the total gravitational force as a linear superposition of the forces contributed by the sources) to Einstein's general theory of relativity, which is "an astonishing *non*linear theory of even greater mathematical elegance" (Penrose 1987a, 34).

The solution must come from integrating quantum theory and general relativity, hence quantum gravity. Most people working on these problems are changing the structure of the fields (superstrings, more dimensions, and so forth). Penrose is one of the very few who suggest revising the structure of quantum theory.[10] This is justified by an appeal to the considerations discussed above about the specialness of initial singularities, "an *observational fact* of quantum gravity!" (Penrose 1987a, 35). It leads to his moral: "*the true quantum gravity must be a time-asymmetric theory*" (Penrose 1987a, 37).

Penrose does not have that theory (yet), but he offers a suggestion. The "linear superposition of states will cease to be maintained by nature as soon as the states become significantly differently coupled in to the gravitational field" (Penrose 1986b, 50). "The idea is that, in a sense, Nature abhors complex linear combinations of differing spacetime geometries!" (Penrose 1987a, 44). This seems to have testable consequences, like a prediction of minimal bubble sizes in bubble chambers, measuring devices to detect tracks of elementary particles (Penrose 1986a, 144). The theory will be "non-local in a way that fundamentally affects even the very fabric of spacetime. I do not expect, except perhaps at some temporary provisional level, that we should be able to get away with a theory which describes objective reality taking place *within* some ambient spacetime" (Penrose 1987a, 45).

The reality of state vector reduction fits well into a view which holds the direction of time to be real, while the denial of reduction fits easily into Hawking's approach without an objective direction of time.

Penrose (1987b, 1989) even suggested that this approach might result in an understanding of the nature of consciousness. Life thrives on minute effects in chemistry. Similarly, Penrose speculates, consciousness might be a phenomenon that thrives on minute effects in physics which happen at the transition from the quantum realm to the realm describable by classical physics.

2.4. IMPLICATIONS FOR SCIENCE AND THEOLOGY

We have seen three very different approaches. In this diversity at the frontier, cosmology seems open to metaphysical influences. This might be one of the few areas where science and religion are involved in genuine intellectual dialogue, or where there may even be a conversation between three parties: theology, science, and metaphysics (2.4.1). The diversity also has implications for the way theology should deal with science, at least with cosmology (2.4.2).

2.4.1. *Metaphysics and the Variety of Cosmologies*

According to the philosopher of science Imre Lakatos we can describe science as guided by research programs, more or less coherent series of theories, characterized by a hard core—the set of hypotheses which is kept fixed. Other hypotheses can be added or changed according to theoretical or empirical needs. These hypotheses form a protective belt around the core, and are where we find the major developments within a program. Development is not haphazard, but is guided by a long-term research policy, the positive heuristic. Theoretical science has a more or less autonomous development, guided more by the awareness of the unsatisfactory character of the theory at each moment than by specific experimental results. Mathematics has a central role in that theoretical development.

The works of the cosmologists we have discussed exhibit the characteristics of a research program. Although we did not discuss their work in its development, it really consists of a series of articles which build upon, but also modify, the ideas within a basic continuity.

These cosmologists agree for their hard core on certain elements, like the validity of the Big Bang theory after 'the first fraction of a second'. Therefore, they also agree on the standard problems of this model, like the need for an explanation of the observed homogeneity of the Universe and of the observed inhomogeneities in the Universe. They also all agree that the Copenhagen interpretation of quantum mechanics is unsatisfactory, since the notion of an observer makes no sense for the Universe as a whole.

Characteristic for Penrose is his idea that spacetime points are only an approximation, to be replaced by some more fundamental non-local entity. This was most clear in his mathematically-defined notion of 'twistors', out of which he tried to construct spacetime points and particles. Although there is no explicit proposal for such an entity in his recent work on time asymmetry and quantum reality, it seems that the basic conviction has remained the same. Penrose has expressed a preference for discrete entities, like spin, which is either up or down, either left-handed or right-handed, over continuous entities like position. In the twistor program he stated as his long term goal "that ultimately physical laws should find their most natural expression in terms of essentially *combinatorial* principles, that is to say, in terms of counting or other basic manipulative procedures" (Penrose 1972, 334). This is less explicit in the work discussed above, but might still be assumed as a guiding idea. In that sense, Penrose's approach has a Pythagorean flavor.

A second element is his emphasis on the reality of time asymmetry. A third element in the comparison with the others is that Penrose allows for unrealized possibilities, as is most clear in his description of the Creator picking one universe out of many possibilities, but is also implied in his view of superposition of many states to one in quantum theory.

Hawking bases his work on another branch of mathematics, path integral formalism. This fits very well with his view of quantum mechanics, which accepts the simultaneous reality of all possibilities.

A second element in Hawking's approach is his view of time as something of secondary relevance. It is a feature of human description but is not too relevant for the reality itself. As far as time is concerned Hawking seems to be in line with Einstein. However, Einstein would probably have preferred Penrose's view of quantum reality over Hawking's.

Linde sides with Hawking on the realization of all possibilities. However, they are not realized simultaneously as in Hawking's approach, but consecutively in different bubbles. Penrose's idea that there is a natural reduction of the state vector would be no problem in this view.

As far as time is concerned, Linde is closer to Penrose in that time is asymmetric, although not necessarily unfolding—Linde speaks favorably of the Eastern view that the absolute does not evolve in time. The asymmetry of time is visible in his emphasis on inflation, without a similar deflation processes, and a tree of bubbles formed consecutively. Linde's philosophy could be labelled Darwinian, in that the explanation of our observable Universe is built upon the chance formation of many bubbles and the subsequent selection of those fit for inflation. We happen to be in one of those bubbles that survived for a reasonable time. His account is also Darwinian in that the process is still going on; it is not merely something that happened once in the past.

The different programs have, in part, different problems to solve. Penrose needs to explain how reality becomes classical through a natural reduction of the state vector. Hawking, on the other hand, needs to explain why observers see a definite universe instead of the fuzzy superposition of many states that is his view of reality. For Penrose the question is why the fundamental time asymmetry is mostly hidden; in other words, why time-symmetric physics (Newtonian, relativistic and quantum physics) works so well. For Hawking the apparent asymmetry needs to be explained on the basis of a symmetric theory and symmetric boundary conditions.

From this we can see that these cosmologists also disagree in their view of the data. For Penrose, the time-asymmetric phenomena reflect a time asymmetry of reality in need of incorporation into the framework of physics. For Hawking the time asymmetry is, in principle, an illusion. His aim is not to incorporate the asymmetry, but to explain time-asymmetric phenomena away—as consequences of our way of perceiving, not as features of reality.

The difference in perspectives is also a difference in criteria, clearly visible in the way Hawking criticizes Penrose's introduction of the arrow of time as "rather *ad hoc*. Why should the Weyl tensor be zero on past singularities but not on future ones? In effect, one is putting in the thermodynamic arrow by hand" (Hawking 1985, 2490). Second, Penrose's procedure is based on classical general relativity, not on quantum gravity, where singularities might be different or non-existent. Finally, it "does not explain why the cosmological and the thermodynamic arrow should agree."

The last criticism lost its force when, in a "Note added in proof," Hawking accepted a conclusion of Page (1985) that the two arrows need not agree, even within Hawking's theory. Further, Penrose offers an argument for why the two arrows of time should concur. According to his view the cosmological arrow and the thermodynamical arrow should both have their ground in the new law which restricts initial conditions. The second objection is correct, but holds for all current theories. To blame Penrose for not having a quantum theory for gravity is beside the point and neglects Penrose's related work on the interpretation of quantum theory.

Hawking's first criticism, his objection to the *ad hoc* character of Penrose's proposal, is circular. Hawking objects to making a difference between past and future, putting in an arrow of time "by hand." This criticism would be correct within his program, where the arrow of time is believed to be something outside the basic structure of reality. However, the criticism misses the point of Penrose's program. Penrose is impressed by the asymmetry of time in nature, "one of the long-standing mysteries of physics" (Penrose 1979). In his view this is an aspect of reality which has escaped physical description so far. That his theory recognizes a difference between past and future singularities is not surprising; it is essentially what Penrose is trying to do. Besides, Hawkings ignores the actual arguments for a difference between initial and final singularities, although Penrose (1979, 1981a, 1982a, 1986a) does offer reason of a technical nature.

According to Lakatos, "one may formulate the 'positive heuristic' of a research program as a 'metaphysical' principle" (Lakatos 1970, [1978, 51]). Lakatos uses the term " 'metaphysical' as a technical term of naive falsificationism: a contingent proposition is 'metaphysical' if it has no 'potential falsifiers' " (Lakatos 1970, [1978, 47, n.2]).

For the cosmological programs discussed in this chapter, the ideas are not only 'metaphysical' in the sense that these ideas are beyond dispute, at least each within its program. They are also metaphysical in the classical sense, as they are about issues like relation between potential and actual existence, the nature of space and time, the (dis)similarity of future and past, and the contingency or necessity of the Universe. Those metaphysical elements are most clearly visible in the positive heuristic as ideas guiding the direction of the research, and hence influencing what will be the next step in the development of the program.

The different programs seem all to assume that the unity of Nature (whatever that might mean) implies a unity of description, in this case of quantum and spacetime physics. Hawking states (1980a; 1988, 165) that there are three possibilities: a complete theory, an infinite sequence of theories, or no theory and no description or prediction beyond a certain limit. Apparently he does not take seriously the possibility that there might be two equally defendable theories or sequences of theories which are different in their conceptual structures.

A point of philosophical interest is whether it will be possible to make a choice between Linde's, Hawking's, and Penrose's programs based on criteria which are acceptable to all. These programs might produce theories which are acceptable according to those shared criteria—for instance, that the theory should reproduce quantum theory, general relativity and thermodynamics in their respective domains of validity. In that case, the theories might be empirically equivalent, at least with respect to our present-day empirical material.

That leaves us with three possibilities. 1. The programs are in a more complete sense equivalent, and there may exist a way of translating the concepts and structures of the one into the other. Or they might be conceptually so different that they are conceptually (logically, metaphysically) incompatible. In the latter case, it might be that 2. future observations or experiments will rule out all but one, or that 3. the empirical equivalence remains preserved and hence the programs will co-exist as different possible approaches.

For the possibility of equivalence one might point to the equivalence in quantum physics of the wave formalism invented by Schrödinger and the matrix formalism invented by Heisenberg. However, this kind of equivalence between the programs is unlikely. The differences are very fundamental.

The programs might be examples of programs which yield theories that are "logically incompatible and empirically equivalent" (Quine 1970). Empirical equivalence means that the different theories have the same corroborated predictive power. Even though such empirical equivalence might not persist if we would be able to do observation at distances as short as the Planck length (10^{-33} meter, where quantum gravity is supposed to influence strongly the structure of spacetime), it is something we have to reckon with in our present account of cosmological theories. If such a diversity at the level of theories is persistent, the whole idea of knowledge as being true due to a correspondence with reality becomes problematic.

It is not amazing that at the level of abstract theories, at a considerable distance from the phenomena, we might have more than one option. Framing theories is a creative and constructive enterprise. There is no *a priori* reason why only one construction must fit the bill. This has been described as the underdetermination of theories by the data. There are quite trivial examples, which in fact boil down to the problem of induction: even a hundred observations which fit on a straight line are insufficient to establish that the relation is a straight line—it might meander between the observed points. Cosmology as presented in this chapter provides more interesting examples.

The presence of metaphysical ideas as partly guiding research is possible due to the underdetermination of the theories by the present data. Such metaphysical differences about the nature of time or between the possibilities and the actualized realities seem to be persistent. It might be that one of the programs would become the new scientific consensus, due to new observational evidence or through explanatory successes which are unmatched by the others. But even then, there could be different interpretations as long as people hold different metaphysical convictions. Differences in formalism have disappeared in standard quantum theory, but it still has its variety of interpretations.

A Locus for the Influence of Theology on Science

The general issue of the relation between science and theology will be discussed in Chapter 5. For now I want to consider only the implications of underdetermination, which provides room for metaphysical influence in scientific research.

At the intellectual level the relation between science and theology has mostly been a monologue by science addressed to theology, not the 'reciprocal influence' suggested by the often-used terms 'dialogue' or 'interaction' (Lash 1988, 204f). Science leads our understanding of the world. However, the presence of metaphysical influences in the construction of the most abstract theories about our Universe gives an opening for an influence from religious convictions to scientific research. If one has a strong theological interest in history, one would prefer a metaphysics which incorporates time asymmetry. Hence, one would prefer to work on a scientific program which fits that interest, as Penrose's program does. If one's religion is less focussed on history and more on a belief in God as the ultimate, atemporal transcendent Ground, then one might be looking for something more like Hawking's approach. Metaphysical diversity on issues such as the nature of time and reality means that we can achieve consonance in some cases by opting for that scientific program which best fits our theological ideas.

I am not claiming that the scientists involved do have these religious convictions. They are probably atheistic or agnostic. Nor do I mean to imply that theologians should give the scientists advice. The details of their work are much too complex for cheap advice. I defend the view that the religious and philosophical convictions held by the scientist might be reflected in the research program he pursues. A professional theologian or philosopher might be of some help in making as explicit as possible such religious convictions and their metaphysical background. I am not suggesting that there is a strict relation, that the one logically entails the other. Such relations are quite rare, between such different fields as science and theology. As already stated, even if only one of the research programs survived the next decade, there would still be almost the same variety of metaphysical views, perhaps now presented as different interpretations of the theories produced in that single research program.

2.4.2. *Theology and the Variety of Cosmologies*

The fact that there is a plurality of programs pursued in cosmological research beyond the Big Bang theory has some implications for the way we can relate the results of science to theology.

1. The temporal cosmological argument (1.3.1) for the existence of God, on the basis of a beginning of the Universe, turns out not to be univocally supported by science as research goes beyond the Big Bang theory. Some theories refer to a beginning; others (such as Linde's) are without an absolute beginning, and still other theories present a view in which the 'beginning' loses its special status as a feature of reality (Hawking's). It is not amazing that theologians and philosophers are not informed about current cosmological research, but it is a serious failure if we neglect the limits of the theories we use.

2. Many in 'science and religion' focus on methodological issues, but science is also theologically relevant for its content. For instance,

Hawking has a quite different view of the nature of time than Penrose. That implies a different view of history and processes, which bears upon many theological issues.

3. Many authors contributing to 'science and religion' restrict themselves to the areas where science shows consensus. This is much less secure than it seems. For instance, the Big Bang theory suggests a certain view of the 'beginning' of the Universe. However, a more detailed study of scientific research shows that the interesting issues are not in the Big Bang theory, but just beyond its limits, in current research. And, even worse, though the different programs accept the Big Bang theory within its domain, they nonetheless disagree about many issues of interpretation of the Big Bang theory because they envisage a different further development of the scientific understanding of the Universe. This raises the question about the relevance of the established scientific theories for theology.

If one leaves the domain of consensus, one has to face the plurality of approaches in the forefront of research. This is not only the case for cosmology, but holds also for other areas of fundamental physics such as the interpretation of quantum mechanics or of thermodynamics.

In 'science and theology' should we restrict ourselves to the most promising ideas (but how do we know?), pick the idea that best fits our personal view (but that is arbitrarily selective), or wait till there is consensus (which might take a long time)? If we look primarily for intelligibility, as I suggest with the notion of constructive consonance (0.2, 5.5), we can take a look at as many approaches as we can, to learn from each what we can and cannot meaningfully say about theological concepts. If we look for credibility, we should be willing to face the scientific approach that is the hardest to encompass; a kind of reverse eclecticism: take science where it hurts most (Eaves 1989, 203; see 5.5.3). In any case, we may have to accept the provisional nature and uncertain status of all theological models, even if they have been built upon the availalable scientific consensus.

2.5.   EDGES, CREATION, AND NOTHING

In this section I will focus on the notion of *creation out of nothing* in the context of cosmologies like those of Hawking. The absence of a beginning of time in some theories has been taken by some writers to imply the absence of a creator. I will argue that this rests on a view of God and God's role in creation which is not the view of most developed theologies. The second issue is the claim that physical cosmology is not able to describe creation out of nothing, as claimed, for instance, by Hawking. I will argue that this physical concept of 'nothing' is not identical to the philosophical concept. This brings us to the contingency of existence, which I take up in the following chapter. Theories such as Hawking's might get closer to a 'complete explanation of the Universe', an answer to the traditional metaphysical question of why the Universe is as it is. This too is a question I will take up again in the next chapter.

Creatio ex nihilo traditionally has two components: origination and dependency at all moments. Deism, in general, emphasizes only the first, God's role in the beginning. However most of the recent cosmologies emphasize a structural similarity of all moments. Therefore the understanding of *creatio ex nihilo* as dependency, which might be seen as the counterpart of God's sustaining activity, fits in more easily with recent cosmological ideas. If we're looking for a religious interpretation, theism fits better than deism.

This doesn't answer the fundamental question of why, in the first place, we should consider a religious interpretation, even one involving a notion of a transcendent God. An interpretation of transcendence will be developed in the next two chapters. Some non-scientific reasons for preferring such an interpretation will be given, after discussing the prospect of complete theories—a prospect which would suggest that we need nothing beyond the scientifically knowable universe— in the next chapter.

2.5.1. *Edges and Deism*

> the conclusion of the effort, at least so far: a universe with no edge in space, no beginning or end in time, and nothing for a Creator to do. (Carl Sagan 1988, x)

For Carl Sagan the issue is simple: if Hawking is right that there is no absolute beginning of reality, than there is no need for a Creator. This is quite similar to the argument of others that a beginning in the Big Bang sense supports belief in a Creator (1.2.1, 1.3). However, it is not the only possible position. Quite a number of theologians and others have argued that the two—a physical beginning and belief in God—are relatively independent (1.2.4, 1.2.5, 1.5).

We might picture God as the great watchmaker who constructed the world and wound the spring—before letting it run by itself according to the original design. In relation to such an image of God the beginning is very important, for it is there that the watchmaker did his (or her) job. This kind of theological imagery was popular in the seventeenth and eighteenth centuries and it is perhaps still the most widespread image, aside from that of God as 'an old man up there'. Belief in the watchmaker-God has been labeled 'deism', in contrast to theism, which holds that God is also actively involved in the processes of the world at later moments. Contemporary theologians have, in many different ways, argued that it is of major importance to see God as related to the present. A purely deistic concept of God is not a serious option within contemporary theology, because such a God would not be relevant to us and the ways we shape our lives.

The removal of a beginning would imply that the watchmaker God is not a defendable image. That seems to be the essence of Sagan's remark. However, it is not a death blow to theism, since this is not the kind of God theism defends. For some theologies it's even the other way round. For instance, process theology, a theological strand which developed on the basis of the philosophies of Whitehead and Hartshorne, argues that there is no absolute beginning, but only an eternal process in which the world and God exert influence on each other. This concept doesn't fit the Hawking theory either, because its view of the nature of time is very different. But the example of such a theology, which is intellectually quite well-developed, shows that theology is not necessarily tied to an absolute beginning, an edge to time.

Whether it is possible to develop a theological view which fits the whole picture, not only the edgelessness but also the nature of time and the determinism and completeness suggested in the Hawking cosmology, remains to be seen. But Sagan's argument 'no edge, hence no God' is not decisive. Aside from the possibilities which might still be present in the context of the Hawking cosmology, we need to keep in mind the status of this cosmology. As argued above, there is a genuine pluralism in contemporary cosmology, and this pluralism is at its strongest where cosmologies touch on the most fundamental metaphysical questions. Hence, we could opt for a cosmology which still allows for such an edge, a beginning of time, as Penrose's cosmology does.

2.5.2. *Out of Nothing*

Hartle and Hawking interpret their own proposal for the wave function of the Universe as allowing the probability "for the universe to appear from Nothing" (Hartle and Hawking 1983, 2961). Here

I will argue that the Hartle-Hawking theory does not describe such an "appearance out of nothing", taken in its absolute sense. Neither do other theories, such as those of Vilenkin. I will argue below that the Hartle-Hawking theory can be interpreted in the sense of *creatio ex nihilo* (creation out of nothing), but that this theological notion should then be understood as a view of the Universe as being sustained by God at every moment rather than as a cosmogonic expression.

There is one sense in which this theory can most clearly be understood as creation from 'nothing'. As was explained above (2.3.2), ordinary calculations often assume a state at one moment and laws to calculate the state at another moment. In such situations one might say that the second state arises out of the first state. There is in the Hartle-Hawking approach at the timeless level no reference to a state other than the 'resulting' state. As it is compact, it is the only boundary present in the calculation. The theory gives a precise meaning to the notion of 'nothing' as the absence of other boundaries in the calculation.

However this should not be misunderstood as appearance out of nothing. Appearance is a temporal notion, which does not fit with this level of description. Expressions like 'tunnelling from nothing' are of a mixed nature, and not suitable to describe the basic idea of this theory. Tunnelling connotes a temporal process, while the 'from nothing' applies to a kind of time-independent actuality.

The 'nothing' is not an absolute nothing. One "must still grant the existence of quite a body of pre-existing laws of Nature in order to get away with this trick" (Barrow 1988, 231; similarly Heller 1987, 421), for example quantum laws and fields as well as mathematical logic. The 'nothing' which has a precise meaning in the context of this proposal is not an absolute 'nothing' in a more philosophical sense.

There are serious problems when one tries to combine the language of probabilities with the notion of 'nothing'. I will first formulate two objections in general terms, and then formulate one in the terms of the quantum cosmology of Hartle and Hawking.

1. The probability of throwing a head when tossing a coin is one half, but a fifty percent chance of getting an actual head is there if and only if someone tosses a coin, if and only if one of the possible outcomes is realized. A mathematical idea of getting a universe from nothing does not give a physical universe, but only the idea of a physical universe—assuming that there is a difference between the Universe and a mathematical idea about the Universe. There has to

be some input of 'physical reality'. Perhaps that is an aspect of the nothingness, but that makes it into a physical entity and not nothing at all.

2. Physical probabilities, as exemplified by radioactive decay, start with something, an initial situation (a particle in space and time) becoming another situation (other particles in space and time). The probability is the chance that the transition from Situation 1 to Situation 2 happens during a certain interval of time, or that the particle is found in a certain volume of space, or something of that nature. Even if one reduces the entities in the first situation as much as possible (no energy, no matter fields, and so forth), talking about probabilities only makes sense if there is some measurable structure (like time) present in the first situation.

These two arguments are both contained in the description from within time. It is difficult, if not impossible, to get outside that when talking about probabilities. That also shows up in the third, more technical, argument.

3. Before interpreting a wave function as an amplitude for probabilities, the normalization must be established. In the case of a single particle, without creation or destruction, the wave function is normalized by requiring that the integral of the probabilities over the whole space must yield 1 at any moment: the particle must be somewhere. Hartle and Hawking use something similar for the wave function of the Universe (Hartle and Hawking 1983, formula 4.3). It is the requirement that the probability of having a metric at a three-dimensional spacelike 'surface' is 1. If this is the way normalization is achieved, the wave function gives the amplitude, not that a state arises from nothing, but that a certain state is there, given that there must be a metric, a universe.[11]

Interpreting the Hartle-Hawking wave function as giving probabilities for appearance out of nothing is too strong. Rather, more defendable and modest, this approach "determines the relative probability of universes corresponding to different classical solutions" (Hawking 1984a, 377).

2.5.3. Creation as Cosmology or as Dependency

Traditional theological ideas about creatio ex nihilo have two poles. On the one hand they refer to cosmogony, the coming into being of our Universe. On the other hand they denote an eternal sustaining by God, ultimate dependence at each moment. Chris Isham states that the latter "is somewhat decoupled from modern scientific thought" (Isham 1988, 376), a view that is probably widely shared among theologians and scientists. A recent exception is Pannenberg, who argues that the notion of inertia (or mass) in physics is at odds with the theological idea that the world is continuously sustained by God (Pannenberg 1981, 1988c).

In my view, the Hawking cosmology lends itself much more to an interpretation in terms of sustaining than of making. The basic entities are the three-dimensional spaces with their material content (fields). Therefore, these are to be seen in this context as the basic entities of creation, the 'what' that is created. The calculations of their relative probabilities can be performed on the timeless level. It is not that one results from the other or comes after the other. From the timeless perspective they are all co-eternal, or they are all created 'timelessly'. Hence they all are equally related to the Ground of Being.

Another way to argue for the same conclusion: this scheme does not have an initial event with a special status. There is no way to pick one slice as the first of the sequence. Hence, all moments have a similar relation to the Creator. Either they are all 'just brute facts', or they are all equally created.

This view of God 'sustaining' the world in all its 'times' has been transformed by Isham into another image: "one can almost imagine the universe . . . being held in the cup of God's hand" (Isham 1988, 405).

To summarize: this theory allows for a precise interpretation of *ex nihilo* (2.5.2), and it fits better with the idea that every space (with content) is equally created by God than with the idea that God created 'in the beginning'. Questions about the relationship between the two components of *creatio ex nihilo* follow. Understanding it as a cosmogonic process seems to single out a certain event as having a special relation to God. Sustaining tends to stress the similarity of all states in their relation to God. Theologians who want to defend both components of *creatio ex nihilo* need to clarify the similarity and dissimilarity between the first and the later states in their relation to God. In the theory discussed here there is no moment with a special status, and therefore the cosmogonic interpretation loses its force.

2.5.4. *Theology in the Context of Hawking's Cosmology*

The different cosmologies described in this chapter provide different contexts for theological thought. A theology which fits one cosmology need not be in accord with the other cosmological research programs. Hawking's cosmology, as one of the well-developed contemporary programs, does not fit theologies with a strong emphasis on processes in time. Amazingly, this quantum cosmology seems much closer to two seventeenth-century views. The cosmology might perhaps be made consonant with traditional reformed theology, which saw everything as predetermined by God. It might also be combined with a Spinozistic view of God and the world, where the world is one of God's eternal modes of being. As does the traditional reformed view, this approach accepts strict determinism. In a sense, the Spinozistic view fits even better, as the Universe acquires in Hawking's cosmology some of God's characteristics, being timeless, eternal, and 'necessary'.

There is one major difficulty in case one tries to combine Hawking's cosmology with a Christian view of the world. In the way it has been presented here, the theory is about three-dimensional spaces with material content. They may be ordered in time-sequences, but that is secondary. Therefore, the model lacks continuity between subsequent events, like the reading of the first and the second word of a sentence. One might evoke God as the one who gives continuity, but that means God 'filling the gaps'. In the major Christian traditions there is a sense of continuity, because God's great deeds in the past (Exodus, the convenant on Sinai, Incarnation, Resurrection) are supposed to have relevance for today and for the future. In a Christian perspective, the past has to be taken up into the present in some way.

A final word of caution: this theory is not to be taken as *the* conclusion of science today. It is still in development, and it is one program among others, although one of the most elegant and coherent schemes. The special feature of the Hartle-Hawking scheme is the absence of a boundary as its proposal for a boundary condition. This absence of a boundary could be a model, of limited validity, for reflection on *creatio ex nihilo*.

COSMOLOGY WITH OR WITHOUT GOD

3.1. INTRODUCTION

> The only way of explaining the creation is to show that the creator had absolutely no job at all to do, and so might as well not have existed. We can track down the infinitely lazy creator, the creator totally free of any labour of creation, by resolving apparent complexities into simplicities. (Peter Atkins 1981, 17)

Is God an element in the explanation of the Universe? Or is God unnecessary for the explanation of the Universe, and hence superfluous? Or is a God beyond the Universe ruled out, since the Universe is everything? This chapter deals with three different topics, mainly related to traditional arguments for the existence of God. At the end (4.6.1) the main conclusions are recapitulated and integrated into the main drift of this book.

I first look at a topic related to the argument from design, the 'anthropic principles'. Our place in space is not special; we are not the center of the Solar System, nor of the Galaxy, nor of the Universe. However, it has been argued that our Universe is a very special universe among the possible universes. Other universes would not allow for life. Is our Universe special? If it is, so what? Does this show that life is the purpose of the Universe? Does it indicate divine design?

Science seems on the brink of explaining everything. Atkins, for example, expects science to explain everything, even the coming into being of the Universe and its dimensionality. There would be no role left for a creator. Section 3.3 considers the expectations about complete theories, and the tension between unity and diversity. Section 3.4 deals with contingency. Contingency, in contrast with necessity, means that something about the Universe could have been different. We will consider whether the initial conditions and the laws can be considered contingent, and whether they may be in need of a non-scientific explanation (3.4.1), whether contingency is a notion which fits science (3.4.2), and the contingency of existence—'Why is there anything at all, and not nothing?', (3.4.3).

We then turn to the question whether a God beyond the Universe can be a meaningful notion or is excluded by science. Such a notion of transcendence implies, as far as science is concerned, a certain agnosticism with respect to that transcendence (3.5).

The final section recapitulates the different arguments for and against the existence of God as discussed so far. A second-order argument about the intelligibility of the Universe is also considered. All these arguments are found wanting. They always involve additional assumptions. We cannot escape our own limitations and the ambiguities due to them.

3.2. DESIGN AS EXPLANATION: ANTHROPIC PRINCIPLES

"The most miraculous thing is happening. The physicists are getting down to the nitty-gritty, they've really just about pared things down to the ultimate details, and the last thing they ever expected to happen is happening. God is showing through. . . . "
. . . "Mr. Kohler. What kind of God is showing through, exactly?"
(Dialogue between a computer freak and a professor at a divinity school in *Roger's Version* by John Updike [New York, 1986, 9]).

3.2.1. *Weak, Strong, and Participatory Anthropic Principles*

The anthropic principles,[1] or the coincidences with which they are related, have been used in scientific and metaphysical explanations for characteristics of the Universe. It will be argued here that anthropic principles do not function properly in scientific explanations. Either the contribution is trivial, as is the case for the so-called Weak Anthropic Principle (3.2.3), or the contribution is metaphysical, as is the case for the various strong anthropic principles (3.2.4). Nor does anthropic reasoning provide arguments from science in favor of metaphysical positions such as the existence of God (3.2.5). Rather, the anthropic principles are, or presuppose, certain metaphysical positions which, once accepted, imply certain views of the Universe. This does not exclude the possibility that the existence of life provides information about the Universe we happen to live in.[2] However, this is at the level of data, which might be called anthropic coincidences.

The *Weak Anthropic Principle* (WAP) states that what we see must be compatible with our existence. We see a Universe with planets because we depend on planets. We see a Universe which has existed for some billions of years because it took billions of years to develop beings which are capable of thinking about the age of the Universe. It has the nature of a selection rule: our observations are biassed in favor of situations where we exist.

The *Strong Anthropic Principle* (SAP) has been stated thus: "The Universe must have those properties which allow life to develop within it at some stage in its history" (Barrow and Tipler 1986, 21). This is not a statement about what we actually observe but about the class of possible universes.[3] There are different ways to argue for this principle. One has been given by the physicist J. A. Wheeler when he related the existence of the Universe to the existence of observers in the Universe. This particular version has been called the *Participatory Anthropic Principle* (PAP). Others have related the necessity of the conditions for life to design, and hence to a creator who prefers to create a universe with life, or even sentient and conscious life.

3.2.2. *Anthropic Coincidences and Explanations*

Some examples of anthropic coincidences will be given, as well as a few explanations which invoke the Weak Anthropic Principle. The next section will evaluate this type of argument, and hence the Weak Anthropic Principle.

Size and Age of the Universe
The Universe is enormous in size when compared to human dimensions, even when compared with the human enterprise that reaches farthest: space-travel. The age of the Universe is more than a million times the typical age of a human civilization. This might result in feelings of insignificance, as forcefully expressed in the science fiction story *The Restaurant at the End of the Universe* by Douglas Adams. He describes a terrible machine which destroys the soul: the Total Perspective Vortex. It makes one see the whole infinity of

creation and oneself in relation to it. The effectiveness of this machine shows that life cannot afford to have a sense of proportion (Adams 1985, 71).

However, other things being equal, the age and size of the Universe might be related to our existence. We need certain types of atoms, like Carbon and Oxygen. These atoms are produced by nuclear processes in stars. Some of these stars exploded. Such supernova explosions were instrumental in producing heavier elements and spreading them around. Our kind of life became possible only after the interstellar gas had been enriched sufficiently with heavier elements produced and distributed by these processes. Biological evolution took another couple of billions of years to produce complex, intelligent, observing, and amiable beings—us.

Turning this description upside down, it is argued that intelligent observation by natural beings is only possible after a couple of billion years, say ten billion years. Thus, such beings can only observe a universe which is at least ten billion years old. Along this line, WAP offers an 'explanation' for the observed age of the Universe. Such a universe must then also have a size of ten billion light years in all directions, hence the size is also 'necessary' for our existence.

Density of the Universe

The Big Bang theory assumes certain initial conditions. Prominent among them is the average density of the Universe. A universe with a much larger density would have collapsed at an early stage, while a universe with less matter would have been too diluted to allow the formation of stars.

A WAP 'explanation' turns this around. We can only exist in a universe which does not collapse too early and which also allows the formation of stars. Thus, our existence implies—and hence 'explains'—that we observe a nearly flat universe, or at least a nearly flat region of the Universe.

Dimensionality

We happen to experience our world as having three spatial dimensions as well as one time dimension. Why? "One possible answer is the anthropic principle" (Hawking 1988, 164). Two-dimensional creatures would be separated into two halves by any canal running through the body, say for digestion or the circulation of blood. In higher-dimensional worlds planetary orbits would be unstable.

Many other arguments for various aspects of the initial conditions of the Universe and the laws applying in our Universe can be found in *The Anthropic Cosmological Principle* (Barrow and Tipler 1986).[4] The Russian cosmologist Rozental (1988), among others, offers many examples of the explanatory use of weak anthropic arguments as a selection rule in a context with 'many worlds'[5].

3.2.3. *Evaluation of the Weak Anthropic Principle*

The Weak Anthropic Principle is in itself true but devoid of relevance. Take the following simplified example:

1. Assume that we know that life depends on liquid water.
2. We observe the existence of life, for instance ourselves.
3. WAP then predicts that our environment, our planet, will have a surface temperature between zero and hundred degrees centigrade. This explains the temperature on our planet.

This is no explanation. It is merely the common use of evidence: we observe A (life, 2), we know that A and B go together (1, life needs liquid water), and hence B (3, there must be liquid water). This does not explain why A and B are there, why there are living beings and planets with the right temperatures, nor does it explain why A and B go together. The anthropic reasoning repeats the first assumption: the two go together. There is nothing wrong with the argument, but there is no reason to call the WAP "a principle".[6]

The explanation of an event is in general something different from the explanation one offers when asked 'How do you know?'. From the existence of this book you, as a reader, can infer the existence of its author. You can show the book when challenged by someone else to explain how you know about that person. However, the book does not explain the existence of the author. It only provides the grounds for your belief in his existence. Retrograde reasoning justifies beliefs, but it does not explain why the situation was that way. "Instead of saying that I am here because my parents met, I say that because I am here I know that my parents met. . . . From the present state of the world one can obviously make all sorts of highly probable, sometimes certain, conjectures about its distant past" (Gardner 1986, 22).

'Backward thinking' has other difficulties. Feinberg and Shapiro (1980) used the example of the Mississippi River—which is awfully well fitted for the Mississippi Valley. If one were to put the Amazon

River in its place one would run into all kinds of trouble, like misplaced bridges and the flooding of New Orleans. One could suppose that the Mississippi River was designed for its valley. The mutual fit between river and valley has, of course, a regular explanation: the flow of the water follows the shape of the valley. Weak anthropic explanations seem inappropriate. Science might find more classical explanations for those features for which an anthropic argument has been advanced. This has already happened several times. Inflation reduced the number of unexplained features of the Big Bang theory. It explains, for instance, the density and expansion velocity. The number of dimensions might turn out to be a necessary consequence of a higher-dimensional theory which has only this low temperature appearance. Heinz Pagels (1985b, 38) even sees anthropic reasoning as dangerous to the scientific enterprise, since it detracts from the real job of science, finding a fundamental explanation.

Anthropic arguments employ something that we do not yet understand, complex life and consciousness, to explain something else. These arguments tend to take for granted that our kind of life is the only way that entities can have the complex structure which appears to be necessary for making observations and reflecting upon them. However, there might be totally different forms of 'life' which we cannot yet imagine. Weak anthropic arguments invoking possible worlds seem to allow anything to be different, except for the form observership could have. In a world with another structure the conditions for life could be different.

Weak Anthropic Principle with Many Actual Worlds

The Weak Anthropic Principle might explain something if it were combined with the assumption that there are 'many worlds', regions which were different with respect to the relevant property (such as the mini-universes in Linde's cosmology). The realization of a property with a non-zero probability becomes very probable if there are many occasions, and it becomes certain if there are an infinite number of occasions. If there are an extremely large number of monkeys typing for some time there might be one flawlessly typing a Shakespeare play—as well as many more typing the same play almost flawlessly. However, this does not explain the typing monkeys (the many worlds), nor the possibility and probability of the event.

A weak anthropic argument with many worlds does not explain why we have precisely this Universe and not one which is slightly less isotropic. It would be more probable to pick one of the many versions of the play which are complete except for one misplaced punctuation mark. As Penrose argues, if the Universe were only contrived for the purpose of having life the arrangement could have been much less precise.

Hawking opposes anthropic arguments invoking many worlds with the principle of economy. If other universes are separate from our own Universe, and thus have no observable consequences in our Universe, they might as well not exist. They can be "cut out of the theory" (Hawking 1988, 125). If they were related they would be part of one universe, and hence should obey the same fundamental laws. In the same book Hawking used an anthropic argument for the effective dimensionality observed: intelligent beings could be present only in regions with three dimensions. The crux is that different regions are part of one universe governed by one fundamental law. This law allows for different expressions, in this case dimensions, at low energy. One could still argue that it would be more economical to do away with unobservable regions of another dimensionality, but cutting these regions away would make the resulting theory less economical as it needs an additional principle.

The metaphysical issue with theological significance in discussions of the Weak Anthropic Principle is not so much whether the principle of selective observation is valid and useful but rather the relation between the actual and the possible. Both Linde and Hawking (2.3) take it that all possibilities of a theory are realized, and then they can find a job for a weak anthropic selection rule to explain certain features of our observations as typical for regions in which observers can exist.[7] Penrose seeks a way to express his conviction that there is a natural process which reduces the many possibilities to one realized possibility.

3.2.4. *The Strong Anthropic Principles*

The strong anthropic principles state that any possible universe must have the properties for life (or intelligent and observing life).[8] This is a statement not only about the observable Universe but about the class of all possible universes; it leads to an explanation of properties of the Universe in terms of purpose: a property that is necessary for life is necessary for the Universe. Such teleological approaches have a long history, but they are not widely accepted in contemporary science.

Strong anthropic arguments have some disadvantages.

1. Properties of other possible universes are untestable, as we do not have access to those other universes. Either they are not actual, only possible, in which case we are unable to set up an experiment in which we make them actual, or the other possibilities are actual, and one could think of them as bubbles or other domains within a single universe. But as long as those domains are much larger than the observable Universe this offers no testable consequences. A third form of many possible universes might be based upon the Many Worlds Interpretation of quantum theory (see 2.3.3). All the possible outcomes co-exist in a fuzzy reality. Any concrete observation is always made in a specific branch—and does not give access to the other branches.

Strong anthropic reasoning cannot rely on testable consequences about the class of possible universes (or of domains within a universe). Its appeal must be based upon the coherence of the view which it supports.

2. Anthropic arguments are quite restrictive in their predictions about possible universes, if 'life' is taken to be 'life as we know it'. However, life in its richness is only partly understood. This is even more the case for consciousness. To seek to explain properties of the Universe by reference to life or consciousness is like asking the lame and the blind to guide each other. Besides, other forms of life might develop in zillions of years in completely different stages of the Universe, or other forms of life might be possible in other possible universes.

3. SAP explanations are also vulnerable to the future development of scientific theories. Successive theories have, in general, fewer and fewer unexplained parameters (constants or boundary conditions). As we will see below, some scientists are searching for a complete theory, perhaps even one without any arbitrary parameters—without invoking any reference to the necessary existence of life. If they were to succeed the set of consistent possible universes would contain only one element.

If applied on a small scale, as in 'planets must have properties which allow for the development of life in some stage of their history', a strong anthropic principle is surely false. This example illustrates the nature of the SAP; it is like the old teleological arguments: everything must have a function, and therefore the Moon must be populated, as the ancient philosopher Plutarch argued (Raingard 1934). Although we are no longer able to maintain that the Moon is populated, we can still claim that the Moon has a function for life, for instance in the development of life on Earth through tidal effects. A teleological view of the Universe is not implied by science. It is a metaphysical view, which fits in well with belief in a Creator who likes living beings and therefore created one or more 'universes'— an idea which might be called the TAP or Theistic Anthropic Principle.

A version of strong anthropic reasoning which seems to have more basis in science is the Participatory Anthropic Principle (PAP), introduced by J. A. Wheeler (Wheeler 1977; Patton and Wheeler 1975). It builds upon the interpretation discussion about quantum theories. As I mentioned above (2.3.3), quantum theory has as its basic entity a state vector (or wave function) which describes a superposition of many states. However, we do not observe such superpositions, but only more definite states. One of the proposed solutions for this tension between the many possibilities and the one actuality is that the act of observation changes the state vector from describing a mixture to one describing the one observed state. Observation makes reality definite; some even defend the view that observation now makes the past definite. But what is an observation? A measurement apparatus would still in principle be subject to a quantum theoretical description in terms of a superposition. How does the apparatus get its definite reality? Some, including Wheeler, have pursued this line to the moment where consciousness comes in. The PAP supposes that it is observation by conscious beings which gives reality to all the preceding stages.

If this interpretation is applied to the Universe, and if the Universe is subject to a quantum mechanical description, this leads to the conclusion that a universe needs to develop conscious beings who observe the early universe. Otherwise it would not come into existence. We are not mere creatures, but "central participators in the great cosmic drama" (Eccles 1979, 31).

Wheeler's view is based upon a sound knowledge of quantum theory, a disputable, but not necessarily wrong, interpretation of quantum mechanics, and a preference for the question of the origin of the Universe above the question about the difference between an observer and an observed system. The characteristics needed to qualify as an observer are unclear. "Was the world wave function waiting for millions of years until a single-celled creature appeared? Or did it have to wait a little longer for some more highly qualified measurer—with a Ph.D.?" (Bell 1981, 610). It also seems a bit odd that regions of the Universe with observers would be different from regions without them, even though the differences would not be observable (Penrose 1989, 295). Both the Strong Anthropic Principle and the Participatory Anthropic Principle are metaphysical principles. The supposed necessity of life has not been established as a fact independent of specific metaphysical positions.[9] Hence, these anthropic principles do provide an alternative to the idea of divine design, but not an especially compelling one.

One might accept the necessity of life (SAP) because one believes that one of God's purposes in creating the Universe was to create humankind after God's own image. Upon such a theological perspective anthropic considerations should be insufficient, according to the cosmologist Don Page (1987), for a complete explanation. It would be hubris, excessive pride, to assume that humans are the main reason the Universe is as it is. God could well have had other purposes.

3.2.5. *Anthropic Coincidences and Divine Design*

In some discussions of the anthropic principles two ideas are juxtaposed: *either* design, and hence God as an explanation, *or* many worlds with a WAP explanation for the properties of our world.[10] The theistic explanation should be considered as equally respectable as a WAP explanation. It might even be preferable. John Polkinghorne, a professor of theoretical physics who became an Anglican priest, calls the ideas about other worlds metaphysical speculations.

> A possible explanation of equal intellectual respectability—and to my mind greater economy and elegance—would be that this one world is the way it is because it is the creation of the will of a Creator who purposes that it should be so. (Polkinghorne 1986, 80).

Such an apologetic defense of God's reality does not work:

1. The argument assumes that the anthropic coincidences are here to stay. However, some of these features, which apparently point to design, or perhaps even all of them, might find more traditional scientific explanations in future theories. That is what has happened for the traditional design arguments based on intra-cosmic adaptedness. The inflationary scenario has already led to some erosion of anthropic coincidences, making the argument for theistic design or many worlds less forceful.

2. According to Hugh Montefiore, design is simpler than, and hence to be preferred to, a weak anthropic selection working on

many actual 'worlds'. The latter "is infinitely more complex in so far as it postulates an infinite number of universes" (Montefiore 1985, 38). This is a widespread objection against theories which work with a plurality of 'worlds'. It appeals to a philosophical rule of 'economy', often ascribed to the fourteenth-century William of Occam: one should not introduce more entities than necessary to explain the phenomena.

But here the 'economy' rule is misapplied. The many worlds are not introduced 'by hand'. Take again the example of planetary systems. The standard theory explains planets as remnants of an original cloud which collapsed to form a star. This theory works well for our Solar System and fits in with our knowledge about stars and their formation. It seems more complex, more *ad hoc*, to reject the possibility of other planetary systems, although perhaps not observed, than to accept their existence. It would need an additional rule if one would accept this theory of planetary formation and reject the possibility of other planetary systems.

It is simpler to accept a theory in its predictions beyond the observable domain than to draw a line, if a theory works well for the accessible domain, and if the theory is simple and coherent. The issue of simplicity is not about the number of entities predicted by a theory but about the structure of the theory. Does a theory need more separate rules to include those entities or to exclude them? Some cosmological theories, like Linde's (2.3.1), are simpler if one allows for the existence of many domains. Simplicity is not a simple count of entities: one Creator or many universes.

3. One of the attractive features of the anthropic coincidences as a basis for a design argument appears to be the concrete nature of the evidence. Rather than using 'design' it is based upon the improbability of certain numerical values.

However, we don't have the opportunity to find out probabilities by trying many universes. We are therefore limited to the use of *a priori* probabilities for 'order' and 'disorder'. In this context Michael Ovenden (1987, 105f) pointed out two ambiguities. First, the order perceived depends upon the properties considered and hence is partly subjective. Second, in a deterministic world, like the world of classical physics as well as most quantum cosmologies, every past or future state is implied by a complete specification of the present state. Hence, changes in the order we ascribe to the system are due to our selection of parameters considered. This is not directly applicable to the anthropic coincidences, which deal with parameters for the whole process and not with parameters changing in time. Nonetheless, the subjective nature of the improbability ascribed to the anthropic coincidences must be dealt with if one is to sustain a definite argument from design on the basis of those improbabilities. Ovenden asks whether we are thus, in seeking evidence for design, simply seeing ourselves, involved in "a pointless exercise in narcissm" (Ovenden 1987, 106). Pointing out the subjective component in an anthropic design argument need not result in the opposite extreme, as if there were no mirror into which Narcissus looked. Even more strongly, not Narcissus but 'the mirror' is the object of scientific research. However, we consider probabilities with respect to a constructed model of possible universes, that is, possible values of these constants.

Paul Davies (1983a, 1984, 1988) has argued that one might be able to explain how all physical structures have come into being without appeal to a creator. However, we would still need to explain the laws which were used in these explanations. "The laws which enable the universe to come into being spontaneously seem themselves to be the product of exceedingly ingenious design" (Davies 1984, 243). This would suggest a purpose which includes the consequences of these laws: us.[11] Aspects of a complete explanation of existence and the contingency of the laws of physics will be discussed in the next sections, both in defense of a persistent 'mystery of existence' and in relation to the alternative view that there might be only one logically possible set of physical laws—and hence no room for design.

We might even push the issue beyond the specific form the laws have to the general lawfulness of the Universe. The emphasis is, according to the philosopher of religion Hugo Meynell, "on the explanation for the intelligibility of the world, rather than on accounting for the gaps in that intelligibility" (Meynell 1987, 253). Such an argument from intelligibility cannot be combined with arguments based on specific design. The final section comes back to this general issue of intelligibility in relation to the preceding discussions (3.6).

My rejection of a theistic design argument based on the anthropic coincidences does not imply that belief in a Creator is wrong, nor that all possibilities of a theory should exist. It implies merely that this way of doing the apologetic job does not work. We need to take more seriously the idea of more worlds as well as the possibility of more complete scientific theories. It seems that the theological interpretation does not follow from the anthropic coincidences.

Rather, once one has a theological understanding of reality, the anthropic coincidences can be seen as expressions of God's providence (as in Bosshard 1985, 209). The underlying coincidences and the whole approach point to the way in which the scientific understanding of humans is an understanding in the context of their world, including the cosmological Universe. Humans are, in a sense, children of the Universe. But that doesn't clearly point to a Universe designed for the sake of humans, nor, as pointed out by Rolston (1987, 257), does it imply that there is nothing but nature.

3.3. COMPLETE THEORIES: THE ONE FORGETS THE MANY

> Confronted with an emotionally satisfying mathematical scheme which is 'simple' enough to command universal assent, but esoteric enough to admit no means of experimental test and grandiose enough to provoke no new questions, then, closeted within our [conceptual] world within the world, we might simply have to believe it. Whereof we cannot speak thereof we must be silent: this is the final sentence of the laws of nature. (John D. Barrow 1988, 373)

3.3.1. *Complete Theories: The Ideal of Unity*

There are three components in current arguments for complete theories: mathematical consistency, the actual presence of all possibilities, and esthetic criteria.

Mathematical Consistency: The Problem of Infinities
Quantum physics is very successful. Its predictions have been confirmed to a very high degree of accuracy. However, it has one problem, aside from the interpretation issue discussed above (2.3.3). Take, for instance, quantum electrodynamics, the theory which describes a world of electrons, positrons (anti-matter particles resembling the electrons), and radiation. In this theory the mass of the electron turns out to be infinite. Hence, our mass would be infinite as well, which is in disagreement with observations.

Theoretical physicists have found a trick, called renormalization, to get around this problem: subtract infinity somewhere. This procedure can be defined rigorously and it works. It implies that the resulting mass is not a prediction of the theory but taken for granted.

If the same trick were needed over and over again in calculations the theory would be useless; it would not predict anything. A renormalizable theory is a theory which needs this trick only once, and then the theory produces finite results in all other calculations. Quantum electrodynamics is such a renormalizable theory, tested and confirmed to a very high degree of accuracy.

Particle theories which incorporated more particles turned out to be plagued by infinities which were not that well manageable. The Dutch physicist Gerard 't Hooft showed in the early 1970s that only theories of a specific type were renormalizable, and showed how the trick worked for such theories. Since then theories of the different nuclear forces have followed this path, both the Weinberg-Salem theory for the weak interactions and the quark theory for the strong interactions. The more recent developments towards Grand Unified Theories (GUTs), which integrate nuclear and electromagnetic forces, are also within this class of renormalizable theories.

As history has shown, the requirement of having a theory with manageable infinities, a renormalizable theory, is rather restrictive. And it seems artificial, a trick to sweep the problems under the rug.

One step further would be a theory without problems, one which predicted finite results for all possible observations. Such finiteness for a theory is, surely, a stronger restriction than renormalizability. And the restrictions become even more severe if the theory has to include gravity as well. There are, as far as I know, no theories of which it has been shown that they are finite under all circumstances. However, there are some theories which might have this property. The best candidates today are called superstring theories, and their number is quite small (Green 1986). Six theories satisfy the known conditions of consistency, and of those six three are perhaps equivalent. "Ideally it will turn out that there is only one" (Schwarz 1987, 654).

The idea might be clear even without going into the interesting and difficult details of the proposed theories: requiring that a theory produces finite results for all possible observations is very restrictive. This, combined with more obvious forms of mathematical consistency, might mean that there is only one possible theory which describes the particles and interactions in a universe.

It is assumed throughout this kind of scientific work that the laws can be formulated mathematically. I am not sufficiently well-informed to be certain that there are no other assumptions taken for granted. Through such assumptions there might be an *a posteriori* component in the selection of the single possible theory. But the possibility of a very limited set of mathematically consistent theories deserves to be taken seriously.

A Universe with All Possibilities Present

Linde imagines the Universe as consisting of mini-universes, bubbles "of all possible types" (Linde 1987a, 627). Hawking has a quite different proposal for the structure of the Universe at large. In his view the many possibilities which are part of the quantum description of the Universe are all equally present.

The actuality of all possibilities, in one way or another, implies that an explanation does not need to claim that certain features are the only possible outcome of the preceding processes. It is sufficient if those features are possible, for then they will be realized somewhere. "This problem is still difficult, but it is much easier than the one we have been trying to solve" (Linde 1987b, 68).

Without this assumption, that all possibilities are actual, a complete explanation would not work. We would be left with an incompleteness, as the theory would not specify which possibility is the actual one. However, this assumption alone isn't sufficient. The presence of all possibilities is always the presence of all possibilities of a certain theory. The question remains: why one theory and not another?

Simplicity and Esthetics

There are variants of Einstein's theory of General Relativity which are compatible with observations as they stand today. Nonetheless, these variants are not considered to be as good as Einstein's theory. Judgments like this are based on criteria such as coherence, simplicity, and elegance. Similar judgments are made in discussing more recent cosmological theories. When M. A. Markov states that his proposal for an oscillating universe has no problem of origin, the underlying judgment that an origination is a problem relies on considerations such as the presumption that an abrupt beginning upsets the coherence and continuity of physical descriptions. Hawking also defends his proposal as the most reasonable idea, a universe without edges, which is self-contained. The test is whether the proposal fits the observations, but "it may initially be put forward for aesthetic or metaphysical reasons" (Hawking 1988, 136).

As I see it, those reasons don't only arise "initially", in the process of discovery. Esthetic and metaphysical arguments are still present in the criteria for theory evaluation. Accepting such criteria in addition to the requirement of consistency might reduce the number of possible initial conditions (as in Hawking's proposal) and laws, within the not too distant future, perhaps even to only one package.

3.3.2. *Diversity in Nature: The Many*

"We actually made a map of the country on the scale of *a mile to the mile!*"

"Have you used it much?", I enquired.

"It has never been spread out, yet," said Mein Herr: "the farmers objected: they said it would cover the whole country and shut out the sunlight! So now we use the country itself, as its own map, and I assure you it does nearly as well." (Lewis Carroll in *Sylvie and Bruno Concluded*, Chapter 11)

There is one general objection against the expectation of a simple complete theory: our world is so complex. Could a complete theory be fair to that complexity, or would it be complete only due to a great amount of abstraction, leaving many of the particular characteristics of our world outside its scope? The English philosopher of science Mary Hesse holds, that for "the explanation of *everything* there must in a sense be a conservation of complexity, in other words a trade-off between the simplicity and unity of the theory, and the multiplicity of interpretations of the few general theoretical concepts into many particular objects, properties and relations" (Hesse 1988, 197).

Could one have a manageable complete theory which covers everything in all its details? Or would that be like the map which used a mile for a mile? If it aimed at being complete in all three dimensions it would be even more unmanageable. Actual maps are useful because they depict the relevant features, with respect to its purpose, and disregard all other details.

The study of complex systems, for instance the weather, is as much a respectable branch of science as research on unified theories. Two catchwords in recent developments are 'chaos' and 'fractals'.[12] This study does not deal with the actual content of such research but emphasizes the diversity in reality as a contrast to the quest for a unified and complete theory. Freeman Dyson, a major theoretical physicist, prefers 'the jungle' with all its richness over the few barren 'mountain peaks'. He contrasts two styles in science, one aiming at unity and looking inward and to the past, the other looking outward and to the future, and thus welcoming diversity. Unifiers have a passion for simplicity. "Diversifiers are people whose passion it is to explore details. They are in love with the heterogeneity of nature and they agree with the saying 'Le bon Dieu aime les détails' " (Dyson 1988, 44f). Dyson acknowledges the progress in theoretical physics, but he hopes that a final statement of the laws is an illusion. Otherwise, "I would feel that the Creator had been uncharacteristically lacking in imagination" (Dyson 1988, 53).

Dyson combines two ideas. The one is that diversity is as important as unity, a topic I pursue in this section. The other is that diversity and complexity show up most clearly in the course of time, hence in relation to the future. I'll return to his speculations about the cosmological future in Chapter 4.

3.3.3. *The One and the Many*

The tension between unity and diversity is a classical problem in philosophy. In different forms it pervades other areas of life, like politics and family life. The third-century neoplatonic philosopher Plotinus is associated with an emphasis on 'the One'. Primacy of the unity goes with a top-down approach. Reality, with its diversity, is like an illusion, since deep down there is no diversity nor individuality. As far as there is diversity it is not good. The Good and the One are together on the divine side beyond being. Nominalism, a philosophical tradition that arose in the late Middle Ages, is the symbol for emphasis on diversity. This school of thought advocates a bottom-up approach. The diversity of things is the reality we encounter. Unity is our contribution in the process of description.

Most philosophy focusses on unity, on general structures of arguments, on the features common to all being. There are a few notable exceptions, like existentialism and Bertrand Russell's logical atomism. Bertrand Russell holds the Universe to be "all spots and jumps, without unity, without continuity, without coherence or orderliness or any of the other properties that governesses love" (B. Russell 1931, 98). Existentialism and Russell's atomism are quite different. But both deny that ultimate meaning exists objectively in reality. That fits in with the denial of unity.

Christian theology, when compared with philosophy in general, is more concerned with particulars, especially in relation to our own being. The theologian Langdon Gilkey is wary of demands for total coherence and intelligibility. For our human experience existence is mysterious; "the incoherent and the paradoxical, the intellectually baffling and morally frustrating character of our experience, reflect not merely our lack of systematic thinking but also the real nature of creaturehood, especially 'fallen creaturehood' " (Gilkey 1959, 37).

However any comprehensive theological scheme is as much an attempt to think the diversity within a unity as a complete scientific theory would be. They both remain open to a further consideration of their unity, and the way that unity deals with the diversity. Gilkey's statement should not be misconstrued to suggest that theology has no interest in the unity of an encompassing view. But Christian theologians should in my opinion remain open to the diversity of experiences. And this not only through a coherent scheme of thought, but despite the confusing aspects of existence, like evil. As I see it, the problem with 'complete theories' is that they might go with values which overemphasize unity and neglect diversity. Both unity and diversity should be part of a satisfactory view of the world. Three elements of the Christian tradition might be useful in this context. The particular person Jesus became understood as the Christ with universal significance. The idea of the trinity combines unity and diversity in God. And the doctrine of creation might be helpful, as it locates the unity in the transcendent creator while allowing for diversity in the created world.

To sum up this section, there is progress in theoretical physics and cosmology towards a very limited number of encompassing un-ified theories. However this completeness and unity are achieved at a very abstract level. The variety in the physical world is left out of sight through a process of abstraction and generalization. Christian theology needs to find ways to express both unity and the value of particulars. It has some resources in its own tradition, especially in christology, the doctrine of the trinity, and the doctrine of creation. I will say more about this in my final chapter on God.

3.4. CONTINGENCIES AND THE MYSTERY OF EXISTENCE

> any contemporary discussion regarding theology and science should first focus on the question of what modern science, especially modern physics, can say about the contingency of the universe as a whole and of every part in it. (Wolfhart Pannenberg 1988c, 9)

An event, property, or state of affairs is contingent if it is possible but not necessary: it could have been different. Pannenberg, Torrance, and many others have used the notion of contingency extensively in the dialogue with the natural sciences (Schipper 1986). They correlate the contingency of the world with divine freedom. God might have chosen differently, for example no world at all, or a world with different ingredients (laws and initial conditions). Strong emphasis on such a contingency of creation correlates in most instances with a voluntaristic understanding of God. A very extreme version might imply that God is not bound by anything; God could do something logically contradictory or wicked. Many theologies avoid such consequences by including goodness and rationality (logic) in their concepts of God. If, analogously, relationality were included in God's being, as it is by process theologians, God could not lack a creation either. Such a view has no need for a contingency of the existence of reality.

Contingency has been used in arguments for the compatibility (at least) of belief in God with science. Such arguments are similar to arguments from complete scientific theories against belief in God. They deal with the empirical nature of science and the quest for causes.

Empirical science arose, according to Whitehead (1926), when God was conceived of as endowed with "the personal energy of Jehovah and with the rationality of a Greek philosopher". The properties of the world would not have been deducible by thought alone. Upon such a view of the rise of modern science, science and belief in God were allies rather than enemies. One could question this view of the history of science, and point to other factors, like the development of technology. Besides, the argument does not support the conclusion that science and theism should remain allies. But the empirical approach is still part of science. Would this provide evidence that we deal with a world which is contingent? Or is the empirical approach similar to simulations of a model airplane in a wind tunnel test? If the calculations are too complicated, empirical testing may be easier, but its usefulness would not prove the contingency of the features studied.

Another approach focusses on explanation or causation. If something is inexplicable from within the world, one might seek causes beyond the world. That was essentially the structure of the cosmological argument from a beginning (1.3.1). Similarly, one could attempt to trace the contingency of the initial conditions of the Universe, or of its laws, or even of its existence, to a being beyond the world.

I will not go into the philosophical and theological discussion about contingency and its relation to concepts of God. The question for this study is whether cosmology might contribute to such arguments by showing the contingency of the Universe. Robert Russell (1988a) introduced a distinction between global and local contingency, the first characterizing the world as a whole and the second particular events within the world. Cosmology seems a suitable ground for discussions of global contingency. Russell made further distinctions, which I adopt in my own way.[13] Different aspects of the Universe can be thought of as either contingent or necessary.

1. The *initial conditions* of the Universe, or other determinants of the characteristics of the Universe, are a candidate for *global empirical contingency*.

2. The *theories* that apply to the Universe might represent *nomological contingency*, the contingency of the specific laws valid in the Universe.

3. If the *existence* of the Universe is inexplicable, that might be looked upon as reflecting *global ontological contingency*.

3.4.1. *Contingency of Initial Conditions and Laws*

Most theories allow for more than one set of initial conditions. Within the theory they are all, if considered *a priori*, equally likely. Otherwise one would have an extra law. This kind of contingency might disappear if physics and cosmology formulated a theory without initial conditions, or, what amounts to the same thing, are possible in only one configuration. That is the claim of the Hartle-Hawking cosmology. It is a package deal: if you follow the scheme you must stick to it; there is no room for negotiations about details (such as initial conditions) once the scheme is accepted.

There might be more than one possible *theory* for a universe. However, as we have seen (3.3.1), mathematical consistency turns out to be rather restrictive. For example, we couldn't have a universe with only electrons and positrons as well as radiation, unless we accepted renormalization, the trick which brushes the infinities under the rug. But theories aren't equal; some are considered *a priori* more plausible than others. Esthetic criteria apply more easily to theories than to initial conditions. Implicitly, one assumes that esthetic criteria such as simplicity can be applied to reality, and hence that its 'creator' has esthetic preferences. The contingency of initial conditions disappears once one accepts the Many World Interpretation of quantum mechanics (2.3.3) or any other formalism which ascribes existence to all possibilities. The contingency of theories, or of separate laws of physics, disappears as well, at least in quantum cosmologies like those of Hawking (2.3.2) and Tipler (4.3).[14] In their approach, every consistent sequence happens. Each sequence is describable by a differential equation, and hence by laws of physics. The classical laws of physics are just those regularities that are found to hold along that sequence which corresponds to a universe of the type we experience. Not all laws are equally probable, but all possible laws exist; those with high probability 'exist more', in a way which is hard to imagine. The classical laws have a high probability because they correspond to sequences which have a high probability according to the universal wave function.

What contingency is left? "All the contingency in quantum cosmology is in the wave function, or rather, in the boundary conditions which pick out the wave function which actually exists" (Tipler 1989, 239). The Hartle-Hawking proposal which requires compactness, in a sense the absence of a boundary, is one proposal resulting, hopefully, in a wave function (see 2.3.2).[15] Tipler proposed a Teilhard Boundary Condition requiring a certain future boundary. This would, probably, result in a different unique wave function (4.3). This example brings us back from the contingency of the laws to the contingency of boundary conditions. But they are no longer conditions on the boundary, say of positions and velocities at the initial boundary. They are conditions about the kind of boundary considered; there may be none (Hartle-Hawking) or there may be a future 'omega point' (Tipler, see 4.3). This is sufficient to pick out the scheme to be followed. There are some additional assumptions aside from contingencies which reside in the choice of the shape of the boundary (compact, or a future point). One is the existence of the material universe, a reality corresponding to the theory (see 3.4.3). It is also assumed that that Universe "is susceptible in its entirety to mathematical analysis" (Isham 1988, 401). Isham lists four more specific assumptions.[16] "These are strong assumptions, and they will of necessity be satisfied in any 'universe' predicted by the theory. Like most things in life, theoretical physics does not yield something for nothing, and what you get out is what you put in" (Isham 1988, 402). This illustrates that theories are bounded by the concepts used and the assumptions made. Some limitation might be

removed in subsequent theories, but similar assumptions seem unavoidable (see also 3.5.2 on conceptual boundedness).

As a description without any contingency would do away with
the fundamental role of experiments in science, it would do away
with the argument that theology and science must be friends because
the theological idea of contingency has made science possible (Torrance 1981a). Nor would there remain ground for an argument for
God's existence based upon designed features of the Universe.

But we can still be grateful for things we understand. If such a
complete theory were possible, it would show that the Creator had
only one type of universe available, given the rules of logic and
mathematical consistency combined with God's esthetic preferences.
So what? This is similar to the question of whether God had a choice
among possible worlds, as seems Leibniz's view, or whether God's
nature implies that God necessarily creates the best, in a moral sense,
as seems Spinoza's view (Hubbeling 1987, 148). As far as I can see,
God's personhood is not dependent on these kinds of contingencies,
except for a strong voluntaristic idea of God. Local contingency, at
all instances of time, might be more relevant, at least for a theological
view developed below (Chapter 6), but not so much to allow for
God's freedom as to allow for human responsibility. However, that
is not directly involved in the discussion with cosmology. The contingency of existence might be important, as it would reflect God's
will to have a creation.

Cosmology supports neither contingency nor necessity. As we
will see in the next subsection, both are meaningful in the context
of a well-defined scientific theory or philosophical system. Both are
also valuable as components in our understanding of creation: necessity as a language for reliability. There is no need to emphasize
contingency over and against necessity, except for the mystery of
existence itself.

3.4.2. *Science, Contingency, and Necessity*

Science works with a *methodological* principle of sufficient reason,
the guideline 'one should always seek reasons'. Science is a quest for
reasons, and for clear expressions of such reasons. This principle
cannot be abandoned if science is to be science. However, as stressed
by Munitz (1974), this methodological rule should be distinguished

from the *metaphysical* principle of sufficient reason, which states that there must be such reasons, whether we can find them or not. This latter principle is outside the range of science, although it might be seen as supported by the instances where science has been successful in its search for reasons. Quantum physics might be interpreted as a branch of physics where the metaphysical principle appears not to be valid.

The methodological principle of sufficient reason implies that contingency is always outside science. Something which seems contingent might be shown by future science to be unavoidable, given certain circumstances. And science attempts to show that those circumstances are necessary as well. Science is a quest to remove contingency as far as possible.

But science is in practice also at odds with complete necessity. In trying to explain everything, science always traces properties or events or rules back to other events, boundary conditions, or laws. Certain rules are used in that process of explanation, laws of physics and logical and mathematical rules. Even if the chain does not go backwards in time, there is a chain of 'more fundamental' explanations—explanations which are based on laws and boundary conditions of wider applicability and greater simplicity.

If someone, like Peter Atkins, Heinz Pagels, or Stephen Hawking, claims to be near the end of the chain, providing an explanation on the basis of the most simple principles, it remains legitimate to ask 'Why those principles?'

The principles might be justified by showing that they agreed with all observations. Such a justification would fail to do two things which would be needed in order to show within the context of science that the Universe is necessarily the way it is: 1. It fails to show the impossibility of a different set of principles, leading to a different universe. 2. It fails to show the necessity for the existence of anything that corresponds to those principles, since all evidence is *post factum*.

There might be other sets of principles which would fit the observations equally well. The theories would be complete, but not necessary, although the observations would be explained if they fit all possible theories.

Work on complete theories fits well within science. But the claim that science offers the ultimate explanation, and hence that the Universe could only have been the way it actually is, goes beyond science. The belief that we are close to a complete explanation could nonetheless be justifiable, due to the success of the program and the simplicity and elegance of the assumptions.

3.4.3. *The Mystery of Existence*

God blessed one formula in some creative act. (Charles Misner 1977, 96.)

Why is there anything at all that behaves according to the mathematical rules written down in the *Physical Review*? Some, like Atkins, maintain that chance phenomena are a sufficient explanation. I disagree. As argued above (2.5.2), even physical theories about creation as a quantum fluctuation of 'nothing' need an input of actuality. The probability of throwing a number below seven with a die is one—it is certain—but there is an outcome only if there is an actual die which is thrown. This contingency remains beyond physics.

Frank Tipler (1989; also Barrow and Tipler 1986, 154ff) defends another argument for the necessary existence of the Universe, which he bases on computer metaphysics. He considers the possibility of a perfect simulation of the Universe. Any perfect simulation is indistinguishable from the real thing itself; these can therefore be equated. The program 'Universe' has subprograms simulating humans. These 'humans' would not be able to find out about the computer simulation; they believe that the simulation is real. Therefore, concludes Tipler, a simulation which is sufficiently complex as to contain thinking observers as subsimulations exists necessarily. Therefore the Universe exists necessarily. This argument serves two further functions. First, there is no remaining contingency. Second, and more important to Tipler, it means that the Universe has one of the traditional defining characteristics of God—necessary existence, not being dependent upon anything else.

I do not agree with the conclusion. The necessary existence is one which is ascribed to the 'Universe' (simulation) by the subprograms representing humans. It is an argument post factum: if we exist then, necessarily, the Universe exists, because we are part of it. It doesn't establish the necessary existence of the Universe in itself, but rather the necessity of its existence given the existence of humans. In a sense, the argument reaffirms that contingency and necessity are terms which apply relative to a framework (see 3.4.2). Relative to a framework in which we exist the Universe necessarily exists—but such a necessity has a *post factum* character. Relative to a framework which allows for nothingness, an 'outside' or 'beyond' with respect to anything in the Universe, the contingency of existence seems unassailable.

I have for a long time considered this to be a stop-gap, a last resort for the theologian if there is nothing else to claim, the 'God of the ultimate gap'. I still doubt whether this contingency of existence is useful in a cosmological argument for the existence of God. It seems equally possible to accept the Universe as a brute fact, which just happens to be.

But nonetheless, this contingency is related to a sense of wonder which I have felt increasingly while studying these ideas. It has been described aptly by the physicist Charles Misner:

> To say that God created the Universe does not explain either God or the Universe, but it keeps our consciousness alive to the mysteries of awesome majesty that we might otherwise ignore. (Misner 1977, 95)

To understand the Universe as a gift, as grace, is a way to interpret this sense of amazement and to relate it to an understanding of God. It can be used to express the idea of God's love for the world: God creates it freely. That is one major aspect of *creatio ex nihilo*, the world's dependence upon a God who is ontologically transcendent with respect to the world.

It is in this context that the difference between theism and pantheism is most clearly visible:

> We might perhaps define theism best by understanding it as that conception of God where the world is the product of God's free, self-conscious creative and sustaining activity. This definition involves that God does not require the world for the realization of his being, because God creates the world freely. (Hubbeling 1963, 10)

The mystery of existence offers a possible interpretation of transcendence. One can agree with the possibility without considering it a relevant option. I do not think that science offers any reasons for preferring a theistic or a pantheistic option. However, I do have theological and ethical reasons. 'Holism', a contemporary label for pantheism, tends to underscore the brokenness of the world and to overemphasize harmony and unity. As I will defend in my final chapter, prophetical criticism fits better with a metaphysics which incorporates a radical notion of otherness, of transcendence. A difference between the Universe and a Beyond is needed to formulate the critical tradition which we have inherited and which is still worth preserving.

3.5. CONCEPTUAL BOUNDEDNESS AND TRANSCENDENCE

> there is a dimension of Reality that is beyond all actual or possible conceptual analysis and rational comprehension. (Milton Munitz 1986, 235)

The quest for a single complete theory of the Universe expresses the belief in the coherence and unity of the Universe. This might raise the question as to what one would mean by 'God' as a term intended to refer to something beyond the Universe. Is such a beyond not ruled out by defining the Universe as everything? As I will explain, this is based on confusion about the meaning of the term 'Universe' (3.5.1). Following Munitz (1986) the term 'Universe' will be used here for the largest system accessible to science. One can conjecture a beyond, but that beyond is not accessible to scientific knowledge (3.5.2).

3.5.1. *The Universe as Everything*

> The Cosmos is all that is or ever was or ever will be. (Carl Sagan 1980, 4)

Transcendence is primarily a relative term: something transcends something else when a certain norm is applied. God surpasses humans in love, knowledge, power, but not in number. Humans surpass worms, at least in certain respects like weight. If this is true, is it meaningful to talk about God as transcending the Universe? Is the Universe not, by definition, all there is?

Transcendence is primarily a spatial metaphor which assumes boundaries that can be transcended. Whether this imagery is, as theological imagery, conceptually clear can be questioned. But it deals with something important, the notion that God is beyond our grip, unpossessed and independent, as a person, an 'elusive' presence. If the Cosmos is by definition everything, is there anything not included in such a notion of Universe?

A notion such as 'all there is' is notoriously ambiguous—at least when compared with most scientific concepts. It is quite possible to give it a meaning which implies that God is included. However, defining the notion 'Universe' in such an encompassing way does not do justice to the subject of this study—the relation between ideas about God and scientific theories about the Universe. Such definitions obscure the question of whether there is a distinction between the Universe as studied by science and what is meant by 'God'.

For the purposes of clarity I stick to the definition given earlier (2.3.1): the term 'Universe' refers to the largest system considered in the context of a specific scientific theory (Munitz 1986, 55). Different systems have been called 'Universe' during the history of cosmological thought. However, as soon as they were considered to be part of a larger system the term lost its applicability to the smaller systems—galaxies are no longer 'island universes'.

This definition implies that we do not have access through science to anything beyond the Universe, even though we can argue about other possible universes. As soon as, within a scientific discussion, the existence of anything 'beyond' is assumed the scope of the term 'Universe' is widened: it immediately swallows such a 'beyond'. In so far as God is an ordinary cause among others, or known as other beings are known, God could not be understood as transcendent with respect to the Universe. The definition implies scientific agnosticism with respect to a beyond. "The Boundless is neither observable, intelligible, nor known" (Munitz 1986, 184).

3.5.2. *The Boundless Beyond Conceptually Bounded Cosmologies*

| The penalty of knowledge is doubt. (Edward Harrison (1985, 275) |

In his *Cosmic Understanding* (1986) Milton Munitz gave a philosophical analysis of scientific cosmology. The Universe as it is known, as an intelligible unit, is a product which results from the application of a conceptual scheme. This should not be misunderstood, as if reality owes its existence to concepts. It is an epistemological point: all theories about the Universe are constructs which use human concepts. Conceptual boundedness is inescapable if one wants to achieve intelligibility. We aim at transcending the conceptual limitations of a theory by entering another conceptual scheme which has its own boundaries. A similar point is made by Harrison in his *Masks of the Universe* (1985). Each understanding of the universe is a mask which is held in front of the real, but in itself unknowable, Universe.

We could stop here. However, Munitz eloquently suggests "a dimension of reality 'beyond' any account of the known universe (or any of its contents), of which we can have a mode of awareness that is not hemmed in by the constraints and ever-present horizons of

cosmological knowledge" (1986, 229). The epistemological endless-
ness of the cosmological search might be due to an ontological "ultimate boundlessness or indeterminability at the very heart of reality"
(Munitz 1986, 229). This reality would not be conceptually bounded
the way the Universe is, nor would it be bound by anything beyond
itself. 'Boundless Existence' is not the name of an object or entity.
It does not fit into the standard use of language.

> We shall be driven, consequently, and at the end, to silence, al-
> though the 'talk' on the way, if at all helpful, will have its value in
> making the silence a more pregnant one, and indeed the occasion
> for having an overridingly important type of human experience.
> (Munitz 1986, 231)

One can summarize Munitz as attempting to point to something
which epistemologically transcends all our knowledge—something
which is, however, at the heart of reality, hence ontologically immanent. It fits in with the classical theme of 'learned ignorance', the
title of a book by a theologian of the fifteenth century, Nicholas of
Cusa. As knowledge increases, the awareness of ignorance increases
as well. Edward Harrison (1985, 274) even suggests that the learned
ignorance increases faster than the knowledge. He bases this conjecture upon the historical observation that the more knowledge a
theory about the Universe incorporated the shorter it lived. The
mythical views lived for millennia, and Newton's for some centuries.
But, as is one of the main tenets of this study, the Big Bang cosmology based upon Einstein's General Relativity is in the process of
being succeeded by quantum cosmologies within a few decades after
its establishment.

Harrison suggests that the burden of ever-increasing learned
ignorance might be "supportable when we derive from unlearned
ignorance unquestioned faith in the cloud of unknowing, whether
it be God, the Universe, or Unigod" (Harrison 1985, 276).

3.6.   RECAPITULATION AND CONCLUSION

3.6.1. *The Argument So Far*

1. *The beginning of the Universe and of time*—part of the Big Bang
model of the Universe—turns out to be outside the domain of validity of the Big Bang theory (2.2.1). A theory which integrates par-

ticle theories and space-time theories in a new way is needed. There is no consensus yet, but there are a number of proposals. These have different consequences for the apparent beginning. Linde's approach allows for a beginning of the observable Universe, but it does so in a framework which assumes an eternal substrate in which such bubbles appear from time to time. Hawking's proposal does not introduce such an eternity, but has no absolute beginning either. Rather, the whole Universe is timeless. Time, and the associated idea of a possible beginning, are phenomenological concepts and not fundamental features of the Universe. Penrose, the third cosmologist discussed in Chapter 2, seems to propose a cosmology which resembles in this respect the classical Big Bang model. However, this is basically a consequence of the present stage of development. He too considers it likely that our notions of space and time have to be modified very significantly in any adequate theory. An argument from the beginning of the Universe to a preceding creator is not supported by contemporary cosmology (1.3.1). If one thinks of God in relation to these cosmologies one should not follow Deists who only consider an initial creator, active 'in the beginning' but irrelevant at later moments.

2. *Design* is at stake in discussions of the anthropic coincidences (3.2). That seems attractive for theology because here humans are explicitly part of the scientific considerations. However, it turns out to be on rather shaky ground. The coincidences may find regular explanations. Or the coincidences might be favorable to us in our 'world' without being of universal significance, just as our planet happens to have the right temperature for life. Hence, they may be either necessary (and explainable) or a chance phenomenon (and hence happening occasionally). These two options reappear in many of the discussions; for example we can understand the Universe as self-organizing or as basically chaotic. Design seems a third mode of understanding. However, an external design in a supernaturalistic interventionalistic form would never show itself that way. If design works through necessity and self-organization one might, with a deistic image, envisage the creator-watchmaker sitting down, planning carefully ahead before setting the thing up. If design operated via chance one might invoke the notion of the farmer sowing in the reasonable expectation that some of the seeds will bear fruit. Hence, it is possible to integrate both positions (that the anthropic coincidences reflect our ignorance or that they express a real contingency of the properties of our world) in a theistic perspective. On the other

hand, both the expectation of their explainability and of a fundamentally chaotic and chance aspect of the Universe can be incorporated in other metaphysical views as well.

3. *Contingency and necessity* are both meaningful in the context of a well-defined scientific theory. However, as we saw above (3.4), a general argument about the contingency of the features of the world, whether the initial conditions or the laws, is beyond science. Neither seems in itself preferable from a theistic point of view.

4. This applies also the the laws of the Universe. The quest for *complete theories* (3.3) suggests the possibility that there might be only one logically consistent set of laws. These would therefore be necessary. However, this assumes that the Universe allows for a simple and unified mathematical description. An assumption of the intelligibility of the Universe is corroborated by the successes of theories formulated in the language of mathematics, but the unity is partly due to the scientist who develops the universal theory and abstracts from the diversity of things in the Universe. Besides, the unifier never escapes the conceptual boundedness of his unified theory (3.5).

5. The strongest case for a theistic argument seems to be based on the *existence* of the Universe. Some scientists claim to deal with that as well, but their arguments are inadequate (2.5.2, 3.4.3). Existence itself, with or without a beginning, seems inexplicable within science. A theistic explanation assumes the unexplained existence of God. Accepting the existence of something is at least as good a possibility.

There seems to be no strong basis for an argument from the theories of scientific cosmology to God, whether from the beginning, or from the anthropic coincidences, or from the contingency of the laws or the initial conditions, or even from the contingency of existence.

The opposite, a clear argument against God, is not supported either. Carl Sagan, who argues on the basis of the absence of a beginning, and John Gribbin, who announces the end of metaphysics (see 0.1), misunderstand the theistic idea and disregard the limitations of cosmological theories. It is not only that there are so many theological positions. There are also, once we move beyond the standard Big Bang theory, different proposed quantum cosmologies. This implies that there are no single clear-cut answers on issues like whether there was a beginning. The differences are due to different assumptions, which are themselves more or less metaphysical.

3.6.2. *The Intelligibility of the Universe*

We could avoid the uncertainties caused by the variety of research programs in cosmology by focussing on the points they have in common. However, these programs suggest very different ontologies. The common element seems epistemological; they all provide an intelligible universe. I will now turn to this 'second-order' common element.

What is it about the Universe and about us that makes it possible to think in an orderly way about it, in other words, to frame adequate mathematical theories? Doesn't that suggest an epistemological design argument for the existence of God? Hugo Meynell has proposed such an epistemological argument in his *The Intelligible Universe*. Its datum is the remarkable fit between our mental capacities and the structure of the Universe. It concludes that "there is something analogous to human intelligence in the constitution of the world" (Meynell 1982, 68).

The argument is not without its problems. Firstly, one might doubt whether it is true that the world is intelligible. Who understands quantum mechanics? Many are able to work with the formalism. But 'understanding' is ambiguous.

> *Examiner*: What is Electricity?
> *Candidate*: Oh, Sir, I'm sure I have learn't what it is—I'm sure I *did* know—but I've forgotten.
> *Examiner*: How very unfortunate. Only two persons have ever known what electricity is, the Author of Nature and yourself. Now one of them has forgotten. (Oxford University science *viva*, c. 1890, quoted by Barrow 1988, 193)

Almost everybody knows that a light switch affects the light. Many believe they understand it. But those that continue questioning may well raise difficulties for understanding. Electricity is manipulable, and well describable by Maxwell's laws. Understanding in the sense of being able to work with them is one thing; understanding in the sense of grasping the origin of the laws is quite a different matter.

Secondly, the fact that mathematics is so adequate in theoretical cosmology might be like the amazing fluency of natives in their own language. Modern cosmologists have been trained to use mathematics, so why should one be surprised if they use it and find it effective for the problems they deal with? It might well be a property of their approach or of the problems they select. The scientist makes his (or her) models of the world. Why would it be surprising that the models are mathematical? However, this rebuttal seems too easy. Science has an effectiveness which is also felt by those not trained in mathematics.[17]

Thirdly, the fit could also be understood in a different, say evolutionary, way. A variant of the question is how it comes about that we are able to understand our environment. As Terence Penelhum argues against Meynell, most mutations have led to adaptations that are beneficial to those that have them without endowing them with cognizance of the enviroment, but the capacity for knowing is another possibility which may be advantageous to those who have it. It is a remarkable result, but "so are all other adaptive mutations when you think about them" (Penelhum 1987, 289). Meynell's defense rests on the observation that the world should have had the intelligible structure before beings with the capacity to grasp that structure evolved. "The question still remains, of how there came to be an intelligible world in the first place" (Meynell 1987, 251; cf. 1982, 90).

Fourthly, the apparent intelligibility and lawfulness of the Universe might be due to selective observation, a WAP effect. This seems to me the strongest objection as it is able to cope with Meynell's objection against the evolutionary explanation. I will give two examples from cosmology and one more colloquial.

One could imagine an infinite chaotic universe, with some temporal eddies of regularity and intelligibility. Complex organisms might exist only in these eddies, and hence observe such eddies. Linde's cosmology implies such a universe.

In quantum cosmologies, on the Many Worlds Interpretation, all possible sequences of states co-exist. Some are regular, say describable according to the Wheeler-DeWitt equation. Other sequences are totally unintelligible. There is no law, or, as Tipler explains (Tipler 1989, 239), all possible laws of physics co-exist. They have, however, different probabilities. The more regular ones turn out to have a higher probability, and hence are more significant. A more accessible example is light. Light moves in a vacuum along straight lines, rays—a supreme case of intelligibility, it seems. However, weird physicists have discovered that they can describe light also as moving along all possible paths from its source to the place where one observes it. These paths may take significant detours. There is no intelligibility for each path, they are just allowed. The observed intelligibility, the straight rays, is the consequence of interference. For a wave of light that has followed some path, there always is a wave which has had a slightly shorter route. These interfere and cancel each other. The straight one is the only one which is not cancelled by interference. In a sense, the procedure implies a shift in the level of intelligibility. The claim is no longer that each path is intelligible. Rather, the whole "least action" formalism is the unit which is now considered intelligible.

A more colloquial example. One might think that intelligible economic development correlates to a strong central planning agency. However, a free market economy may, in principle, also lead to an overall intelligible development even though there is no overall planning. One could interpret this by formulating 'freedom' as the overall principle. However, one could just as well conclude that the principle is 'no principle'. This is the line of thought behind John A. Wheeler's quest for 'law without law'.

John Barrow described two interpretations of the trend in fundamental physics. One interpretation understands the abdication of many laws first regarded as distinct and separate as a development towards an ultimate unified theory of everything. "But it may be that our undoing of the catalogue of Nature's laws will take us down a different road, which will lead us to the recognition that there is no such ultimate theory of everything: no law at all" (Barrow 1988, 297).

The argument from intelligibility is circular, as is the argument which invokes the principle of sufficient reason to argue that everything that exists should have a cause. Methodologically, scientists approach the world assuming that they can find reasons, in other words that the phenomena are intelligible. However there is no reason within science to assume that their quest be effective. Quantum theories might be understood as describing events without reasons, if one assumes that one state is actualized out of many possibilities. Intelligibility assumes something about the Universe which is, though in more neutral terms, almost as strong as Meynell's conclusion that "there is something analogous to human intelligence in the constitution of the world" (1982, 68). The difference is due to the vagueness of the expression "analogous to human intelligence", not to the ascription of intelligibility to the world, which is equivalent to the premiss.

The further development of the argument from intelligibility in the world to a divine intellect is certainly beyond science. Science seems part of the argument, as justification of the belief in the world's intelligibility. But this view of science is not beyond dispute. Intelligibility might be a consequence of the way scientists deal with their object of study and their criteria of intelligibility. Furthermore, intelligibility as regular behavior might be a feature of the part of the Universe that is observable to us, but not of the Universe in its entirety.

Our knowledge is limited both in extent and conceptually. One might, as Munitz does (3.5.2), suggest an unbounded existence beyond our knowledge though at the heart of reality. However, the conclusion must be one of scientific agnosticism. We are driven to silence. At least, we cannot claim knowledge about anything epistemologically transcendent. Too often science has been used in ways which suggest that we can know God through ordinary experience or through science. However, does such knowledge exhaust human thought and life? It seems to me that moral and esthetic values inhabit a domain of reality other than scientific knowledge.

The agnosticism of Munitz has old roots in theology, in what has been called the *via negativa*—understanding God by contrast with what God is not. The other traditional approach, the *via analogiae*, understands God primarily by pointing to aspects of experience which are analogous to what we hold of God, for instance a human example of self-giving love taken as referring to the immensely greater self-giving love of God. The distinction was made (in 0.2) between faith dealing with the presence of God in the ordinary world and faith emphasizing the apparent absence of God. Given the first position one might expect that it is possible to find support for belief in God in the features of the world. In my view there are no unambiguous arguments of such a nature.[18]

Two options are available for a theist who accepts the failure of the cognitive arguments. Firstly, one can give up arguing about it. Such fideism (belief is like taste, not subject to dispute) need not imply that we neglect science completely. We could use the particular cosmology of the day, such as the Big Bang as image of an initial creation, without making our theology dependent upon the science of the day (Carvin 1983 and 1988). Secondly, we could use precisely the ambiguity at the level of our knowledge, in combination with injustice and imperfection as more existential ambiguities of our lives, as the reason why we introduce the hypothesis 'God'. This resembles the way in which Harrison needs faith to cope with the burden of learned ignorance (3.5.2). I will say more about this in 6.1.

PART TWO

Constructing Theology in a Scientific Culture

> Only humble preaching in the belief that we are given
> to understand little and only within a conceptual model
> accessible solely to our culture can bring the Word
> closer to those for whom it would be difficult to accept
> that knowledge of the relation of man to God was given
> to us in an easy and finished manner, whereas knowl-
> edge of the Universe is acquired with such great effort.
> (Michael Heller 1986b, 36)

The first part of this book, 'A Common Quest for
Understanding?', dealt with ways in which others have
related cosmology and theology, using cosmology either
as support for belief in God or as showing the contradictory or superfluous nature of such beliefs. Again and
again arguments turned out to be inconclusive. Absolute
certainty is not the hallmark of scientific answers, because
they are our constructions, even though science provides
credible answers. The second part deals more explicitly
with knowledge as a construction. This will be transposed
to theology, especially in Chapter 5.

The second part is also theologically different from
the first part. We started with theology and science as
similar enterprises, involved in a common quest for understanding. We did not find unambiguous evidence for
harmony between the ways the world is understood by
science and by theology. Besides, other functions of theology might be more important in our culture. A prophetic theology requires a contrast between reality as it is
and the vision of reality as it should be. Chapter 4, on
eschatology, considers other proposals, especially those of
the cosmologists Freeman Dyson and Frank Tipler. But
it also introduces the major theological decisions underlying my own position. The final chapter integrates the
methodological stance with the material of the preceding
chapters into an incomplete and tentative view of the relevance and meaning of God.

ESCHATOLOGY AND THE COSMIC FUTURE

> The end of the cosmos will be something new too. The question that remains is whether the anticipated heat death constitutes a sort of cosmic Good Friday, and whether it makes sense to hope that beyond it lies an Easter for the universe. (Ted Peters 1988, 292)

4.1. THE MEANING OF ESCHATOLOGY

An introduction to TV cartoons showed a recently married couple sitting on a couch. This is what he had always imagined married life would be: "sharing important things". She understands that as "sharing our hopes and dreams, making plans for the future", but he meant "watching smurfs".

These divergent attitudes, relating enjoyment to the future or the present, are widespread. I side partly with him: married life is relevant in the present, and not only through its contribution to the future. I also side partly with her, for it is about hopes and dreams (values) and about plans (possibilities).

A similiar duality of future and present is also basic to a discussion of eschatology and science. Theological eschatology is not futurology dressed up as theology; eschatology should be, in my opinion, a theological counterpart to axiology, the reflection upon values. Such reflection has a critical component, judgement, and an evocative component, conversion. Instead of guessing what will be next, the task is to detect what is going on in the events that take place and to determine in which direction we should go.

It is not realistic to relate the future on a cosmological scale, counted at least in billions of years, to perspectives for humankind. The evolution of life is only a few billion years old; humanity only a few million years or much less, depending on where one wants to draw the line. The cosmological time span is so enormous that future evolution, if continued, will result in descendants which we would not recognize as such. The following is, as far as humanity is related to the far future, more a thought experiment than a realistic description. However, it may reveal something about the content of religious convictions.

The cosmologist Steve Weinberg (1977, 154) poses the challenge clearly: the Universe faces future extinction, either as an infinite future of extremely low temperature in an open universe, or as a finite future of increasing heat while the Universe recollapses. Weinberg concludes that the more the Universe becomes understandable, the more it also appears to be pointless. There seem to be two options if we want to save meaning in the face of such expectations.

1. We could dispute the pessimistic view of the future. Frank Tipler and Freeman Dyson, two scientists, defend more optimistic views of the possibilities for life in the far cosmological future. Dyson points to the similarity between his interest in continuing diversity and the process theology of Hartshorne. We will compare Dyson's view (4.2.2) with the recent contribution to process eschatology by Marjorie Suchocki (4.2.3). Tipler seems closer to Teilhard de Chardin, suggesting a completion of everything in 'the Omega Point'. He also argues for the determination of the present by that Omega Point, thereby suggesting similarities with Pannenberg's theology. This Omega Point has attributes which make it appropriate to name it 'God', according to Tipler (4.3).[1]

2. We could alternatively separate theological eschatology from ideas about the far future. I will consider the role of time in contemporary cosmologies (4.4) before developing a sketch of an axiological eschatology (4.5).

4.1.1. *Two Types of Eschatology*

> And the Lord God will wipe away tears from all faces. (Isaiah 25:8 [cf. Revelation 7:17; 21:4])

The two theological models distinguished in 0.2 suggest two possible ways of comprehending eschatology. Eschatology may be understood as theological reflection concerning the *finiteness, creatureliness*, of existence, or as reflection concerning *injustice*, one might say the *brokenness* of existence. Both concerns might be developed in a temporal sense, but need not be.

The primary opposite of finiteness seems to be existence without limits. If eschatology is understood as a theological imaging of the future, either of individuals beyond death or of the whole world, it might reflect a desire for unending existence, for immortality. We may distinguish between objective immortality, in which our contributions continue to exist either in reality or in God, and subjective immortality, the continuation of our own subjectivity as a center of feelings.

Subjective immortality is more disputed. The process theologian Schubert Ogden, for instance, holds that belief in subjective immortality obscures the difference between God and man. It would mean the rejection of finite creaturehood, of our limitations, instead of living from God's grace (gift) and call (demand) (Ogden 1975, 161). Belief in subjective immortality might detract from this life and this world. Should one not be satisfied with a contribution to God through one's life, for the sake of God's glory?

In an atemporal eschatology one could accept finitude, but imagine this world without the anxiety and estrangement caused by finitude. Would that be a kind of perfection of this world, an affirmation of the goodness of its existence and of the relations which fill that existence, without destruction? I will try to incorporate this perspective of perfection in my eschatology (5.5).

Marjorie Suchocki, another process theologian, agrees with Ogden that belief in unending existence may detract from a strong affirmation of this life and this world. However she emphasizes another dimension of the doctrine of immortality, the overcoming of evil. According to Suchocki we need subjective immortality, the continuation of the person as a center of feelings, aside from objective immortality in God's experience, in order to allow for compensation for suffering (Suchocki 1977, 1988).

Another theologian, Carl Braaten, emphasizes that an eschatology implies that nothing is as it should be; everything is called to conversion and promised fulfillment. This, according to him, is connected with an ontology according to which the essence of things lies in their future (Braaten 1974, 6). He expresses three basic elements of this type of eschatology: 1. judgment on the present: it is not as it ought to be; 2. appeal to action as response to judgment; and 3. consolation in contexts of injustice, failure, and suffering.

Eschatology expresses the ground for consolation and conversion. Eschatology is, in this sense, almost the worldly component of a *theodicy*, a defense of the compatibility of a good God with the evil in the world: unfair suffering of the poor will be compensated, while the wicked will be judged.

There are, at least, two classical traditions concerning the issue of theodicy (Hick 1966; Heyward 1982). The Augustinian tradition offers *another place*: heaven as a spiritual realm where all will be well. The Irenean tradition is developmental, with the perspective of *another time*. The Augustinian tradition takes evil with deadly seriousness; humans are unable to do anything significant against it: God does the job. The Irenean style emphasizes growth through obstructions; evil has a pedagogical function. The process will, finally, bring humans to the likeness of God—there is a "determinism of the happy ending" (Heyward 1982, 127).

Carl Braaten (1972) distinguishes between an existentialistic understanding of transcendence as a dimension of depth in the present, and a historical understanding as the influence of the future on the present, two strands somewhat similar to the 'other place' and 'other time' distinction made above. The existential-ontological view can be found in the writings of the theologian Paul Tillich during his later years in America, when he did not address a specific historical situation, but rather the general human situation of alienation. The historical-eschatological style is more explicit in Tillich's religious-socialist writings in the European context before his exile. According to Braaten, one cannot combine these two strands in Tillich. 'Mysticism' and 'history' contradict each other. Braaten opts for the second, as the first lacks the interest in specific events in history. Robert Hensen defends the importance of depth in Tillich's thought, an eternal presence of Being. A more temporal sense of depth is a sideline in Tillich's writings. This line should have been stressed more, according to Hensen, since it is this line which makes the theology relevant to life as lived in the temporal reality (Hensen 1967, 212–17). I will suggest a coherence of the dimensions of depth and of time building on the possibility of two descriptions, one from within the flow of time and another considering the whole of space-time. That need not imply an escape from the particular reality we inhabit and shape through our decisions. Rather, it intends to emphasize the present as the locus of eschatology.

4.1.2. *My Method of Relating Science to Eschatology*

Emphasis on the second type of eschatology implies certain ideas about the adequacy of an eschatological proposal in its relation to science. The following summarizes my methodological approach for this chapter.

1. *Physical science cannot express the content of the critical dimension,* the judgement on those who did not do what should have been done. The relevant values do not follow from the sciences, nor does science offer concepts to express them. Science is not the first conversation partner for the normative issue.

2. *Science could help envisage a metaphysical conceptual space in which the possibilities of unending existence, appeal for conversion, and/or consolation might be formulated.* The essence in the future (Braaten, Pannenberg) or the Omega Point (Tipler) are examples of such metaphysical schemes, which give a certain shape to reflections on normative issues.

3. *A metaphorical wealth of images to express consolation and judgement is not sufficient. We need to make intelligible the meaning of eschatology.* That meaning is not purely intra-linguistic: it is a claim about a possible interpretation of the reality we live in.

One may take these together as:

4. *An eschatology which is cognizant of the science of our time is not a translation of the expression eschatology had in another time.* We do not need counterparts for the flat Earth with the heavens above, the angels, the purgatory, or whatever.

We should seek an understanding of reality which is adequate with respect to science and to the theological function of eschatology, capable of expressing the concern for justice and love.

This methodological principle may be illustrated with an analogy from physics. Newton's ideas about space, time, and gravity were superseded by Einstein's. There is no continuity at the level of ontology, of conceptualization of reality, although those ontologies are claimed to underly the experiences of reality. There is continuity at less abstract levels in the order of knowing, for instance the predictions for the orbits of planets. Similarly, we need not aim at continuity at an abstract level which is several interpretative steps away from actual life. Continuity with the traditions of the Bible and the early church should be at the level of the life as lived. The more abstract levels are to a greater extent constructions, although intended to describe the reality underlying lower levels. Constructions, or interpretations, may change quite drastically even though 'the facts' remain the same.

Both 'fundamentalists' and those who reject the fundamentalist understanding of Christianity often make the error, I think, of conflating the levels. They take the original form of expression of the concerns to be as important as the concern itself. Everything has to have a counterpart in the new formulation. They take the images to be the facts, but forget about their fundamental function. A modernization of images might be successful for the most part, but is nonetheless a complete failure if the images lose their capacity to express the concern for justice and love.

4.1.3. *Cosmological Futures*

> Look out of the window: everything you see is frozen fire in transit between fire and fire. Cities, equations, lovers, landscapes: all are hurtling towards the hydrogen crucible. (John Fowles 1980, 20–21)

The Second Law of Thermodynamics (Appendix 2) has been interpreted as predicting an ultimate state of equilibrium for the Universe, 'heat death'. However one need not appeal to this very general—and, in its applicability to the Universe, dubious—law in considering the future of the Universe (see Appendix 6.1). The Big Bang theory has two possible extrapolations: either the Universe continues to expand ('open'), and we have to face a very cold future, or the Universe will start to contract at some stage and will collapse to another state of extreme density and temperature ('closed'). The description becomes more detailed when one takes the future of the material content of the Universe into account, as has been done more recently (see, again, Appendix 6). If there is sufficient time, the material contents of the Universe will change drastically. The result in the long run in an open universe might be a diluted mixture of radiation, electrons, and positrons.

4.2.   DYSON AND PROCESS ESCHATOLOGY

4.2.1. *Dyson's Future*

The physicist Freeman Dyson sees no 'escape from frying' in a closed universe, but he is quite optimistic in case our universe is open. When space gets colder it becomes easier to have a signal distinguishable from the background noise, and hence to have life which stands apart from the events caused by the background radiation, if life is able to adapt itself to those circumstances (Dyson 1982, 379). There has been a tremendous evolution of life over the past few billion years. If this continues in the same fashion there seems to be no limit to the variety of life-forms. Dyson assumes that the basis for life is structure, and not the properties of particular molecules, and thus that it is possible to change the architecture of life, including its size and constituents (1979b, 453).

In the long run all sources of free energy will have been exhausted. However, the temperature of the environment decreases as the Universe expands. In a low temperature environment less energy is needed for processes, but they take longer. Dyson makes a quantitative proposal for the slowing down of metabolisms. An organism or society could exist with a finite amount of energy, but its temperature would increase due to its metabolism. It would be unable to get rid of the excess heat sufficiently fast (Dyson 1979b, 455). The problem in an open universe would not be how to keep warm, but how to keep cool!

Hibernation provides a way out. The metabolism might be active during limited periods of time, but the radiation of waste heat continues during periods of hibernation. If the cycles of activity and hibernation are well chosen, survival might be possible for an infinite time with a finite total energy (Dyson 1979b, 456). According to Dyson's proposal an organization as complex as the human species today needs, from now till eternity, the amount of energy that the Sun radiates away in eight hours.

Such an immortality would be unsatisfactory if the total storage capacity for information were finite (Dyson 1979b, 456). It is impossible to store an infinite amount of information in digital form, since the number of constituents (particles) accessible is finite. However, Dyson argues that a few objects can provide an, in principle, unlimited analog memory. For instance, one could determine more and more digits of the angle between two stars, and use these additional digits for the storage of information. I have doubts about this proposal for the storage of information,[2] but let us continue with Dyson's view.

Transmission of information between different societies implies the use of energy (electromagnetic radiation). Due to the increasing distances more energy is needed for the transmission of the same amount of information. This increase is matched by a decrease in energy cost of the radiation when the background temperature decreases. Dyson calculates that communication between two societies could continue forever even on the basis of a finite amount of energy (Dyson 1979b, 459).

4.2.2. *Dyson's Theology*

Dyson envisages "a universe growing without limit in richness and complexity" with "life forever" (Dyson 1979b, 459). This future is not easy. There are many challenges, like the decay of atomic matter (protons). But it might continue in the form of a plasma of electrons, positrons, and photons.

One of Dyson's fundamental values is interestingness, which expresses itself as challenges and diversity. That implies a very positive view of a universe in which survival is possible, but difficult. Dyson even elevates this to "a principle of maximum diversity", which would underly the construction of the Universe (1988, 298). This even suggests a sort of answer to the questions of Job, since tragedy and stress are consequences of the desire for maximal diversity.

Mind is more interesting, and hence more valuable, then matter. It has, on Earth, infiltrated matter and thereby become a moving force in the process. "The universe is like a fertile soil, spread out all around us, ready for the seeds of mind to sprout and grow. Ultimately, mind will come into its heritage" (Dyson 1988, 118). It is beyond our capacities to understand mind when it has expanded its reach far beyond the human scale; one could call it God. Mind operates in quantum events, in human experiences, and as a mental component of the universe. Dyson believes in a purpose which has to do with the future. This purpose too might be called God. God is "inherent in the universe and growing in power and knowledge as the universe unfolds. Our minds are not only expressions of its purpose but are also contributions to its growth" (Dyson 1988, 294). Dyson's view emphasizes increasing diversity. Dyson contrasts this with the view of Paul, who subsumes the diversity of the creation under the unity of the creator (1 Cor 12:4–6).

Dyson's view is interesting and valuable in my opinion, especially for its emphasis on particulars (see above, 3.3.2). However there are a few issues which I find unclear or where I disagree.

Dyson uses dualistic language, 'mind invades matter'. This appears somewhat strange, as he takes life to be a consequence of structure, and not something additional to it. Mind is also manifest at the quantum level, as the capacity to make choices (297). Hence, mind and matter seem like two poles in all entities. Coherence suggests such an understanding of Dyson's view, similar to the ontology of process philosophers such as Hartshorne, to whom he refers favorably in his book.

Dyson appears monistic about the purpose and the process. He believes in a purpose, which one could call God. God is inherent in the Universe and is growing as the Universe unfolds. However, if the purpose is to be found completely in the unfolding process, the distinction between the actual process and its purpose is lost. The purpose loses its function as an aim in reference to which choices can be evaluated. Dyson's principle of maximum diversity is not really identical to the process; it is more like an eternal principle. In a theological image, one could say that God's will (the purpose of diversity) is constant, but that God's action is in flux, the process. Dyson does not care too much about the unity of God. However, such a unity offers the possibility of expressing coherent values or purposes as distinct from the actual diversity in the course of events.

Dyson suggests a theodicy based on a principle of maximum diversity. If maximum diversity is the perfection, perfection is only possible if all tensions which can be co-present are present. Failures are in themselves no contribution to diversity, but the possibility of failure is a risk that is necessary in a non-deterministic process moving towards maximum diversity. Such a theodicy justifies unsuccessful efforts. A major sin in such a perspective is passivity, avoiding participation in the process.

Is it a satisfying theodicy? I am not sure, but it does at least part of the job. It could be used as a model for unending existence (objective immortality), since one's contributions make a slight impact on the process. As for the second type of eschatology, Dyson's cosmology suggests some norms; his emphasis on diversity, for example, reflects itself in his preference for small and flexible technological projects. Action in response to a judgement discerned might be meaningful and effective. Is it also a satisfying framework for consolation? Not all suffering is for a greater good; we might destroy our species, and thereby, maybe, slow down the infiltration of mind into the universe. However, Dyson believes in a happy ending; no imaginable catastrophe is final for mind as such. Failure is not the end, all risks are moderated: the process will win.

His view of the cosmological far future is rather speculative. So are all discussions about the far future. But it seems to me more realistic to assume that the situation in the far future is lifeless. I also doubt whether a future as envisaged by Dyson is sufficiently relevant to present contexts of injustice. Besides, some further clarification of the relation between mind and matter, and of that between purpose and process, seems needed.

An explicit theological and metaphysical approach which shares many features with Dyson's view is process theology. Dyson does see a similarity between his view and the theology of Charles Hartshorne. I now turn to the work of Suchocki, who combines the understanding of the world developed in the process philosophy of Whitehead and Hartshorne with a strong emphasis on eschatology for the sake of justice.

4.2.3. *Suchocki's Process Eschatology*

> To work toward justice is to work *with* the dynamics of reality. Divine power assures it. (. . .) Since modes of justice are thus grounded in reality, and are really achievable, then hope is appropriately a component in all our efforts toward achieving our visions of justice. (Suchocki 1982, 89)

Marjorie Suchocki envisages a relational structure of existence. Each entity is a creative unification of many influences from the past into a unity. The entity, once formed, becomes part of the 'many' for another unification. The physical pole is the feeling of the total past; the mental pole expresses the immediate future this entity aims at, and hence how the past is appropriated to form this specific new unity.

The realm of possibilities has, according to this view, power. It has its own form of actuality, the actuality of God. In God the possibilities come first (God's primordial nature). God is completed by the apprehension of other actual entities (God's consequent nature). The possibilities do not really begin, but are in a sense eternal, a model for God's eternity. God is not a mere collection of possibilities. "God is the actuality in reference to which the possibilities receive value" (1982, 38). "God's knowledge of possibilities is God's valuation of possibilities, ranking them into harmonies of order, beauty, and goodness" (Suchocki 1982, 73).

Eschatology is, in the presentation of Suchocki, directly related to the power of God. Justice refers to good actions, but also to a redress of evil and a restoration into wellbeing.

If justice is to be sought, it must be understood as achievable. But we have no experience of full justice, and certainly not of a justice which also includes a full redress for past suffering. Process

theology locates such a full justice in the nature of God. The Kingdom is in its full harmony in God. Suchocki defends a continuation
of the subjectivity of worldly entities even as integrated into God.[3]
Every entity will enjoy the unity of the One; justice, also as compensation for injustice in the world, is real for the subject in God.
The justice in God reflects the harmony of the primordial possibilities
in God, now with some possibilities actualized. God is always able to
achieve harmony as God incorporates entities from the world in God.

That might be nice for God, but does it count for us? What is
the effect of the kingdom in God upon us? (Suchocki 1982, 87 and
191; 1988, 115–134). The justice in God influences the world
as God influences the world, because it expresses itself in the
God-given initial aim towards a possible mode of harmony and justice
in the temporal world. "The temporal work toward the kingdom of
God is not separate from the eternal establishment of the kingdom;
likewise, the eternal establishment of the kingdom affects the temporal possibilities for ways in which to live justly and with love"
(Suchocki 1982, 174f).

The process-theological view is, of course, much more detailed
than presented here. It really offers a metaphysical scheme in which
many notions can be articulated very well. It seems to incorporate
most of Dyson's insights, about the value of diversity and interactions which take that diversity seriously, about matter and mind
(physical and mental poles), and about optimism.

I have doubts about the process metaphysical scheme. It singles
out time as the most important parameter, while I will argue below
(4.4) for a more restricted emphasis on time. Time is certainly the
basic parameter of one approach to reality, but that need not be the
only approach.

Understanding God as the source of possibilities and values
which rank those possibilities is no mean feat. I will argue below that
that is needed in a metaphysics which supports the second type of
eschatology. But the metaphysical scheme of process theology implies
that God is not the source of actuality. There are always other actual
entities; God is involved in the process of transformation of those
entities. This makes the explanation of evil despite the goodness of
God easier: evil exists despite God. It implies that process theology
drops the notion of *creatio ex nihilo* (see 1.5.2), and thus the metaphysical uniqueness of God as a category sui generis.

Could one not develop a view which has God also as the source
of actuality, even while preserving the emphasis on relatedness as

in the process theological scheme? Conceiving of everything as
grounded in God might make the explanation of evil harder, since
everything has its source in God. But would it not, precisely for the
same reason, also offer a stronger expression of ultimate trust? We
will return to these issues in the final chapter.

In Dyson's view the process will bring about more interesting
and diverse worlds. In Suchocki's proposal we will be saved in God,
even with continuing subjectivity. Our acts make a difference with
respect to the degree of discontinuity between the actual entity and
its perception by God. The certainty of Dyson and Suchocki is comforting. But neither form of optimism seems a consequence of the
scientific knowledge about the structure of reality. They are, at best,
possible ways of understanding and rendering reality based on a
theological assumption of trustworthiness as the ground of that
reality.

4.3.   TIPLER'S OMEGA POINT

> As religions agree that what is ultimately important is the eternal
> continuation of intelligent personality (ultimately God's), not the
> particular racial form it happens to take. If the Omega Point The-
> ory is true, life shall not perish from the Cosmos, but shall grow
> into the Omega Point. (Tipler 1988, 327)

John Barrow and Frank Tipler, in their major book on the anthropic principles, propose, in addition to the anthropic principles
discussed above (3.2), the Final Anthropic Principle (FAP): once life
(intelligent information-processing) comes into existence it will never
die out. Tipler has explicitly related the continuation of life into the
indefinite future to moral and theological ideas, for example that
the FAP would be necessary for a naturalistic ethics (Tipler 1988).
Tipler suggests that Pannenberg's cosmology might be a good model
for the determination of the present by the future. Furthermore,
this cosmology is able to incorporate both collective progress and
individual resurrection (Tipler 1989).

I will first take a look at Tipler's cosmology (4.3.1). The melioristic nature of Tipler's universe, which is essential to the view of the
Omega Point as an evolving God, seems at odds with other assumptions and the suggested relation between ethics and the indefinite
continuation (4.3.2). Tipler proposes a Teilhard Boundary Condition, and thereby formulates a cosmology which, apparently, comes
close to Pannenberg's notion of God as the power of the future. This
brings us to discussions on resurrection and determinism (4.3.3).

4.3.1. *Tipler's Cosmology*

The Omega Point and Life

Stars and planets might, in the far future, be swallowed by a galactic black hole. However intelligent life may be able to change the orbit of the Sun by manipulating asteroids or small comets. Barrow and Tipler defend this notion, and extrapolate that "intelligent beings could eventually gain control of cosmological systems on the largest scales" (Barrow and Tipler 1986, 646).

That life could escape disasters due to local dynamics, such as collisions, seems not too unreasonable. The same objective could also be achieved through space travel, probably with less investment of resources. The possibility of influencing the Universe on the largest possible scale, even the spacetime structure of the whole Universe, is a quite optimistic extrapolation. It seems unncessary for the survival of life, but might be necessary for the formation of an Omega Point where life will encompass the whole Universe.

An open universe might have an infinite future. A closed universe has a finite time ahead. In both situations there are two different possibilities for the causal coherence of a universe in the far future. It might be that observers moving in different directions become unobservable to each other because they are too far apart. This separation need not be due to distance; gravitational effects might also make future communication impossible, as is the case between the inside and the outside of a black hole. Such a future in which events get 'out of touch' is the generic case for model universes in general relativity. However, in some peculiar cases the future boundary is a 'point' in a pictorial representation developed by Penrose. Every part of such a universe belongs to the causal past of that 'point'. This is called an *omega point*. An observer reaching such an omega point would be able to get information about everything that has happened.

Barrow and Tipler use capitals, Omega Point, if an omega point is reached by life. They argue that life will encompass the Universe, and hence life will be *omnipresent*. It will regulate all matter and manipulate the evolution of the Universe as a whole; hence *omnipotent*. Both properties are necessary if life is to bring it about that the Universe evolves into an omega point, for without manipulation it would probably end up differently. Life will, once it reaches the Omega Point, be able to know everything knowable; hence life will be *omniscient* (Barrow and Tipler 1986, 677; Tipler 1988, 322).[4]

Life is understood as information processing. This allows for a definition of subjective time on the basis of thoughts; each unit of thought, or bit of information processed, equals one unit of subjective time. Barrow and Tipler argue for a speeding up of the processing of bits. They conclude that one can have an infinite amount of subjective time (a subjectively eternal future) while having a finite future when counted in physical time.[5]

They argue at length that 'life continuing forever', as defined by them, is compatible with the laws of physics and the conditions in the far future in a closed universe (Barrow and Tipler 1986; Tipler 1988; 1989). 'Shear' might be the source of energy; shear being distortion of space, like torsion in a thread. Information must be stored in states with increasingly higher energies, since the energy of the state needs to be above the increasing background temperature in the contracting phase of a closed universe. This has consequences for the kinds of elementary particles which have to be assumed. Aside from assuming (or predicting) that the Universe is closed and assuming (or predicting) a certain particle spectrum, they also need to assume (or to predict) that time is unidirectional (Barrow and Tipler 1986, 674).[6]

If the technicalities are right, intelligent life might continue forever. However, this does not seem to imply the truth of the Final Anthropic Principle, that intelligent life will continue forever. Is it not possible that advanced technological cultures always destroy themselves, for instance by exhausting their natural resources and polluting their environments? This objection does not hold for Tipler's second approach, which directly introduces the Omega Point instead of assuming that life will create one.

The Omega Point as Boundary Condition

Tipler has also introduced the Omega Point as the boundary condition which determines the structure of reality. ('Boundary condition' is a generalization of 'initial conditions'. The latter specify the way a system has been prepared initially.) It is a boundary condition at the same level of abstraction as the Hartle-Hawking boundary condition. Hartle and Hawking require the absence of a boundary, and hence compactness. Tipler requires that the future boundary is an Omega Point. He calls this the *Teilhard Boundary Condition* (Tipler 1989, 239).

On this approach, it is not life that brings about the Omega Point. Rather, the Omega Point as boundary condition implies a certain wave function, assuming that there is one and only one such wave function. Certain complex phenomena described by this wave function are, at another epistemological level, described as life. They contribute, according to the description at that level, to the evolution of the Universe into the Omega Point. However, at the most fundamental level these developments, including the contributions ascribed at a higher level of description to life, are necessary consequences of the wave function which has been picked out by this boundary condition. The Omega Point determines the wave function, and hence everything. Yet Tipler contends that this need not be understood as classical determinism. I will come back to the issue of determinism below, when I compare Tipler's ideas with those of Pannenberg. As Tipler has it, "the ultimate future guides all presents into itself" (Tipler 1989, 240).

4.3.2. *Tipler 1: Progress and an Evolving God*

Tipler argues (1988, 316) that:

a. Morality requires life.
b. "*if* ultimate meaning is to reside somehow in the physical universe itself, then a necessary condition is for life of some sort to continue to exist."
c. Thus, indefinite survival is a necessary condition for a naturalistic ethics to be possible.

The first statement is about life and morality at the same moment. How does he get from the necessity of life now for ethics now to the necessity of indefinite continuation of life for ethics now? For that is the conclusion, not that the indefinite survival of life is necessary for the indefinite continuation of ethics. The bridge appears to be the notion of 'ultimacy' in the second premiss. This works if 'ultimate' is understood as a temporal notion.

'Ultimate' could also refer to the most basic elements, beyond which there is no analysis possible, say the axiomata in a mathematical system. That is, as I understand it, its meaning in most theologies. Tipler seems to exclude such an understanding on the basis of his explicit ontological reductionism. If there is nothing outside spacetime, there cannot be an atemporal category of ultimacy.[7]

However, the meliorism in his system needs such an atemporal notion of value or a physical notion of progress, implying indeterminism. Assume for the moment that the Universe is deterministic.

Tipler has stated that "the most basic stuff of the universe . . . is completely deterministic" (1989, 235; I will come back to other aspects of Tipler's work, which seem more indeterministic, in the next section, 4.3.3). In a deterministic universe there is no increase of information, at least if information is measured according to some objective standard, such as how many numbers one needs to specify the state of such a universe. Take the example of my children's toys. It always take three numbers to specify the position of each toy in the room (distance from two walls and height from the floor), whether we experience the distribution as disorder or order. Our evaluation of the distribution as orderly might be based on criteria like simplicity. But it cannot be based upon the amount of information, for that remains the same. For Tipler information is all there is; the Universe can be understood as a very complex computer program, and all properties are ultimately reducible to the stuff of physics. It is unclear how we could ever have progress, once one combines determinism and reductionism.

To arrive at a melioristic cosmos, we might introduce a form of dualism. There is a sense in which the Universe will be better than it was. That could refer to certain norms, like simplicity. It could also be based on a difference between information processing and ordinary physical processes, say between life and non-life. Meliorism appears to be dualistic. Tipler's confessed ontological reductionism can be maintained only if he assumes a form of indeterminism which allows for progress as the increase of information.

Tipler's progress towards the Omega Point is understood by him to provide a model of an evolving God. At the Omega Point life encompasses the whole Universe, and could be described with the attributes of omnipresence, omniscience, and omnipotence. God is not 'in the beginning', nor atemporally transcendent, but will be at the Omega Point. Since the Omega Point is not a point of spacetime, but rather its boundary, God could be said to be transcendent, outside space and time. Its definition also implies that the Omega Point is formally equivalent to the entire collection of points of spacetime. In that sense, the Omega Point is also immanent in every point of spacetime (Tipler 1988, 322). Tipler's proposal

> leads naturally to a model of a God Who is evolving in His/Her immanent aspect (the events in spacetime) and yet is eternally complete in His/Her transcendent aspect. This transcendent aspect is the Omega Point, which is neither space nor time nor matter, but is beyond all of these. (Tipler 1989, 231)

Tipler uses 'God' in two ways: as a concept for a static and transcendent limit, and as a concept for the evolutionary, immanent process of approaching that limit. This raises three questions.

1. Why should we take these two notions as referring to one God? The Omega Point is the future boundary, and equivalently the whole of all events. However, it is not equivalent to single events which constitute the process of approaching that limit.

2. Is the notion of immanence satisfactory? Individual events are immanent in the whole, and hence in the Omega Point. But the reverse, the way the whole is present in each individual event, is unclear, unless one already invokes the notion, to be discussed in the next subsection, that the Omega Point determines everything.

3. Is the notion of transcendence satisfactory? Transcendence is a relative notion. The Omega Point transcends all individual points in space and time. But it is not transcendent in the more radical sense of transcending the framework of space and time; rather, it is that whole framework. That gives a pantheistic flavor to Tipler's proposal. This seems a logical consequence of Tipler's confessed ontological reductionism.

We could, if we dropped the ontological reductionism, combine Tipler's cosmology with an Irenean view. Humans are created incomplete, like infants which have to mature. They are in God's image (Genesis 1:27), but their destiny is to be both in the image and in the likeness of God (Genesis 1:26). Tipler's theory might be a cosmological model for the developmental process of the creation towards a final state of perfection, while maintaining a notion of God as having the omni-predicates all along—not an evolving God but creation evolving towards likeness of God. The main deviation from Tipler's interpretation is with the ontological reductionism, which excludes for him a God transcending the physical Universe.

4.3.3. *Tipler 2: Resurrection and Determination by the Future*

I concluded my description of Tipler's proposed Teilhard Boundary Condition with his statement that "the ultimate future guides all presents into itself " (4.3.1). Tipler (1989) also argues that the Omega Point, assuming its existence, is an appropriate source of hope. It implies continuous progress as well as individual resurrection!

Progress and Resurrection

Life forever is in Tipler's cosmology a collective eternal worldly progress. If there is to be an Omega Point there must be further forms of life beyond *Homo sapiens*. They will be further developed in knowledge and wisdom. The extinction of *H. sapiens* is, according to Tipler, only an evil in a racist—perhaps we should say speciesist—value system. We should be satisfied if the most valuable things, especially the expansion of knowledge and wisdom, continue. The continuation of life and its progress in knowledge and power is a consequence of the Omega Point, which is assumed as the boundary condition.

Individual resurrection will be possible close to the Omega Point. The defining characteristic of an omega point is that all worldliness of particles and radiation converge upon a 'point', and thus become causally connected. Hence all photons which have been scattered in different directions by the movements of a certain individual will come together again.

> The light rays from those people who died a thousand years ago are not lost forever; rather, these rays will be intercepted by the Omega Point. To put it another way, these rays will be intercepted and intercepted again by the living beings who have engulfed the physical universe near the Omega Point. All the information which can be extracted from these rays will be extracted at the instant of the Omega Point. (Tipler 1989, 230)

Whether all information has been preserved in the light rays is a technical discussion; according to Tipler, the capacity for the processing of information will increase so fast that all possibilities, including all human genomes and all possible human memories, could be simulated by 'brute force', computing power. As Tipler has it, "resurrection is likely to occur even if sufficient information to resurrect cannot be extracted from the past light cone" (Tipler 1989, 249).[8]

It might be that close to the Omega Point sufficient information will be available to reconstruct details of lives of individuals from the past. The closer one gets, the better the information, and thus the more perfect the possible simulation. Using the identity of indiscernables Tipler identifies a perfect simulation with the process simulated (see above, 3.4.3). Hence the possibility of being perfectly resurrected as a reconstructed simulation close to the Omega Point.[9] This might seem a bit late. However, since the Omega Point is in subjective time infinitely far in the future, there still will be an infinite amount of subjective time for the resurrected individual if resurrected at some, even if small, objective time before the Omega Point.

Such a resurrection as a perfectly recontructed simulation will not remain a mere possibility. If life is to reach the Omega Point it needs to have, supposedly, a drive for as much knowledge as possible. It will therefore reconstruct from the information available the processes of the past. Tipler concludes that "the hope of eternal worldly progress and the hope of individual survival beyond the grave turn out to be the same. . . . The Omega Point is truly the God of Hope" (Tipler 1989, 250).

Tipler reaches the conclusion of eternal worldly progress in two ways. First he assumes the Final Anthropic Principle, resulting in the conclusion that there should be an Omega Point (Tipler 1988). Second, he assumes the Omega Point as the determining boundary condition for the wave function of the Universe. This boundary condition then implies the Final Anthropic Principle (Tipler 1989). Both approaches are fine, and the whole is mutually consistent. However, Tipler does not escape the introduction of, at least, one of these rather speculative assumptions. Future developments in scientific cosmology might support the assumption of the Teilhard Boundary Condition, especially if Tipler would explain observed features of the Universe (or predict new observations which are subsequently corroborated) which would be unexplainable in the context of competing cosmologies.

Tipler's proposal includes two forms of resurrection. Every event is included in the whole of spacetime, and thus in the Omega Point in its timeless transcendence. This is similar to the objective immortality in the mind of God as described above (4.1.1; 4.2.3). Tipler envisages also subjective resurrection as reconstruction close to the Omega Point. One might object that this resurrection lacks the transformatory aspects of the resurrection as expected by some believers. Someone who is continuously suffering pain while living on Earth does not hope for a perfect copy of these experiences, but rather for a perfected life without handicaps and pain. This longing for a more perfect resurrected life has been incorporated in Tipler's proposal (Tipler 1989, 246f). Resurrection is depicted as an intentional process, the construction of a simulation by the living beings of that far future. They might well make slight changes in the simulation— either out of compassion, in order to avoid unnecessary suffering of the resurrected person, or out of prudence, because healthy and pleasant resurrected beings would contribute best to their own lives.[10]

The changes made in the simulations might even be necessary if those resurrected beings are to contribute to the growth into the Omega Point.

Tipler, Pannenberg, and Determinism

There is a superficial similarity between Tipler's understanding of the Omega Point which, as a boundary condition, determines everything, and Wolfhart Pannenberg's understanding of God as "the power of the future" and "the all-determining reality".

Determinism is a complicated issue. For a definition we could follow William James who stated in an 1884 lecture at Harvard Divinity School:

> What does determinism profess? It professes that those parts of the universe already laid down absolutely appoint and decree what the other parts shall be. The future has no ambiguous possibilities hidden in its womb: the part we call the present is compatible with only one totality. Any other future complement than the one fixed from eternity is impossible. (James 1956, 150; quoted by Earman 1986, 4f)

Earman has reformulated this in a more technical way as Laplacean determinism by invoking possible worlds which satisfy the same physical laws obtaining in the actual world. Determinism means that any two worlds which agree at one time also agree for all future and past times (Earman 1986, 13). It is clear that determinism is thus bound up with the notion of time. The definition might be widened by allowing other subsets of the Universe to replace the world-at-a-given-time. Indeterminism thus means that information about a subset of the universe does not uniquely determine the rest of the universe.[11]

It should be noted that such definitions make it meaningless to speak of indeterminism with respect to the whole of space-time or the whole Universe. It is trivial that whatever happens happens (see Earman 1986, 10–12).

Tipler has stated that the most basic stuff of the Universe "is completely deterministic" (1989, 235). However he also claims for a number of reasons that his quantum cosmology should not be understood as deterministic in the classical sense.[12]

1. One reason which has been put forward by Tipler is that quantum cosmologies in general do not admit a global concept of time. Therefore there would be no way to implement the definition of determinism (1989, 240). The fate of this argument shows the

difficulty of dealing with current research: Tipler has already refuted his own argument.[13] The objection that time is not well defined is true for quantum cosmologies in general. However, Tipler has discovered that the Teilhard Boundary Condition implies a global parameter which can be taken as time.

2. A second reason is, as Tipler calls it, the "evolution contingency". In Newtonian physics there is a spacetime—as background, like the stage of a theatre—and processes going on in that spacetime. If the processes were to stop suddenly, that would establish a discontinuity which breaks the laws. This is a detectable event, because the background spacetime is still in its place. However, in Einstein's general relativity and subsequent spacetime theories the spacetime is not such an independently given background entity. It comes with the processes. If the processes were to stop completely there would be nothing, no background against which the disappearance would be measurable. It would therefore not break any laws.

The undetectability of a less than maximal (future) extension is similar to the idea discussed earlier, that it would be undetectable if the world, including the spacetime background, had been created only a few thousand years ago, with all the traces of history like trees with rings (see Chapter 1, note 3). This contingency is mostly resolved by the implicit assumption that the *future and past maximal extension* is the one which is actual: spacetime and the processes are extended as far as possible according to the laws.

One could object that the assumption of the actuality of the maximal extension, over and against all less than maximal extensions, is rather trivial. However, Tipler is right in noting that it is an additional assumption, which is never included in the initial conditions or the total past history. It is a specification about the continuation of the topology, and might be seen as containing an infinite amount of information—as infinitly many lesser extensions are excluded.[14]

Thus, the Omega Point theory is not deterministic, at least as long as the assumption of maximal extension has not been made. We shall assume in the remainder that this assumption has been made.

3. The quantum theory allows for the calculation of probabilities for all possible states and sequences of states. Tipler therefore speaks of "guidance, so to speak, not rigid control" (Tipler 1989, 240).

However, Tipler adheres to the Many Worlds Interpretation of quantum theories (see above, 2.3.3; Tipler 1986a,b). According to this interpretation, all possibilities encoded in the wave-function have an equal ontological status; they all happen. It therefore seems to me that the appeal to quantum probabilities does not free Tipler from the appearance of determinism.

Contingency remains, however, as the contingency of the wave-function—and hence of the Omega Point, the Teilhard Boundary Condition. In quantum cosmology the collection of all possible wave-functions is the set of possible worlds. It is contingent which universal wave-function is actualized—Tipler's, Hawking's, or another one. But the possible worlds of classical physics, the spacetime configurations and matter-fields, are no longer contingent. All these space-time configurations and matter-fields, as encoded in the universal wave-function which is picked, are equally actualized (Tipler 1989, 236f).

This does not suffice as a refutation of determinism for the Omega Point theory. It only states that the Omega Point theory, and the corresponding Teilhard Boundary Condition, are not neces-sary—within the collection of competing quantum cosmologies. However, *the Omega Point theory, as the combination of the basic procedures of quantum cosmology, the assumption of maximal extension, and the Teilhard Boundary Condition* excludes, upon this view, any remaining contin-gency of spacetime, particles, and processes.

4. The strongest argument against a deterministic view of the Omega Point theory has to do with the relation of the whole to its parts. There are two ways to look at the Omega Point.

If one starts with the whole universal wave function, the 'com-plete picture', everything is given—that is, trivially, its completeness. This suggests determinism, but is of course the trivial form: every-thing that has happened has happened. This is, in a sense, the atem-poral understanding of the Omega Point—as the wave function which is beyond space and time.

If one starts from the spacetime points, or similar entities at a lower level, the case is different. The Omega Point appears, in this perspective, as the future boundary. The whole is not completed until the Omega Point has been reached. It turns out that no subset, say the present and its past, is sufficient as information to determine the remaining spacetime points and the corresponding material fields. Every point is needed as information in its own right. Even the subset 'all but one point' is insufficient to determine the wave function at that point. In that sense, looking back upon the James definition of determinism given above, the theory is not deterministic within space and time.

As became clear in the final argument about the non-deterministic character of the Omega Point theory, every point is essential to complete the whole. None can be omitted, or it would not be that whole that is called the Omega Point.[15]

As a consequence, every individual act or decision receives an infinite weight, an absolute yes-or-no character. Either it fits into the universal wave function which corresponds to the Omega Point, and then it corroborates the expectation of such a future completion. Or, if it did not fit into the universal wave function which describes the Omega Point as a whole, there would be no Omega Point. The completion would be lost; the whole Universe would never be able to reach the Omega Point. It is a package deal: one is fully in or fully out; and not just oneself, but with one's decisions everything is. This repeats the contingency of the universal wave-function as all the contingency that has been left in such quantum cosmologies. In that sense there is no freedom, except for the freedom to follow the rules or the freedom to lose everything. One could also say that there seems to be no room for play, for 'adiaphora'. Adiaphora is a term that has been employed in relation to the many quarrels and schisms in the history of the Christian churches. Occasionally it has been realized that not all differences were about important issues. For example, salvation might be compatible with more than one way of celebrating the liturgy. Adiaphora refers to those things that can be done in more than one way without being heretical. Tipler's cosmology—the assumption of a quantum cosmological scheme with maximal extension and the Teilhard Boundary Condition—does not seem to leave room for adiaphora: everything is necessary for the fulfillment of the whole, and hence for salvation, the achievement of the Teilhard Boundary Condition. It might be indeterministic according to any well-defined temporal notion of determinism, but it does not leave much room between what is possible and what is necessary for the desirable fulfillment. The only freedom left is the freedom to leave Tipler's cosmology, the Omega Point universal wave-function.

To reformulate this remark: it seems difficult to incorporate a notion of forgivingness. Evil might be only apparently evil, if it fits into the universal wave function which describes the Omega Point. Or else it destroys the Omega Point, and hence Tipler's God. That there might be evil which is real, which destroys the path towards fulfillment, but which is subsequently overcome, opening anew a path towards fulfillment: that is hard to envisage in this scheme. The overcoming of evil seems to require a more dualistic concept of God and the Universe.

The theologian Wolfhart Pannenberg (1989) has welcomed Tipler's cosmological work as raising "the prospect of a rapprochement between physics and theology in the area of eschatology" (Pannenberg 1989, 255). However, Pannenberg appears to be more interested in the reality of freedom, contingency in the present, and in the correlated tension between the reality of evil and the overcoming of evil. God is envisaged as "the power of the future" in order to avoid the destruction of freedom in the present. "A being presently at hand, and equipped with omnipotence, would destroy [human] freedom by virtue of his overpowering might" (Pannenberg 1971b, 242). Contingency is important in Pannenberg's theology as metaphysical expression of human and divine freedom (Pannenberg 1970; 1988c; 1989, 269).

God as "all-determining reality" is a notion, also used by Pannenberg, that seems to come closer to Tipler's conception of God as the Omega Point. According to Pannenberg the final destiny is certain. Pannenberg therefore has had to face the challenge which this poses to human freedom and real novelty, contingency in history. Freedom is a very complicated issue—does one freely choose to do good, once one's actions are determined by what one thinks best? Pannenberg acknowledges a tension between divine power and human freedom, and similarly between certainty about the end and the reality of evil, and attempts to resolve these tensions by locating God's omnipotence in the future, by envisaging the creation of creatures with freedom, by understanding God's power as love, and by stressing the imcompleteness of present reality (Pannenberg [1988, 323] in response to charges or challenges of determinism by Cobb [1988], Ford [1988], Clayton [1988] and Polk [1988]). Tipler does not seem to accept the tension between divine power and human freedom. He uses a more monistic unity of God and the Universe and seems to see no problem in a somewhat limited notion of freedom. He thus appears to stand closer to Spinozistic pantheism or the supralapsaristic strand in Calvinism than to Pannenberg's theology, or for that matter any theology which emphasizes history.

A significant gain of Tipler's approach is the precision achievable by using physical and mathematical concepts in envisaging the Universe, both as a whole and as parts which are to constitute that whole. More detailed studies should clarify the similarities and differences between the approaches of Tipler and Pannenberg, as well as the possibilities for further convergence of these approaches.

Apart from asking for its credibility as a claim about the future of the Universe, one may ask whether Tipler's cosmology provides an acceptable eschatology. Tipler's proposal does provide a temporal eschatology responding to finiteness by suggesting resurrection in time as well as the inclusion of all finite existence in the whole of spacetime beyond space and time. There might even be the possibility of improved resurrection, and hence a happier future life. The specific notion of time used to define an infinite future in a finite proper time appears quite acceptable in this perspective.

Whether we consider Tipler's ideas too speculative or whether we take them more seriously, at least they have the advantage over many theologies of pressing for a more precise, incisive, and fruitful discussion of themes like determinism, freedom, and the reality of evil in the light of future fulfillment.

4.4. TIME AS A FLOW AND TIME IN ITS ENTIRETY

Big Bang cosmology has been related to theological ideas with respect to the beginning of the Universe, to its contingency, and to its dynamic nature. This latter emphasis has its roots in the dialogue between theology and evolutionary biology, but Big Bang cosmology is often invoked as an additional scientific discovery which shows the dynamic, evolving character of the Universe. For example, "astrophysics adds its testimony to that of evolutionary biology and other fields of science. Time is irreversible and genuine novelty appears in cosmic history" (Barbour 1989, 143). Most discussions about the future assume such a dynamic nature of the universe.

However, some cosmologists, and certainly most quantum cosmologists, interpret their own field quite differently. As Stephen Hawking expressed it in an interview with *Time* (8th February, 1988), "the universe would not be created, not be destroyed; it would simply be. What place, then, for a Creator?"

There are three challenges from modern cosmology to the notion of a dynamic, evolving Universe. Firstly, physics seems to do without the notion of a unique present. All moments qualify as a possible present. Hence, there is no way to incorporate the idea of a flow of time. Secondly, almost all fundamental physical and cosmological theories deal with whole possible histories of a system aside from, or perhaps instead of, describing the system as evolving in time. And thirdly, in most quantum cosmologies time is a phenomenological construct and not a basic aspect of reality (4.4.1). There are two descriptions of the Universe possible. From within time it is described as changing. But the Universe can also be considered as a spatial and temporal whole. This perspective might be labelled timeless or from outside time, *sub specie aeternitatis*. 'Timeless' means without the flow of a present, it is not the denial of temporal extension. I will argue that the presence of those two different perspectives offers opportunities for theology (4.4.2).

4.4.1. *Time in Cosmology*

Time is a terribly complex subject, discussed in many philosophical treatises. A few remarks, mainly following the discussion by Peter Kroes (1985), can be found below in Appendix 5.

The Absence of a Flowing Present

There is a commonsense awareness of the present as a special moment, the boundary between the past and the future. This present is 'moving' towards the future as 'time is passing away'. What is this special moment in the context of physics and cosmology? Is this an objective phenomenon or is it mind-dependent? If it is mind-dependent, not independently present in physical reality, how do we reconcile mental events, which have the property of 'becoming', and physical events without that property? It could also be held that there is no becoming in the mind—but why then is the illusion so persistent? If we opt for an objective, mind-independent view, we need to face the question of whether the flow of time can be made part of the physical description.[16]

Kroes concludes that the language of physics is, at least at present, unable to deal adequately with the notion of a flow of time (Kroes 1985, 211). In their study of physical reality physicists eliminate those aspects that make phenomena unique, including the unique 'here' and 'now'. An objective theory of the flow of time would do precisely the opposite, as it would single out a unique moment of time as the present. Subjective, mind-dependent, theories are, still according to Kroes, not better off.

Time in its Entirety in Spacetime Descriptions

We can compare a universe to a movie film, each frame representing a three-dimensional universe at a certain moment. We can take either the perspective of the viewer, who sees all the pictures successively in time, and hence sees action, movement, 'evolution', or the perspective of the manufacturer, who handles the whole film as a single entity, for instance in selling or storing. The film still has a 'story', but there is no movement, no action or 'evolution'. The same holds for books. Physical descriptions possess a similar twofold quality. But that need not imply determinism—although this does seem to be implied by the example of a film.[17]

Within physics there are often two descriptions.

1. We see this feature in the Hartle-Hawking quantum cosmology (2.3.2 and Appendix 4), where we could calculate the states by using a differential equation and an initial state, but which also has a timeless level of calculation without reference to previous states. This theory is exceptional in that the timeless level of description is about individual spaces, say individual moments.[18] That approach raises some questions of its own, especially about the continuity of our experiences. However, the presence of two descriptions is not restricted to this theory, which is still in a preliminary phase.

2. General Relativity, which is the theory behind the Big Bang theory and hence the basis for the notion of a dynamic universe, has four-dimensional spacetime as its most fundamental entity. This level of description is like having the whole film: all moments are equally present; there is nothing like flow or movement. It is, however, often possible to decompose the four-dimensional description into a description of three-dimensional space evolving in time (Misner, Thorne, Wheeler 1973).

3. Physical theories as different as Newton's mechanics, thermodynamics, and quantum theories have been formulated in terms of abstract spaces which represent all possible states of the system by points. A trajectory, a line of such points, represents a possible 'history' of a system. At this level of description, the theory is not about evolving systems, but about whole histories represented by the different trajectories. I say more about this in Appendix 5.

4. Light takes the fastest path from a source to a receiver. In a homogeneous medium this is a straight line. One very useful description is in terms of all possible paths, with the addition of a selection rule (principle of least action) to determine which path is actually taken. As before, the physical description works with com-

plete 'possible histories'. Such principles of least action are very pervasive in physics. This idea has been incorporated in the path integral formalism, which is extensively used in contemporary field theory (particle physics). It is at the basis of Hawking's approach, but is also utilized in works of other physicists discussed in this book.

Both the difficulty of giving a physical expression to the flow of time and the prevalence of a timeless description imply that we cannot appeal to modern cosmology and physics to support the claim that we live in a dynamic, evolutionary world.[19] However, the conclusion need not be merely negative. The availability of two different perspectives also offers some opportunities for theology, as I argue in the next section.

Time's Ontological Status in Quantum Cosmologies

If a theory deals with spacetimes, or complete histories, time remains as an order parameter from one side of history, its beginning, to the other side, its end. Yet even such a status for time is disputed in quantum cosmologies. In general terms, once space and time become subject to description in terms of quantum physics they lose the property of definite location in space and time. What would a moment in time be if it didn't have a definite location in time?

Andrej Linde understands time as a phenomenological notion which can be introduced by an observer inside a 'bubble', if the bubble is sufficiently long-lived (1985b, 289; see 2.3.1). Time is also a phenomenological construct in the cosmology of Stephen Hawking. Time, as a parameter ordering different states representing universes at a single moment, could be defined on the basis of the fields and the geometry of the respective states (see 2.3.2). In both cosmologies the notions of time and spacetime are approximations which are not valid for 'small' spaces, where quantum effects are important.

James Hartle, Hawking's co-author in the first technical exposition of his ideas on quantum cosmology, has developed these ideas in a somewhat different direction. He considers two options. The first is to abandon the notion of spacetime, and thereby time.[20] We are left with features in the present which are interpreted as records of the past, but that past might well be an illusion. Hartle rejects this as an overreaction to a technical problem in the formalism of quantum mechanics. The alternative is to assume that spacetime (not to be split as space-time) is fundamental, and to develop a fitting way of calculating quantum probabilities.[21] As a consequence, some features of ordinary descriptions are lost; among them causality and the idea that the Universe has a specific state at a moment of time. His formalism allows, in principle, the prediction of all possible observations. But it does not allow for an organization of those possible observations into a series of spaces at subsequent times. Spacetime is essential, on this view; causality and separate moments of time are approximations.

A more fundamental role for time seems involved in the work of Roger Penrose (2.3.3). He suggests that it is quantum physics that is only approximately valid. Time might therefore be meaningful for small spaces as well. However, the most fundamental formalism will not have objective reality in space and time. Rather, these notions will be consequences of more fundamental entities.[22]

Frank Tipler follows an approach more similar to those of Linde, Hawking, and Hartle. He too considers time to be a phenomenological construct. "At the most basic ontological level, time does not exist" (Tipler 1989, 237). We observe only relationships between objects in space and the theory encodes all possibilities at once in the wave function of the Universe. However, as explained above (4.3), Tipler assumes a boundary condition which requires all classical paths to terminate in an omega point. He therefore needs a well-defined time (as ordering parameter) in at least one series of subsequent spatial universes. The possibility of a temporal ordering seems more or less accidental in Hawking's cosmology. By contrast, Tipler's cosmology requires such a possibility; it has been shown by Tipler that the Teilhard Boundary Condition implies the existence of a global time.

Time's status is, at least, disputed. Time might still have some fundamental status, but it might also be recognizable only for 'large spaces'. Anyhow, such cosmologies are not directly in line with evolutionary biology's conception of a dynamic and evolving Universe. Theological insights developed in dialogue with the evolutionary understanding of the natural world are not directly extendable to the dialogue with cosmology. The Big Bang model is often presented as describing an evolutionary universe. That is a possible representation. However the more speculative ideas at the frontier of cosmological research, and even the standard theory of space-time (General Relativity), suggest that the evolutionary presentation is one of limited validity, and not the most fundamental one.

One might object, against taking the 'timeless' view seriously, that timelessness is a feature of those theories, and need not be a feature of the world. However, we do not have access to the world independent of our theories. Theories generate our ontology, the way we take the world to be. Hence, in taking these cosmological theories seriously we need to consider the timeless perspective they suggest.

4.4.2. *Eternal and Present: Theology in Two Perspectives*

Almost all current theologians who take science seriously opt for a dynamic picture. Often, cosmic evolution is considered as an extension of biological evolution (Peacocke 1987b, 37; Moltmann 1985). When the physical view of time is discussed, there is a strong emphasis on the flow of time and the asymmetry of time. This is especially true for process theologians (such as Griffin, 1986). An exception is the physicist and Anglican priest John Polkinghorne, who sees an analogy between the duality of a timeless level of description and a description from within time with the duality in theology between 'the God of the philosophers', emphasizing static perfection and remoteness, and 'the God of Abraham, Isaac, and Jacob', with its danger of too much anthropomorphism. "A true account will hold the two in balance" (Polkinghorne 1988c, 6; see also xiii). In this section I try to find such a balance of theological notions related to the two physical descriptions.

Opportunities of the Two Descriptions

Philosophical theology and theoretical science occupy some distance from commonsense experience. At that level both descriptions of evolution through time and whole 'histories', might be useful. They each allow for different clusters of associations, and thereby help us to see the world differently. However they each have their disadvantages. Combining both perspectives in relation to the present seems to me the most promising theological approach. The precise meaning of all the terms is dependent upon the further system in which the ideas participate.

A description *within time* takes history and evolution as basic. Evolution is here a broad category, including cosmic, stellar, geological, and cultural change. This resonates with a theological emphasis on 'Heilsgeschichte' (salvation history). *Creatio ex nihilo* is most easily associated with questions about ultimate origins, hence cosmogony. *Creatio continua* will be the theological doctrine that deals with God's relation to the processes of change, especially God's relation to the emergence of novelty. Time is always there. Contingency is primarily about events; instead of the events that happened something else could have happened, and the events of the future are still open possibilities. Initial conditions could have been different. Necessity seems reflected in the laws, the same for all moments in time. Value is easily related to the future: the qualities of a decision will be judged by the consequences. Hence, one has a teleological or utilitarian kind of ethics. The eschaton, say the Kingdom of God, is closely related to the future. God's relation to the world is most easily formulated in terms of immanence or temporal transcendence (having existed before the world, or luring us towards a better future).

The *timeless perspective*, or better, the perspective that incorporates the whole of time, might be understood as a view *sub specie aeternitatis*, a 'bird's-eye view', the whole of history as if seen from beyond. *Creatio ex nihilo* is not correlated with questions about the origin. Rather, it reflects a question about the ground of everything. (For an atemporal understanding of 'ground' one could think of the role of axiomata in a mathematical system: they may come first in arguments, in the order of knowing, although they are, historically speaking, formulated only after some time. They are not prior to the system in the order of being. They are the ground of the system, within the system.) *Creatio ex nihilo* might also be understood as an expression of God sustaining the world at all moments. *Creatio continua* could also express this notion of sustaining, or in more traditional terms, God's *conservatio*. However, it is stripped of the emphasis on change and novelty, which attaches to it in the other perspective. 'Novelty' is not a concept that fits in with this timeless perspective; it belongs to the other language.

Time is more explicitly seen as part of the created order. Contingency is primarily the ontological kind: why is there anything at all? The contingency of the laws is more explicit: why this package and not another? The events are no longer seen as contingent: they are all necessary relative to the whole of history. Value must be understood as being there for every event, just by being part of the whole web—or perhaps even more primitively, just by being. This lends itself more readily to a deontological view of ethics, as expressed in Immanuel Kant's second formulation of the categorical imperative, the ground rule for his ethical system, which states that one should never treat others only as means towards ends. They are always ends in themselves. Eschatology is less connected with the future, and more with God's transcendence. Transcendence is less easily understood as temporal (before and after the world); rather it is a radical beyond, as if in a completely different dimension.

Both these approaches are in danger of missing something essential. The perspective incorporating the whole of time might result in a conservative, *status-quo* affirming, understanding of eternal values, and thus divert attention from concrete contexts of injustice and suffering to a timeless and eternal 'other place'. Doing without the perspective from within time would mean the loss of concreteness. It might mesh with a more purely Platonic philosophical approach or with an Eastern perspective, but Christianity has emphasized the value of particulars, and the importance of God's activities in the world, for instance in the history of Israel. Taking only the timeless perspective might, as with the emphasis on unity (3.3), make it difficult to maintain this characteristic of Christianity.

However, we need not confine ourselves to the description from within time. The timeless perspective also allows the expression of important convictions. It is especially valuable as it may open our thoughts to the possibility of something other than the temporal, and hence to considerations about God's transcendence. An evolutionary faith is in danger of subsuming present suffering and injustice under a future happiness, and thus becoming the optimistic expectation of 'an other time'. Furthermore a combination of the two perspectives might be more valuable than a mere juxtaposition of them. Prophetical criticism appeals to God's otherness or transcendence: that is its Archimedean point, from which to criticize the present.

The View *Sub Specie Aeternitatis*

Speaking about God in a spacetime framework which takes in the whole at once doesn't exhaust what one could say about God as the Eternal One. It only offers an entrance. In the previous chapter the realization of conceptual boundedness led to a suggestion of a beyond, 'Unbounded Existence' (3.5.2). With respect to the whole of time one may make a similar suggestion, of a beyond which has an atemporal transcendence, the Eternal. This is not caught in the description. From the scientific perspective it can be, at most, an assumed supplement 'out of the plane of the spacetime description'. This notion of atemporal transcendence, and the correlated view of the whole of time, might be useful as an understanding of God. An ethical analogy has been developed by Sutherland.

As Sutherland argues, a view *sub specie aeternitatis* is not one that can be attained definitively. But it can be a notion which expresses the intention to aim at an understanding of the human affairs that goes beyond any limited outlook, whether of an individual, of a community or even of humanity (Sutherland 1984, 88). The idea functions like the transcendental regulative ideas of reasons, as directing the understanding towards a certain goal.

The unattainability, the transcendence, is essential. Sanity requires allowing self-questioning in relation to a perspective other than one's own. If this 'other perspective' were accessible, like a list of eternal values, it might result in fanaticism without self-questioning. The idea of the eternal as referring to something transcending even one's most cherished beliefs keeps faith open (Sutherland 1984, 110).

God's Eternity

The statement that God is eternal may be understood in two ways: 1. that God is everlasting, hence God has an unending duration; and 2. that God is timeless, hence without duration.

Nelson Pike discusses the second option in his *God and Timelessness* (1970). This view was held by Boethius, Anselm, Thomas Aquinas, Schleiermacher, and many other important theologians, according to Pike, who analyses its logical relations with other doctrines, like *immutability*, *omnipresence*, and *omniscience*. He finds it possible to maintain timelessness, but with consequences for the interpretation of those other attributes, consequences which he does not like. He discerns in it a Platonic influence with hardly any scriptual basis. "What reason is there for thinking that a doctrine of God's timelessness should have a place in a system of Christian theology?" (Pike 1970, 189–190). I see two reasons why timelessness might have such a place:

1. Time is part of the created order. This is Augustine's view of *creatio cum tempore*, and seems a reasonable interpretation of most contemporary cosmologies. It might be combined with the rejection of a straightforward cosmogonic interpretation of *creatio ex nihilo*. Hence, it is not meaningful to talk about God as if there was time before the creation: God as everlasting.

2. The presence of a timeless description, where the whole is a unit including all moments, suggests that it is possible to talk about the relation of God to this whole—and not God at one moment to the Universe at that moment, differentiating moments in God.

I therefore maintain that it is useful, at least in part, to under-stand God's transcendence with respect to space and time as time-lessness. This emphasizes God's unity with respect to the world. It doesn't exclude an order, perhaps even a flow, within God, which could be labelled God's time. As my teacher in philosophy of religion, Hubbeling, liked to ask: how otherwise could God enjoy music? If music is not enjoyable when all notes are played at the same moment, God's perfection, also with respect to esthetical appreciation, requires that God has God's time.[23]

4.5.   PROPOSAL FOR AN AXIOLOGICAL ESCHATOLOGY

> But the true longing of humanity is not for an afterlife; it is for the establishment of a justice here and now that will make an af-terlife unnecessary. (John Fowles 1980, 30)

The cosmological views of Dyson and Tipler focus on the future. However, mind is continuously present in Dyson's proposal, while Tipler suggests an atemporal presence in each moment. And, al-though they both suggest a theology of an immanent evolving God, they also appeared to need some form of dualism between purpose and process, between the physical reality and the norms with respect to which the cosmos is evolving, hence between the temporal and some atemporal values.

4.5.1. *Heyward: Praxis and Present*

Transformation as personal conversion or social change is an important theme in many, especially evangelical or political, theo-logies. Natural theologies arising out of experiences with the natural world mostly lack this element; they tend to overemphasize the actual state of affairs as one deserving wonder. However, a theologically adequate natural theology should, in my opinion, attempt to disclose the possibilities for transformation of the natural order.[24]

Eschatology has been understood by some theologians as "an expression of our standing in every moment in face of the eternal, though in a particular mode of time" (Paul Tillich 1963, 395).

These two themes, transformation and present, are emphasized in Isabel Carter Heyward's 'theology of mutual relation', which she developed in discussion with the Irenaean and Augustinian traditions while paying attention to Elie Wiesel's questions and remarks arising out of his experiences with the Holocaust. Is it possible to justify God in the presence of burning children?

'Irenaeus' stands for a developmental view. To struggle and to cope with evil is part of the process of growing, of maturing. Emphasis on the process might offer relief from the evil we do, as all things are supposed to work together for the final good. Such a view is in danger of diverting our attention from present responsibility to the anticipation of a future perfection which will appear in any case, effected by God. An 'Augustinian' view takes evil very seriously. The worldly process will not lead to perfection; the perfection is to be expected in a more spiritual realm, solely effected by God. Such a view discourages humans from knowing and doing what is good in the world, to make a difference. Both views diminish the relevance of the present, and of our activities in the present, by locating perfection in another time, a future state of maturity, or another place, a heavenly state of bliss. As Heyward argues, if we imagine that the future is already created, or predestined by God, we thereby dismiss our responsibility for what happens (Heyward 1982, 129f).

Her theology of the present has a strong praxiological emphasis. We act in the present; our responsibility lies here. She opposes escapism to heaven or to an indefinite future. She also rejects ontologizing, especially top-down ontologies which give being (essence) priority over action (relation, existence). That should not, in my opinion, exclude a conceptual, ontological expression of such a theology.

An adequate theology should explicitly deal with the possibilities available in the present, the realm of transformation of the natural order. Eternity has to touch that present, and should not be envisaged as some 'other time' or 'other place'. The present is the locus of actions and decisions. Eschatology should function for the orientation within that realm of possibilities—and that leads to axiology, reflection on values guiding decisions in the present.

4.5.2. *Sketch of an Axiological Eschatology*

This chapter started with two basic types of eschatology (4.1.1), focussing on: 1. perfection, for instance the overcoming of finiteness in unending existence, either objectively (in God or world) or subjectively; and 2. justice.

Cosmologies which emphasize the future, like Dyson's or

Tipler's, may provide frameworks for the expression of such eschatologies. However, the more optimistic cosmologies are rather speculative. And they are not completely satisfactory, especially for the second type of eschatology, as the relation between that future and a present state of injustice is rather remote. Besides, Tipler's cosmology appears to leave no room for behavior accountable in terms of morality, due to its emphasis on necessity. I prefer a framework which emphasizes the present and is especially open to the second type of eschatology.

In the further interpretation of a present-oriented eschatology which deals with injustice, three elements were mentioned: 1. judgment on the present, a valuation; 2. appeal to action in response to that judgment, conversion; and 3. consolation in contexts of injustice, failure, and suffering.

In order to develop an adequate eschatology which correlates with the concern for justice, especially with the dimensions of judgment and appeal, we need to develop a metaphysical scheme which is *au fait* with science. Such a metaphysics should allow a theology which is primarily prophetical, aimed at critically relativizing the status quo, and evoking a response. Such a theology requires the recognition of a difference between what is possible and what is actual. The future is one which we make, not one which is definitely enfolded in the cosmic process. God might be understood as the source, or even the locus, of the values and the possibilities. This proposal corresponds basically with the much more detailed process theological view presented by Marjorie Suchocki (4.2.3).[25] Four elements are needed: 1. The *present* is the central state of reference, and not a far past or a far future; 2. Each actual present is correlated with a *set of possibilities*, alternatives for the near future of that present; 3. The consequences of the different options in a given present are to *some extent predictable*; and 4. There is a reference *frame for evaluating* the different options, an orientation on the space of alternatives.

With respect to 1., the unique moment which is the actual present is not caught by the language of physics. To take the present as a basic notion implies that one reaches beyond the scientifically describable. It seems preferable to do so, as it is the locus of existence, the locus of decisions and actions, the locus where God should be relevant, if relevant anywhere.

Total determinism eliminates 2. There are no alternatives; there is no morally accountable behavior. Nobody can make a difference for the sake of justice.

As to 3., unpredictability of consequences, which would follow from total indeterminism, would eliminate accountability as well. There should be a partial predictability, at least a reasonable expectation of the consequences for the near future, if one prefers one alternative for action over another. In actual practice, the predictability of complex systems like the weather is limited. In most cases, predictions are better for the near future than for the far future. The study of complex and chaotic systems has developed rapidly over the last decade (Gleick 1987; Pagels 1988). Chaos sciences seem to offer possibilities for a scientifically adequate expression of a limited predictability while denying the possibility of a complete predictability, as one can never, in principle, know with sufficient accuracy all relevant conditions.

If, and this is a very sizable if, the epistemological unpredictability in chaos theories is integrated with ontological indeterminacy as a possible interpretation of quantum physics, one might perhaps be able to formulate a framework in which the conditions 2. and 3. are fulfilled.[26]

With respect to 4., the existence of moral, esthetic, or other, criteria relevant to the choices is the most a-scientific. It is transcendent with respect to the spacetime framework. It might bring in the Augustinian 'other place' as a reference, relevant to the steps towards the near future.

The first type of eschatology (4.1.1), which deals with metaphysical finiteness, has as its temporal form 'immortality'. Objective immortality as a contribution to the processes in space and time seems to be built into the cosmologies of Dyson and Tipler. These two cosmologies of unending growth are rather speculative. Other scenarios do not have a similarly optimistic future within the spacetime framework. This raises the question of whether one can develop a different understanding of perfection.

Perfection could be understood as an affirmation of the goodness of finite being, an affirmation despite the anxieties of finite life. Such an affirmation seems to need a theistic understanding of present reality, seeing it as grounded in a good God. Theism also offers another possibility for objective immortality aside from the optimistic vision of eternal progress. From a theistic perspective one might interpret everything, the whole of spacetime, as embedded in, or as

a whole related to, God's eternity. This requires an atemporal understanding of God's eternity, as suggested in the preceding section
(4.4). Such an eternity is, by construction, intimately connected with
each present.

I therefore suggest that we understand God both as the ground
of reality and as the source of values and possibilities. The first
element, God as the ground, expresses the affirmation of the goodness of finite reality and envisages a locus for objective immortality.
The second component, of possibilities and values, corresponds to
the call for conversion for the sake of a more just future. In such a
way one could combine the dimensions of depth and future, of
mysticism and history.

The process-theological view distinguishes between these two
functions ascribed to God. The possibilities and values are located
in God's primordial nature. All actuality is *post factum* received in
God's consequent nature. In the final chapter an attempt will be
made to combine the two functions, together with notions developed
in previous chapters, and hence to envisage God as the source of
actual existence (the ground of being), and as the source of transformation (the ground of becoming; of possibilities and values).

THEOLOGY AND SCIENCE: THEIR RELATIONSHIP AND THEIR METHODS

5.1. INTRODUCTION

Is theology a scientific, or at least a rational, enterprise? Some have defended a methodological similarity between theology and science, and have used this similarity to support the status of theology among the sciences. This approach does not provide the fruits expected. Even if theology and science followed the same rules, the resulting theology need not be related to the results of science. Besides, a strong emphasis on the similarities between theology and science might result in insufficient consideration of the differences, especially the existential components in theology. The emphasis on similarities as an argument for the credibility of theology presupposes acceptance of the norms represented by scientific research as valid for an enterprise like theology.

The model proposed in this study, constructive consonance, is not primarily an argument for the rationality of theology. Its scope is the credibility of theology in its relation to the natural sciences, especially cosmology. Some form of mutual consistency seems required, but a strong methodological similarity between theology and science is insufficient and unnecessary. Credibility needs to be based upon an adequate method for relating the scientific and the theological enterprises.

Philosophy in this century has made, at least in the English-speaking world, a turn from the world of experiences and things to the world of language. The meaning of words is visible by the way they are used in certain language games or linguistic practices. In the philosophy of science there has been a turn to history and sociology. Thomas Kuhn's *Structure of Scientific Revolutions,* first published in 1962, has become the symbol for an emphasis on radical change in scientific understandings of reality. The reference to revolutions suggests a political model of scientific change, instead of the traditional emphasis on the rationality of scientific progress. Far more radical than Thomas Kuhn are David Bloor and Barry Barnes, who replace the philosophy of science by a 'strong program' in the sociology of knowledge, according to which the standards of science are determined by socio-political factors.

There has also been a reaction against the apparently relativistic and subjectivistic tendencies of these linguistic and sociological approaches. There is a turn to ontology, an attempt to discuss the way the world is, and to epistemology, focussing on the process by which we come to know. Notions like truth, reference, and reality often signal this side of the philosophical debate. These different approaches in philosophy have been carried over to discussions about the relation between theology and science.

Authors like Ian Barbour, Arthur Peacocke, Janet Soskice, John Polkinghorne have labelled their own position 'critical realism'.[1] They emphasize continuity within science and theology, and the reality-depicting nature of both enterprises. They are open to development in the expressions of doctrine, but want to avoid the relativism which seems to follow from the emphasis on revolutions in our understanding. As they see it, such relativism would reduce theology to an anthropological phenomenon, like story-telling and day-dreaming, projecting human desires upon some inaccessible realm.

Others have emphasized an understanding of both science and theology as *interpretations* of reality. Langdon Gilkey (1970) will be my main example of a linguistic-cultural approach along these lines. Gilkey emphasizes, certainly more than the critical realists, the differences between theology and science, even the independence of the meaning of religious statements from facts (5.3.1). Mary Gerhart and Allan Russell (1984) stand for an epistemological approach. They reject the idea that cognitive claims are threatened by revisability; change in ontology is a consequence of the process by which scientific and religious knowledge is created. Such approaches to the nature of science and religion go along with less interest in an orthodox continuity with 'the tradition'; any interpretation is primarily located in present experience and reflection (5.3.2).

European Protestant theology has been more restrained in its dealings with the natural sciences. A few characteristics, as present in writings of the German theologians Christian Link, Eberhard Jüngel, Wolfhart Pannenberg, and Jürgen Moltmann, as well as of the Scottish theologian T. F. Torrance, will be discussed briefly (5.4).

Pointing to methodological similarities or dissimilarities between science and theology does not provide a method for relating science and theology, although some of the authors discussed do offer opinions on that as well. The final section of this chapter sketches constructive consonance as a method which relates scientific and theological ideas (5.5). Consonance, because humans desire integration, or at least coherence, and because belief in God as the One suggests a certain harmony between ideas about the relation between God and the world and the scientific knowledge of that world. Constructive, because the harmony is not readily found, but, like all human knowledge, is a construction.

5.2. CRITICAL REALISM IN THEOLOGY AND SCIENCE

5.2.1. *Metaphors and Models in Science and Religion*

A defense of critical realism along a linguistic route has been offered by Barbour in his *Myths, Models, and Paradigms* (1974) and, more recently, by Soskice in her *Metaphor and Religious Language* (1985). They both explicitly defend cognitive functions of religious language by arguing for a similarity between science and religion. For example, both employ models and metaphors (Soskice; Peacocke 1987a, 22), or at least, the open-ended, essential role of models in science is comparable to the role of metaphors in religion (Barbour 1974, 14).

Even if one agrees on the similarities one may ask whether these really contribute much to the justification of the realistic interpretation of religious language. Sharing tools, an image used by Peacocke (1984a, 51; 1987a, 27), is insufficient as an argument. Tools can be misused—a hammer can be used to hit someone on the head. Hammers may also be used in the same way for very different purposes, say making toys and making prisons. Regular scientists share tools with astrologers and 'creationists', but that does not, according to the regular scientists, justify astrology or 'creation-science'. The crux is the justification of religious language as being about a reality.

In her defense of theological realism Soskice emphasizes the role of experience, community, and interpretative tradition (Soskice 1985, 149). Scientists are able to make references as members of a particular linguistic community, within which names, like Columbus, and words, like neutrino, have a certain meaning. A referential claim is, in most instances, based on other people's experiences. Christians too rely upon the experiences of others, for instance mystics, interpreted in Christian language. Peacocke emphasizes experience (past and present) and the mediating tradition which "provides the links of referential usage and repeated and new experiences that enable us to refer to what the initiators referred to, even though we may have revised our models through continuous reinterpretation" (Peacocke 1984a, 47). Peacocke considers the continuity back to the original introduction of a scientific term, its baptism, essential to its ability to depict reality (Peacocke 1987a, 20).

The appeal to a linguistic tradition is a strange argument for realists, who explicitly reject the strong program in the sociology of knowledge, which emphasizes the dependence of knowledge upon community and tradition. Besides, critical realists like Soskice and Peacocke heavily emphasize continuity. Their approach harmonizes with theological strands with a strong emphasis on tradition, Catholicism and Anglicanism, but introduces a significant difference from science. Continuity is, in my opinion, neither a necessary nor a sufficient condition in science. One can develop another referent, despite a continuous tradition. Replacing bit by bit may, after sufficient changes, result in an entity which has no pieces in common with the original entity. Take cosmology: the changes in notions of what we consider to be gravity, from medieval cosmology to Newtonian cosmology with gravity as action at a distance, and then to Einstein's cosmology with curved spacetime, will be followed by a further development in quantum cosmology. There is a form of correspondence for the mathematical theories since Newton: a new theory should be able to explain, in the appropriate domain, the phenomena which were explained previously. However, does that imply the continuity of a referent? What is that continuous referent behind gravity as an action at a distance and gravity as an effect of a curved spacetime? Do these cosmologies refer to 'the same' thing? Anti-realistic accounts of Christianity provide an example of a development within the continuous linguistic tradition of Western Christianity, but critical realists like Peacocke and Soskice hold that they do not refer any more to the same reality (God). However, it seems undeniable that anti-realistic accounts are also in a continuity of links.[2] A case for 'referring to the same' should be based upon the contents and contexts of the referential acts.

The appeal to tradition as mediator of experience seems to reflect an orthodox interest, the justification of churches with a strong emphasis on the Christian tradition. However, in the secular debate about the meaningfulness and truth of the Christian beliefs this is only possible if the experiences themselves are justified, for example through the historicity of the empty tomb (Soskice 1985, 140) or the factual nature of mystical experiences (Soskice 1985, 138ff.; Peacocke 1984a, 37f). These authors assume a separate class of experiences which would be 'religious', and which allows for real reference to God "just as it is nature we really refer to and discover in the sciences" (Peacocke 1984a, 48).

'Religious experience' is a complicated topic outside the scope of this study. How is one to establish that there really is such a separate category of experiences which gives access to reality? One might well argue that religious experiences are ordinary human experiences interpreted religiously. The argument of critical realists seems circular: taking a realistic stance about religious experience they conclude that there is a religious 'dimension' of reality and that religion has access to that dimension, similar to the scientific access to the real world.

The linguistic approach fails as it focusses on the forms of language, instead of the issues themselves. When it turns to the issues, it takes the religious experiences as religious data, quite independent of their interpretation.[3] Furthermore the conclusion is rather trivial: metaphorical language "can be referential" (Peacocke 1987a, 25). Of course; if a person is described as a dog, this is intended to depict some aspects of the character of that person. The issue is not whether metaphors can be referential, but whether religious metaphors are.

5.2.2. *Science and Religion as Knowledge of One World*

A causal argument for theological realism is also used, apart from the more social-linguistic argument. Something can be referred to, if it enters into a causal relation with us, as that which caused a certain state of affairs (Soskice 1985, 137). She suggests that the cosmological arguments of Thomas Aquinas, which describe God as the origin and cause of all there is, constitute such a causal link which provides sufficient ground for a referentially-realistic stance about

'God'. Religious experience, although perhaps unconvincing to atheists, may also serve as such a pointer, God being that which has
caused a certain experience in me or in others. Realism with respect
to entities of scientific theories has also been defended on the basis
of the use of those entities in further experiments. Ascribing reality
to electrons seems the natural attitude for someone who uses these
entities in electron-microscopy (Hacking 1983, Peacocke 1987a,
17f). The application to religion is not as explicit as the application
of the argument about causes behind experiences. Religious tech-
niques, like prayer, have not been invoked in this context. The argument from further use might result in a pragmatic defense of a
religion by pointing to the ability of its adherents to cope with life.

Critical realism is, at least, in need of further clarification. More
important for my argument here, it doesn't offer a methodology for
relating science and theology; they are only put side by side as two
similar activities. Ian Barbour's classic study on *Myths, Models, and
Paradigms* ends with suggestions for the study of religion (Barbour
1974, 172ff), but gives none for the interaction between theological
conceptions and theories and observations from the natural sciences.
Methodological parallelism becomes a justification and clarification
of the nature of faith and theology.

Critical realism has not only failed to yield a model for relating
the two enterprises; it appears unable to do so in its present form
because of the separation between the sources of religious knowledge
and those of scientific knowledge. At its core, it is a two-way approach. The two ways of exploring reality may share tools, but that
does not by itself diminish the separateness of their contents.

However, Peacocke and Polkinghorne have, among others, contributed to interactions between scientific and theological contents.
The central issue, in this respect, is not 'realism', but the conjecture
that both science and religion deal with the same reality. Peacocke
and Polkinghorne envisage a hierarchy of order and complexity up
to the human and the personal—a hierarchy which is apparently
present both in the world as a hierarchy of systems and in our
cognitive enterprises, a hierarchy of sciences, humanities, and theology. There is no reason to discriminate among the levels; subatomic
particles are as real as social reality (Peacocke 1984a, 36). Peacocke
and Polkinghorne do accept the ontological unity of everything, with
the more complex consisting of units of a less complex type. They
also accept the heuristic, methodological value of reductionist strat-
egies: we learn a lot by taking systems apart. However, they reject

epistemological reductionism. Certain properties exist at higher levels which do not exist at lower levels of the description, as wetness exists for large aggregates of water molecules but not for single molecules. Consciousness might be such a property. Furthermore, theories at higher levels have a certain autonomy with respect to theories at lower levels.

Theology refers, according to this approach, to a higher, or even the highest, level in the hierarchy (Peacocke 1979, 367–371). Theories at a higher level have to respect findings at lower levels; biology cannot accept descriptions which violate the conservation of energy, a law of physics. But theories about higher levels cannot be translated completely in lower-level terms. Similarly, theology has to adapt itself to the discoveries of science, but is not subservient to these (Peacocke 1984a, 51; 1987a, 28).

The issues of hierarchies and reductionisms are complex. Eric Juengst (1986) points to some difficulties, especially in asserting the autonomy of theories at higher levels, and of properties of more complex systems in combination with ontological reductionism. Juengst suggests that theology should not be understood as the topmost in a hierarchy, as if it were the extreme among the natural sciences. Juengst refers to biology, where genetics does not fit in a hierarchy from molecular biology through histology, physiology, and ethology up to ecology and evolutionary biology. Rather, genetics is the discipline which, by staying outside the hierarchy, weaves the different levels together. Similarly, theology could be conceived of as 'exploration of the ultimate meanings of things', and therefore as the source of all the sciences.

The 'one world with a hierarchy of levels' position seems, at least partially, independent of further arguments about critical realism for science and theology. I am not too confident that it is adequate with respect to the actual relations among the sciences beyond general statements about biology versus physics. And this concept of the relation between theology and the sciences forces one into stances on reductionism and emergence which are, at least, non-trivial.[4] Most important, to me, is the way in which theology is understood in such a program. By lining it up with the sciences in one hierarchy, theology is understood to be, at least in some important aspects, similar to the sciences. And the claims of theology are supposed to be in line with the claims of the sciences. This metaphysical approach is in danger of neglecting the more existential functions of theology as well as its critical tension with 'the facts' (see above, 0.2, 4.1.1, 4.5, and below in 5.5 and 6). I will therefore attempt to describe the relation between theology and the sciences in a somewhat different way.

There appear to be two interests behind critical realism. The emphasis on continuity with initiating experiences and the tradition of the church seems to result in a kind of Anglican orthodoxy. The constructive dimension of theological and scientific conceptuality, expressed by the qualifier 'critical', seems somewhat overwhelmed by the desire for realism as orthodoxy, which is reflected in the emphasis on depiction of reality. The reference is held to be unchanged, though the terms with which one refers are reformable (Peacocke 1981, xi–xii). Historical continuity is preferred, against the possibility of radical change, especially for theology. The other major interest behind critical realism seems to be the seriousness with which the ideas are treated. If theology were mere myth or only the peculiar language game of a particular community, why take it seriously? That seems the main question to be faced once we distance ourselves from the realistic program.

5.3. SCIENCE AND RELIGION AS INTERPRETATIONS

5.3.1. *Gilkey: the Function of Myth in Culture*

The American theologian Langdon Gilkey defends, for example in his *Religion and the Scientific Future* (1970), mythical language as unavoidable and essential for any culture, providing an expression of its self-understanding. Theology may be defined as reflection on the mythical symbols of a tradition or culture. Myths are not outdated fables. Mythical language uses multivalent symbols referring in some way to the transcendent or sacred. Its "meanings concern the ultimate or existential issues of actual life and the questions of human and historical destiny" (Gilkey 1970, 66).

Traditional religious language incorporates facts as well as a reference to the transcendant or sacred. Myths of creation tell about a transcendent creator as well as about the early history of the world. The sciences have discredited the factual content of myths, and thus forced a change in our understanding of the nature of mythical truth. In this way, science contributes to a purification of our understanding of the nature of religion. Religion has become symbolic truth, "nonassertive of matters of fact" (Gilkey 1970, 35), though still asserting something. However, the separation between the factual and the symbolic meaning has endangered the meaning of religious language. Science seems to send the following message to theology: you can "neither be part of us and be *valid,* nor separate from us and maintain any *meaning*" (Gilkey 1970, 33).

Gilkey rejects a new coalition with the facts. If conclusions of science, for example biological evolution, are used as basis for religious convictions, they become scientific myths and cease to be scientific theories (Toulmin 1957). Science does not lend out its prestige, certainty, and meaningfulness beyond its proper domain. Such scientific myths share the uncertainty of all myths.

Gilkey sees the grounds and uses for religious discourse in our culture by considering the confidence in science and in its application to the problems of humanity. Science as a form of human inquiry "points beyond itself to a ground of ultimacy which its own forms of discourse cannot usefully thematize, and for which religious symbolization is alone adequate" (Gilkey 1970, 41). Recent philosophy of science has stressed human dimensions in science, elements of conviction and commitment, a passion for understanding, and the unavoidability of assumptions, for instance of an ideal of order. Gilkey criticizes the naive understanding of science in worldviews related to science;[5] science is too much presented as objective, without genuine presuppositions, and as the sole avenue to reality. Gilkey focusses on the role of the knowing subject.

Our understanding of the destiny of our scientific culture relates to certain myths. Dominant myths in our culture have been the liberal view of progress and the Marxist one of a dialectic process. These used multivalent language and spoke of universal and ultimate structures. They have, by now, lost most of their status (Gilkey 1970, 74f; 1987, 58). The world is often perceived as directionless. The new myth is the new scientific humanity, in principle able to know the secrets of things and to control the forces of nature, for example, to free the world from hunger and war. Underlying this is a belief in human autonomy; humans give meaning to a meaningless world. Gilkey labels this (using an archaic notion for a contemporary line of thought) a gnostic myth. As Gilkey understands gnosticism, salvation was related to spiritual knowledge—from a Christian perspective, an old heresy (see Appendix 8). In the modern form of this myth, knowledge is expected to resolve the ambiguities of existence and action; knowledge makes "free *from* evil rather than free *for* evil" (Gilkey 1970, 77). There is an apparent inconsistency in this scientific (gnostic) myth: humans are, as subjects, assumed to be completely free and, as objects, to be completely intelligible. Gilkey suggests that the symbols of humans as dependent creatures and as *imago dei* make more sense of this mix of determinism and freedom. There are ambiguities in the modern myth for "good intentions seldom achieve full realization"; even stronger, "they create unintended evils as often as intended goods" (Gilkey 1970, 91). Repentance and forgiveness are needed, acceptance of humans and the world even with their ambiguities. Religion can criticize the myths of a scientific culture and offer a more adequate alternative.

The mythical images of deities are replaced in philosophical reflection by abstract notions which appear to be more universal and more ultimate. However, this procedure is self-denying. For the philosophical concepts "define the most permanent and universal characteristics of the given system of things, but they have difficulty expressing anything that transcends that system as its ground, source, or end" (Gilkey 1970, 112). As Gilkey remarks, "*if* the divine is to be in any sense transcendent to the system of the given world, philosophical language must in turn transcend itself into another form of speech" (1970, 177), a post-reflective mythical, multivalent language.[6] This does not deny the need for philosophical reflection. With respect to science and religion he concludes that "some form of mediation through ontology is unavoidable" (Gilkey 1970, 182).

We can distinguish between the content of science, the process by which it discovers or constructs that content, and the function of science in a wider cultural environment. Gilkey emphasizes the latter, the way science relates to the myths of a culture. All cultures, those with science included, have aspects which could be called ideological or religious (Gilkey 1987, 51). This cultural context is important, but not the subject of the present study. In relation to the cultural function of religion, Gilkey has emphasized language. The role of language in Gilkey's understanding of science and religion has been criticized (Gerhart and Russell 1984, 5f). He is charged with reductionism, from more or less coherent structures to myths as the vehicles of expression, and of suggesting an arbitrariness about scientific and religious ideas by neglecting the reasons why certain 'stories' are taken seriously—their explanatory relation to certain experiences.

These criticisms do not do complete justice to Gilkey's overall position. He has paid explicit attention to the process of scientific discovery, and stressed the unavoidable role of systematic philosophical formulations, though he expects such systems to fail, as they play down the ambiguities of existence and the elusiveness of the transcendent.

Gilkey, with his emphasis on the existential and cultural function of religious ideas, deals with aspects which are in danger of being neglected when the cognitive relations between science and theology are discussed. However, Gilkey's rejection of a religious dimension in the facts and theories of science, say evolution, is not all that should be said about matters of content. Without deriving religious notions from the facts, religious notions can still be explicated while using the facts, and they must in some sense be coherent with these facts. This is even more so because existential positions implicitly or explicitly assume wider, one could say metaphysical, views of the world.

5.3.2. *Understanding as a Metaphoric Process*

In *Metaphoric Process: The Creation of Scientific and Religious Understanding*, a professor of religious studies, Mary Gerhart, and a professor of physics, Allan Russell, emphasize change. "Both in science and in religion old truths do not last forever" (Russell and Gerhart 1984, 69).

They argue that understanding should not be explained with relatively simple notions of fact, like 'the cat is on the mat'. In science we deal with many objects of which we have no direct experience, or a direct experience which is not very informative for our understanding, for example in the experience of stars as dots of light. The more sophisticated forms of experience are mediated by understanding. As they argue, everybody sees, at the level of direct experience, the Sun rising, although those that accept the Copernican understanding of the Solar System understand the events as reflecting the rotation of the Earth.[7] There may be conflicts between our direct experiences and our theoretical understanding, for instance of a brick as consisting mostly of empty space. In many cases, the tension is resolved while the theoretical understanding is maintained. But the theoretical understanding may also be abandoned due to certain experiences.

Gerhart and Russell see science and religion as different fields of meanings. Explaining the meaning of a word involves reference to other words, which again may require further explanation. The meaning of a word is the configuration of relations among the elements of the responses (Gerhart and Russell 1984, 93). Such a configuration of relations is part of a larger network, a "field of meanings". Such a field of meanings is not a purely linguistic feature; it is the conceptuality which has arisen out of and shapes our experiences, it expresses our understanding.

New knowledge exists in two varieties. On the one hand we have extension of the conceptual network by analogy from something known to something not yet known. New knowledge of the previously unknown is constructed in such a way that it automatically fits into the existing scheme. Analogy introduces no tension in the field of meanings because it deals with some meanings which were still flexible, the thus far unknown.

On the other hand, if we insist on an analogy between two understandings that have already been formed and are embedded in their own field of meanings, we may introduce tension. Such an analogy is a metaphor; it is not found but created by reforming the fields of meanings (Gerhart and Russell 1984, 113). It is by such a metaphoric process that genuine new knowledge comes into existence. In that sense, we create the world, as we understand it, by creating the understanding; that world is distorted with respect to the world of ordinary experiences. Creating new metaphors is, often, a trial balloon, an experiment with ideas.

Gerhart and Russell now argue that: 1. Science and religion are different fields of meaning, but have the same epistemological structure. The same processes, analogical extension and metaphoric creation, are involved in the formation of new knowledge. And 2: Relating concepts from the scientific field with concepts from the religious field is also such a metaphoric process curving the existing world of meanings. By being related they are each strengthened. Theology is needed, since it gives a theoretical status to experiences of limit and transcendence. A claim to truth is less probable for any understanding which does not relate the two fields.

The proposal of Gerhart and Russell, which has only been sketched very superficially here, emphasizes the similar epistemological structure of science and religion. This is not, as it is for the critical realists discussed above, a similar relation to language or to facts, but rather a similar process of development of new knowledge—by extension and reformation. One can raise the question of whether the parallelism holds. Is there not a difference between scientific development and religious change? More importantly, does the similarity in the process thereby make the claims themselves more reliable?

5.4. THEOLOGY AND SCIENCE IN EUROPEAN PROTESTANTISM[8]

5.4.1. *Beyond Barth: Torrance, Link, and Jüngel*

In the preface to his first volume on creation in his *Church Dogmatics* (Barth 1945) Karl Barth deems the natural sciences irrelevant with respect to the biblical and Christian understanding of God's creation. His discussion of the doctrine of creation closely relates to the first two chapters of Genesis. Some subsequent theologians have, in different ways, attempted to combine Barth's theology with the natural sciences. I will not deal with their writings as interpretation of Barth, but only with these views in themselves.

T. F. Torrance

The Scottish theologian Torrance[9] emphasizes that theology should be understood as a science similar to the other sciences. However, the similarity is purely formal. All sciences intend to be about reality. The appropriate method for a specific science, including theology as the science of God, is determined by the reality it intends to investigate.

Torrance has developed the parallelism with physics extensively. He understands Barth's contribution to theology as an integration of the Patristic emphasis on God's being and the Reformation emphasis on God's salvific acts. This, according to Torrance, is similar to recent work on a unified field theory which would integrate the particle and wave theories of matter and light. Barth has been somewhat more successful; the beauty and structure of Barth's thought indicates "that he has penetrated rather deeply into the underlying organic relations in our understanding of the God-man-world manifold" (Torrance 1984, 280; cf. 1976, ix; 1984, viii).

However, in the end Torrance envisages more than a mere parallelism. Geometry was originally a branch of mathematics, rather externally related to physics. But in modern cosmology with its concepts of curved spacetime it has become the heart of physics. Similarly, natural theology as theological reasoning based upon reason and worldly experiences was externally related to theology based upon revelation. But now it must become part of the core of positive theology. That will imply a change in its structure, "for then physical statements and theological statements will be intimately correlated" (Torrance 1984, 281). We still lack the cognitive instruments, which "may bring to light and represent for ourselves the profound harmonies and symmetries of the divine grace in which is enshrined the inner logic of God's creative and redemptive operations in the universe" (Torrance 1984, 282).

The methodological parallelism is based upon realism; knowledge is that which does "correspond to the given reality" (Torrance 1969, 116). A method should be governed by the material content of its knowledge.

How do we ever have access to that reality in itself? This problem of all knowledge is well known in the formulation given to it by the philosopher Immanuel Kant. A theological answer has been that we have access to God because of God's self-revelation to us. The problem then becomes how one would ever know that something which might be God's self-revelation really is such a revelation. Is God's self-revelation self-authenticating? That might be convincing for a believer, but is not convincing to an outsider. Such a form of realism as present in Torrance's work is in danger of disregarding the unavoidable constructive nature of our knowledge. The relation between content and appropriate method would justify a separate theological approach only if it had been established that there is a separate theological dimension of reality. Torrance assumes two dimensions, a natural and a spiritual one, which overlap (Torrance 1985a, ix).

If such a parallelism were established, it would offer a justification for the term 'scientific theology', or, as also used by Torrance, 'theological science'. But it would not result in a way of relating the different fields, theology and the natural sciences. However, Torrance does want to go beyond a mere parallelism. He has discussed specific issues especially contingency and order, and space and time. Spacetime is, according to Torrance, a depth structure which is objective though invisible. This is similar to the objectivity of theology (Torrance 1976, 187f). The analogies between the different dimensions of reality are a consequence of the overlap between the different dimensions.

A major problem for arguments based upon parallels or overlap between two enterprises is that partial analogies need not be significant. The apparent overlap between astronomy and astrology does not imply that they both make credible claims about reality.

Torrance may be understood as representing the first type of theology, as distinguished in the introductory chapter (0.2): faith being about a hidden dimension of reality in its relation to the material world. There is, though somewhat obscured, a deep harmony there—a harmony which may shine through.

I will now discuss the continental neo-Barthians who seem to be more aware of the problems surrounding any appeal to reality. They also differ in theology. Instead of a harmony of the spiritual and the natural, they point more to the 'brokenness' of creation. One might say that Torrance joins Barth in his emphasis on the possibility of true knowledge about God if theology follows its own methods (whatever they may be). Christian Link and Eberhard Jüngel do not deny this, but emphasize much more the impossibility of natural theology and the limitations of any theology.

Christian Link

In his *Welt als Gleichniss* (1976) Christian Link rejects natural theologies which would include God as an explanatory complement to the scientific understanding of the world (1982, 365). One should not proceed from a general understanding of God to the specific biblical revelation, but explicate the universal scope of the particular truth claims of the New Testament, *in casu* that Jesus is the truth.

Link makes a distinction between an academic and a catechetical tradition in natural theology. The first argues that the Christian ideas are, in essence, common to rational humanity—and hence for the validity of 'the book of nature' as a source of revelation. The second doesn't aim at a formal understanding of God and revelation, but attempts to see God in all experiences, including those recounted in the New Testament as parables. This is "faith seeking understanding", to use Anselm's famous dictum: making something known from that which is believed. The theoretical tradition should pursue this second use of natural theology.

Link relates the problem of natural theology to the doctrine of God. For example, Luther's notion of the *deus absconditus*, the hidden God, is understood as expressing the limitations of secular reasoning: it cannot find God in the world (Link 1982, 31). The conclusion is not primarily about God's absence but about the possibilities of reason. But that need not imply that a coherence of knowledge and

faith is impossible unless one takes the specific European developments in thinking to be definite and unsurpassable. Link rejects the
idea of an absolute hiddenness, an infinite qualitative distinction
(Kierkegaard), because it would deny the possibility of knowing God
as God.

Christology, the reason-provoking encounter of God and humanity, should be the locus for natural theology. A simple natural
theology in continuity with our worldly experiences is impossible
without loss of the strangeness which is an essential characteristic of
Christian theology. Such a natural theology would also misjudge the
reality of suffering, the brokenness of creation. The 'new creation'
can only manifest itself in contrast, in the suffering of creatures.
Link refers in this context also to the ecological crisis as a universal
Good Friday.

One should not ask how a human could get outside, to the
external, hidden God. Rather, according to Link, one should ask
how it becomes possible that the world is experienced as creation,
and that God allows encounter, since "the word has become flesh
and lived among us" (John 1:14).

Link sees a parallel between the trinitarian understanding of
God and three religious interpretations of experiences of the world.
Christology relates to God's suffering in the world. God as the creator
relates to God's hiddenness in the world. And the Spirit relates to
God's future in the world. These themes are too complex to deal
with in a few lines. However, these aspects of suffering, hiddenness
and future should not be neglected in the dialogue between theology
and the natural sciences.

In comparison with the positions discussed before, Link has the
advantage of not needing to overemphasize the perfection 'showing
through'. Link's position does not result in a mere debate about God,
but about God and the world, and thus needs to introduce themes
like hiddenness, suffering, and the like. Issues of content and
method are integrated in this way.

Eberhard Jüngel

Jüngel is one of the few other 'Barthians' who have reconsidered
the possibilities for a theology which takes the world as relevant.
One of his major criticisms of traditional natural theology is its orientation on the actual, and God's presence in that actuality of the
world. It thereby lacks attention for the transformation of the natural
order, the possibilities, that which the world might become. Theo-

logically, revelation is understood by Jüngel to mean disturbance and renewal, the opening up of new possibilities (cf. Webster 1986, 120, 123ff; Jüngel 1975a [1980, 175], 1975b [1980, 196]).

A second issue of interest is his criticism, against Wolfhart Pannenberg, of arguments from the world, especially from the human, to God, as if there were a worldly necessity of God. Jüngel proceeds by assuming that theology is "confronted with a truth when the worldly non-necessity of God is asserted" (1983, 17f). It is not a disadvantage or a mere additional fact. Rather, it affects the whole theological understanding. A worldly necessity of God correlates, according to Jüngel, to a God understood as determining power, and hence to the denial of freedom. The worldly non-necessity of God expresses the understanding of God as powerful through love. The worldly non-necessity of God should not be translated into a contingency of God, a 'less than necessary'. Jüngel uses the expression "God is more than necessary", meaning that necessity as a category "does not reach as far as God" (Jüngel 1983, 25). Necessity is not applicable because it is always necessity in relation to a certain context.

Taking the world as a parable of God is, according to Link and Jüngel, theologically legitimate. Parables are not mere additional stories. They tell about God and about human life in relation to that God. They define or explicate, in an analogical or metaphorical way, some of the meaning of the 'God', of 'loving one's neighbor', and the like. If the world can be understood as a parable, this seems to me to imply, perhaps going further than Link and Jüngel, that scientific ideas about the world can be used to give semantic meaning to theological terms.

5.4.2. *Moltmann and Pannenberg*

Jürgen Moltmann and Wolfhart Pannenberg have developed positions which are much more critical of Barth's theology. We will first turn to Moltmann's almost popular *Gott in der Schöpfung (God in Creation,* 1985) before making some remarks concerning Pannenberg's writings.

Jürgen Moltmann
Moltmann envisages a doctrine of creation which emphasizes relatedness within the world (ecology), within God (social trinity), and between God and the world. During the national socialist

period in Germany, natural theology as providing knowledge of God had to be rejected. However, now the issue is not the knowledge of God but of the creation, which is in crisis ecologically (Moltmann 1985, 11).

I doubt whether the distinction works. The issue then was also the understanding of the world, of the nature of race, and so forth. And the contemporary ecological crisis is, basically, also a human crisis. Pollution is a threat to many species, but not to all microbes. To label it a crisis is to add certain values, probably in favor of more complex organisms like mammals. Hence, one could say that both then and now the issue is the understanding of the world, with a strong human component to it. In both cases we also deal with knowledge of God in order to know what to do in the world, to discern the way. Knowledge of God was not detached from reality then, nor is it now.

Moltmann considers himself to be doing "theology of nature", asking what our concept of God contributes to our understanding of nature, in opposition to natural theology, the contribution of nature to our knowledge of God. This is a standard political move on the German theological scene. However, Moltmann does not appear to be consistent. He uses sciences to argue for the relationality of the world, and from that he argues for the relationality of God.

Moltmann intends to distance himself from the anthropocentric elements in the Christian tradition. He therefore stresses that the creation narrative does not end with the sixth day, and thus with the creation of humans. The seventh day, the Sabbath, is the end of the creation. The intent of history and evolution is, according to Moltmann, to make the creation into a house of God, to bring it to the joyful feast of a universal Sabbath. The Sabbath blesses and reveals the world as God's creation. In his section on evolution Moltmann describes humans (1985, 197) as: 1. The last creature before the Sabbath, embodying all other creatures; 2. the complex system which includes all simpler systems of the evolutionary process, because humans have arisen out of them; and 3. *imago mundi*, a microcosmos which represents the macrocosmos before God.

The transition from exegetical statements, like the first one, to claims which present themselves as natural science, like the second, is in need of methodological clarification. The example, for instance, implicitly assumes the identifiability of the concept of 'kind' in Genesis 1 with the concept of 'species' of modern biology, an identification also assumed by 'creationists', but heavily disputed.[10] The second claim is not in line with contemporary evolutionary theory. Every extant creature, even contemporary single-celled organisms, has a lineage going back to single-celled organisms. Humans are just one of the current forms, like the end of one branch of the evolutionary tree. Even if humanity is understood as recapitulating the previous forms in its own lineage, it certainly does not recapitulate those in all other lineages. Humans do not incorporate mice. Nor are humans dependent upon all other species. Humans arose without influence from the Australian marsupials, although there have been common factors in their developments, both genetically and environmentally. Humans could well continue to exist without marsupials, even though many children would consider the non-existence of kangaroos a serious loss.

The theological conclusion uses the 'scientific' statement about humans including all the simpler systems to conclude that humans represent the whole of creation before God. Is the inclusion necessary? If marsupials like the kangaroo are not included in the human system, would that imply that they should not be represented before God the way bacteria living in our intestines are? The premiss about the inclusion is wrong, and would, if true, not be necessary. One should formulate other reasons why one considers non-human life to be worthy of defense.

Moltmann's theology has a strong anthropocentric orientation to it, even though he explicitly intended to develop a non-anthropocentric theology. Even his most cherished non-anthropocentric concept, the Sabbath, is a term that has been taken out of the context of social life. Nature does not have a seventh day of the week. If it is the Sabbath which reveals the world to be creation (1985, 20), the criterion might make the social world into God's creation, but does not really apply to the world described by the natural sciences. Moltmann overcomes the anthropocentrism of traditional theology by treating all non-human reality as if it were human reality, a sociosystem.[11]

Aside from anthropocentrism, it might have been better if Moltmann had developed his view more systematically. There are many nice images in his theology of creation, and especially a vivid use of biblical elements like the Sabbath, but it lacks a coherent methodology and metaphysics.

His emphasis on God's presence in nature implies some specific problems. One is the seriousness of suffering. Furthermore 'God in creation' might result in an overestimate of the strength of nature,

and thereby result in a misjudgment of risks. I will suggest below
(6.3) a theological justification of care for the natural world in a
framework which stresses God's transcendence.

Wolfhart Pannenberg

Wolfhart Pannenberg is more explicit in the systematic development of his theology.[12] He seems to relate science and theology
cognitively in two ways, which could be labelled inductive and de-
ductive. Both reflect his interest in the universality of theological
claims.

1. An inductive-apologetic approach is most clearly present in
his anthropological writings.[13] Secular anthropology needs a religious dimension; the finiteness of human existence suggests, in contrast, infinity. This dimension correlates to an external reality.

2. Inference from theology to claims about the world is more
explicit in his discussions of physics and biology. For example, "the
theological affirmation that the world of nature proceeds from an
act of divine creation implies the claim that the existence of the world
as a whole and of all its parts is contingent" (Pannenberg 1988c, 8).
It is this stance which allows for "theological questions to scientists"
(Pannenberg 1981). It also bears upon the nature of science. "If the
God of the Bible is creator of the universe, then it is not possible to
understand fully or even appropriately the processes of nature without reference to that God" (Pannenberg 1981, 4).

God is cognitively necessary; the sciences are incomplete (inductive approach), and must be incomplete (deductively seen from
theology). If "nature can be appropriately understood without reference to the God of the Bible, then that God cannot be the creator
of the universe, and consequently he would not be truly God and
could not be trusted as a source of moral teaching either" (Pannenberg 1981, 4).

Does his quest for a religious dimension in secular understanding
imply that he opts for an understanding of God as a complement
to, and present in, our reality? This seems to fit with his description
of God as the "all-determining reality" and with the (apparent?)
determinism from the future, hence the determinism towards a
'happy ending'. Such a view might express God's trustworthiness in
promises, which could be comforting. But how does Pannenberg
avoid the theological dangers of such an approach, the loss of sen-
sitivity to evil, injustice, and imperfection, and hence of judgement,
and the danger that we fail to hear a call for conversion, for doing

whatever we can do against injustice and evil? This relates back to the distinction between two types of theology (0.2). Pannenberg fits in a 'mystical' approach to the relation between theology and science, which emphasizes God's presence in the world as described by the sciences and thus tends to develop a metaphysical theology in which ordinary reality is closely connected with a 'hidden' religious dimension. Another position, which could be called 'prophetical', deals rather with God's apparent absence, or at least the ambiguity of the data. I will, in the next chapter, come back to this distinction (6.1).

A more specific methodological question concerns the selection: which science does the theologian use? Is there any way in which it is governed by rules? This does not hold for Pannenberg alone, but becomes important for any theologian who really engages in the natural sciences. For instance, Pannenberg's theological anthropology has been criticized for its use of outdated science and its neglect of genetics.[14] Which branches are relevant, and which positions within those branches? We will come back to this issue at the conclusion of the next section.

5.5. CONSTRUCTIVE CONSONANCE

In this section I try to present my own position, which could be characterized as a quest for theology in critical coherence with science. The differences between theology and science are essential, if one looks for a prophetic aspect to theology (5.5.2). Criteria for credibility of a theology which is constructed in a critical consonance with the sciences will be developed in dialogue with three major ideas about the meaning of truth: correspondence, coherence, and pragmatism (5.5.3).

5.5.1. *A Recapitulation of My Argument*

On Theology

Theology should not be misunderstood as a pre-scientific answer to questions now better answered by science. For example, 'creation' is, in most theological systems, not a term referring simply to an event in the beginning (0.1; 1.4; 1.5; Appendixes 7 and 8).

I suggest a distinction between two types of theology, which we could relate to a sense of God's presence or a cry because of God's absence. The first is reflection upon faith which deals with a hidden (spiritual, transcendent) 'dimension' of reality and its relation to the ordinary world. The existence of that other, more perfect, dimension is expected to shine through in the material world. The second type of theology takes up the experiences of imperfection such as injustice, and expresses the concern for justice and love. The first type defines Christianity by a certain metaphysical stance or worldview, and subsequently turns to the existential consequences. The second gives primacy to the existential side, and judges a metaphysical scheme by its capacity to incorporate the concern for justice and love (0.2). I see judgement of the present, appeal to conversion or action, and consolation as aspects of eschatology (4.1.1). Theologies cannot be restricted to biblical issues. Any contemporary relevance of the stories of Israel and Jesus requires a bridge between the setting of the stories and the present situation. Additional assumptions of a philosophical nature are unavoidable (0.2).

On Science

The limits of the Big Bang theory have often been neglected. For example, the 't = 0' moment is not within the domain in which the Big Bang theory is reliable, nor does it form the boundary of that domain (2.2.1). There are several proposals for theories with a wider explanatory scope. There is, as yet, no consensus about the way ahead (2.2.2; 2.3). This is taken to be representative of science: there is an area of consensus, but also a diversity of opinions on the direction of further development. Outsiders to cosmology should realize both the limited domain of the consensus and the diversity, without using either for a cheap dismissal (2.4.2).

There is a variety of research programs in cosmology. They differ in expectations about the most promising approach, but also in their underlying view of reality. The diversity is partly due to different assumptions, for instance about the nature of time and (quantum) reality. Such assumptions are metaphysical, not only in the sense that they are unquestionable within the context of a program, but also that they relate to the general characteristics of being and experience. These programs also differ, therefore, in the definition of the problems to be solved and in their criteria for theory evaluation. They are, at least with respect to our present knowledge, incompatible with each other but, perhaps, nonetheless equivalent in explanatory power (2.4.1).

The diversity among contemporary research is similar to the

discontinuities in the history of cosmological models. Pacholczyk (1984) argues that previous pictures were never generalized but rather discarded. Michael Heller agrees with respect to specific world models, but not for cosmology as the science of non-local, or global, phenomena. As a science it is "also about unverifiable assumptions which are indispensable in order to render such a science possible" (Heller 1986c, 69). The diversity of programs and discontinuities in the history of models of the Universe exemplifies the constructive side of science. Theories, and certainly theories at some distance from ordinary experience, are constructions using certain concepts and are dependent upon certain assumptions.

Even if there were a scientific consensus on the best approach, there still is the possibility of a variety of interpretations. This is the case for the probabilistic features of quantum theories, as well as for the role of time in all physical theories. An example closer to the religious issues under consideration: the equivalence of the Universe to a vacuum, and hence the possibility of its origination through a vacuum fluctuation, can be invoked as support for an atheistic stance, the Universe being something accidental, or for a theistic stance, or even for an understanding of the Universe as an illusion.

On Metaphysics

John Gribbin suggests that the end of metaphysics has arrived (0.1). I don't assume a single, well-developed metaphysical scheme, like the Whiteheadian scheme of process theologians. Rather, I point out the relevance and meaningfulness of issues which are generally considered metaphysical. Some positions discussed, like the strong anthropic principles, are themselves clearly metaphysical in their assumption of an essential role of mind or purpose in the Universe. The programs of Andrej Linde, Stephen Hawking, Roger Penrose, and Frank Tipler (2.3 and 4.3) are closely connected with different ideas about the nature of quantum reality, and of time, and with different appreciations of finitude or compactness. The point is not only, as the theologian Langdon Gilkey has argued on many occasions, that the scientific enterprise as a whole is based implicitly upon assumptions about the knowability of the Universe, assumptions themselves beyond science. There is also, at least at the frontiers of scientific research, a diversity which can be traced back to different specific metaphysical ideas. One might argue that this variety disappears once consensus on the best scientific theory has been reached. I doubt whether this really holds for the issues considered here. Firstly, these cosmological theories are at such a distance from direct observations that additional assumptions are needed. This is the point well made by Heller (1986c) when he describes cosmology as dealing also with its own assumptions. Secondly, we have other areas in physics where consensus on a theory has been reached without being parallelled by a similar consensus on the interpretation. This is especially clear with respect to the nature of reality in quantum theories and the nature of time in thermodynamics. A consensus theory in quantum cosmology would probably share in these disputes about correct interpretation.

Theology is not identical with metaphysics. I draw attention to the existential and evocative dimension. An incomplete theology can well neglect metaphysical issues. But a well-developed systematic theology needs metaphysics and anthropology. It deals with humans, and needs to reflect upon such anthropological issues as freewill, the social nature of humans, and much more. But it considers these humans in a wider context, in relation to 'God' or 'the whole', or 'the ultimate', or whatever concept is fitting in that context. One cannot even consider human actions without dealing with an underlying view of reality, for instance of time and (in)determinism. Metaphysical notions are necessary in order to make intelligible what is meant by certain theological statements.

There is no exclusive order of the three components discussed: theology, science, and metaphysics. Metaphysical assumptions influence science, but science also influences the way the most fundamental structure of the world is seen. Any theology is dependent upon metaphysical views, but religious and moral convictions may also impel people to hold certain views. Hence, in dealing with theology and science at the cognitive level, considering matters of content, one has to deal with three components: theology, science, and metaphysics. None is fixed, all three are constructions—though each with a different status and relation to experience. There is more besides these. For example, epistemology comes in at the moment one deals with the relation of ideas to experience.

On the Relation between Theology and Science

The possibility of consonance is an assumption which is made for general reasons, such as a quest for coherence in human understanding, and for theological reasons, such as an expected unity in our understanding of God's creation, the world. Such consonance is not found, but can be constructed. It involves the sciences, theology, and philosophical notions. Meanings of terms change, and hence a new understanding of reality develops (0.2; 1.2.5; 5.3.2).

Mary Hesse writes about relating science and religion, that "the main issue is not one of scientific 'realism', but one of communicative strategy" (Hesse 1981, 287). That fits well with the acknowledgment that we are dealing with a constructive project built upon the assumption of consonance (as well as on other assumptions specific to the particular theology under consideration). Arguing for the truth of religious convictions on the basis of scientific theories has failed too often. In the dialogue between science and religion, it is more promising to focus on intelligibility than on truth. If there is a plurality of scientific views, as is the case in quantum cosmology, one could attempt to set forth the core of one's convictions in as many of these frameworks as possible, in the same way that beliefs have been presented in many different languages and cultures.

After intelligibility comes credibility as the next step towards truth. The credibility of a theological view will be enhanced by a clarification of the concepts involved, but it needs more. Embedding theological ideas in a web with the most credible scientific and philosophical ideas might contribute to their credibility.

Claiming parallels, for instance between Genesis 1 and the Big Bang, runs the risks of neglecting the context and function of the different contributions. Comparison becomes possible only after translation into a common language. The proposed components for the parallel must be representative of their respective contexts (1.4.2).

One aspect that might easily be lost when one emphasizes the parallels between science and theology, or even their consonance, is the critical aspect, judgement, which should, I believe, be part of an adequate eschatology. However, science might help to envisage a metaphysical conceptual space in which possibilities of conversion and consolation can be articulated. In this context, the issue is not a translation of the images of another time. Rather, we seek a new understanding of reality which is adequate with respect to science and the theological function of eschatology, capable of expressing the concern for justice and love. This is illustrated by an analogy from physics. Einstein's theory of general relativity is conceptually not in continuity with Newton's view of space and time. However, the theory is continuous with the Newtonian tradition at the less abstract level of description of, for example, planetary orbits, despite the radically different conceptuality (4.1.3).

5.5.2. *The Priority of Dissimilarities*

Essential Dissimilarities

In a discussion on religion and science Nancey Murphy suggests the image of a crossword puzzle (Murphy 1989). Theories are compared to words. A solution is constrained by clues, representing external constraints, and mutual consistency of the words. The language used in solving the puzzle is an analogy for the conceptual scheme within which scholars work at a given moment. Changing language is not common practice in puzzle-solving, but might be considered in principle.

Murphy compares science and religion to "different regions or sections in the puzzle", perhaps opposite corners. The model suggests the possibility of direct overlap and of connection via a region belonging to another discipline, say history or metaphysics. When theology was dominant, say in the Middle Ages, one could understand it as occupying the upper left-hand corner, the part where one starts. The image places theology and science completely on the same level. They have the same type of truth, and of experience.

I want to emphasize the difference in function between theology and science. As Gerhard Theissen wrote,

> scientific thought is corrected by reference to facts; faith must contradict the oppressive force of facts. Science subjects itself to the 'facts'; faith rebels against them. (Theissen 1985, 4)

Science and theology have a different relation to reality; the one describes and explains, while the other should look primarily for possibilities for transformation towards justice and perfection. They relate differently to experiences, at least if judged by the possibility of achieving consensus on 'the facts' or 'the experiences'. They also regard changes differently. In general, changes in science appear to be development if not progress in knowledge. It is not clear what would constitute similar progress, in the long run, in theology, and even less clear whether such progress actually occurs. Theology changes, perhaps, more in relation to its contexts, the *condition humaine* that it faces.

All in all, the differences seem sufficiently important to search for another understanding of their relative location than that offered by the puzzle image. One solution would be to take them as unrelated. This has been a quite common position among Protestant theologians. Such a complete separation runs into two problems.

Firstly, theological language is in danger of becoming unintelligible, at least outside its own closed world. It resembles a language-game with its own internal rules and meanings unrelated to the outside world. In actual practice the isolation is avoided by implicitly allowing certain human experiences into the game, often those of a more existential nature. However, if the separation is thus taken as being less strict, why should the experiences which have been systematized in science be excluded?

Secondly, a complete separation runs the risk of making theology irrelevant. The human world is a part of the world as studied by the sciences. If theological thought neglects the world as dealt with by the sciences, it will also be unable to deal adequately with the human world. The dissimilarities were justified with the words of Gerhard Theissen, "faith must contradict the oppressive force of the facts". That is the main reason why science and religion should not be treated as identical. However, it is also the main reason why they should not be divorced from each other. Theology has to be related to the facts in order to be intelligible and relevant.

How can Theology and Science be Related yet Dissimilar?

It is easier to criticize others than to propose proper ways of relating theology to science. The quest is certainly not finished. However, it seems to me that the explicit consideration of metaphysical elements makes it possible to formulate a theology which is open to the results and methods of science and nonetheless maintains its critical possibilities. Hence, the total project involves three fields: science, theology, and metaphysics. Each field has its own internal considerations. Here, we consider their interaction. Science has parts which are, in practice, beyond change. Whatever religious or metaphysical ideas one has, no sane scientist disputes the scientific consensus about the Solar System or DNA molecules. However, science is not all consensus. There is, by necessity, uncertainty and dispute at the frontier of research. And there also exists, at least for some fundamental branches of physics, a continuing debate about the proper interpretation of the formalism. Both uncertainties come together in the recent developments in cosmology considered in this study. In that respect, science can be influenced by metaphysical and religious ideas. On the other hand, the metaphysical ideas are dependent upon results from the sciences and upon contributions from other branches of philosophy such as epistemology. Religious ideas have roots that stretch far back in time. However, they also change in the dialogue with the sciences.

Hence, I envisage three webs of beliefs (Quine and Ullian 1978), each related in a fundamental way to the other webs. However, in order to avoid the 'one puzzle' image, these webs are not in the same space. Rather, one can imagine beliefs in the scientific web as knots linked by inferences. Some of those inferences are very straightforward, for example a logical deduction. Others are rooted partly in certain metaphysical beliefs. They connect the web of beliefs on which science focusses with a 'second-order' web in which the knots represent metaphysical assumptions. They might also relate in such a way to a third web, convictions of a religious and existential nature. The webs are separate in the sense that the mutual connections within each system of beliefs are of major importance. However, the scientific web is also linked to the other webs, not only specific beliefs but also to their constitutions as a whole, because it influences the kind of connecting inferences which are accepted in the scientific web. And in the end one cannot deny that the three form a single web, though one which consists of many rather different layers.

The idea can be expressed in other ways too. When discussing Peacocke's idea of a hierarchy of levels with theology being the highest level, I mention the alternative proposal by Eric Juengst, who contends that genetics does not fit into one of the levels within biology. Rather, it owes its importance to the way it integrates the different levels. Similarly, one could not relate theology and science in a linear order, the one at the outer boundary of the other, but rather as different, but intertwined sets; theology integrating aspects into a tentative worldview.

My own theological proposal, as presented in the next chapter, is intended to be an example of such a theology which is constructed in relation to metaphysical and scientific notions, but which also maintains a distance with respect to the 'scientific facts'.

5.5.3. *Truth and Credibility*

Not all systems of scientific, metaphysical, and theological ideas fit together. There must be criteria. However, criteria are themselves assumptions, or based upon assumptions, which makes it impossible to avoid circularity. I nonetheless propose three criteria. They are dependent upon my general assumptions, like the quest for integration (0.1), but as criteria not restricted to my own theological proposal, developed in the next chapter. The first and second consider the intelligibility, or clarity, of the notions used; the third its theological adequacy.

First, and easiest, comes *consistency*, which results in the formal possibility of a position. A theological position has to aspire to internal consistency. It also needs to aim at consistency with those elements from science (or other enterprises outside theology) which it takes into consideration. I will return below to the consequences of the diversity of the sciences and of approaches within some sciences. Consistency seems rather trivial. However, it can have serious consequences. For example, if one accepts the Hartle-Hawking cosmology, one cannot understand *creatio ex nihilo* as an initial creation at the beginning of time (see 2.5).

Mutual consistency is a minimal requirement, which is sufficient in arguments for the formal possibility of certain beliefs. However, it is insufficient in our age, where the meaning, relevance and truth of religious beliefs are in dispute. The more prominent questions concerning beliefs are, in my opinion, different: 'What does it mean?' 'Why should I bother?' 'Is it true?'

The second element in constructing a theology which takes science seriously concerns the question of (semantic) *meaning*. The meaning of 'love thy neighbor' is explicated through the story of the Good Samaritan. Concepts may be made intelligible in a more specific way by expressing their meaning in terms of a scientific theory. Since science is considered to be intelligible, it can be used to make theological notions clear. For example, the meaning of *creatio ex nihilo* as cosmogony can be set forth by using the language of science. Using the Big Bang cosmology one can suggest as its meaning an initial creation at 't = 0'. Another meaning, that of sustaining, can be made clear in terms of the Hartle-Hawking cosmology (2.5). If meanings are thus formed, one improves the coherence (consistency and integration) of the religious and the scientific ideas.

Expressing the meaning of a theological concept in terms of a specific theory is, of course, risky. Firstly, it may miss some essential elements of the theological content. Secondly, the scientific theory may itself turn out to be wrong. That affects the theological concept's credibility, to which we will return below, but does not diminish the possibility of making it intelligible. The flat Earth has been ruled out in an age of air traffic. However, the idea of a Heaven 'up there' still has some intelligibility (though no credibility). As far as intelligibility is concerned one can be quite permissive with respect to the science used; once one is after credibility it becomes crucial which science is used.

Thirdly, in constructing a theology which is consistent with science and intelligible through its association with science, one should not forget the *relevance,* the existential function of a religion. If theology were merely another kind of science, or an intelligible and consistent fiction, there would be no reason to bother with it. Each religion has its own traditions, its own stories or myths, which convey values, attitudes, and so on. Any theology, as an intellectual construct, appropriates such myths. For example, there are stories of prophets calling for conversion. The eschatology that I have begun to develop (4.5.2; see also 6.2) needs a way of talking about possibilities for transformation and about values, in order to incorporate what I perceive to be important convictions. The criterion of relevance makes the difference between science and theology.

These three elements are, in my opinion, required for any significant theology which takes science seriously. They do not guarantee the truth or credibility of such a proposed theology, although they play a role in the assessment of credibility. The remainder of this section will deal with the way in which truth, or at least credibility, might be thought of in relation to the criteria mentioned. It will be argued that a correspondence view of truth is not useful. A coherence view of truth relates to the first and the second criterion, consistency and the creation of meaning through coherence. A pragmatic view of the truth relates to the third criterion.

Truth as Correspondence with Reality

The commonsense understanding is that statements are true if they correspond to facts, that is, to reality. Such a view of truth encounters problems. For instance, it does not allow for hypothetical statements ('if . . ., then . . .'), nor for counterfactuals ('If Napoleon had won the battle, he . . .'). And, how is one to compare statements with 'the way things are'? The relation between the sentence 'it is raining' and the actual falling of drops of certain liquid is certainly not one of mirroring. The questions become even more abundant once we move from isolated statements about possible observations to systems of statements as complex as scientific theories.

It seems an often-neglected truism that 'realism' is not a single position, but exists in many varieties, each in response to different objections. I assume realism in an ontological sense; there is something real. This may be disputed, and has been disputed in recent cosmology by Barrow and Tipler (1986, 155),[15] but existence of some external reality seems nonetheless an assumption shared by most ordinary people, scientists, and theologians.

Are theories adequate descriptions of that reality? Does, for instance, the term 'electron' really refer to an entity in that reality? Such questions are not about reality in itself, but about the relation between our knowledge and reality.

A maximal claim could be that scientific statements are true because they correspond to the way the world is. Statements fall into two basic classes: true and false. The adequacy of this view for science is very disputable (Harré 1986). For example, all scientific theories are revisable; they are probably not completely correct. They should all be counted as false, upon this strict view. An adequate description of science needs to overcome such a 'black-and-white' distinction between true and false; some theories are 'less false' than others.

A more moderate claim is that the best scientific theories are, perhaps progressively, approximately true and/or that their central terms are genuinely referential and/or that the approximate truth of a theory explains its predictive successes (Leplin 1984). Notions like approximate truth and progress are, however, not trivial. And, the discontinuities in the history of theoretical science suggest the possibility that current theories might be in need of significant revision, even though they are successful. To recall one example given before, Newton's theory of gravity was superseded by Einstein's. There is continuity in explanatory and predictive success, but the theories suggest different ontologies. They seem to refer to different fundamental realities. Whether terms in theories adequately refer to reality, and whether reality resembles the description given in the best current theories, is disputable—and obviously not soluble in a work such as this.

In the case of cosmology there is a genuine diversity of approaches and a significant distance from observations.[16] They depict reality quite differently. What should we do? In relating science to theology one should keep in mind that theories are revisable constructions. The diversity of perspectives makes a realist stance, even if qualified with notions like 'approximate', useless for the theories considered here. On the other hand, these theories are successful. We should, in my opinion, take scientific theories as credible, but probably incorrect, proposals for possible ways of understanding the nature of reality. Current theories deserve to be taken seriously, as the best available today, but not too seriously, for they will change.

Realism as a close correspondence between theories and reality seems too strong a claim. But it seems a reasonable policy to treat the best theories as if they described reality accurately, and to consider the implications. Truth as correspondence with reality is a metaphysical notion. The correspondence theory of truth rings true as far as the meaning of truth is concerned, but does not in itself provide criteria for assessing the truth of a statement. It seems more profitable to consider the epistemological issue: when are we justified in accepting some theory or theology as true? The term 'credibility' carries this connotation.

Coherence and the Domain of Science

A criterion-oriented view of truth is the coherence theory of truth (Rescher 1973). Coherence combines consistency and integration of the proposed ideas in a connected system which is also sufficiently complete. Rescher proposes coherence as a regulative principle in the process of screening competing truth claims in a large but inconsistent set of 'data'. We don't start with a grasp of 'the whole truth', but rather we work our way through the material in order to select the better candidates for truth. "The truthfulness of a truth-candidate is thus an issue for *contextual* determination and becomes a matter of fitting it amongst others in its environment" (Rescher 1973, 41).

Consistency and the construction of meaning through coherence satisfy well the coherence criterion of truth. Consistency is required for coherence, but consistency is trivial if the meaning of scientific and religious terms would be unrelated. Hence, consistency, if it is to be an effective criterion, assumes some coherence of meanings.

Coherence is an incomplete criterion as long as there is no domain of ideas specified within which coherence should be sought. The credibility of theology depends upon the credibility of the science used and upon the uniqueness of the construction. If we were to use a 'flat Earth' geography we would certainly not attain credibility. However the issue is actually more complicated. There is a diversity of sciences with, *prima facie,* different metaphysical views, for example with respect to time (4.4). There is also a diversity of approaches within a science, for example in cosmology (2.3). Should we follow those scientists who seem to defend views closest to our own religious outlook, or should we rather consider science "where it 'hurts' most" (Eaves 1989, 203)? There seems to be four positions:

1. *Eclecticism:* we take whatever fits best. This attitude is present in much religious misuse of speculative scientific statements, such as those of David Bohm and John Wheeler. Such a selection of the science used might contribute to the intelligibility of our view, but makes no additional contribution to credibility.

2. *Cheap dismissal:* we need not pay attention to science, since scientists are not sure themselves. Theologians can hold whatever opinions they like. As long as scientists cannot reach consensus, anything goes. This neglects the partial consensus among scientists. Though there is some variety of positions, many alternatives have been ruled out. Hence, to dismiss the sciences because of a lack of consensus is not really warranted.

3. Cautiously *wait and see* what becomes of the consensus. This is, for example, the position advocated by Ian Barbour (1989) and Harry Shipman with respect to inflationary theories and more speculative ideas in cosmology. "Viable theologies need not, at the moment, even be consistent with such ideas, since these ideas are speculative at this time" (Shipman 1986, 9). There is, I admit, no strict need for consistency. However, the consensus is not that clear and safe either. For example, the Big Bang theory allows both for a view which is timeless (if developed along Hawking's line) or for a view that has an arrow of time (if developed along Penrose's line). And one might wonder whether any current consensus is stable.

4. *Reverse eclecticism:* take the worst possible case. If we solve it, we have really made progress. This is the real challenge, and hence the real opportunity for credibility.

All in all, working towards coherence of theology, science, and metaphysical notions seems a reasonable strategy. In constructing such coherence, or consonance, not all contributions have equal initial plausibility. In general, it is much less likely that the science gives way than that the theology does. However, this is not as absolute as it seems. Even within the sciences one comes across such differences, for instance between the hard core and the auxiliary hypotheses of a research program, to use the terms of Imre Lakatos. And similarly for a religious view, some elements can be of enormous weight, while other elements are less relevant.

Relevance: Pragmatic Truth?

So far I have argued that the first two elements mentioned, consistency and coherence, can both contribute to the credibility of a proposed theology which takes science seriously. What about the third element, the more specifically religious one: relevance?

Relevance might be related to a pragmatic view of truth. Upon a pragmatic view, the usefulness or effectiveness of a certain theory provides a reasonable ground for considering the theory as true. If we can use 'electrons' in TV tubes we assume that the concept 'electron' as it appears in the theory refers to something in reality. In this case, usefulness is used as a criterion for truth, which is itself taken as correspondence to reality.

The notion 'relevance' introduces values. Sticking to the same example used above, I opt for a 'prophetic' distance between the facts and the values as an ingredient in any theology which deals with the scientific description of the world, because of the realities of imperfection and injustice in this world. The pragmatic justification of a specific religious view, by its effectiveness in coping with the world, is thereby less tied up with a correspondence view of truth. However, this pragmatic component is important in evaluating proposals for a theology which deals also with the sciences. Whether this pragmatic credibility relates to truth depends upon the connotations ascribed to 'true'. Can values be true? One could, as I am willing to do, concede that one doesn't deal here with credibility in relation to truth as correspondence with facts. However, this would be due to the limited scope of the notion 'true'. Values may not be true; they are nonetheless important, and not beyond dispute.

Returning to Correspondence

Truth as correspondence between ideas and reality is not directly attainable. I therefore turned to coherence and pragmatic justification. Taking these as criteria, one might still hope that the credibility thus supported is credibility with respect to truth about reality. This transition is, again, not without its implicit metaphysical assumptions. Moving from coherence as a criterion for credibility to coherence as effective in getting at reality assumes, at least, that reality is coherent. And the same holds for the pragmatic justification; it assumes that lies cannot be effective in the long run; the world supports honesty.

We are unable to side-step the constructive, and therefore provisional, character of our ideas. The next chapter presents my own attempt at expressing a theological view in critical coherence with the sciences. I hope that it may also be read as an example of the method defended here.

GOD

> The ubiquitous absence of 'God' in ordinary life is this sense of
> non-existing, of mystery, of incalculable potentiality; this eternal
> doubt that hovers between the thing in itself and our perception
> of it; this dimension in and by which all other dimensions exist.
> The white paper that contains a drawing; the space that contains
> a building; the silence that contains a sonata; the passage of time
> that prevents a sensation or object continuing forever; all these are
> 'God'. (John Fowles 1980, 27)

In the first chapter I distinguished two models of theology. The
first considers the world as showing some of God's perfection. God
is thought of as present, and harmony between ideas about God and
ideas about the world is expected. The other model is primarily one
of reflection upon the apparent absence of God, as an interpretation
of evil.[1] Considering the first type of theology, the debatable issue
is whether God exists. In that context, God's absence becomes an
atheistic notion. The second type of theology uses a different notion
of absence, which one could interpret prophetically, for instance as
a critical judgement effected as withdrawal. It could also be interpreted more in line with the wisdom traditions as an "elusive presence" (Terrien 1978).

For the first type of theology, reflection upon the nature of
reality, the results in the preceding chapters (as summarized in 3.6)
were negative on a number of issues. Cognitive arguments for the
God hypothesis *remoto Deo* are not too successful (6.1.1). They might
show the possibility of such a God, but fall far short of providing
an argument for God's existence.

If theology is primarily about living with the irrationality of the
world then the God hypothesis acquires much more significance,
although cognitively it is still, from our point of view, only an option.[2]
The elusiveness of God becomes a significant part of such an understanding of God (6.1.2). The understanding of 'God', once we

accept the hypothesis 'God', will be developed further by recapitulating themes from earlier chapters and attempting to integrate them into a coherent whole (6.2).

In the final section, the understanding of 'God' thus developed is related to the 'integrity of creation' concept, and contrasted with a different understanding of God in some documents on justice, peace, and the integrity of creation as produced in the context of the World Council of Churches (6.3).

6.1.   A HYPOTHETICAL GOD?

6.1.1. *There Are No Cognitive Arguments for the Hypothesis 'God'*

Does contemporary science lead to God or require God to be complete? An affirmative answer has been defended in many ways, for instance by arguing for the necessity of a religious dimension in secular anthroplogy (Pannenberg 1962 and 1983), by pointing to one or more forms of the contingency of the Universe (Torrance, Jaki), by referring to Gödel's theorem in mathematics—on the existence of some undecidable propositions in each formal logical system (Jaki, Torrance)—and so on.

No Argument for God can be Based upon Incompleteness
The Beginning. The Big Bang theory suggests a 'beginning' a finite time ago. However the domain of the theory does not reach that far; particle theories are not known for the very early Universe, and an even worse shortcoming is the lack of a consensus about a theory which integrates quantum physics and spacetime physics. Penrose's proposal in quantum cosmology might be understood as similar to the Big Bang picture. However, Linde's cosmology is basically eternal; the apparent beginning is the 'birth' of a domain through a quantum fluctuation, followed by the subsequent growth in a period of rapid inflation. Hawking's cosmology implies a finite four-dimensional universe. But time is just a parameter; a beginning with reference to such a parameter is an artificial feature and does not correspond to an 'edge' of reality.

Anthropic Coincidences as Empirical Global Contingency.   Some have explained features of the Universe by reference to anthropic principles (3.2). But the data to be explained, the anthropic coincidences, are eroding. Some data have found ordinary scientific explanations, for instance through the introduction of the inflationary idea into cosmological models. Other coincidences may in future be explained by theories of quantum gravity. The Weak Anthropic Principle merely states that one can go by inference from consequences to circumstances, for instance from human existence to a certain kind of environment. It does not explain either humankind or the environment; it only explains our knowledge about the environment as knowledge based upon a consequence, humans existing in that environment.

Stronger anthropic principles, which suggest that any possible universe must have the properties for life or consciousness, are beyond science. There is a teleological version, often called the Strong Anthropic Principle (SAP), which is like the old metaphysical idea of plenitude. Applied intracosmically the principle is wrong; the Moon is not inhabited. Another version, the Participatory Anthropic Principle, extrapolates enormously a disputable interpretation of quantum physics: minds in the Universe give definite reality to the Universe, also to its earlier stages, by observing the Universe. It 'solves' the origination problem at the expense of a mind-matter problem of cosmic proportions.

The anthropic principles do not give compelling explanations for the coincidences. This suggests that a theistic explanation, *design*, might be appropriate. However, the erosion of the data and the possibility of the existence of many worlds make this strategy equally unsuccessful. Besides, design is, upon further reflection, not an explanation at the same level as chance or necessity (3.6.1).

Global Ontological Contingency. Why does the Universe, with a finite or an infinite past, exist? It has been argued that the most simple answer to this question is the theistic answer. For example, Richard Swinburne argues that that is a much simpler assumption than accepting the Universe as a brute fact which just happens to be (see 1.3.2.). Even if one agrees with Swinburne, contrary to the claims of some cosmologists and popularizers, that the contingency of existence is beyond science, such a comparative case for the theistic answer is not independent of scientific understanding. And it must be granted that modern cosmology works with theories which have an appealing beauty and simplicity to those who have the training and ability to understand them.

My discussion of the above three kinds of argument suggests that scientific cosmology cannot be used in apologetic arguments for the existence of God. On the other hand, it does not exclude the possibility of a transcendent God either.

No Argument Against God can be Based upon Completeness

It has often been claimed by scientists and popularizers that the hypothesis 'God' is ruled out, or at least made superfluous, by contemporary scientific understanding. But I have analyzed some specific instances of this contention, and found them wanting.

The Mystery of Existence.   The origination of the Universe has been described as a quantum event. However the possibility of quantum fluctuations assumes a physical vacuum with certain properties. And quantum theories use the language of probabilities, which is only intelligible if one has a measure: for instance the probability of a certain decay is 0.5 per day. Even the most extreme 'nothing' of the physicists is not an absolute Nothing devoid of any properties and measures. Even if theories are perfect and complete, they do not answer the question of why there is anything which behaves according to those theories. The mystery of existence is unassailable. It remains possible, therefore, to understand the Universe as a gift, as grace.

Unified Theories and Abstraction from Diversity.   Theoretical physicists and cosmologists are making progress towards more comprehensive and less arbitrary theories. Avoiding infinity as a prediction for observable quantities turns out to be a very restrictive requirement. If that is combined with esthetic criteria, like simplicity, it might result in a small number of theories which are possible *a priori*. However, this completeness and unity are achieved at a very abstract level. The variety of the physical world is omitted through a process of abstraction and generalization. This one-sidedness is heuristically powerful, but should not lead to a reductionistic stance, as if the diversity of particulars were not also a reality.

God is unnecessary as explanation of the details of the theory, as they are fixed by the requirements of consistency and simplicity. This has consequences for any appeal to contingency as a major category for understanding God's creative activity. However, necessity might be the correlate of God's trustworthiness. God might still be the source of the reality described in the theory, and hence of the validity of the theory. There are classical debates about God's relation to goodness and to the laws of logic. Is God constrained by goodness and by logic and mathematical consistency? Many would agree that goodness belongs to the essence of God. God is not constrained by consistent and unified theories; rather, unity and consistency can be thought of as reflections of God's nature in God's creative work.

Complete Theories and Conceptual Boundedness. Epistemologically, complete theories are always dependent upon certain concepts. Conceptual boundedness is unavoidable if one wants to achieve intelligibility. The conceptual boundaries of a theory are transcended by entering the conceptual scheme of another theory. One could stop here. However, one could, with Munitz (1986), think of something beyond these conceptually bounded cosmologies. By definition, we never will have scientific knowledge of that reality, for that would mean having it in a conceptual scheme. The reality hinted at epistemologically transcends all our knowledge, although it might be at the heart of all reality.

Conclusion

Cognitive arguments for the existence of God fail, as well as similar arguments against the existence of God. This is in line with more general conclusions regarding contingency and knowledge. I have argued that science is equally at odds with contingency and with necessity (3.4.2). What is understood as contingent in one perspective might be necessary in another perspective (4.4). And all knowledge is construction constrained by reality. It is like a web of belief (Quine and Ullian 1978): constrained at the boundaries where it touches reality, but constructed according to some organizing principles, and hence with some variation, especially for the beliefs which are at some distance from the fixed boundary. The hypothesis 'God' might be seen as either one of the possible organizing principles, or as a belief which is at a significant distance from, and therefore not too much constrained by, reality as understood through science.

Arguing without the God hypothesis, *remoto Deo*, does not result in a cognitive argument for the existence of God, one could say *pro deo*. The possibility of thinking God is not excluded, but there are no interesting reasons to use that possibility, or at least no good grounds for the introduction of that hypothesis.

Some are satisfied with a public argument for the possibility;

they have their own, perhaps fideistic, resources for the belief itself.[3] However, I think that a different type of theology, which thematizes God's prophetic absence/elusive presence, also allows for a different public argument for the God hypothesis.

6.1.2. *Absence or Elusive Presence of God in the World*

There seem to be three types of response to the apparent absence of perfection.

1. One could *deny the imperfection.* Many in the 'New Age' movement seem to hold that the world is in itself harmonious; apparent imperfections are consequences of wrong perceptions of the world. Fritjof Capra states that all crises in our society, whether inflation or violence, are facets of one crisis, which is a crisis of perception (Capra 1982, xviii). If we described the world appropriately, we would overcome these crises and find harmony. Berman (1981) suggests that the modern period is characterized by a loss of meaning due to a wrong metaphysical view, especially the splits between matter and mind and between facts and values. He too expects a drastic change in our perception of reality, leading to a *Re-enchantment of the World.* It is a certain view of redemption, of value: life in harmony, intimacy, beauty, community, is possible if we try to see the world that way.

There are other perspectives offering value in this world. The expansion of life and consciousness envisaged by Tipler (4.3) or the continuous complexification envisaged by Dyson (4.2) may be understood as alternative immanent redemptive visions and the same could be said for a more modest visions of progress, both technologically and politically.

The possibility of perfection might also be envisaged as located in 'another place' or 'another time'; hence in a somewhat more dualistic religious metaphysical scheme. If this perfect realm is somehow a discernible reality in our ordinary world, such a view results in an expectation of harmony, and hence a denial of the real absence of justice and perfection. Such a view might result in a 'critical-realistic' (or naive-realistic) approach to theology and science: science is scanned for hints about that other reality, for explanations of apparent failures, and so on. According to this view, absence of harmony would suggest an atheistic absence of God.

2. The opposite standpoint is well expressed, in the context of reflections on cosmology, in Weinberg's conclusion to *The First Three*

Minutes: the Universe becomes more and more comprehensible, but in the same movement its *pointlessness* becomes ever clearer. We are left to ourselves, without being part of a grand harmony, whether as initial design or as an expectation about a pleasant future. Weinberg mitigates his conclusion a little by suggesting in his final sentence one way of transcending the absurdity: "The effort to understand the universe is one of the very few things that lifts human life a little above the level of farce, and gives it some of the grace of tragedy" (Weinberg 1977, 155).

3. The *ambiguity* of the world, and hence of arguments from the world to harmony or tragedy might be taken as an intermediate position. One could take the possibility of perfection and justice as a conjecture, a hypothesis about a better world, or about this world made better. It would be similar to Edward Harrison's conception of the burden due to increasing awareness of ignorance, the so called learned ignorance. The burden might be bearable if one assumes more or less naively, from outside the scope of learning, "faith in the cloud of unknowing, whether it be God, the Universe, or UniGod" (Harrison 1985, 276; see 3.5.2 above).[4]

Such a conjecture remains a conjecture; there are, in the world, no clues to its truth; that was my conclusion in the first half of this section. It is somewhat like Kant's regulative ideas: it is itself beyond the claims based upon experience, but is nonetheless an idea which is important in relation to experience in the life that is lived. The absence of God is not denied, but rather reinterpreted as an absence which cries out for presence—and hence for change.

All three options are actually lived, and hence practically livable. However, I do not consider them equally compelling; I opt for the third, intermediate position: the conjecture of a different possibility.[5]

The first position, the presence of harmony despite its apparent absence, has two disadvantages. It seems insufficient, as it takes the sting out of evil by making evil something apparent or something that exists for the sake of a greater good. And as I argued above, it seems unsuccessful. I do not have any argument against the second position, except that it might paralyze the person who holds it. It might take away any incentive to do something which would make a difference. I prefer to assume a transcendent reality, a possibility for perfection and justice. It places us at the boundary between the freedom of the second position, in which there are no constraints, and the lack of freedom of the first position, which has the happy ending as part of reality.

How can one trust a hypothetical God? Can one worship a hypothesis? Is this way to God adequate with respect to the seriousness with which a real God should be taken?

The hypothetical is part of the order of knowledge, not of being. To give an example from physics: quarks are assumed to be the smallest constituents of protons, neutrons, and other particles. As knowledge, the quark theory is hypothetical. However, the quarks are supposed to be at the heart of the matter, in the order of being. All theories of science are proposals, but not mere fantasy: they purport to be about the way the world is. We never have direct access to ontology; theories propose ontologies.

Science has generally been understood as a critical and rational enterprise, especially since Karl Popper introduced the emphasis on falsifiability. There may be engagement in science, but no strong commitment to certain ideas. Everything is in principle open to criticism and revision. Yet there is also, as successfully argued in Kuhn's *Structure of Scientific Revolutions,* a commitment to a particular approach, a basic understanding of the nature of problems and solutions, of the way the world is, a 'paradigm'. This commitment to a paradigm is much less open to rational criticism and revision. There are, of course, mediating positions like Lakatos's methodology of scientific research programs, which attempts to describe the rationality of fundamental changes using the distinction between progressive and degenerating research programs.

The argument for the God hypothesis involves, as I present it, a decision which is like a commitment to a paradigm or program. We may argue that the choice made is reasonable, but in the end it cannot be decided by argument. The understanding of such a God, as developed in the next section, is much more open to revision. There is engagement with a certain metaphysical scheme, but it can be discussed and evaluated in many ways: its internal consistency; its consistency with other fields of knowledge, including the natural sciences; its coherence; and also its adequacy with respect to the preceding understanding of theology as being about imperfection and injustice.

6.2.   CONSTRUCTING A CONSONANT 'GOD'

Once the symbol of God is introduced it should be given content in an intelligible way. This section suggests some facets of an understanding of God which is appropriate both to contemporary cosmology and to the way the task of theology has been envisaged above. It is, of course, not intended to deal with everything that has been or could be said about God; rather, it follows some lines of thought to develop one possible minimalistic framework which could be fleshed out with additional religious imagery.

Before turning to the content, it should be made clear that such an understanding of God remains revisable. The cosmology itself is not fixed; the Big Bang theory does not provide the definitive context for metaphysical thought, while there is a variety of research programs going beyond the limitations of the Big Bang theory. Contingency and necessity turned out to be both relative to the approach at any moment. Agnosticism with respect to transcendence beyond our conceptual schemes (3.5) reminds us that any proposal for an understanding of God is always limited by the conceptual scheme used.

However, the tentative nature of any proposal should not rule out the attempt to make a proposal. In the constructive phase, we should bracket the relativizing, which is appropriate to the way one adheres to the proposal, and act with engagement, but also with openness. It is a thought experiment, testing ideas by thinking them through.

The proposal is intended to fill the symbols with intelligibility by using whatever science has discovered (also in principle revisable) about the world we live in. That seems to be more appropriate than a proposal which uses our ignorance. Ignorance is just that; it does not contribute to anything positive. If God is claimed as the answer to our ignorance of the moment, it will be a 'god of the gaps', always retreating as gaps are closed.

First let's look at the 'location' of God: is God best conceived of as transcendent in a temporal sense, or is a spatial metaphor more adequate? I will defend the view that *present transcendence* captures the valuable moments of the different possibilities. I propose to understand God metaphysically as the *principle of otherness*.

6.2.1. *God's Locus: Present Transcendence*

God's transcendence has been referred to in this work in a number of ways. Epistemological transcendence with respect to our conceptual systems correlates to the revisability just mentioned. Here I'm more concerned with ontological transcendence: how could one conceive of God's location relative to our world?

To phrase the question in such a way introduces a spatial metaphor, location, and the related spatial metaphors of transcendence and immanence. A problem with these metaphors is that they look straightforward, but turn out to be confusing once we attempt to develop them conceptually. Before entering that debate it should be said that transcendence as a metaphor is intended, among other things, to express the idea that God is independent, 'beyond our grasp'. The question then becomes how such a God is related to the world.

There are different ideas about God's 'location relative to the world', combined in almost all logically possible ways in different theological schemes. For the sake of clarity I simplify by distinguishing four basic types.

Immanence. Some emphasize God's presence in the processes of nature. This is pantheism, if God and nature are thought of as co-extensive, God being identical with the whole. God evolving with the evolutionary processes in the Universe is often a variant within the immanentistic emphasis.

Temporal Transcendence: God as Creator. If God is understood as the Creator in a temporal sense, God is in some way preceding the Universe. This leads to the question rejected by Augustine: what was God doing before God created the world?

Temporal Transcendence: God as the Eschaton. God is also understood as the one who completes and perfects the creation, in whom everything has its destiny. Pannenberg used the term "power of the future" for God; process theologians consider God as luring the worldly processes to greater harmony. God will be complete if the world has been 'felt', perceived, and integrated, in God's consequent nature. The theme of 'another time' was already introduced above (4.1.2), and may be understood as correlating to an Irenean type of eschatology (Hick 1966).

'Spatial' Transcendence. God has also been understood as located in 'another place', Heaven. This corresponds to the 'Augustinian' type of eschatology (4.1.2, Hick 1966). There is a Platonistic strand in such a conception, the contrast between the realm of eternal ideas and the realm of transient objects. A location of that 'other place' within our spacetime co-ordinates is not intended, at least not by

more sophisticated representatives of such a position. If one wants to develop the image geometrically, one should rather think of the possibility that our three-dimensional space[6] is embedded in a higher dimensional 'space' as a surface is embedded in a three-dimensional world. God could be the center and the world like a spherical surface, hence God would be at an equal distance from all places. God could also be conceived of as a higher-dimensional reality, which created space within God's space. If God's reality has at least two dimensions more than our reality, this might lead to a logically satisfactory model for God's omnipresence (Van den Brom 1982).

All four positions carry valuable insights as well as specific problems. The strength of the immanence idea is that God is here. A God as creator before the temporal world has the advantage that God is conceived of as the source of our temporal reality. That implies the problem of evil, but may give strength since reality is imagined as having its roots in God, and hence being trustworthy, livable, and worthwhile. A God imagined as our destiny is perhaps equally comforting, and also provokes insight into the difference between where we seem to be heading now and where we should be heading—to God's reality. A God who is imagined to be 'up', outside our framework of spacetime, fits our understanding of the whole of spacetime as an entity which one could imagine seeing 'from the outside', *sub specie aeternitatis*. That makes God the ground of the whole temporal and spatial reality from 'beginning' to 'end'. Even time is something created with the created world, as Augustine suggested by way of a solution to the 'before' question. God is, on this view, different from the world, as Plato's world of ideas is different from the actual world.

I propose to emphasize the present as God's primary locus. If God is pushed to a distant past or future then God may be irrelevant. Such options are in danger of ending up with a God who is no-where instead of now-here.[7] However God is not identical with the present. The other options emphasize God's difference from the present, as origin and destiny as well as something outside the temporal realm. A suitable term for this combination of ideas might be to understand God as *present transcendence*, a transcendence different from but intimately related to each present. One could also use a more metaphysical term, and call God the principle of 'otherness' with respect to each state of affairs.

Eschatology was understood to have at least three functions

(4.1.2): 1. judgement on the present: it is not as it ought to be; 2. appeal to action as response to that judgement; and 3. consolation in contexts of injustice, failure, and suffering. These three aspects may be included in the understanding of God as present transcendence, as otherness.

6.2.2. *God's Nature: Values, Possibilities, and Actuality*

The process-theological view as represented by Suchocki (4.2.3) understands God as the locus of values and possibilities. I propose to add a third component: God as the source of actuality.

God as the Locus of Values

Scientists have values, and these values are relevant to their work. Esthetic preferences may lead to a certain approach; mutual cooperation requires other values. However, the theoretical formulations of natural sciences are not intended to refer to values. They describe what is, but do not prescribe what ought to be.[8] We encountered the dualism between facts and values already when Dyson's and Tipler's visions of the future were discussed. I argued that Dyson needs a distinction between the purpose, his principle of diversity, and the process. Tipler is in need of a yardstick (values) to measure the progress of the physical universe as it approaches the Omega Point. These values are external to the spacetime Universe described in cosmology.

Values are, of course, internal to humans. It has been attempted to explain them evolutionarily, with many interesting results. However, even if one can describe their origination and their adaptive advantage in the process of natural selection (an advantage which co-operation with non-kin sometimes seems to have[9]) values remain of a different type, metaphysically speaking, from skin color or whatever else is explained adaptively. And values are certainly external to the world as understood by physics and cosmology.

A common distinction in the ethical literature is between teleological and deontological theories (for example Frankena 1963). A teleological theory takes as the standard for morally good behavior the non-moral value that is brought into being, for instance the total amount of happiness of the people involved. A deontological view may consider an act morally right even if it does not lead to the best result, just by the nature of the act. My position has a deontological component. Actions are morally right if they contribute to the overcoming of imperfection and injustice. Imperfection is a non-moral category, but justice is unavoidably moral. This is not to say that the effect of a certain action is irrelevant, but that its effect is also evaluated with respect to some moral standards aside from non-moral notions of perfection (harmony, beauty).

Locating values in God has three advantages, besides fitting the prophetic criticism of the present as not being according to God's vision:

1. God is conceived as eternal. Hence God is beyond temporality, and thus beyond any specific situation. That seems to lead to a satisfactory understanding of values; values which are, as such, situation-dependent are no values, but words hiding opportunism. Values are themselves always abstract; they bring the non-situational into the moral deliberation concerning a concrete situation.

2. God is traditionally understood as perfect and just, two terms exemplary for moral and non-moral values. Non-metaphysically one could add love as a supreme value which is thought to be embodied in God. This might have its expression, in the terms used here, as the desire to bring about justice and perfection. The philosophical triad of Goodness, Beauty, and Truth also seems appropriate.

3. God is beyond our grasp. This is radical transcendence. As defended by Sutherland for the view *sub specie aeternitatis* (see 4.4.2), it implies a relativizing of our claims. We cannot appropriate the ultimate values as if we knew them exhaustively. In principle, this should imply that a fanaticism which does not allow for the possibility of being wrong is ruled out.

Judgement compares to what could have been, and hence to something external to what can be found historically. Anthropologically, imagination is involved. Judgement introduces through its values a ranking of the different possibilities which could have been but were not, and of the different possibilities which still are possible for the near future. Ideally, if we intend to make a difference, we base our action in the present upon such a ranking. That also requires, of course, a conceptualization of 'possibilities'.

God as the Locus of Possibilities

Physics offers two ways to consider the present in a wider perspective; the present can be understood as part of a sequence in time, hence in a perspective which might be called evolutionary or historical, and it can be considered as part of the whole of spacetime. In the first perspective, a present lies between its near past and its near future. There is continuity and novelty with respect to that past. God can be related to the origination of the whole process, the initial push, existentially (creation) and in terms of values (covenant). God can also be related to the future, both as bringing it about, as in the theology of Wolfhart Pannenberg who calls God the power of the future, and as providing a vision of harmony, as in process theology.

There is continuity, but there is also novelty with respect to preceding events. In physics, changes are considered to be in need of an explanation, but continuity is often taken for granted. For example, Newton introduced the law that an object remains at rest or remains moving at a uniform speed, if there are no forces acting on it. Evolutionary theists want to express how we can conceive of God as working in and through chance and selection in the course of evolution.[10] Pannenberg has called for a revision of the idea that continuity is automatic, related to the notion of inertial mass, which suggests too much the self-preservation of entities instead of their dependence for conservation upon a transcendent cause (Pannenberg 1988c, 9).

Novelty is less clear in cosmology. Processes happen, and hence new phenomena occur. But they could have been predicted on the basis of the preceding state of the system, and hence they were in some sense already included in those preceding states (except for singularities). As we saw in the discussion of Tipler's cosmology (4.3), a deterministic system has no real novelty; a specification of the state at any moment fixes the state at all earlier and later moments. Big Bang cosmology is, in principle, deterministic after the initial Singularity. Quantum theories of gravity and cosmology share, at least in their current state, in the interpretation difficulties of ordinary quantum theories. Determinism is a concept within the philosophical interpretation of scientific theories. It could be understood as a reflection of God's trustworthiness, God's constancy. It could also be reconciled with God as the one who brings about the new events, if one could have God 'foresee' the novelty to be, described from within time, and if this 'foreknowledge' becomes part of the regularities and initial conditions.

However I opt theologically for the meaningfulness of human choices: we can make a difference. That seems irreconcilable with the complete determinism of classical physics, although it requires some determinism, for one's decisions are supposed to have certain effects. The issue requires much more study of the interpretations

of quantum mechanics and thermodynamics (predictability and determinism), and of the relation between physical reality and con-
sciousness/will than can be undertaken here.

Some who would like to support the hypothesis 'God' through
contemporary science have put forward empirical contingency as a
major theme (Torrance, Jaki, Pannenberg). Inner-worldly contingency would provide hints for dependence on, and determination
by, another reality, God. This approach fails (6.1.1). However that
need not be a problem for such theological positions, for necessity
can be ascribed to God as the source of order, of continuity, of the
trustworthiness of reality, and whatever features reality is supposed
to have.

On the other hand, if one rejects the argument from empirical
contingency and argues for the God hypothesis on the basis of its
existential and axiological relevance, one ends up with the need for
such an inner-worldly contingency. There must be different options
for human action, or else judgement and call to action are meaningless. This is at stake when some cosmologists assume the actuality
of all possibilities, not only globally as in Linde's cosmology, but also
locally, as do those like Hawking who adhere to a Many Worlds
Interpretation of quantum theories—for that is deterministic, a denial of choice.

The future that will be is one among the possibilities; the possibilities are not themselves all in the future. One way to interpret
transcendence as a beyond of a non-temporal nature is as the set of
all possibilities either for each individual present or, if one considers
whole universes at once, possible complete Universes.

God as the Source of Actuality

Theologically, *creatio ex nihilo* was seen to express some basic ideas
about God as the good creator of everything; the 'nihil' as denial of
a reality independent of God. It expresses God's transcendence, as
a creative being transcends its works, but expresses also God's relatedness to the world (1.5), for the world is God's work.

Creatio ex nihilo should not be understood as referring to an event
of origination, for that is not in line with contemporary cosmology
(2.5; 6.1.1). The negative conclusion could be stated more generally:
every beginning is a limit of the theory, it need not be an edge of
reality. The Universe might be without an edge, either eternal—the
apparent beginning being a local phenomenon like birth—or

smooth—the apparent beginning being a consequence of our notion of time, like the North Pole as an edge of the map but a smooth place on the globe.

Creatio ex nihilo may be understood metaphysically as an expression of global ontological contingency, the mystery of existence (3.4). One can understand the Universe as a gift, as grace. *Creatio ex nihilo* should be understood as applying to all moments of time, not just a first moment. One can envisage a relation between God and the whole of space and time (4.4), and, as argued for the Hartle-Hawking cosmology, with each individual state (2.5.3). God might be understood as sustaining the world at all moments, being equally related to all moments.

I distinguished between three functions of eschatology: judgement, appeal to action, and consolation. This third element gives the strength to strive for values, and correlates also to the understanding of God as the source of what is. It is the affirmation, despite evidence to the contrary, of the value of this reality.

Some have understood this as a certainty about a happy ending, a metaphysical warranty that God will make everything come out all right. Cosmological visions of a nice future (Dyson, Tipler) are the worldly correlates of such a vision—especially Tipler's because of its emphasis on necessity. However, an interpretation of the affirmation that the reality rests in God as to imply a bright future for the world is dubious, both scientifically and theologically, at least with respect to theology as understood here: as a response to God's apparent absence.

There are some scientists who do opt for an optimist scenario, but they have to make many disputable or disputed assumptions. It is as with the issue of the beginning: some defend an absolute beginning, but others don't. One could, of course, take the easiest way and assume that those who defend the nicest perspective are closer to the truth. But it is more defensible to consider the worst possibility, and hence to face the possibility that life and consciousness will exist for only a finite span of time, though perhaps a long span. If the future turns out to be livable forever, there is no problem, but it does not seem a reasonable ground of hope in the here and now.

Theologically, the suggestion that God will bring about a bright future, a determinism of the happy ending, takes away our responsibility for what will happen. There is, independent of the happy ending, some truth to that: we are not responsible for the cosmological future, or even for the future of the Sun: it will burn out in some five billion years. But it is assumed in the theology presented here that we can make a difference with respect to the present and its near future. Therefore, one should not introduce the image of God over-riding our failures.

Further, if God uses our failures one might be led to the conclusion that God uses imperfection and injustice as a means to a higher good, and hence that imperfection and injustice are only apparently real, for they serve the greater good. This conflicts with the assumption of their reality, made when the theology developed here took its starting point in the experience of God's apparent absence.

As a fourth reason against the location of hope in a bright future, it is at too great a distance. The next few generations, say children and grandchildren, have relevance by virtue of their relation to us, and hence they set before us the issue of our immediate future. Beings a few thousand generation hence, or even much further away, do not inspire us to do something about the quality of their lives. The same holds also for the future as a source of comfort: it might justify one's present suffering if one expects one's children to profit from the suffering. But does it offer any consolation to know that life will continue indefinitely, and be able to expand and manipulate the whole cosmos? As argued in detail by Hilhorst (1987), the ethical intuition that the future should be livable beyond the next few generations, with its implications for environmental policies and the like, can only be grounded in the present values we ascribe to life.

The affirmation that God is the ground of being, the source of actuality, should be understood as an affirmation about the present and not about some remote past or future. Affirming goodness, despite evidence of imperfection, may help us overcome our anxieties. God as the ground of actuality might be a mystical complement to the previous two issues, values and possibilities, which might correspond to prophetical judgement and appeal. These three should go together and reinforce each other. That brings us to the question of their unity.

6.2.3. *God's Unity*

God's unity, understood as the coherence of the three aspects discussed above, is an assumption. Unity, as the unity of cosmological and axiological thought, might well be the characteristic for religion, especially for one who recognizes the autonomous nature of natural science and of ethics in our time. Categories like 'the holy', 'grace', and 'forgiveness' do not belong to cosmology or axiology; they have their meaning only in the process of interweaving these two. Different religious views might, perhaps, be characterized by the way they shape the unity, without tension as, for example, in most New Age approaches or with a prophetic contrast as defended here. Process theologians like Suchocki, for instance, tend to accept only the first two elements, values and possibilities, in God's primordial nature; actuality is secondary, arising in God's consequent nature as the entities of the world are felt by and included in God (4.2.3). However the assumption of the unity of values, possibilities, and actuality is a valuable element in the construction of the proposal. It integrates the prophetical components, emphasizing judgement and action, with the mystical component, the consolation of being rooted in God.

The notion of *otherness* embraces the unity of the three elements. God as the principle of otherness stands in contrast with imperfection and injustice as realities in our world. By contrast, God is to be understood as perfect and just, as the embodiment of the ultimate moral and esthetic values. God stands also in contrast with what is actual, by worldly standards. This finds expression in the understanding of God as the locus of the other possibilities. The other possibilities, together with the way they relate to the values, provide the vision for this world. God as otherness stands also in contrast with finite and dependent being, the way things in the world are. God is beyond time, and in that sense eternal. Independent, God can be the source and ground of what is dependent.

A relational understanding of this otherness is expressed in the term *present transcendence*. The otherness as such is not mere negation, as if it had nothing to do with the here and now. As otherness, God is related to each present. God's distance, His transcendence within present relation, makes it possible that entities have a specific identity. If the distance were lacking they would become instances of God's self-identity, and lose their value as particulars.

That brings us back to the theme of unity and diversity in cosmology. Cosmology tends to emphasize the unity of the whole spacetime. There is also a trend towards unification of partial theories into one encompassing theory. We can affirm this in theology, as a reflection of the unity of the God who is the creator of reality (spacetime) and of the regularities (unified theories). However, we should also affirm theologically the existence of diversity, which should not be dismissed. That would be a loss to the completeness of the scientific project, an incompleteness which has recently found a partial remedy in studies of chaotic systems. It would also be a loss to the theological project, as it denies the value which we ascribe theologically to particulars (3.3).

In the Christian tradition God's unity has been thought of as a *trinity*. It is possible to develop the metaphysical image of God as the principle of otherness in a trinitarian way, although that does not, of course, claim identity with the whole tradition of trinitarian thought. God the Father, the Creater of Heaven and Earth, might be understood as a parallel to God as the source of actuality. The Christ, exemplifying love, may be correlated with the values which have their locus in God. The Spirit might be an appropriate term for God as the locus of possibilities, since the Spirit may be understood as that which opens possibilities whenever necessary.

The view presented here can also be applied to develop a rudimentary Christology as a formulation of the unity between this threefold concept of God and the world. Christ is not understood, as in some cosmological Christologies, as the universal principle (logos) of rationality of the cosmos. Jesus Christ can be interpreted as the presence of this threefold otherness in finite reality. In Jesus's life and sayings values became visible, for instance the love for one's neighbor. Jesus used the possibilities for transformation according to those values—an effective transformation, for instance when he stayed with the tax collector Zacchaeus (Luke 19:1–10). There is also an immediacy of consolation and strength in the presence of Jesus, for instance in the stories in which he forgives sins, or when he says to one of those crucified with him that that person will be with Jesus in Paradise immediately (Luke 23:43).

Doctrines of the Spirit are less well developed. However the Spirit might be understood to represent the presence of the otherness within humans, making visible possibilities and valorizing them, as well as offering strength and consolation by instilling and affirming in humans the sense of dependency upon a good source.

6.3. CONSTRUCTING A CONSONANT WORLD

The preceding section gives my outline of a metaphysical understanding of God as the principle of otherness, intended to be capable of doing justice both to the task of theology and to the scientific understanding of the world. My approach starts from the experiences of imperfection and injustice. After developing the metaphysical view of God we need to return to the world, to see how this view relates to practice. If God's prophetic absence from the world is the interpretation of those experiences, the task becomes 'to make God present' in the world, or, as Heyward (1982) calls it, 'to god' the world. The world is not God, and it will never be God either. But the values and the possibilities, which constitute the concept of God I have just introduced, are intend to yield the transformation of the world to greater conformity to the values intended, and hence to the goodness of its source.

Justice, peace, and the integrity of creation are the terms used by the churches in the contemporary reflection upon global issues such as poverty, the possibility of nuclear destruction, and environmental concerns. The theology sketched in this chapter offers a possibility to express these concerns in a coherent way. Justice, peace, and integrity are all ideal notions; they oppose experiences which we do have on Earth, experiences of unjust economic relations, war, and pollution. They represent God's otherness, and more specifically they belong to the values contrasting (judging) the way things are. The churches could contribute to the further clarification of these values in themselves.

There is the danger that this may be forgotten with regard to the Integrity of Creation. This would lead to theologies which deny the reality of the brokenness of creation and introduce too much continuity between God as the source of the creation and the world as it is. Emphasis on God's immanence in nature and on the interrelatedness of God and nature have been proposed as better views of nature and God. Such views are supposed to contribute to the solution of environmental problems. For example, a recent theological report for the World Council of Churches, 'Towards a Theology of Nature and a Theocentric Ethic', argued for the value of the non-human environment/nature by arguing for God's presence in all creation (WCC 1987a, 41). Integrity of creation is seen as having three nuances; among them that the natural order has an integrity which is observed as interconnectedness (Hall in WCC 1987b; WCC 1987a, 42).[11] That might lead to the misleading idea that there are no real tensions or conflicts between entities in that natural order for they all become part of, and are thereby subsumed under, the whole. In the approach followed above, God's prophetic absence is reflected in the brokenness which is present; the integrity is primarily a notion in contrast with the world, and hence an element of the principle of otherness. The diversity in nature, with its inner tensions, is a more explicit part of this scheme.

If justice, peace, and integrity are the values by which options will be evaluated, they need to be complemented by an actual quest to perceive the possibilities. That requires concrete analysis considering many aspects, for instance the social, the economic, and the technological. This requires, of course, contributions by specialists on these topics.

In the theological perspective presented here, these options have their ground in God as do the values. It becomes a major task of the theological contribution to integrate these two, to insist on the evaluation of possibilities with respect to values. Our evaluation, and hence recommendations and actions, never coincides with God's valuation of the possibilities, but we can only try to integrate the possibilities and the values, in as detailed and serious a way as possible.

Ultimately the goodness of the world is affirmed by postulating God as the source of reality. In the end, this is close to the affirmation of the integrity of the creation. However the goodness, or integrity, or inter-relatedness, is not perceived, but postulated. It thereby re-emphasizes our active role: as we affirm the integrity of creation as a value and as a theologically postulated reality, we commit ourselves to contribute to that integrity.

APPENDIX 1

A BRIEF SKETCH OF THE BIG BANG THEORY

Reliable introductions include the books by Weinberg (1977), Silk (1980), Reeves (1981), Trefil (1983) and Pagels (1985a). Somewhat more technical is Narlikar (1988). Among first-rate textbooks on the topics are those of Weinberg (1972), Misner, Thorne, and Wheeler (1973) and Wald (1984). North (1965) provides a scientifically and philosophically very well-documented history of cosmology from 1900 until the early 1960s. I don't bother with references to ideas that can be found in most books on astronomy and cosmology.

1. ASTRONOMICAL OBJECTS

The Earth is a *planet*. The Sun is a *star*. Stars seem to move in circles around the Earth, making one revolution in 24 hours. The planets seem to follow a more complicated path. Astronomical theory until the eighteenth century was mainly about explaining these paths of the planets. Newton's law of gravity provided the explanation for the orbits as a dynamic equilibrium between gravitational attraction and centrifugal forces due to velocities.

The Sun, a medium-sized star, is 300,000 times (all numbers are given approximately) as massive as the Earth. The next nearest known star is 43.10^{12} kilometers away, that is 300,000 times as far from us as the Sun is from the Earth. Interstellar distances are counted in light years. One light year, the distance light travels in one year, is ten thousand billion kilometers. The nearest star is 4.3 light years away from us.

Besides the things seen, there are many *things unseen*, more difficult to observe. The Universe is filled with dust, particles, clouds, protostars, and the like. Dark clouds can be observed because they absorb light from sources beyond them. Astronomy was limited in the past to observations using visible light, since that passes the atmosphere and can be detected by the human eye. Radio astronomy developed after World War II. In recent years other parts of the electromagnetic spectrum have revealed new phenomena, often with instruments high in or outside the atmosphere. Physics has discovered other particles, like neutrinos. Astronomers have started making neutrino observations.

When the eye gets accustomed to the dark, a white band, *the Milky Way*, can be seen. It looks as if we are in the center of a disc of stars. We are in such a disc, but not at the center. The Sun is in the plane of the disc, but at about two-thirds of a galactic radius away from the center. Our *Galaxy*, as the Milky Way system is called, has spiral arms in which most of the stars are located.

All the stars that can be seen with the unaided eye belong to the Galaxy. In the beginning of this century there was a discussion whether 'nebulae', fuzzy patches in the sky, were clouds within our Galaxy or objects outside our Galaxy and comparable to it, 'island universes'. Many nebulae turned out to be other *galaxies* far outside our Galaxy. The Andromeda Galaxy is one of our nearest neighbors at a distance of 2 million light years. The stars do not fall to the center of a galaxy because they move around it, just as the planets move around our Sun. The Sun makes one revolution around the galactic center in 250 million years. Galaxies are ten times more massive than the sum of the observed stars and gas. There exists dark, yet undetected, mass extending far beyond the stellar distribution.

We know of about a hundred billion (10^{11}) galaxies in the Universe, about as many as there are stars in our Galaxy. In cosmology galaxies are often taken to be the basic reference points in the Universe. Stars are born within a galaxy and leave their remnants for reprocessing within the same galaxy.

Galaxies exist in *clusters*. We belong to the Local Group of about 20 galaxies. There are clusters of several hundred large galaxies accompanied by smaller galaxies. Even clusters are not scattered evenly throughout the Universe. They are organized in superclusters (clusters of clusters).

Some radio sources with a pointlike optical appearance, detected in the 1960s, were baptized *quasars*, quasi-stellar radio sources. Such objects are a few billion light years away. The energy output of a quasar exceeds that of all the stars within a normal galaxy. But the active region of a quasar must be very small, less than a millionth of the diameter of a galaxy. Most explanations assume the existence of a black hole in the core of a galaxy. Quasars represent the Universe in an earlier stage of its history, since it took time for the radiation to reach us.

2.   COSMOLOGICAL OBSERVATIONS

It is not trivial that it is *dark at night*. If the Universe extended to infinity, we would expect contributions from very distant stars or galaxies. Individually they don't contribute much, but the number of sources increases with the distance. It is like standing in a forest, next to a tree (the Sun). At the side of that tree, the tree is the dominant feature in sight. Looking in other directions you see trees everywhere. Not a single line of sight escapes from the wood. Instead of trees we should see stars or galaxies everywhere, making the sky glow like a stellar surface. This is called *Olbers's Paradox* (Jaki 1969; Harrison 1987). The assumption of an infinite and static universe seems to be false. "A successful cosmology must be able to explain Olbers' paradox, and the Big Bang theory satisfies this fundamental observational requirement" (Silk 1980, 56).

Evidence for *expansion of the Universe* is based on the Doppler effect. If a source is approaching a receiver, subsequently emitted waves are gaining on each other. More waves are received each minute than there were emitted. For sound this results in a higher pitch, for light in a shift towards the blue end of the spectrum. In the absence of overall structure one would expect that some sources would be moving towards us, and therefore shift to the blue. Others would move away, hence shift to red.

Almost all radiation from galaxies is *red-shifted*. This implies, if interpreted as a Doppler shift, that these galaxies are receding. The observed velocities are nearly proportional to the distance. This is the Hubble law. The first measurements indicated an increase in velocity of 150 km/sec for each additional million light years (Mly) distance. Changes in distance measurements now give a best value of 15 to 30 km/sec per Mly.

The almost linear relation between recession velocity and distance in the large gives the impression that we are looking at the results of an explosion: fast-moving particles are found far away, slower particles are much nearer to the center. This seems to place us in a central position. However the linear relationship between distance and velocity implies that the same impression will be obtained from any point of space. Take for instance a series of galaxies along a line:

```
<--·      <-·           ·        ·->      ·-->      ·--->      ·---->
```

(The single point is our point of view, arrows indicate the velocities.) If we take another point of view and consider our new home as at rest, we should modify the picture by subtracting the velocity of our new home from the velocities indicated. The picture becomes:

<----·   <---·   <--·   <-·   ·   ·->   ·-->

Both pictures exhibit the same feature: all galaxies seem to be receding from the point taken to be stationary, and all with velocities proportional to the distances. Consider a cake with raisins. When the cake expands the distance between the raisins grows. If we neglect the boundaries of the cake, every raisin could imagine itself to be the center of the distribution of raisins, seeing all other raisins receding with velocities proportional to the distance.

In 1965 Penzias and Wilson published observations on a radio noise which could not be ascribed to any local source. This *cosmic background radiation* comes from all directions. The spectrum is characterized as 3 K radiation, since it corresponds to the radiation that would be emitted by a body at a temperature of 3 (or more precisely 2.7) degrees Kelvin above the absolute zero (0 K = $-273°$ C). Since the radiation cannot be ascribed to localized sources, it is considered to be of cosmological origin. If this radiation is red-shifted as well, it must have been produced in a stage with a higher temperature.

The cosmic background radiation is very *isotropic;* the variation with direction is very small. Isotropy and *homogeneity* (being the same at all places) appear to be good approximations on a cosmological scale.

The Universe is locally not homogeneous and not isotropic. The existence of clusters and superclusters of galaxies implies that up to that scale there remain deviations from homogeneity. Cosmological theory should explain both the observed homogeneity in the large and the inhomogeneities.

Hydrogen is the most common visible element in the Universe. *Helium,* second element in the chemical periodic system, accounts for about 25% of the visible matter. The other elements are available in much smaller quantities. The helium abundance is almost the same in very different places (older and younger stars, interstellar gas, other galaxies). The other elements show local variations in abundance. Theories of stellar evolution make it possible to calculate how much of each element is produced during the life-span of a star and during supernova explosions. These theories are in good agreement with the observed abundances except for helium and a few other light elements, such as lithium and deuterium. These light elements are seen as remnants of an earlier phase. Hence, the Universe as a whole must have had the conditions for nuclear fusion: hot and dense.

The relative *densities of particles* in the Universe seem to need a cosmological explanation. There are a few hundred million times more photons (the 'particles' which constitute electromagnetic radiation, in this case mainly the background radiation) than protons and neutrons, the main constituents of ordinary matter. Neutrinos might be as abundant as photons. Anti-matter appears to be absent, although physical theories are mostly symmetric, making it as likely to see anti-matter as matter. (Anti-matter consists of particles with the same mass, but opposite electric charge. The anti-electron is called a positron. Together they can mutually annihilate into radiation, or be formed out of radiation. Recent theories, so-called GUTs, allow for asymmetry between matter and anti-matter.)

Formation of *structures* (stars, galaxies, and so forth) seems to be against the Second Law of Thermodynamics, which states that in a closed system entropy increases ('order decreases'; see Appendix 2). But the release of energy in the form of photons implies that the system which forms structure is not a closed system. The photons carry entropy away, leaving a situation with more organization. (This issue is explained at a popular level in the book by Reeves [1981]; Frautschi [1982] offers a more technical account.) If this is to be possible, the surrounding space must be cooler to get rid of the excess (binding) energy. Why is there such a temperature difference? Why is not everything (mass, energy, temperature) spread out more evenly? An explanation can be based on the expansion of the Universe. The temperature in space decreases as its volume expands, creating the *non-equilibrium* necessary for the formation of structure. This is similar to Olbers's paradox and its solution.

Although the observations and arguments are much more specific, this brief sketch already gives the major picture: the Universe had a dense and hot phase a long time ago. That accounts for the nuclear fusion (light elements) and the background radiation. The temperature of the background radiation dropped as a consequence of the expansion. This made possible the difference between the background and specific clumps of matter (stars).

3.   COSMOLOGICAL THEORY

Special relativity was formulated by Einstein in 1905. The word
'relativity' has been a source of much misunderstanding. The theory
deals with the things which are *invariant,* even if considered by different observers. An example in classical terms: if we wanted to
measure the position of a point in a room, the answer would depend
on the co-ordinate system used. It makes a difference whether we
use the door or the corner as the origin which serves as a point of
reference. But if we calculate the distance between two points, using
the Pythagorean law

$$d^2 = x^2 + y^2 + z^2 \tag{1},$$

the two measurements give the same result. Distance is invariant
with respect to the choice of co-ordinate system.

In special relativity all laws are formulated in an invariant way
for all observers moving with a uniform velocity with respect to each
other. One invariant is the velocity of light, which is also the maximum velocity, denoted by c. Distances are not invariant, but there
is a new invariant,

$$d^2 = x^2 + y^2 + z^2 - c^2.t^2 \tag{2}$$

(x, y and z denote three orthonormal spatial co-ordinates, t stands
for time). Space and time are together described by a four-dimensional spacetime, although space and time are not as similar as the
three spatial directions are.

It turns out to be impossible to incorporate the Newtonian theory
of *gravity* in special relativity (Misner 1973, Chapter 7). We have to
depart from special relativity and especially from the notion of
straight lines. This implies that in formulas like (1) and (2) there
arise terms which mix co-ordinates. Including gravity implies that
we need to use spacetime in a way which we depict by saying that it
is curved. Only empty space, including empty space inside a spherical
distribution of mass, behaves like a flat space. Locally physics can be
done in a special relativistic way, but there is no global flat co-ordinate
system. Similarly every piece of the Earth can be depicted on a flat
map, but there is no single flat map possible covering the whole
surface in a continuous one-to-one correspondence.

Extending special relativity to incorporate gravity leads to *general
relativity,* as proposed by Einstein in 1915. This theory relates the
metrical tensor—the extension of formula (2) with all possible mixed

terms x.t *etc.* — to the energy tensor, which describes the energy and mass distribution as the source of gravity. It is the physical theory of gravity. This theory contains other well-tested theories (Newtonian gravity, special relativity) as limiting cases. It is formulated in a mathematically consistent and elegant way. Three observations about deviations from the Newtonian theory confirmed the theory quite early. Einstein derived a small effect on the orbit of Mercury, which had been known for some time but remained unexplained within other theories. The theory predicted also an amount of bending of light. During a solar eclipse in 1919 this bending of starlight passing near the Sun was confirmed. The third early prediction, red shift of light due to gravitation (and not to velocity like the red shift in the Hubble law) has been confirmed today with high accuracy. There have been many other experimental tests (Misner 1973, 1129; Will 1979). A binary pulsar (double star system) has recently provided extremely accurate confirmation of relativistic phenomena (Taylor and Weinberg 1989). The theory of general relativity can be considered as well established by observations independent of cosmology.

General Relativity Applied to the Universe as a Whole

Albert Einstein found a solution to the equations for a homogeneous and isotropic fluid in 1917. His solution implied that the Universe was expanding. Since this seemed untenable to him, he modified his equations by adding one term, the cosmological constant, so making a static (but unstable) solution possible. After Hubble established the expansion of the Universe, the original solution appeared to be better and Einstein abandoned the cosmological constant. However, the constant still has a place in some recent theories, although it must be extremely close to zero in our Universe.

Another apparently static solution was discovered by the Dutch astronomer Willem de Sitter in 1917. The De Sitter solution presupposes that the sum of the rest mass of the matter and the pressure is zero. Since rest mass is always positive and no known substance has a negative pressure equal to that, both quantities must be zero. The De Sitter solution can also be interpreted as describing an empty universe which contracts since past eternity until some finite radius for the universe, and expands indefinitely afterwards. During the phase of expansion the De Sitter solution is in accordance with the Hubble law. It is formally attractive, since there is no moment at which the model breaks down. However it is unrealistic, as it does not allow for the presence of matter. Recently, the De Sitter solution has become popular as a description of the Universe in a very early stage.

The original equations of general relativity, together with the assumption that the matter distribution in the Universe is homogeneous and isotropic, admit three types of non-static solutions, all with an 'initial moment' of infinite density. These solutions were independently discovered in the 1920s by Friedmann, a Russian meterologist and Lemaître, a Belgian astronomer and priest:

1. A universe with positive spatial curvature, a *closed* universe. 'Closed' means that two parallel light rays would, if continued indefinitely, cross each other. The life span of such a universe is finite, as well as its volume. Such a universe can be imagined as the surface of a sphere of one dimension more than normal space.

2. A universe with zero spatial curvature, hence a universe with a Euclidean spatial structure, 'flat'. Light rays which are parallel remain so forever.

3. A universe with a negative spatial curvature, a spatially *open* universe. Parallel light rays diverge. These spaces are difficult to depict. The volume and life span is infinite.

FIGURE 3.   Relation between time and size for different universes.

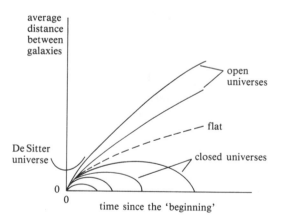

The choice among the three models depends on the mean density of the Universe. There is a *critical density*, which corresponds to a universe with zero spatial curvature. If the density exceeds the critical density, the Universe has a positive spatial curvature (is closed). If the density is lower, the Universe is open. The total density due to the observed matter is about 1% of the critical density, but dark matter is at least ten times as abundant. The density is known to be between 0.1 and 2 times the critical density, so the Universe is nearly 'flat'. A very closed universe would not expand for billions of years, while a very open universe would be too diluted to be livable. The choice between the three models is not relevant for discussions about the early phases of the Universe, but it is relevant to ideas about the future (Appendix 6). We are still on the left side of the diagram.

It is easy to calculate back to the beginning of the expansion if one assumes a constant rate of expansion. The assumption of a straight extrapolation is not completely correct but it is sufficient for our purposes. The age thus calculated, the Hubble-age of the Universe, is today about 15 or 20 billion years. Neither corrections nor other methods of calculation change the conclusion that some time between ten and 25 billion years ago there was a state of extreme density.

For some time it was believed that the initial Singularity was the consequence of the unrealistic assumption of homogeneity and isotropy. However, since 1966 singularity theorems have been proven, especially by Hawking and Penrose. These theorems imply that, under certain general assumptions, singularities are unavoidable in general relativity. The theorems leave three options open: the Universe has an initial singularity, the conditions do not hold, or general relativity becomes invalid near the singularities predicted by that theory. A slight modification would not remove the singularities, but a fundamentally different theory, like a quantum theory of gravity, might perhaps be free of singularities. This is the Big Bang theory in its *metrical formulation*. It gives the impression of an infinite density in the 'beginning' and expansion until the present.

Particle Physics in the Big Bang Theory

The temperature during the 'first' few hundred thousand years was so high (above 3000 K) that atoms were not stable: electrons and nuclei were mostly separated. Interactions between radiation (photons, light) and particles were so intense that the mean free path of a photon was very short. Therefore, the Universe was not transparent to photons. (We cannot see below the surface of the Sun for the same reason.) By optical means it would have been impossible to see anything before the decoupling of matter and radiation. "By convention, this event marks the end of the big bang" (Pagels 1985a, 256).

The preceding centuries are not very interesting, except for the 'first few minutes'. *Nuclear reactions* happened when the temperature was a few billion degrees and the density was high, between one second and a few minutes after the 'beginning'. The observed abundances of deuterium, lithium, and helium give information about this phase.

Continuing bangwards we enter the era of elementary particle physics. The *leptonic period* started about one ten-thousandth of a second after the 'beginning'. Photons had sufficient energy to produce light particles, like electrons, in combination with their antiparticles. The neutrinos were released. They did not interact substantially with matter any more, just like the photons of the background radiation a few hundred thousand years later. If we were able to detect the neutrino background, we could 'look' back to the Universe in 'the first second'.

Before that there had been a period during which heavier particles, like protons and neutrons, were produced and quarks might have been around as free particles. This is a bit more vague since the theory of strong interactions is not as well developed as the theory of weak interactions, though it can still be considered part of the standard theory. To describe the *preceding* bit of time, more speculative and less well-tested theories are needed, as discussed in Chapter 2.

The 'standard model' is able to explain almost everything observed, such as the expansion, the cosmic background radiation, and the abundances of elements. The explanations, which are much more quantitative and precise than has been presented here, are based on theories which have been tested outside cosmology. A few initial conditions remain unexplained.

4.   THE STEADY STATE THEORY

The Steady State theory (Hoyle 1948; Bondi and Gold 1948), an alternative to the Big Bang theory, incorporates the Hubble law on the expansion, but without the "definite moment of 'origin' of the Universe, as it is in the Friedmann cosmologies" (Hoyle 1980, 7). Bondi and Gold started from the perfect cosmological principle: the Universe should look on the average the same to all observers regardless of *place and time,* differing in this latter assumption (time) from the homogeneity in the Big Bang theory. Expansion seems to dilute the matter. In the steady state conception this is matched by the spontaneous occurrence of new matter in empty space, 'continuous creation'. This was included in the Einstein equation, the basis for general relativity, by adding an extra field. The predicted rate of creation is so low that it is compatible with present knowledge on matter in intergalactic space. Looking backwards in time there is no increase in density, for part of the matter did not exist in the past.

The Steady State theory offers no simple explanation for the 3 K radiation, although Hoyle claims that the theory can account for it by considering the energy produced in stars. Other objections arise from the observed distributions of galaxies and quasars.

This book is not the place to judge the pros and cons of the Steady State theory, but to evaluate the ways cosmological theories are related to metaphysical and religious convictions. Hoyle's ideas on these issues have been discussed above (1.2.3). As an informed outsider I follow the majority in accepting the Big Bang theory as the better theory, at least after the first fraction of a second. In this book the Big Bang theory is assumed *within its domain*.

5.   PROBLEMS AND DEFINITIONS IN BIG BANG COSMOLOGY

Problems Already Solved

The first problem for General Relativistic cosmology was, according to Einstein (1917), that it did not admit a static solution. That was the reason why he changed the theory by adding a cosmological constant. The expansion was confirmed in 1929. "Thus ended the first great cycle of apparent contradiction to General Relativity, test, and dramatic vindication" (Misner et al 1973, 707).

In the 1940s the age calculated from the observed expansion was less than the age ascribed to the Solar System. Partly because of this, the Steady State theory had a good hearing. In the 1950s a better understanding of certain objects observed in nearby galaxies, which were used as distance indicators, led to a drastic adjustment of the age of the Universe, as calculated in the Big Bang theory. "Thus ended the second great cycle of an apparent contradiction to General Relativity, then test, and then dramatic vindication" (Misner et al 1973, 710).

Questions Still Open

Within the standard model there is no successful treatment yet of the *inhomogeneities* which lead to the formation of galaxies and clusters. There are also the *initial conditions.* Why that temperature? Why that density? Why the observed ratio of millions to one between the numbers of photons and baryons (protons, neutrons)? Why no anti-matter?

The density parameter is between 0.1 and 2, relatively close to 1, the threshold between closed and open. This is called the *flatness problem,* as the threshold corresponds to a flat universe. This is more puzzling than it seems, because every deviation from flatness now must arise from a much smaller deviation in the past, like 1 part in 10^{14} at 1 second after the 'beginning' (Dicke and Peebles 1979).

There is also a *horizon problem.* If the Universe has a finite age, say 15 billion years, we only have information from a finite region, extending 15 billion light years in all directions. We have a horizon. Two galaxies or quasars near our horizon in opposite directions are outside each other's horizon. There cannot have been any causal connection between them during the whole past of the Universe, at least according to standard physics, since the causal horizon grows proportionally to the time since the 'beginning', while the distance scale grows with a lower power of time due to the deceleration of the expansion. We do observe the same physics at both places, not only with respect to the laws, but also with respect to the information they provide about the past history of the Universe. It seems amazing that the temperature of the background radiation, the density of galaxies (deviations from homogeneity), and other cosmological data are the same in all directions, if there has been no causal connection between different regions.

Besides these initial conditions there are the more general questions: Why three and one dimensions (space + time)? Why the laws that are applied to the constituents of the situation? Why these particles and forces?

Limits of General Relativity

Standard cosmology is based on general relativity. Ordinary quantum theory is used in the Big Bang theory, for example in analyzing nucleosynthesis. But gravity itself is not quantized. There is a tension between general relativity, which is deterministic, and quantum theory, which is probabilistic. Aside from the esthetic urge for unification, consistency seems to require a modification of general relativity and/or quantum theory.

Definitions

So far I've referred to the 'beginning'. There is a risk of begging important questions when we drop the inverted commas. The term points to the moment of infinite density and temperature which follows from an extrapolation backwards of the observed expansion, at least in the context of the three possible types of metric discovered by Friedmann and Lemaître. This moment (if it existed) is called the *Singularity*.

The notion 'Big Bang' has been obscured a bit too. Pagels calls a moment 300,000 years after the Singularity "the end of the big bang" (1985a, 256). Although there are good arguments for calling the period up to this moment the Big Bang, the common use is that the Big Bang is a moment rather than a period. I will use the term *Early Universe* for the period described by the standard model. This starts with the hadronic and leptonic eras and ends with the decoupling of photons and matter. The *Very Early Universe* is the period between the Singularity and the beginning of the standard model. To justify the distinction: the standard model uses theories which have been tested independent of cosmology. Future experiments may extend the scope of theories tested outside cosmology, but there remains a distinction between such a standard model and ideas beyond it.

There is confusion over which moment should be called the Big Bang. Some use the term to refer to the Singularity. Others (Gribbin 1982, 32) take some moment where our explanations concerning the Early Universe begin. I agree that the latter is a better usage. As, alas, common usage is not very exact, and a definition like this one is easily tripped over, I will avoid the term for most of the discussion.

There is still another specific moment which is used as a boundary for the possibility of normal physical explanation, the *Planck time*, calculated from the constants of quantum physics and gravity as 10^{-43} second. Before this moment quantum effects affect gravity in ways not yet known. The Planck time lies between the Singularity and the beginning of our explanations concerning the Early Universe.

In short:

t = o	Singularity
then	phase in which a quantum theory of space-time is needed; space and time might be undefinable.

$t \approx 10^{-43}$ seconds	Planck time
then	spacetime can be treated with the well known theory of general relativity; theories about matter not known, or at least not tested independent of cosmology. This phase and the preceding one could together be called the Very Early Universe.
$t \approx$ one billionth of a second	theories of matter and of spacetime known and tested independent of cosmology. (Location of this boundary depends upon one's view of particle theories.)
then	Early Universe.
$t \approx 300{,}000$ years	the Universe becomes transparent, formation of stars and galaxies takes place after this moment.

The Big Bang theory is often extrapolated to 't = o', the Singularity. However, the theory is reliable only when the underlying theories of both the structure of space and time and the behavior of matter and radiation are known and corroborated by evidence independent of cosmology. In that sense, the Big Bang theory is not a theory about the origin of the Universe, but rather a well-supported theory about the evolution of structures in the Universe from, perhaps, one billionth of a second up to the present.

Theories beyond that limit of a fraction of a second after the extrapolated 't = o' of the Big Bang models, are more speculative. The boundary might be pushed back, for instance when proton decay would be established (see Appendix 6), or when the planned Superconducting Supercollider would add significantly to our experimental knowledge concerning particle theories. But such developments on the experimental side will not remove this kind of boundary to our knowledge.

APPENDIX 2

THE SECOND LAW OF THERMODYNAMICS

1. THERMODYNAMICS AND ENTROPY

Thermodynamics arose in the nineteenth century in relation to the quest for a maximally efficient conversion of heat into usable forms of work, for example in a steam engine. Two laws were discovered to be basic.

The *First Law of Thermodynamics* is the conservation of energy. Heating a system, or doing work on a system, for instance, by lifting or compressing, implies an increase in the energy of the system and a decrease in the energy of the environment. This rule is symmetric, energy increase on one side implies decrease on the other side, and vice versa. It seems as if we could completely undo an increase in energy by taking out the work and heat which had been put in first. This suggests the possibility of a *perpetuum mobile*, even though one which is unable to do any work on other systems.

The First Law need not imply problems for 'naturalistic' accounts of the origination of the Universe. The total energy of the Universe might either be zero, undefinable, or not conserved if the Universe as a whole is not the kind of unit the First Law applies to (see 2.2.2).

Many ordinary experiences do not exhibit the symmetry which seems suggested in the First Law. Moving into a third-floor apartment takes a lot of work. However, bringing the same stuff down again does not energize; rather, it again takes hard work. Bicycling uphill takes a lot of work, which results in additional speed (kinetic energy) once one goes downhill. However, this process is not perfect, especially on an unpaved road. Not all energy is put to work again; some is lost as a consequence of friction. This energy heats the road. The energy that can be used for work is called *free energy*.

The Second Law of Thermodynamics states that free energy always diminishes, though total energy remains constant (as expressed in the First Law). Some energy is converted into heat, which cannot be reconverted into work without loss. Free energy can increase if new energy is imported from elsewhere. That is how life on Earth is sustained by energy from the Sun. The Second Law therefore only applies to closed and isolated systems, systems without exchange of matter, energy, or volume with other systems.

Another notion, *entropy*, is closely correlated with the difference between total and free energy. It thus expresses the amount of non-usable energy. Hence, decreasing free energy correlates to increasing entropy. The *Second Law* is therefore also formulated as: *entropy* always increases. The entropy of a system, say a box of gas, remains constant once the system is in total equilibrium. If there are no temperature differences nor other sources of potential energy, the system cannot do any work. In this situation the entropy would be maximal for that system.

2.   THE ASYMMETRY OF THE SECOND LAW

The Second Law of Thermodynamics is well established. It is nonetheless a peculiar law relative to the rest of physics, for example classical mechanics. First, it introduces the system as a whole. One can ascribe energy and velocity to each individual particle, but entropy is closely connected with properties of the whole system, for example its volume.

Second, the law describes processes as happening in one way: entropy increases, free energy decreases. That is in line with many ordinary experiences. But the other basic laws of physics are all symmetric. We do not consider it necessary that the Earth spins the way it does; it could well have been the other way round, with the Sun rising in the West. The Second Law seems a phenomenological law, which summarizes properties of larger systems, like amounts of gas consisting of billions of billions of atoms. How can this law suggest that processes happen in a specific direction, and exclude the reverse of these processes, if the underlying physics which describes the atoms and their movements and collisions allows for such a reversal? One explanation sees it as a consequence of preferring certain configurations, while disregarding the microscopic level.

Think of a deck of cards. It might be ordered, say according to suits and numbers. Let us call this A. It might also be disordered; to be called B. The Second Law is similar to the effect of shuffling: an ordered state A tends to become disordered, B, while the reverse happens very rarely. The asymmetry is not due to something special about state A. Each possible sequence is, fundamentally, equally probable. The issue is that there is only one sequence which gives the order described as A, while there are many sequences which we lump together as disorder, state B. There is a subjective element involved: the decision to set aside the sequence 1, 2, 3, 4, 5 . . . as ordered, and to consider sequences like 3, 1, 4, 2, 5, . . . and 3, 5, 1, 2, 4, . . . as in disorder.

A similar argument applies to a box of gas. All molecules might be on one side. Specific distributions of the molecules, whether all on one side or of specified molecules (assume them to be distinguishable, which they aren't) on the left and others on the right, are all equally probable. There is, if one considers the system microscopically, no tendency (Second Law) towards any particular distribution. But there are more distributions in which the gas occupies the whole volume than there are with all the molecules in one corner. That explains the tendency of a macroscopic development from 'all on one side' to the occupation of the whole box.

Hence, the Second Law, the continuous increase in entropy until equilibrium, can be interpreted as a consequence of probabilities. A system will, if it is in a less probable state, probably move towards a state with a higher probability until it is in the most probable configuration. It is, upon this view, not impossible that we would find all the atoms of a gas on one side of the room, but it is extremely improbable, even if we waited for the whole 15 billion years since the apparent beginning of the observable Universe.

If the Second Law expresses the movement towards the most probable states, why aren't we yet in such a state? Why is there disequilibrium, the order which allows for stars and life? There seem to be two possible answers; either it is a fluctuation, or a consequence of special initial conditions:

1. A special distribution is possible, though not very probable. It might arise during the reshuffling process. Ludwig Boltzmann, around the turn of the century, defended such a view of the Universe as a whole: the observable Universe is temporal fluctuation of relative order (disequilibrium) in an infinite background of mostly boring equilibrium. Observers are dependent upon the disequilibrium, which makes processes possible. They will therefore only exist during such fluctuations. A standard objection to Boltzmann's idea is the enormous size of the observable Universe. A much smaller fluctuation with observers like us, say a fluctuation the size of the Solar System or the Galaxy, is apparently much more probable. The inflationary scenario provides a possible solution, because the fluctuation now can be conceived of as rather small—having become as

large as the observable Universe due to inflation and the subsequent regular expansion (see Appendix 3).

2. The non-equilibrium might also be a consequence of the way the system had been set up. If we found the ruins of a sandcastle, we would not assume that those ruins had been formed by accident, as a fluctuation, but rather that there had initially been a sandcastle. This line of argument implies that the Very Early Universe should have been very ordered. The high temperatures seem to imply that matter and radiation were in thermodynamic equilibrium. Roger Penrose (2.3.3) therefore suggested that the original source of low entropy is gravity. The subsequent clumping of matter, for example in stars, allows for the processes which increase the entropy of the Universe.

Others have used the need for special initial conditions as support for belief in a supernatural cause of the Universe. However, these arguments are inadequate (1.3.1; 3.2). They neglect the possibility of a natural explanation in terms of laws of physics, perhaps new ones like the one proposed by Penrose (2.3.3). Besides, it may be disputed whether the Second Law is applicable to the Universe as a whole. The Universe, by definition, has no exchange of matter and energy with an environment. However, the expansion implies a non-equilibrium, because the temperature of the Universe as a whole (the background, now circa 3 K) continuously decreases (see Appendix 1).

3.   INTERPRETATIONS

A 'pessimistic' evaluation of the Second Law, as describing the unavoidability of decay which ultimately results in a 'heat death' of the Universe, has been widespread. It has also had an impact on religion (see Hiebert 1966, 1967; Brush 1978; Barrow and Tipler 1986, 166ff). More recently, scientists like Prigogine have emphasized the need for the dissipation of entropy in processes which form structures, like the structures of living beings. This has led to a more positive evaluation of the Second Law as a condition for the formation of structure (Prigogine and Stengers 1984; Jantsch 1980; and in a Christian framework Peacocke 1979, 1984b, 1986a, and Hefner 1984c). Robert Russell has suggested an integration of both views with two different Christian traditions. The 'pessimistic' evaluation would be analogous to the Augustinian understanding of the world as fallen, while the 'optimistic' evaluation of entropy would be analogous to the Irenean view of the world as being involved in a process moving towards the likeness of God (Russell 1984, taking up distinctions made by Hick 1966).

APPENDIX 3

INFLATION

One recent scenario (proposed by Guth in 1981), the *inflationary universe,* solves almost all the problems of the Big Bang theory. The claim is that the Universe expanded enormously, 10^{50} (hundred thousand times billion times billion times billion times billion times billion) times, between 10^{-35} sec. and 10^{-33} sec. after the Singularity, hence long before the Big Bang model becomes applicable.

The inflationary expansion involved velocities far beyond the velocity of light. That is no problem since no energy is transported. Imagine a point on an inflated balloon. With respect to its surroundings *on* the surface of the balloon the point can be considered to be at rest. In relation to an embedding space points move, but there is no point moving within the surface of the balloon: equivalently there is no point of spacetime moving within space.

1. HOW INFLATION SOLVES THE PROBLEMS

Inflation implies that the whole observable part of the Universe arises from a very small region, the parts of which were causally connected before inflation. That solves the horizon problem: everything we observe has been in contact in the past. The origin of the galaxies might be explained by quantum fluctuations in the original region. The inflationary model also explains the flatness of the Universe today. Even if the original region were curved, due to the enormous inflation we see only a very small region, which is nearly flat, just as a small region of the Earth is flat. Inflation predicts the density to be very near to the critical density, and therefore a mass density which is higher than at present visible in the universe. 'Dark' mass might consist of ordinary objects like planets, but also of exotic particles predicted in GUTs and other particle theories. The absence of antimatter is explained, since the particle theories used in inflationary scenarios (Grand Unified Theories, GUTs which integrate the nuclear and the electromagnetic forces) do not conserve the number of baryons (so they allow for changes in the matter-

antimatter balance), while during the non-equilibrium of the inflationary phase the matter type might have become dominant. Monopoles, strings, and other effects of boundaries are inflated away,
hence diluted.

2.   HOW INFLATION ARISES

The different scenarios for inflation (Guth 1981; Albrecht and
Steinhardt 1982; Linde 1982a, b) need a field (a field represents a
kind of particle; this isn't one of the well-known particles) and a
form of potential energy. It's like a ball on a slope: it has kinetic
energy which reflects its movement and potential energy, as it can
roll further down the slope and thereby gain kinetic energy. The
original scenarios needed special forms for the slope; if the slope
were too steep there wouldn't be sufficient time for a relatively long
period of inflation. Especially important is the end of the inflationary
phase, which could result in a significant production of inhomogeneities which would destroy the gains (as an explanation of the
initial conditions of the standard theory). Today it is expected that
inflation occurs in the right way in the right particle theory as a
phenomenon accompanying a phase transition; "all but the last of
the prescribed features, that the potential be part of a sensible particle physics model, are relatively easy to arrange" (Turner 1985,
311). However, "a handful of models that satisfy the prescription
for successful inflation have been constructed" (Turner 1985, 316).

A well known *phase transition* is the transition from water to ice.
There are many such transitions in physics. They can often be seen
as thresholds on the temperature (or energy) scale: above that threshold there is one kind of physics (water behaves as a fluid), below that
there is another kind of physics (ice is subject to solid state laws).
The two different types of physics are part of the same fundamental
physics (in this case quantum mechanics with electromagnetic interactions), but the physics takes different forms in the different phases.
Phase transitions are abundant: the solid, fluid and gas phase are
all within the atomic phase. At higher temperatures the electrons of
the atomic shells get dissociated from the nuclei: the plasma phase.
Further up the scale we have separate protons and neutrons instead
of nuclei. Again further up we probably have a 'gas' of quarks and
gluons in-stead of the protons, and so on.

Phase transitions are often associated with symmetry-breaking. Continuing the water and ice example: in water there is no preferred direction, there is a complete symmetry under rotations (aside from external influences, such as the gravitational field of the Earth); ice has a crystal structure, which has, once the crystal is formed, a certain orientation in space. The continuous rotational symmetry is lost. The crystal could have been formed in a different orientation, but once formed the original symmetry is broken. However, "most of the models for inflation now do not involve SSB [Spontaneous Symmetry-Breaking]" (Turner 1985, 319).

Inflation seems a not too *ad hoc* expansion of the standard theory. Thus elaborated, the standard model explains almost all the features of the Big Bang, features unexplained in the standard model in its original form. Inflation as a component of an expanded standard model is widely supported.

However, it is not an answer to questions about the initial conditions or the origination event. It describes only an epoch in the evolution of our Universe. There remain questions about the Very Early Universe. None of the three cosmologists discussed in Chapter 2 has any objection to an inflationary phase in the early universe. But the significance of inflation is judged quite differently. For Linde, it provides a basic principle of his cosmology, which sees the Universe as consisting of many inflating bubbles.

APPENDIX 4

HAWKING'S COSMOLOGY

In physics, in general, the physical state of a system at a certain moment, t_2, (such as positions and velocities of billiard balls) can be calculated when the state at another moment, t_1, is known, plus the laws which describe the evolution from one state to another. In the Big Bang theory the state of the Universe at any moment consists of information about the material content (particles, represented as fields) and the curved three-dimensional geometry which describes the effect of gravity on space. The state of a universe at one time can, again, be calculated by using the equations *and* as a boundary condition the state at another time. In that sense one could say that one state 'arises out of' another state (Figure 4, left).

In the Big Bang theory the limit of such previous states is the initial Singularity. It turns out to be impossible to specify the data at the Singularity; many different possible universes start off with identical initial singularities (Figure 4, right).

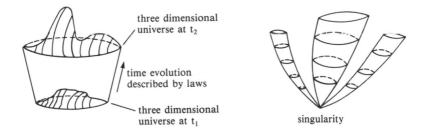

three dimensional universe at t_2

time evolution described by laws

three dimensional universe at t_1

singularity

FIGURE 4. Left: the state of a universe at one moment, depicted as a curved surface, follows from an earlier state and the laws. Right: many possible evolutionary sequences start with a singularity.

In quantum physics the state of a system is no longer a specification of all positions and velocities. The entity calculated in the *theory* is a *wave function* (also called *state vector*), which gives (when squared) probabilities. The wave function for a particle describes the probabilities of finding the particle at a certain position at a certain time. That presupposes the spacetime framework.

Spacetime cannot be presupposed in theories about the Universe. In quantum cosmology the basic entities of the *world* as described by the theory are: 1. *three dimensional spaces* or geometries with curvature. (This is the gravitational part; gravity is expressed as curvature. It is different from general relativity, where the basic entity of the theory is the four-dimensional spacetime, which in many cases can be decomposed into a series of three dimensional spaces.) And: 2. *fields*, representing the material content, the 'particles', in such a three-dimensional space.

In quantum cosmology a procedure similar to the classical approach (state at t_2 from state at t_1 and laws) holds. There is a differential equation, the Wheeler-DeWitt equation (Wheeler 1968; DeWitt 1967), which governs the evolution of the wave function. If one specifies the wave function at one boundary one might calculate the wave function for other moments, hence the transition probability from state$_1$ to state$_2$. In this way one could still look upon it as a description of an evolutionary universe—although the interpretation becomes less clear, as the theory does not describe a single sequence of states but a sequence of probabilities for different states.

One formalism for calculating transition probabilities in quantum theories uses path integrals. We sum over all 'paths' connecting the initial and the final event. A well known case is light: instead of assuming that light goes along the single straight path from A to B we can also assume that it takes all possible paths between A and B. Due to interference all contributions cancel, except for the 'classical' path: straight from A to B. In the case of three-dimensional spaces with fields a path consists of a curved four-dimensional spacetime and a field defined on that spacetime. The spacetime must have two three-dimensional spatial end-surfaces, such that the curvatures and fields match there.

A disadvantage of this description from within time is that we still need to specify the boundary conditions. Therefore, this approach doesn't help very much in discussing the 'creation' of the universe. This is avoided in the Hartle-Hawking proposal (Hartle and Hawking 1983; Hawking 1982, 1984a, b, c, d, 1987).

The elegant and interesting feature of the Hartle-Hawking theory is that one can calculate the wave-function directly without referring to other states or to evolution from such other states. This specific feature of their proposal is very technical, as it needs path integrals over four dimensional spaces (not to be called spacetimes, unless one allows for an imaginary time), but it seems to work.

The only condition is that the three-dimensional spaces are closed (compact), just as the surface of a balloon is closed in two dimensions. If the surface is closed, a single three-dimensional surface is the only boundary of the four-dimensional spaces used in the path integrals, just as the two-dimensional surface of the balloon is the only boundary of its three dimensional volume (Figure 5). The resulting state is the only boundary in the calculation, instead of the two surfaces as boundaries, an 'initial' one at t_1 and a 'resulting' one at t_2, in other approaches.

> By evaluating the path integral over compact metrics, one eliminates one of the two parts of physics, the boundary conditions. There ought to be something very special about the boundary conditions of the universe and what can be more special than the condition that there is no boundary? (Hawking 1982, 571)

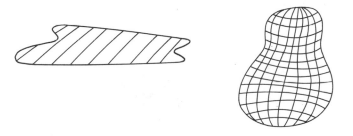

FIGURE 5.   A surface can be non-compact (left) or compact (right).

The trick is not without its repercussions. Ordinary time, with its notion of 'becoming', disappears. We could still see a trace of the traditional time variable in the path integral over four-dimensional spaces which fit at the three-dimensional boundary, but it is an imaginary time variable, and thereby the 'time' dimension is completely on a par with the spatial dimensions. There is no reason to call it a time variable at this level. But there still is the notion of time in the other description. This one can be reconstructed by forming stacks of three-dimensional states. Such stacks turn out to satisfy the Wheeler-DeWitt equation which can be interpreted as describing the evolution of the states, with two complications: there are more stacks than one, and not all slices fit in such stacks.

The calculations are complicated, especially if we include all fields that should be part of a realistic theory. No model describing our Universe exists yet. But there are some results, indicating that the density should, in a simplified model, be close to the critical density (Hawking and Page 1986), and that most universes of this type have an inflationary phase (Gibbons, Hawking, and Stewart 1987).

APPENDIX 5

TIME

1.   SOME ASPECTS OF TIME

Ontological Status

Is time an order inherent in reality, even independent of the presence of objects (the Newtonian view), or an order of successions, hence *a posteriori* with respect to objects and events, but nonetheless a feature of reality (Leibniz), or a co-ordinate introduced by us when we form knowledge? The most famous representative of the latter position is Immanuel Kant, who took time to be one of the 'Anschauungsformen'—*a priori* with respect to knowledge (see, for one of the many interesting discussions on this topic, Heller 1986a). Such issues are present as background to the more specific questions about time, its structure, flow and directionality.

The Structure of Time

What is time's structure? One could ask similar questions about the structure of space, and about order, topology, and metrical structure.

The *order of time* is expressed in common language as 'before' and 'after'. This order is clearly present in the Newtonian view, where time can be represented by a single line. In the special theory of relativity there is only a partial order. Events which can influence each other have a unique order. For events which are too far apart in space and too close together in time to be connected by signals there is no unique order. What is considered to be simultaneous, or earlier or later, is dependent upon the state of motion of the observer. Time and space are integrated in one description; one cannot abstract the temporal order from the spatial distances (Figure 6).

In general relativity a global temporal order is further lost. There are solutions (though perhaps not representing a universe like ours), which have circles in the time-direction. Following such a time-axis in the future direction brings one back to the same point from the past direction. In such a solution there is no linear order, since what happens after an event is also before it.

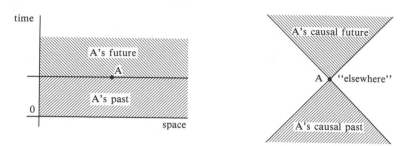

FIGURE 6. Left: in Newtonian physics one can unambiguously decide the temporal order (earlier, simultaneous, later) of any two events. Right: according to the special theory of relativity the velocity of light is finite. The causal past of A are the points which can reach A with a signal of, at most, this velocity. The remaining points, 'elsewhere', may all be considered simultaneous with A, since they cannot exert influence upon A or be influenced by A.

Some cosmological solutions admit a global definition of time. To take an idealized model of the observed Universe as an example: one could define a global time on the basis of the 'evolution' of the Universe, either specified by the curvature or the temperature of the cosmic background radiation. For some observers such a notion of simultaneity coincides with more ordinary notions of simultaneity, as defined through synchronizing clocks (as done in special relativity). But for others the global and the local definitions of simultaneity do not coincide. A global definition of time is equivalent to preferring a special group of observers, which is at odds with the equivalence of all observers as the fundamental idea behind relativity theories.

The evolution of the Universe seems, in our kind of universe, to single out a preferred group of observers—those who observe the cosmic background radiation as isotropic (the same in all directions). "Relative to this group of observers, therefore, we can speak properly of 'the' evolution of the universe" (Kroes 1985, 17). But the "resulting total temporal order of the events has by itself, without reference to this group of observers, no physical meaning whatsoever" (Kroes 1985, 18).

These arguments, based on Kroes (1985, 14–18), lead to the conclusion that the notion of a global time and 'the' evolution of the Universe are observer-dependent, and not a reintroduction of absolute time and an absolute temporal order of all events in the Newtonian sense.

The *topological structure* of time is, according to common sense, like a line. However, as already hinted at above, it might be globally like a circle, or some more complicated topology. Walking around on a circle does not change one's direction, future pointing remains future pointing. But other shapes might not be orientable in that way (Figure 7).

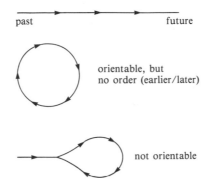

FIGURE 7.   Some structures of time.

One might also imagine time to be discrete, there being some smallest unit of time. Penrose argues, as one of the motives behind his program to develop a physics in terms of twistors, for a rejection of the continuum concept. A small volume seems to contain as many points as a large volume, or even the whole universe, which he rejects. As Penrose sees it, "the concept of spacetime composed of *points* should *cease* to be an appropriate one—except in some limiting sense" (1972, 334). A different approach, but also attacking the simple topology of time as linear and continuous, is taken in the ideas about spacetime foam, proposed by Wheeler (1964) and Hawking (1978). From a distance the surface looks smooth, but that is only apparent; the detailed structure would be highly complex.

Back to the notion of time in the continuous sense. Is it open or closed? One can have both, even within one solution of general relativity theory. Gödel (1949) discovered a solution of the Einstein equation which allows for one description presenting it as open as far as time goes, and another description which has closed time-like curves.

Time Asymmetry
We perceive an asymmetry between the past direction of time

and the future direction; the past seems fixed and given in memories, while the future seems still undecided: we can influence it. Synonyms for this notion of asymmetry are 'the arrow of time', and the 'anisotropy of time'.

The basic laws of physics, such as Newton's and Einstein's laws, along with quantum theory, are time-symmetric. How is the apparent asymmetry to be explained? The standard answer is that the asymmetry is a consequence of the boundary conditions, a statistical phenomenon (see Appendix 2). Hawking seems to see it as dependent upon the mind, a phenomenological construct (see 2.3.2). Others (such as Prigogine and Stengers) argue that the symmetry of the present laws of physics shows their inadequacy. As Penrose has it, the asymmetry should be built into the fundamental laws, as it is a fundamental feature of the world (see 2.3.3.).

2.   TRAJECTORIES AS WHOLE HISTORIES

In 4.4 above I argue that many, if not all, physical theories allow a description which takes the whole of time as the basic entity. The following exemplifies this by a brief presentation of the use of trajectories in physical theories.

Take, as an example, a point moving along a one-dimensional curved line (Figure 8a). Given the setting, a complete description of the system, its state, consists of the position and velocity of the point. The point will move along the line, and hence its position and velocity will change.

This can be represented graphically by a curve in a position-velocity diagram (8b). Such a curve is called a trajectory. Time is a parameter along the trajectory, which represents the whole history of the point, its movements along the line. If the point had started with another velocity or at another place but on the same trajectory we would have a redefinition of our time; the 't = 0' would be located somewhere else. If a point is not on the same trajectory we have a different evolution, hence a different trajectory in the diagram. Some trajectories will be closed: the point repeats the same movements again and again. Others might be open, and hence extend to infinity.

That example concerns a very simple system, but it lends itself easily to generalization. For a system with N particles the phase space has in general 3N dimensions (axes) to describe all positions and 3N

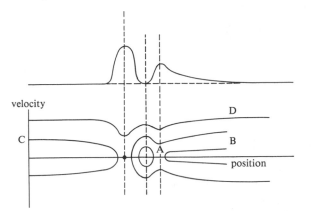

FIGURE 8. Trajectories for a particle moving without friction. A: a particle is
caught in the well, moving back and forth. B: a particle loses its velocity while going uphill and acquires the opposite velocity upon falling back. C: a similar particle coming in from the right. D: a particle
with sufficient velocity to cross the highest barrier. The diagram
shows that there must be some unstable cases, e.g. between
B and D, as well as a stable point (the bottom of the well).

dimensions to describe all velocities. Hence, the dimensionality of
the space is very high for a complex system; a simple two-dimensional
diagram is insufficient. However, the advantage is that the description of the system becomes very simple: it is a single point in such
a phase space. Its history is a line (trajectory), and time is a parameter
labelling the points along that trajectory. The different positions and
velocities of the components of the system are retrieved as projec-
tions of the position of the system (as a point) in phase space on the
different axes.

Physical theories are very fruitfully formulated in terms of such
trajectories in phase space. Formulating a theory as being about the
set of possible histories (trajectories) means that one abstracts from
the specific initial conditions. That is generally done in physics, as
it focusses on the general characteristics, and not on the unique
features of a system. To test a theory we need to make a certain
experimental arrangement and compare the results with those following from the theory, if the corresponding initial conditions are
used to select the trajectory.

APPENDIX 6

THE COSMOLOGICAL FUTURE

This topic is discussed in most of the references given in Appendix 1. A popular book with emphasis on 'dark matter', is Gribbin's *The Omega Point: The Search for the Missing Mass and the Ultimate Fate of the Universe* (1988). Another introduction, which also discusses catastrophes through collisions with asteroids and similar objects, is Close's *End: Cosmic Catastrophe and the Fate of the Universe* (1988). The relevant scientific information is accessible through an article by Dyson (1979b), articles and a book by Islam (1977, 1979, 1983), and the book by Barrow and Tipler (1986).

1. THE SECOND LAW OF THERMODYNAMICS AND THE FUTURE

As probably first pointed out by Helmholtz in 1854, the Second Law of Thermodynamics (Appendix 2) appears to imply that the Universe is running down, using all its free energy. All differences in temperature would in the long run become vanishingly small. As life is dependent upon differences in temperature, life would come to a halt when the Universe approaches its final state of maximal entropy. This prospect has been called the *heat death* of the Universe. *Freeze death* would have been more suitable, since the final temperature in an indefinitely expanding universe will be quite low. This idea had a strong impact on the perception of the world by scientists and philosophers in the nineteenth and early twentieth centuries (Brush 1978). Major scientists like Jeans and Eddington made it an important point in their popular presentations of scientific cosmology.

A number of objections have been raised against the use of the Second Law in arguments about a future heat death. I will list some of these objections. I will then argue that it is possible, and preferable, to avoid the use of the Second Law in reflections on the far future of the Universe.

Objections to the Cosmological Applicability of the Second Law

1. According to the historian of science Duhem, it assumes that the Universe can be understood properly as a collection of isolated particles (Duhem 1954, 288; Barrow and Tipler 1986, 617).

2. A continuous increase in entropy need not imply an end at an upper limit of maximal entropy—the increase might continue to infinity (ibid.).

3. The philosopher of science Toulmin objects to the extrapolation. It is relying on rather indirect evidence to apply a law based upon the working of steam engines to the Universe as a whole (Toulmin 1957 [1982, 38]).

4. Toulmin also warns against linguistic confusion, as a universal law need not apply to the Universe (Toulmin 1957 [1982, 41]).

5. There are reasons to doubt the applicability of the thermodynamic law to the Universe as a whole. The law is based on a distinction between open and closed systems. 'Open' and 'closed' are well defined for ordinary systems with an environment. Systems that exchange matter or energy with an environment are open; in this sense the Universe is closed. Systems that expand (into space occupied by the environment) are open; in this sense an expanding universe seems open. It is this latter form of 'openness' which makes the formation of structure (heavier elements, stars, *etc.*) possible, as the energy and entropy is radiated away into the expanding Universe.

One could also explain this in another way. The entropy of a closed system increases to a maximum value, according to the Second Law of Thermodynamics. This maximum corresponds to the 'heat death' of the system, the state of total equilibrium. A closed system of fixed volume has a fixed maximal entropy. However, as explained by Frautschi (1982), the maximal entropy of any expanding causally coherent region is not fixed. The maximum increases faster than the entropy produced, at least during most phases of the evolution according to the Big Bang model. Hence, the entropy of a region falls steadily behind the maximum.

6. Barrow and Tipler (1986, 619) give an argument on the basis of a recurrence theorem discovered by Poincaré in 1890. If we formulate the Second Law as a statistical feature in Newtonian mechanics, we find that almost any system will approach (and return to) almost any possible state of that system, if there is sufficient time.

There are, as a consequence, as many periods of decreasing entropy as there are of increasing entropy. A statistical understanding of entropy suggests that there might be from time to time a fluctuation in the opposite direction. Hence, there would not be a final heat death, but rather a period of equilibrium followed by a fluctuation which brought the Universe to a state of disequilibrium once more, allowing again for life and activity. The resulting universe has statistically recurring periods of order; hence it is a 'cyclic' universe. However, Tipler has proven a no-return theorem once one considers closed universes in the context of general relativity (Tipler 1979 and 1980). This seems to invalidate the argument against the applicability of the Second Law.

The Second Law of Thermodynamics is a very general statement, which does not lead to specific predictions about the processes that will happen. The law only summarizes a trend which is generally in line with the more detailed descriptions of physical and chemical processes according to other physical laws.

Because of the general nature of this law and because of the disputes about its applicability to the Universe as a whole, it is preferable to base reflections upon the far future of the Universe on more concrete physical theories: general relativity as the theory about the structure of space and time (next section) and quantum theories as the relevant theories about the material constituents of the Universe (section after next).

2. THE BIG BANG THEORY AND THE FUTURE OF SPACE

The Big Bang theory makes the simplifying assumption that our universe can be described as a homogeneous fluid of dust (galaxies). There are basically two classes of models for such universes. If the density is below a critical value, the Universe will continue to expand forever although, because of gravitational attraction, with ever-diminishing velocities. Such a universe is called 'open' (another meaning of open in addition to the two mentioned above). If the density is above the critical density, expansion will come to a halt, and the Universe will start to contract.

The density of visible objects, those that emit light or other detectable radiation, is below the critical density. However there are strong reasons to believe that there is a large amount of 'dark' (as yet unseen) matter. The most specific argument, to my knowledge, is based upon the observed rotation curves of the outer parts of galaxies. These observations, combined with the same physics which makes it possible to calculate the orbits of planets or satellites, suggest that there is about ten times as much mass in a galaxy as expected on the basis of the visible stars. Taking such conclusions into account, the consensus is that the actual density is between 0.1 and 2 times the critical density.

Inflationary models (Appendix 3), which appear to be successful for our observed Universe, predict that the density will be extremely close to the critical density. Whether it is a fraction below or above the critical density depends upon the cosmology assumed for the pre-inflationary phase. The difference today would be so negligible that it is not observable. Although some cosmologists have strong opinions on the case, it seems that there is no reason based on observational evidence to favor one of the two scenarios. If the density were precisely the critical density, a so called 'flat' universe, the basic scenario would be the same as for an open universe: continuing expansion. This possibility is not discussed separately.

If the Universe is *open*, the average distance between galaxies (or other constituents) increases continuously. The background radiation, which has today a temperature of about three degrees above absolute zero, spreads over ever larger volumes. It loses temperature and intensity, approaching absolute zero. This will never be reached within a finite time; the future of an open universe is infinite.

If the Universe is *closed*, the expansion will still continue for a long time. The closer the density is to the critical density, the longer the remaining time until the turning point. The shortest possibility consistent with present observational evidence is about 50 billion years, but it might be much longer, and surely will be if inflation is a correct scenario. The future until the turning point is very similar to the future of an open universe for the same timespan. Once the Universe contracts, its density and temperature (background radiation) will rise. This does not exactly mirror the expansion phase, because the produced radiation (for instance in stars) as well as the irregularities produce a certain pressure. This speeds up the collapse, although not very significantly. A more observable difference would be that all stars might have burned out during the expanding phase. And, if the first phase lasted long enough, the material content might have already changed considerably (see below). However, if there were still stars and atoms around they would fall apart when the temperature became too high. When the temperature is about 300° Kelvin, the sky is everywhere as warm as it is during the day on Earth. When the temperature rises a bit more, free liquid water spontaneously boils and we approach the end of our kind of biology. Above 4,000° Kelvin, atoms fall apart into nuclei and electrons, which implies the end of chemistry. The density increases, and galaxies merge. When the background temperature exceeds the surface temperature of the stars, the star has to adjust its surface temperature and radius, hence to change its structure, while the energy production in the core continues. Perhaps outer layers rapidly evaporate. When the temperature become comparable with the central temperature, "an explosive ignition of the remaining nuclear fuel can disrupt the star" (Rees 1969).

Ultimately, extreme temperatures and densities are reached, as near the Big Bang. The collapsing phase ends with something similar to the Big Bang: the distances become zero, and the density and temperature infinite: a *Big Crunch*.

Some speculate that the Big Crunch for one cosmic epoch might be the Big Bang for another cosmic epoch (Dicus et al; Markov; Petrosian; criticisms, among others, by Bludman, Guth, and Sher). There is nothing in the theory of general relativity, on which the Big Crunch idea is based, to suggest such an extension of the model. Tolman (1934) has shown that an eternally oscillating universe obeying classical (not quantum) theories is incompatible with the Second Law of Thermodynamics. Frank Tipler has proved 'no-return' theorems; the impossibility of an arbitrarily close return to a previous state in any closed universe governed by general relativity (Tipler 1979 and 1980). Each state is unique. Quantum effects might change ideas about a possible future 'beyond the Big Crunch', as argued by Markov. As long as we don't have a theory of quantum gravity, we can't say for sure.

3.   THE FUTURE OF MATTER AND ENERGY

The Future of Stars

Stars balance gravitational attraction with the pressure produced by hot moving particles. But they finally run out of nuclear fuel and become cold objects. If the star is not too heavy (below 1.5 solar mass), it might end as a dwarf, first white but slowly turning to brown and black when its energy is radiated away. It owes its stability to a quantum mechanical effect, which implies that different electrons cannot be in the same state, and hence they cannot be compressed into too small a volume. White dwarfs are small and dense, a million times the density of water.

If the final mass of a star is between 1.5 and 3 times the mass of the Sun, the pressure due to electron-exclusion will not do. The electrons get squeezed onto the protons (cores of the nuclei), making the star consist of almost pure neutrons. The exclusion principle applies again for neutrons. Neutron stars are small, a few kilometers in diameter, and extremely dense, a hundred million times as dense as dwarfs.

If the star is heavier than 3 Solar masses in its final stage, there is nothing that can match the gravitational attraction. It ends as a black hole. Black holes are called black because all radiation (and matter) within their vicinity (within their 'horizon') is captured by their gravitational attraction. However a black hole still exerts gravitational attraction beyond its horizon and might thereby be detectable. Phenomena in some double star systems are explained quite well under the assumption that the unseen partner is a black hole.

Dwarfs, neutron stars, and black holes do not need fuel to provide stability. Planets and other objects lighter than ordinary stars are also stable, as the ordinary strength of materials due to chemical bonds is sufficient to resist gravity.

The Future of Galaxies

In the long run, a thousand billion (10^{12}) years from now, which is a hundred times the present age of the Universe according to the Big Bang model, the sky becomes dark. A galaxy becomes a collection of dwarfs, neutron stars, black holes, planets, dust and gas. Although dark, a galaxy remains a structure held together by gravity, while prevented from collapse by the motion of the objects.

Two bodies orbiting around each other will collapse in the long run, due to the loss of kinetic energy. Moving massive bodies emit gravitational radiation. This is quite negligible under ordinary circumstances, but becomes significant in the long run. Tidal forces (like the influence of the Moon on the Earth and vice versa) also influence such systems. In systems of three bodies, one of the bodies might gain velocity and escape from the system due to a close encounter.

For a galaxy consisting of billions of bodies the close encounters will be very significant. Some bodies might be ejected during the course of billions of billions of years. The remaining objects will form a dense core, which in the long run becomes a single 'galactic' black hole of about a billion solar masses.

The Future of Black Holes

Black holes are absolutely stable, according to the theory of general relativity. However, Hawking discovered in 1974 that they should emit particles and anti-particles. Through this process black holes lose mass. The lighter they are the more radiation they emit. This positive feedback implies that a black hole disappears with a final burst of energy.

Radiating black holes might be compared to ordinary radiating objects. However, their temperature is extremely low: a galactic black hole has a temperature of about a millionth of a billionth degree Kelvin, which is far below the background temperature of 3 degrees Kelvin. Hence, it would absorb today much more than it would emit.

If, due to the expansion, the background temperature drops below the temperature of the black hole, it will start to emit more than it absorbs. The background temperature will become that low after about 10^{30} or 10^{40} years. The emission is not fast; a galactic black hole takes about 10^{90} years to evaporate, a supergalactic black hole 10^{100}. Stellar black holes, if there are any among the ejected dead stars, will have evaporated long before. Each black hole ends with a burst of radiation; "the cold expanding universe will be illuminated by occasional fireworks for a very long time" (Dyson 1979, 451).

There is one way out. If black holes coalesce, forming ever bigger black holes, their temperature drops and their lifetime goes up. If there is no upper limit to the mass of black holes, some black holes might escape evaporation by growing ever bigger, keeping the universe "always entirely matter dominated" (Page and McKee 1981, 45, black holes being considered as matter since they possess rest mass). Barrow and Tipler (1978, 454; 1986, 650) defend the final disappearance of all black holes.

The Future of Rocks, Dwarfs, and Neutron Stars

Quantum mechanics ascribes a small probability to processes which appear forbidden according to classical physics. Nuclear fusion at room temperature and density seems impossible, but it might occasionally happen. An ordinary piece of rock, or a planet like ours, will be transformed by fusion and fission into a piece of iron, iron being the most stable nucleus with the lowest energy per particle, and therefore the natural end product of fusion and fission. All ordinary matter would be transformed to iron after about 10^{500} to 10^{1500} years.

The tunnel effect—quantum theories predict that there is a small probability that a particle is found on the other side of a barrier, even if it lacks the energy to pass over that barrier—also applies to the transition from black dwarfs to neutron stars. A dwarf could by external influences, like a supernova explosion, become a neutron star. Everything that is possible if caused by external pressure, has a finite probability of happening spontaneously. For the transition from dwarf to neutron star, this takes so many years that the exponent in the power of ten would be a number of 76 digits. The transition from a neutron star to a black hole might also occur spontaneously, and this takes a similar amount of time.

If black holes of masses smaller than stars are possible, transition to a black hole and subsequent evaporation also holds for lighter objects. If the lower limit of the mass of a black hole is the Planck mass (20 micrograms, about the mass of a bacterium), the number of years would again be huge; the exponent would be a number of 26 digits. This also holds for dwarfs and neutron stars, since it is much more probable that small black holes get formed within such a star than that the whole object at once tunnels to a black hole state.

After all this formation and evaporation of black holes, the universe consists only of radiation (photons, neutrinos, gravitons and so on), elementary particles and antiparticles (protons, electrons and so on), small pieces of dust (up to the lowest possible mass of a black hole), and fluctuations of the vacuum. Time can still be defined with respect to the decrease in temperature of the cosmic radiation.

The Future of Particles

If the number of baryons (the proton/neutron type of particles) were conserved in all interactions, protons—being the lightest of this type—would live forever, apart from encounters with anti-protons or black holes.

However, black holes have no baryon number. A black hole has 'no hair', no identity determined by its history, whether made up of ordinary matter (positive baryon number), anti-matter (negative baryon number), or radiation (zero). Hence, baryon number cannot be conserved. Another argument for non-conservation of baryon number lies in GUTs, theories which unify electromagnetic, weak, and strong interactions. In GUTs all kinds of particles are described in one scheme. Within most of these theories decay of protons and neutrons into lighter particles like the electron and anti-electron is possible. Such a process is necessary if the theory is to explain the production of an asymmetry between matter and anti-matter in the very early Universe. The first prediction for the lifetime of the proton was 10^{31} years, which corresponds to one proton decay per year for 20 tons of matter. The present experimental limit is not conclusive, but within a few years experiments will determine whether the lifetime predicted by simple GUTs is correct. Other GUTs predict longer lifetimes.

If the proton is unstable all ordinary pieces of matter will be unstable with a similar lifetime. Electrons and positrons, being the lightest charged particles, are absolutely stable if charge is conserved as is generally believed. Some electrons encounter positrons, and these annihilate into photons. In an expanding universe this does not result in a total vanishing of matter density. The density of matter will, under certain assumptions, remain at about 60% of the density of radiation (Page and McKee 1981).

Finally, the universe would consist of radiation (photons, neutrinos), which is hardly interacting, and electrons and positrons. These latter may form bound systems, like atoms, of one electron and one positron, called positronium. These positronium 'atoms' are the only remaining constituents available as building blocks for more complex organization, according to physical theories today.

The Future of Energy

If forms of life or consciousness in such a distant future exist, they must be very different from life as we know it. However, the use of free energy seems a minimum condition. Assuming that technological and social problems are solvable, one can predict restraints on the available energy.

Before settling to the white dwarf state in about five billion years, the Sun becomes a red giant. It will be very hot on Earth. Creatures like us will have to move away. Afterwards, as a white dwarf, the Sun's energy production is less than today. It might be wise to move in again. Anyhow, as the Sun becomes a brown, and later on a black, dwarf, it emits less and less energy. Migration to other stars will be necessary for the continuation of life.

After a thousand billion years, there will be no shining stars in the Galaxy nor elsewhere. The energy stored in rotation can be extracted. Penrose has shown that, in principle, a civilization on a satellite orbiting a rotating black hole could dump its waste in the black hole, and receive energy in return. Since the supergalactic black holes live for about 10^{100} years, this way of extracting energy might perhaps be continued for such an enormous period of time, if the rotational energy is not exhausted before.

If the proton is unstable, each decaying proton produces a few particles with rest mass and energy. In neutron stars, which can be considered as huge clumps of protons and electrons, this would effectively be a new source of energy, which would maintain the temperature at 100 K, far above the background temperature, for the lifetime of the proton, say 10^{31} years (Barrow and Tipler 1986, 648; Feinberg 1981; Dicus et al 1982 and 1983).

Beyond these processes, there are no external sources of energy available. If the decay of matter can be overcome, it remains disputable whether a civilization could survive indefinitely on a finite amount of stored energy. Dyson (1979) defends this (see 4.2).

4.   THE FUTURE IN QUANTUM COSMOLOGIES

Penrose's cosmology (2.3.3) fits most closely into the standard Big Bang picture. He prefers an open universe, but expresses no strong preference as far as I know. He stresses the difference between initial and final conditions, similar to the differences and developments sketched in the preceding description. Hawking's timeless perspective (2.3.2) makes beginning and end alike, not special moments but features of our description.

Linde (2.3.1) might agree with the standard description, but only within a 'bubble universe'. The whole set of bubbles has no clear development or final state; new bubbles will begin as offspring of others. He therefore argues that life appears again and again in new bubbles (Linde 1989). Even stronger: there might be possibilities for travelling, or at least communication, from one bubble to the next (Linde 1989, 353). The condition turns out to be that the vacuum energy density is extremely close to zero. This shows, according to Linde, the potential practical importance of research on the vacuum energy density. But the practical importance is a long-term one: "Unfortunately (or, maybe, fortunately), it may take as much as $10^{5 \times 10^6}$ years until the significance of the current work on this problem will be fully appreciated" (Linde 1989, 358).

This might be related to speculations about *vacuum eschatology*. Some (Coleman and De Luccia 1980; Turner and Wilczek 1982) have speculated about a drastic change of the vacuum, and with it of the types of particles and interactions. Talking about different vacuums sounds strange, since 'empty is empty'. However, a vacuum corresponds to a 'ground level' with respect to which all altitudes are measured. All states with particles are deviations from the vacuum. If another ground level is chosen, all altitudes change. Similarly, choosing another vacuum implies a different world of deviations, *in casu* particles.

The question is whether models have a metastable vacuum like ours (with a lifetime at least in the order of the time since the Big Bang), and whether it is possible that a universe in the course of its evolution gets stuck in such a metastable vacuum. It seems to be possible. If the state we consider as the vacuum today would be unstable (but stable for at least 10 to 20 billion years), there would be another ground state, which would have less energy. There would be a nonzero probability that the Universe would 'tunnel' to that vacuum. Such a transition would start as a bubble of the true vacuum. The bubble would expand with the velocity of light, so we would not observe the new vacuum before it engulfed us. Suddenly, the whole spectrum of particles as well as the whole set of electromagnetic, weak and strong forces would change. On a phenomenological level, the laws of physics would change, although there would be an unchanged set of laws at a more fundamental level. Everything made of ordinary matter would change, and, even worse, the true vacuum would be such that the Universe would collapse immediately. Hut and Rees (1983) analyze the question whether this collapse of our vacuum could be triggered by humans, especially by processes occurring in particle accelerators. Their conclusion is comforting: "we can be confident that no particle accelerator in the foreseeable future will pose any threat to our vacuum."

The last weird thing in this appendix: if we can imagine changing the vacuum of our world, couldn't we also create a 'universe', at least an inflating bubble of spacetime, in the lab? These new bubbles would have their own space and time external to ours; we would not be affected. The question has been considered by Farhi and Guth

(1987). The energy density needed is not accessible by known technology. More fundamental, an initial singularity, which has by definition no preceding history, cannot be produced intentionally. And it is very hard to do without a singularity in creating a 'child universe'. Hence, they conclude that it is probably impossible, at least within the framework of general relativity.

APPENDIX 7

BIBLICAL CREATION NARRATIVES

The following serves as background for the claim in 1.4. that there are no good grounds for substantial parallels between the Big Bang model and biblical narratives. It is not intended as a discussion of different Genesis interpretations, but mainly follows the work of Westermann (1974), one of the major scholars on these texts. Accessible to non-specialists are, among others, the books by Bernhard W. Anderson, *Creation versus Chaos* (1967) and Jon D. Levenson, *Creation and the Persistence of Evil* (1988).

1. GENESIS

Genesis is not a cosmological book. It contains the saga of Abraham, Isaac and Jacob, the patriarchs of Israel, preceded by a primeval saga about the origins of the world, of mankind (Adam and Eve), and of the peoples of the world (the three sons of Noah). I say nothing here about the origin of the Genesis text, since *Beyond the Big Bang* is not about the origins of ideas, but purely about the ideas themselves.

The text, as we have it, presents a universal panorama (creation, flood, all the peoples of the Earth), which narrows down to Israel, one people with a specific history. Most biblical scholars believe that the main emphasis is really the other way round, beginning with the particular experiences of Israel with its God, and then broadening its perspective with the claim that the God of Israel is not a local God, one among many, but the Only One, the Creator of everything. Some scholars have objected to an overemphasis on the soteriological side, since the belief in YHWH as the creator was present quite early. Perhaps blessing and salvation, God's creative and God's historical acts together, are themes of the preaching of God's power, without reducing the one to the other (Westermann 1974). If soteriology is held to be dominant and if creation and salvation, wisdom and history, are thought of as equal themes, there is no doubt that biblical thought about origins is closely connected to the specific traditions and beliefs of Israel. Genesis 1 ends with the blessing of the seventh day, the Sabbath, which is typical for Israel and not part of a universal belief in a God who created the Universe.

The book *Genesis* is structured by *toledot*, genealogies of descendants, narrowing down to Israel while describing the peoples around them as descending from other sons of Noah, Abram, Isaac and so on. The creation narrative ends with the same *toledot*, the only place where it is not about humans. It incorporates the begetting of Heaven and Earth into Israel's past.

A close connection to Genesis 1 is the beginning of the story about the Flood. Many themes return, but now it is not good in the eyes of the Lord (Genesis 6:5). After the Flood, the blessing on procreation recurs, but with a less harmonious relation between man and the animals, allowing man to eat flesh, except for the blood which is supposed to contain the life (Genesis 9:1–7).

As Westermann (1974, 3) points out, two presuppositions have limited the understanding of Genesis 1–11: the assumption that the decisive statements are those of Genesis 1 and 3, understood as 'creation and fall', and the neglect of the theological significance of the genealogies.

The place of Genesis 1 in the 'Urgeschichte' and at the beginning of the 'history' of Israel and God implies that: 1. The world as described in Genesis 1 is not directly equivalent to our world. According to Genesis 3–11, serious ethical deviations have occurred, which are reflected in the order in the world, even bringing it near to a return to chaos in the Flood. 2. Genesis 1 is not primarily giving a general discussion of the origin of the world, but an extension of Israel's experience with its God—in the Exodus, at the Sinai, and elsewhere—to a claim that the God of Israel is the sole power, the Only One, not only for Israel but for the whole world. As such, it is comforting, since this God is known to care for his people, and also demanding, since this God has given his people ethical and other instructions.

'In the Beginning. . . '

Although the word *beginning*, as used in Genesis 1:1, might be a statement about importance, the most natural interpretation is to take it as temporal. This still leaves more than one possibility open: the beginning of the creation narrative, or a heading, summarizing the whole content of the creation narrative. The interpretation depends on the syntactic relations among the first three verses.

Verses 1, 2, and 3 can be three separate sentences, Verse 1 being a heading incorporating Genesis 1 in the whole (Steck 1975, 226). Some translations take Verse 1 as introductory to Verse 2, like: 'When God began to create the heavens and the earth, the earth was without form and void . . .'. According to the Hebrew text, this is a possible reading. Vawter defends it on the basis of other creation legends, which start from "unformed chaos, with no attempt made to account for its presence" (Vawter 1977, 38). Verse 2 describes an initial state, which God has transformed into an ordered cosmos. Von Rad (1964, 36f) has objected to this reading, since then the chaos would be temporally before the creative work of God, which is theologically unacceptable. However, this argument is circular; how do we know that it is unacceptable for the author unless we have understood these verses? Vawter's argument is also circular, since how do we know that there is a parallel in this respect?

Both 1 and 2 might be introductory to Verse 3, making Verse 3 the first statement about God, immediately followed by God's first act. As support, one might point to the beginning of the next story (Genesis 2:4b–7) and to a Babylonean creation story, 'Enuma Elish'. However these narratives lack real parallels to Verse 1 (Westermann 1974, 134f).

Westermann (1974, 130–35) reads Verse 1 as separate, while taking 2 and 3 together. Verse 1 is without parallel in other creation narratives. Westermann takes it to express the intentions of the author, being a title formulated nearly like a song of praise.

Following Westermann and Steck I understand Verse 1 as a heading for Genesis 1, for the whole book of Genesis, and even for the whole Torah (the first five books of the Bible). The 'In the beginning' is not the beginning of the creation story, saying that God created first the heaven and the earth, followed by the subsequent creation of light, dry land, and so on, but it concerns the beginning of history. The essence is not that Heaven and Earth had a beginning, but that the creation of the heavens and the earth has been the beginning of all subsequent history. It sheds light on the history following this creation.

'In the beginning, God *created*. . . '

The verb *bara* is used in Genesis 1 in the heading, in a concluding formula, for the great animals (monsters) from the sea (1:21), and three times in the verse describing man and woman as created after God's image. This verb is used in the Bible only for God. The verb never occurs with an accusative or an expression 'created from. . . '. God creates the whole environment, all of mankind, especially the people of Israel, and also evil (people, the great sea animals). In Isaiah and at other places, *bara* is used for God creating nature and God acting in history, while in texts ascribed to the author of Genesis 1 it is only used as creation in the beginning (Westermann 1974, 137). It sometimes expresses transformation, 'a new Heaven and Earth', or 'a clean heart', which supports the claim that "there is no conclusive evidence in the entire OT that the verb itself ever expresses the idea of creation out of nothing" (Heidel 1942, 89). A major intention of texts with *bara* seems to be that God has a relation with humankind, which is comforting and demanding. The wide extensions, spatial as well as moral, describe God as the sole power. It seems to express that:

1. We and our whole environment, the Universe, derive our existence from the only ultimate power, God, which is comforting and demanding. This does not exclude God's using powerless primordial stuff. 2. Neither mankind nor anything else is like God.

The verb in the sentence, 'In the beginning God created . . .' is essential. The verse is not like 'In the beginning there was a God', saying something about the existence of God. That would be a modern approach. The authors of the Bible took God's existence for granted, and started to talk about God's creative work. Genesis is not primarily a narrative about God as such, but about God's activity as expressed in the world.

'In the beginning, God created *heaven and earth*', that is, the whole environment, near us (Earth) and far away (the sky, the firmament). The way the world is described is clearly outdated: the Earth in the center as a flat dry disk with water around, below, and above the firmament like a dome. It is not reasonable to defend the scientific correctness of the narrative by harmonizing this with modern views. The author expressed himself in the pictures of his time, which are wrong from our point of view. With respect to the general knowledge of his time, the author is not telling his audience much news. Hence, information about the world in itself seems not the intention of the narrative. The text must have been important for other reasons, probably cultic, religious or moral.

Does *Verse 2* imply that God created first a chaos, or even that chaos was already there, independent of Him? One traditional reading is that Verse 1 describes an original, perfect, creation, which subsequently has fallen into chaos (Verse 2). However there is no independent reason for distinguishing between a first and a second creation, with a fall in between.

A second solution sees Verse 2 as a purposeful reminder of another creation story, a struggle between different powers, one of them striving for order, the other the power of chaos. However, this does not explain why the author has retained these older elements. The powers of chaos are thought of as present afterwards, not only as part of a struggle in the beginning (Isaiah 27:1, Psalm 93:3–4). God must defeat them now. This is expressed in the titles of the books by Anderson, *Creation versus Chaos*, and Levenson, *Creation and the Persistence of Evil*. Levenson objects to the doctrine of *creatio ex nihilo* (temporally understood) which has distorted the understanding of the Bible. "In particular, a false finality or definitiveness is ascribed to God's act of creation, and, consequently, the fragility of the created order and its vulnerability to chaos tend to be played down" (Levenson 1988. xiii).

A third view is to interpret Verse 2 as a moment of realism about the negative in God's creation. While incorporating the negative, the context stresses that God is in control—the issue is mastery.

Another view, defended by Westermann (1974, 63), is that the function of Verse 2 is not to describe a 'before', but to seal off God's creative acts from a 'before' that cannot be described.

The phrase *'without form and void'* sounds rather philosophical, as a kind of insubstantial stuff or empty space, but the original Hebrew words *tohu* and *bohu* express something negative and violent. *Tohu* is like a desert, unlivable. *Bohu* appears only together with *tohu*, and in both other contexts (Isaiah 34:11, Jeremiah 4:23) it describes the wrath of the Lord, effected in part by destruction of the land. It should not be mistaken for one of the few remaining wildernesses of our time, a cute National Park. It is desolate and in disorder. The second part, darkness and the deep, is similarly discomforting. Darkness is not a world without physical light, but a gruesome world.

The third sentence might be the spirit of God or a mighty storm. Wind and spirit are the same word, while 'of God' can be a superlative. I don't know any decisive reasons to take it as a superlative, and parallel to the other sentences of Verse 2, or as a contrast, introducing God's presence in the darkness.

The Six Days
In attempts to reconcile Genesis 1 with the timescale of geological

and biological evolution, a day has been understood as an epoch, perhaps quite long. Support is taken from "A thousand years in thy sight are but as yesterday when it is past" (Psalm 90:4). However there is no reason to suppose that the author of Genesis 1 uses 'day' in that sense, unless one assumes harmony with modern science. It is a human-scale unit of time which is used to structure this story about God and the world.

The composition in six days, ending with a seventh day of rest, clearly reflects the idea of a week. Within the six days, there are eight distinctive acts of God, introduced by 'And God said', two on the third and two on the sixth day. There is a parallelism between the first three days and the second three days:

1. light.
2. firmament, waters above and below.
3. dry land and vegetation.

4. Sun, Moon, and stars.
5. birds, fish.
6. land-animals and man.

During the first three days the constituents of chaos—darkness, the waters, and the *tohu* and *bohu*—are brought under control. Here, creation is separation. During the following three days the cosmos is differentiated and filled with inhabitants. Land animals and humans occupy the same living space, which might be a source of conflict (Liedke 1979). Two potential sources of conflict, space and food, have been removed within the narrative. The land animals, unlike sea-animals, birds (Genesis 1:22) and man (1:28), don't receive a blessing with the injunction to be fruitful and multiply. Although it is not our view of biology, the absence of this blessing might be interpreted as a contraceptive. Animals and man receive different prescriptions for food (Genesis 1:29f), both being vegetarians. After the flood the conflict is described as actual (Genesis 9:1–7).

There appear to be at least two *mechanisms of creation*, creation. *through speech* and *through acts*. 'And God said . . .' occurs eight times. It seems to be the mechanism of creation, God ordering "Let there be light," with immediate effect: "and there was light." Although in the case of light this wording seems to support *creatio ex nihilo* (Van Selms 1967, 25), this is not the case throughout. The second day "God made the firmament and separated the waters." And even on the first day, God "made a separation between light and darkness." Verses 7, 12, 16, 21, and 25 are at odds with the emphasis on the suddenness of the appearance of something from nothing after God has said it is to be. 'God said' might be an announcement, even if followed by 'And it was so'. At other places

(Judges 6:38, 2 Kings 7:20) the latter formula is also followed by a
description of the realization of the command, as it is in the verses
of Genesis mentioned above. If the author really had wished to single
out God's way of creating as speech, he would have evaded all those
references to more tactile methods of creating.

Many authors including Von Rad 1964; Bouhuijs and Deurloo
1967; Vawter 1977) stress the tension between the first day with the
creation of light, day and night, and the fourth day with the creation of the sources of that light, as a polemic with other beliefs
which treated the Sun and other heavenly bodies as gods. The
'lights' appear quite late in Genesis 1; they are mere lamps without
names. They are only described as the greater and the lesser light.
The polemical function of the description explains, according to
Westermann (1974, 176), why the author stressed their functions,
to light, separate and rule the day and the night, and to be signs for
the feasts, which is a consequence of having the structure of time
based on Sun and Moon. They don't have some general power of
their own. This reduction of gods to lights "should please every
astronomer. Gods cannot be calculated, lights can" (Van Selms 1967,
45, my translation). A second good reason for separating the light
of the first day from the appearance of the Sun, Moon, and stars is
that it makes a fine pattern in the narrative.

Humankind receives a special place in the narrative, but only a
place in a much wider setting, not even a creation day to itself.
Although Man's special worth has often been defended by pointing
out that he is the last creature, the 'end' of creation, we should realize
that there is still a seventh day; that day is the crown of creation.
The verses on the creation of man and woman are not about the
psychological constitution of humans, but in the first place an expression of man's relation to God. The anthropological element seems
irrelevant to discussing the relation between theology and cosmogony, but the fact that it is more important than the plain cosmogonic
interest is relevant.

In some ancient legends the creator rests after finishing his creation, a kind of inactive presence which expresses the idea that the
creator does not interfere any more and therefore the creation remains in the order it received during the creation (Pettazzoni 1954,
32f; Westermann 1974, 230). The seventh day as the Sabbath has a
different function. The blessing is a legitimization of the specific
Sabbath tradition of Israel, which is a central element in the theology
of the author of Genesis 1 (Schmidt 1967, 155–59). Inactivity of the

Creator to prevent the cosmos from falling back into chaos does not fit, since the God of Israel remains active.

2.   OTHER BIBLE TEXTS ON COSMOGONY

There are other biblical texts which offer or imply a view of creation. Knight distinguishes between six types which coexist in Yahwism, though from different groups or periods. "They thus give voice to the viewpoints and values prevalent in diverse settings: priestly, agrarian, sapiential, prophetic, cultic, apocalyptic" (Knight 1985, 151). Reumann finds "three or four pictures in ancient Israel, three more after the exile, plus half a dozen or more strata in the New Testament" (Reumann 1975, 96). He nonetheless discloses some common features, like praise of God, concern with humans and their existence, emphasis on the ongoing process of God's care, and expectations about a 'new creation'. Here are some of the other biblical references to creation.

In *Genesis 2* the narrative concentrates on the creation of man and woman, while treating the rest as background. The primordial situation is described by negative sentences, describing what was not yet. The creation is formation from inert material, like the work of a potter.

In the *Psalms* references to God's creative works and God's acts during history occur with similar functions—praise of the Lord, comforting man since God founded the Earth—without opting for a single cosmogonic tradition. Both "making" like a potter (8, 19) and "commanding" like a king (33, 148) occur.

In the books of the *Prophets* creation has a modest place. God is primarily the God who has revealed Himself through His acts in the history of His people. To support their preaching about this God, occasional references to God's powerful deeds in creation occur (Brongers 1945). Only in *Deutero-Isaiah,* the anonymous prophet whose ideas are expressed in the second part of Isaiah (Isaiah 40ff), does God as the creator seem to be a constitutive element of the prophet's preaching. Brongers concluded that Deutero-Isaiah's intention has been to bring the people first to the belief in YHWH as the Creator, and then based on this belief to make the transition to YHWH as the lord of history (Isaiah 40:22ff, 44:24–28, 45:12f). 'To create', *bara,* is used in both contexts. The reference to the universal aspect of God is related to Cyrus, a Persian, an outsider, who is bringing the people of Israel back from Exile. So, although the theme 'creation' occurs more in Deutero-Isaiah than elsewhere in the prophets, even for him it has a function subordinate to the proclamation of salvation as an imminent historical event.

In *Job* God's majesty, far beyond human understanding and capabilities, is expressed partly by references to the creation (26, 37, 38). In *Proverbs* there is a minor moral point, for "Who oppresses the poor, insults his Maker" (Proverbs 14:31). More speculative is Proverbs 8:22–31, where Wisdom is said to have been present before all God's works: "Before the mountains were sunk down, before the hills I was born; when He had not made the earth and the fields, nor the first particles of dust. When He made the heavens, I was there" (Proverbs 8:25f). However there is no speculation about any role of 'Wisdom' in the process of cosmogony. The explicit function of this passage is to stress the importance of wisdom for living the life God intended by stressing its temporal priority.

In deutero-canonical literature—books not part of the Hebrew canon but present in the early Greek translation, the Septuagint, and accepted by the Catholic church as part of the Scriptures—there are more philosophical remarks about the creation. In the *Wisdom of Solomon,* God's power is described by "Your powerful hand, who created from formless dust the world" (11:17). In the *Wisdom of Jesus Sirach,* God's goodness and greatness is expressed by a description of the world (42:15–43). "He is the Only One, already before time and until eternity" (42:21). God made it all, but how he did it is not a major concern to the author. The books of the *Maccabees* have the sole explicit reference to *creatio ex nihilo* (2 Maccabees 7:28). This is in the second century B.C.E., so Greek philosophical influence might be present. However, it is not presented in a philosophical context, but for the court of an oppressive king, who has persecuted those who kept to the Jewish traditions. The king tortured and killed six of the seven sons of a woman, because they refused to eat pork. The mother supports her sons by referring to their God as the Creator of the world. When the King tries to seduce the last son to eat of the pork, she advises him to realize that God created the heavens and the Earth from nothing. The reference does not function to explain the cosmos, but to stress God's power as infinitely surpassing that of the oppressive king and so to strengthen the faith in God's ability to resurrect martyrs.

The specific contribution of the *New Testament* to the general notion of creation as a manifestation of God's power and majesty is a Christological understanding of the initial creation. Word and wisdom are starting-points for a Christological understanding of the creation (John 1:1–18; 1 Corinthians 8:6, Colossians 1:15–17, Hebrews 1:2f). The prologue to the Gospel of John is intended to recall Genesis 1: "In the beginning was the Word." This is not so much cosmogonical explanation, as cosmogonical legitimization of Christ. The Old Testament affirmed that the Creator was the God of Israel, the unit of creative works and historical deeds; the New Testament emphasizes the decisive participation of Christ in this unit of past (creation), present and future (new creation, kingdom).

THE HISTORY OF *CREATIO EX NIHILO*

1.   GNOSTICISM AND MARCION

Gnosticism is a name for a wide variety of ideas, so it is certainly incorrect to try to capture it in a few words. Gnostic groups are a bit similar to the theosophical movements and alternative cosmological-religious groups of our time. They assume that there is a spiritual element in the world, especially in man, which needs to be freed from its binding with the material world to return to the spiritual realm, the *pleroma*. In the spiritual realm, one of the lesser powers transgressed a limit and lost some spiritual parts to the material world. The spiritual belongs to God, is part of the divine *pleroma*, more like an emanation from God than like a creation. The material does not belong to God; it detracts from God. The world in its materiality is not good, while in the world the divine is present as the spiritual. The creator of the material world is not the redeemer of the spiritual, while both are lesser powers than the highest God. Ireneus, one of the main Christian opponents of Gnosticism, argued in his five books *Against the Heretics* (180/189 A.D.) for the identity of creator and redeemer.

Marcion (mid-second century) reached similar conclusions as the gnostics, but on a completely different basis. There is not a separate tradition of spiritual knowledge for the initiated. Marcion pushes to an extreme Paul's distinction between 'Law' and 'Gospel' as Old and New Testament. The God of love, the father of Christ, cannot be the severe, just, God of the Jews ('an eye for an eye'), who made the world, with all its evil, from uncreated matter. Marcion accepted only the Gospel according to Luke and the letters of Paul, after changing or deleting all parts which he suspected to be Judaist forgeries.

2.   PLATONISM AND *CREATIO EX NIHILO* IN THE SECOND CENTURY

More information (and detailed references) can be found in the monograph by Gerhard May (1978), which I have drawn upon for this section.

An ontological doctrine of *creatio ex nihilo,* unlike an emphasis on God's power and majesty, is not present in the Bible, nor in Hellenistic Judaism. As argued above (Appendix 7), formulations like 2 Maccabees 7:28 are not directed against eternal materiality, while the presence of primordial matter is not considered a limitation of God's power (Wisdom of Solomon 11:17). Philo of Alexandria, the best-known representative of Hellenistic Judaism in the first century, assumes an active and a passive principle of being, God and matter.

In *middle Platonism* (first century B.C. to beginning third century A.D.) the cosmology of Plato's *Timaeus* is further developed. There are three, ontologically at first equal, principles: God the demiurge who made the world, the Ideas, according to which the world was formed, and the Matter, from which the world was formed. All three are eternal, although the world as formed from the matter was not always considered eternal. In middle Platonism there is a tendency to reduce the number of principles by understanding the Ideas to be thoughts of God. Plotinus, a neoplatonist of the third century, emphasizes the One, and reduces matter from a principle to an emanation from being to non-being. There remain two fundamental differences with Christian doctrine (May 1978, 5): 1. Matter does not arise through a creative act in time but is eternal as is the cosmos; being created is an ontological relation, an eternal generation. 2. In Platonism there is no freedom and contingency in the creative acts of the Creator. Being flows necessarily from the One.

In the Christian gnosticism of *Basilides* (mid-second century) there is, perhaps for the first time, a well-developed concept of *creatio ex nihilo* (May 1978, 84f). Basilides deviates from gnosticism by taking the highest God to be the creator of the world. Besides, he has a negative (in a technical sense) concept of God, stressing the insufficient character of analogical reasoning and hence the dissimilarity between the creation of the world and any worldly process. In later Christian polemical literature, gnostics are accused of using the philosophical cosmology of the Greek philosophers, but for Basilides that is not correct. Basilides's ideas about creation have not had much influence, neither on later gnostics nor on theologians within the church, except for Clement of Alexandria who discusses some of his ideas more academically.

More influential has been the work of Christian *apologists* in the second century, who defended Christian views as the true philosophy. *Justin Martyr* is the first (May 1978, 124) to claim that Plato had taken his ideas for the *Timaeus* from the first verses of Genesis. Justin understands Genesis 1:2 as a statement about disorganized, pre-existing matter. He defends a beginning in time for the cosmos, and therefore a creation of the ordered world. Uncreated matter is not a limitation of God, nor related to the presence of evil, so the Platonic pre-existent matter has no theological significance. Similar nearness to middle Platonism is exhibited by *Athenagoras* and *Hermogenes*. The latter defended the eternity of matter in relation to the origin of evil.

Tatian is the first Christian theologian who thought that the matter, formed by the Logos (the Word, Christ) into a cosmos, to have been generated directly by God (*Oratio ad graecos* 5, May 1978, 152). (Some think he took matter to be an emanation from God [Adam 1965, 155].) Tatian's main argument: ungenerated matter would be a second principle, in some respects equal to God.

Theophilus of Antioch is the first, as far as we know (May 1978, 149), who in opposition to pre-existent matter explicitly and with clear terminology stated: "God created the universe from the non-being to being" (*Autol. I* 4, May 1978, 159). Arguments against the eternity of matter were (May 1978, 163ff): 1. God would not be the Creator of the universe in a complete sense and the divine monarchia not guaranteed. 2. God is ungenerated and hence unchangeable; if matter were ungenerated, it would also be unchangeable and so similar to God. 3. God would not be so great, if he had used pre-existent matter. God would be similar to a human craftsman. God's majesty is that he creates from nothing. The positive affirmation that God's sovereign will is the sole ground of creation brought God's freedom in creation into the philosophical discussion.

Ireneus of Lyons wrote a complete theology against all the 'heretics' of the second century, mainly explaining the Old and New Testament in the perspective of the historical acts of God, from creation to incarnation and beyond. He is not so much interested in philosophical discussion as in asserting, especially against gnostics, that God created the world in a free decision of the will. Word and Wisdom, Christ and Holy Spirit, are the two hands of God which are God's only mediators in the work of creation (*Adv. Haer.* IV 20, 1). God took from Himself the substance, the exemplar and form for the things He made. That God took everything he needed from Himself is not informative about God's constitution, but a denial of any ontological necessities outside God. That God created matter is important, how God did it is not mentioned in the Bible and should not be the subject of speculation, and similarly for God's activity before he created the world. It is decisive that the creation was from nothing and only through God's will (*Adv. Haer.* II 10, 2, 4; IV 20, 2, IV 38, 3). Ireneus, and after him Tertullian, introduced legitimately the voluntaristic traits, which have since been considered to be typical of the Jewish-Christian tradition (Langerbeck 1967, 158), and so, philosophically, the contingency of the created order. Ireneus did not add new philosophical arguments to those of Theophilus, but his biblical-theological whole, of which *creatio ex nihilo* was an integral part, contributed much to the general acceptance of *creatio ex nihilo* as one of the fundamental presuppositions of Christian thought.

NOTES

Introduction

1. R. Hensen brought to my attention the description of 'integration' offered by Anders Jeffner in his *Kriterien christlicher Glaubenslehre* (Uppsala, 1976, 139f). I follow Jeffner's formulation of the 'integration principle' in the text.

2. Occasional references to recent discusssions in the context of Judaism have been included, for example to the proceedings of the 1984 meeting of the Academy of Jewish Philosophy (Novak and Samuelson 1986). Many topics, like the cosmological argument (see 1.3) are common to all three major theistic traditions, Judaism, Islam, and Christianity.

3. See any dictionary under 'natural theology', for instance Van A. Harvey (1964, 158) or K. H. Miskotte in *Die Religion in Geschichte und Gegenwart* (third edition, 1960, 1322–26).

1. THEOLOGICAL RESPONSES TO THE BIG BANG THEORY

1. i. Theories other than the Big Bang theory are motivated by an "atheistic, or simply pagan, or at best agnostic, longing for the eternity of matter" (Jaki 1982, 260). Comment: There are also scientific motives for the development of alternative theories. There are also theists arguing for, or accepting the possibility of, the eternity of the material world.

ii. Proponents of an oscillating universe search for "missing mass", but there is no reason to expect such mass to exist (Jaki 1980, 22; 1982, 260). Comment: There are a number of normal scientific reasons to search for mass which is not visible through light or other yet detectable radiation, for example, the gravitational effects of such matter on the dynamics of galaxies and clusters. To challenge the assumption that all mass is visible is not unreasonable.

iii. The idea of continuous emergence of hydrogen atoms out of nothing, as in the Steady State theory, is "creation without a Creator." This, Jaki holds, is one of the theory's "intrinsic contradictions" (Jaki 1980, 20). Comment: The claim that the Steady State cosmology should have been dismissed as illogical passes over the serious problem that faced the Big Bang model. It predicted at first an age of the Universe which was smaller than the geological age of the Earth. Observations provided a solution for the age problem: distances, and hence the age of the Universe, were wrongly determined. The discovery of the background radiation, which fitted nicely into the Big Bang theory, forced the decline of the Steady State cosmology. Until then it was a reasonable alternative, which fitted some observations better. Besides, "creation without a Creator" is not a logical, but a linguistic problem. 'Sudden appearance without a supernatural, metaphysical cause' is not illogical, unless one already subscribes to Jaki's metaphysical views. And even the 'without cause' is not that strict: the appearance is a requirement of the laws of the Steady State theory, and hence has as much of a cause as quantum events.

Sharpe (1982) gives more extensive, but similar, criticisms of Jaki's approach to the relations between science and Christian theology. See also the references given by Sharpe, and Sharpe's book *From Science to an Adequate Mythology* (1984, 92). In that book, criticisms are complemented by a tentative outline of a theology in relation with the sciences similar to the position I develop in the present work.

2. Frank Shu, in a textbook on physical cosmology, summarized the Big Bang theory by quoting Genesis 1 (as he quotes other pieces of literature), followed by: "So, modern cosmology affirms, in the beginning there was light. And the brilliance of that light has begun to illuminate our understanding of the creation of the material world" (Shu 1982, 387f). Benjamin Gal-Or wrote an interesting integration of cosmology and philosophical reflections with a strong emphasis on time, ending with a view which he considers to be close to the views of Spinoza and Einstein. In passing, Gal-Or remarks that most "astrophysicists, cosmologists and astronomers agree that the biblical account of the beginning of cosmic evolution, in stressing 'a beginning' and the initial roles of *'void'*, *'light'* and a *structureless* state, may be uncannily close to the verified evidence with which modern science has already supplied us" (Gal-Or 1981, 5). More examples of relating the Big Bang theory to Christian ideas are to be found in Allen (1958), Brauer (1958), Green (1985), James (1969), Köhler (1982, 1983), Lovell (1980), Newbigin (1986), and O'Keefe (1980).

3. The idea that God created a world with evidence of a non-existent past is equivalent to the question whether Adam had a navel (and hence evidence suggesting a mother) or whether the trees in the garden of Eden had rings (suggesting growth during preceding years). A famous defense of the reconciliation of a literalist understanding of the Bible with science, by assuming that God had created an apparently developed world, was given by Philip Henry Gosse in his *Omphalos: An Attempt to Untie the Geological Knot* (1857).

4. Some examples with refutations:

i. The observed neutrino production of the Sun is only one-third of that predicted. Perhaps the energy of the Sun is not produced by nuclear processes, but by gravitational contraction (DeYoung and Whitcomb 1980, 153). Comment: The model of the Sun has been modified (a temperature in the core of the Sun of 13.5 million degrees Celsius instead of 15 million and a minor addition of other elementary particles) and now it explains the measured neutrino flux as well as some other phenomena (Faulkner and Gilliland 1985: Faulkner, Gough, and Vahia 1986; Däppen, Gilliland, and Christensen-Dalsgaard 1986; see also Bahcall 1990). Gravitational contraction, the alternative of the 'creationists', leads to an age counted in millions of years, not in thousands, and leaves fully unexplained the observed neutrinos.

ii. Decay rates of radioactive elements can be influenced by physical circumstances. Radiometric dating is not reliable. Comment: The differences in decay rates are small, even under extreme conditions. Along this line one could argue for small uncertainties in the ages, but not for an adjustment which changes billions into thousands. If one argues that the budget of the state should be a few thousand dollars, a cut of a few million in the budget cannot be claimed as support. Instead, it confirms that the budget is on quite another scale.

iii. Stars are supposed to form out of collisions of interstellar particles. This way there would, after three billion years, be a particle of one thousandth of a centimeter. Therefore, this way of star formation is incredible (Slusher 1977, 60f). Comment: Stars are not expected to form through collisions between particles which stick together, but through gravitational attraction bringing the particles closer to one another, making the cloud continuously more dense.

iv. The magnetic field of the Earth weakens. Extrapolated back it can have existed only a short time, otherwise it would have been much too strong (Morris 1974, 157–58). Comment: The data used pertain only to a period of about one century. Older data, obtained by geological research, show a nearly cyclic behavior of the strength of the magnetic field. Linear extrapolation is not applicable.

v. A detailed study of one example has been made by Howard Van Till in his article 'The Legend of the Shrinking Sun' (1986b). Observations presented in 1979 at a scientific conference suggested that the sun was shrinking. These results never appeared as a regular scientific article, since additional studies and a re-evaluation of the original data led to the dismissal of the original claim and to the discovery of an 80-year oscillatory behavior. Among 'creation-scientists' the original data have been accepted without further critical consideration, and extrapolated far beyond their domain. To use the first tentative report as a result "constitutes a failure to exercise appropriate restraint in employing the results of single investigations" (Van Till 1986b, 170). Even worse, with respect to scientific morals, is the way they have disregarded subsequent research, except for one author in the *Creation Research Society Quarterly*, Paul Steidl.

5. Many books on 'scientific creationism', especially in the USA, are related to a famous trial in Arkansas and its impact on education. See Kitcher 1982; Ruse 1982; Frye, ed. 1983; Montagu, ed. 1984, Gilkey 1985.

6. We are here dealing with rejections of the Big Bang theory within the 'classical' domain, in which quantum theories are not supposed to alter radically our understanding of spacetime. The more recent developments which will be discussed in Chapter 2 are of a different nature. They go beyond the Big Bang models, but do accept them within their domain, that is, except for the very early phases (with respect to the Big Bang models).

Hoyle and Alfvén are not the only opponents of the Big Bang model. Halton Arp, for instance, has especially questioned the way velocities have been inferred from spectra. He interprets observations as showing objects which are at almost the same distance but have very different red shifts (Arp 1987; Field, Arp, and Bahcall 1973). (The Big Bang models relate the red shift to the expansion of space, with different red shifts implying different distances). The proceedings of a symposium on the occasion of Arp's sixtieth birthday, held in Venice in May 1987, provide a nice overview of approaches which are somewhat off the beaten track (Bertola, Sulentic, and Madora 1988). In the 1960s Jayant Narlikar, together with Hoyle, suggested that the observable part of the Universe might be a bubble resembling a Big Bang universe within a larger Steady State Universe. Narlikar points to similarities with more recent developments which also accept the Big Bang models within a limited region. As he sees it, "steady state cosmology came on the scene much too soon, before physicists and astronomers were ready for it" (Narlikar 1988, 225). Ellis (1984) gives another review of alternatives to the Big Bang theory.

7. Since the energy is proportional to T^4, 5 K instead of 2.7 K leads to a factor of eleven in the energy, which is 1,100 percent, hence 1,000 percent wrong. If one wishes the opposite impression, one should take $-268°$ C predicted and $-270°$ C observed, a difference of less than 1 percent. Before the discovery of the background in 1965, Peebles circulated a preprint predicting 20 K (Hoyle 1980, 24), which explains the high upper limit.

8. Rahner emphasizes in the general discussion the distinction given in the text: theology and metaphysics as *a priori*, and about the unity or whole, versus science as *a posteriori*, about the plurality of individual phenomena. It would have been interesting if he had considered in this context the challenge from cosmology, as the science which deals with the whole universe. However, he only dismisses the identification of the Big Bang with creation with a brief reference to time. Creation should be, theologically speaking, a timeless creation of time and not an event in time (Rawer and Rahner 1981, 51F). For more on Rahner's view of theology and science see Rahner 1988.

9. Galilei's Letter to Grand Duchess Christina (1615), *Opere* V, p. 319.

10. Russell assumes general relativity with a non-zero cosmological constant and a homogeneous universe filled with matter. In that case there are seven combinations of finitude or infinitude with respect to size, past and future—all possibilities except for a model which is infinite in all respects. The latter would be an 'empty' universe, described by a De Sitter model.

11. Mackie has criticized these arguments against an actual infinite in his *The Miracle of Theism* (1982, 93). For example, an argument against an infinite past goes as follows: if the Universe has an actual infinite past, an infinite stretch of time must have passed in order to reach the present, and this would be impossible. However, this argument implicitly treats the infinite past as a (very long) finite past, when it introduces the impossibility of reaching the present.

12. More precisely, the maximal entropy increases in an expanding universe, and this increase goes faster than entropy production during most phases. As Frautschi (1982, 595) concludes, the universe does not approach a maximal entropy. Rather, the non-equilibrium becomes more pronounced. However, the entropy per comoving (expanding) volume approaches a constant value. Hence, there is a kind of 'heat death' for the Universe according to this reasoning based upon the standard Big Bang model.

13. For criticisms, see Mackie (1982, 95–101) and Hick (1989, 104–09).

14. On etymological grounds (considering the Greek roots of the words) one could argue for a distinction between cosmogony as origination related to fertility and cosmogeny as a more general term, as pointed out to me by Walter Michel. Cosmogeny would better fit the writers of the Hebrew Bible, as they set their view of origins and continuity clearly apart from myths based on sexuality and fertility. However, the subtlety of the distinction between cosmogeny and cosmogony has been lost in contemporary English. I shall use cosmogony as a general term, not implying sexuality and fertility, nor a human contribution through fertility cults, nor a continuity and similarity between the gods and the world similar to the continuity and similarity between parents and offspring.

15. This classification was developed by Barbour (1966; 1968; 1990, 10f).

2.   QUANTUM COSMOLOGIES AND THE 'BEGINNING'

1. At a popular level more can be found in Pagels (1985a), Trefil (1983) and Davies (1984). Narlikar (1988) emphasizes the uncertain nature of recent cosmology in a way accessible to the non-specialist, though with some technical details. Rozental (1988) offers, for those with some knowledge of physics and mathematics, an interesting introduction with emphasis on fundamental laws and constants as well as on the difference between the observable part of the Universe and the Universe itself. Two volumes with excellent technical review articles have been edited by Hawking and Israel (1979, 1987). Convenient entries to current research are conference proceedings, of which were used *Quantum Gravity* and *Quantum Gravity 2* (Isham, Penrose, Sciama 1975, 1981), *The Birth of the Universe* (Audouze, Tran Thanh Van 1982), *Quantum Structure of Space and Time* (Duff, Isham 1982), *The Very Early Universe* (Gibbons, Hawking, Siklos 1983), and *Quantum Concepts in Space and Time* (Penrose, Isham 1986).

2. This equivalence of the Universe to a vacuum was proposed in 1973 (Tryon 1973 and 1984). Tryon's major point was that the total energy could well be zero. Gravity is an attractive force, which can be associated with a negative (binding) energy. One needs to add energy to escape from the gravitational field of the Earth. As one cannot escape from the Universe the binding energy is negative. Tryon still accepted that baryon number (the number of heavier particles like protons and neutrons, and some unstable relatives) was conserved, and hence had to assume that the Universe contained as much matter as anti-matter. Since Tryon's first article the conservation of baryon number has been given up. Contemporary 'Grand Unified Theories' allow for proton decay, as well as for the production of baryons without the production of as many similar anti-particles.

3. Theorems by Hawking and Penrose have shown that singularities are unavoidable under certain general conditions. Linde accepts the existence of such singularities, but "these 'singularities' do not form a global space-like singular hypersurface [volume or point at a certain moment—W.B.D.], whch would mean the existence of a 'beginning of time' for the whole universe" (Linde 1987a, 619).

4. See also 3.5.1. Rozental (1988, 88f) follows a similar approach, reserving the term Universe for 'all being' while using the term 'metagalaxy' for the observable part that originated, according to the standard Big Bang models, approximately 20 billion years ago. There is one significant difference: Munitz defines the term 'universe' in an epistemological way by relating it to theories while Rosental uses the ontological notion of 'all being'. He is therefore more prone to the implicit introduction of additional metaphysical assumptions, like the infinity of the Universe in time and space as well as in diversity (Rozental 1988, 97).

5. Hawking's theory introduces another time-variable, 'imaginary time'. It is in imaginary time that there are no singularities. 'Imaginary' must not be misunderstood as opposed to factual, as the product of imagination. It is a technical term in mathematics for numbers which by definition give a negative result when squared. It has nothing to do with the difference between actual and possible existence or other philosophical notions.

The formula for 'distances' in spacetime $d^2 = x^2 + y^2 + z^2 - c^2 . t^2$ (see Appendix 1) combines the spatial co-ordinates x, y, and z with the time co-ordinate t, but not on a par—the minus sign implies a difference between

the time co-ordinate and the space co-ordinates. This has enormous consequences, for instance that the standard solutions in general relativity may
be finite without edges in the spatial dimensions (like the surface of a sphere),
but do have edges in the time dimension, a beginning and end. Due to the
peculiar properties of imaginary numbers this minus sign disappears if one
takes an imaginary co-ordinate t. Space and time become indistinguishable
in the formula. One can have a solution without any edges, whether in space
or 'time', which now is that imaginary time variable. The question for the
interpretation now becomes: what is the significance of this trick, and of the
thus constructed imaginary time?

Hawking seems to hold that we perceive the Universe in real time, and
in that description it appears to have a beginning and an end, but that the
Universe exists in imaginary time—and in that description the Universe is
without singularities, without beginning and end.

> So maybe what we call imaginary time is really more basic, and
> what we call real is just an idea that we invent to help us describe
> what we think the universe is like. But according to the approach
> I described in Chapter 1 [of his book—W.B.D.], a scientific theory
> is just a mathematical model we make to describe our observations:
> it exists only in our minds. So it is meaningless to ask: what is real,
> 'real', or 'imaginary' time? It is simply a matter of which is the more
> useful description. (Hawking 1988, 139)

The appeal to usefulness has an instrumentalistic tone which seems at
odds with his other writings, for instance about the beginning (or its non-
existence) and God.

6. It can be found in the eleventh book of Augustine's *Confessions*.

7. Section 26 in *On the Account of the World's Creation by Moses* by Philo
of Alexandria.

8. [Added in proof: Penrose's *The Emperor's New Mind: Concerning Com-
puters, Minds, and The Laws of Physics* (1989) gives a vivid and thorough
presentation of these ideas.]

Penrose's cosmological ideas have their background in the twistor program (Penrose 1972, 1975, 1980, 1981b; Penrose and Rindler 1984, 1986).
I will not go into that part of his work. It is an original but not easily accessible
approach, which would take us too far afield. Twistors are not only considered to be mathematically useful. Penrose holds that they represent a deeper
level of reality than spacetime points. Twistors are expected to be at the
basis of both particles and spacetime points. Penrose himself has set forth
his ideas on time, the specialness of the Universe and quantum reality without using the twistor formalism—perhaps in the hope of reaching more
scientists than the small group of those informed about twistors.

9. Tipler (1986b, 247) argues as follows: if there is a sub-system which
can have two states, say up or down, the whole wave-function can be written
down as a product of the wave-function of the sub-system and 'everything
else'. A measurement on the sub-system changes the first term in this product
into the two states 'up' and 'down', but 'everything else' remains the same.
This is in line with Hugh Everett's original proposal (Everett 1957). The
understanding of the Many Worlds Interpretation as resulting in an enormous amount of different worlds, as if everything else also splits, is more
or less due to Bryce DeWitt (DeWitt and Graham 1973).

10. Károlyházy et al (1982 and 1986) have also worked on a kind of

natural reduction of the many quantum possibilities to one more or less classical reality through a change in the quantum formalism in combination with an integration of quantum physics and gravitation theory. Ghirardi, Rimini, and Weber (1986; see also Benatti, Ghirardi, Rimini and Weber 1987, Ghirardi, Nicrosini, Rimini, Weber 1988, and Bell 1987) have proposed a model for a unified description of microscopic (quantum) and macroscopic (classical) systems. In effect, the wave-function reduces itself spontaneously by random 'jumps' towards one corresponding to a possible classical measurement. As they summarize it: "Choosing in an appropriate way the parameters in the so-obtained model one can show that both the quantum theory for microscopic objects and the classical behavior for classical objects can all be derived in a consistent way" (Ghirardi et al 1986, 470). Their proposal does not relate to the integration of quantum physics and gravitational theory, though they suggest that a similar equation might be derived in the context of a quantum theory of gravity (Ghirardi et al 1986, n16). The essential difference is that their approach is a local description of a system, the wave-function being an objective property of the local system, whereas the interaction with the environment was introduced in most earlier approaches to natural reduction (Ghirardi, Rimini, Weber 1987, 3287).

11. There are some technical difficulties as well, as I learned from C. J. Isham. It is not only that the normalization implicitly introduces the assumption that there is a universe (by setting the outcome to one). Under some simple assumptions the outcome of such calculations turns out to be infinite, hence there is no way in which it can be normalized to one. This can also be understood physically. The integration is done while the time variable is still included. This would, even for a single particle, lead to an infinite outcome. "A more plausible scenario is one in which the physical Hilbert space [space which represents all states] is only obtained after abstracting out the intrinsic time variable. This means that, like the concept of real time/Lorentzian spacetime, the probabilistic interpretation of the theory only 'emerges' from the formalism in some sort of semi-classical limit" (C. J. Isham in letter to the author, December 16, 1987). Tipler (1986b) deals extensively with non-normalizability.

3.   COSMOLOGY WITH OR WITHOUT GOD

1. The anthropic principle was introduced in its modern form by Robert H. Dicke in 1961, though Barrow and Tipler (1986) point to many similar ideas in earlier ages as well as in the twentieth century. The distinction between a weak and a strong anthropic principle was made by Brandon Carter (1974). Carr and Rees (1979) wrote the first extensive review article on the subject.

2. Some have also argued for a link between biology and cosmology concerning the origin of life. The probabilities of formation of the complex molecules existing in living organisms are estimated to be extremely low; hence such formation would be unlikely to have happened in the timespan since the Big Bang (Crick 1981, Hoyle and Wickramasinghe 1980). We could conclude against formation of complex molecules by chance or against the Big Bang model. This line of argument is not further discussed here, because

it would force us to include considerable material on the origin of life, a topic on which there is as yet no clear scientific consensus. However the actual argument about the improbability of such formation by chance is quite disputable. And the probability might appear to be low because we still lack an underlying theory (Narlikar 1988, 230). Such arguments seem to present us with a choice between a purposeful God and chance, two options which might well be combined (Bartholomew 1984).

3. Hawking used the term 'strong anthropic principle' for the idea that there are many universes or regions with different laws and 'weak' for different initial conditions. But he also used 'strong' in the sense of purpose: "the strong anthropic principle would claim that this whole vast construction exists simply for our sake" (Hawking 1988, 126). This seems confused. The distinction between laws and initial conditions seems unessential in this context. But the distinction between an anthropic principle working as a selection effect on observations of laws and conditions and one which expresses a claim of purpose seems necessary.

4. There is a more popular exposition in German by Breuer (1981); in French there is a more technical account by Demaret and Barbier (1981). Popular introductions in English have been written by Davies (1982) and Gribbin and Rees (1989). Gribbin and Rees conclude that "the question remains—*is* the Universe tailor-made for man?" (269). Their view is that anthropic reasoning suggests the existence of other worlds (284), though the issue is, in combination with the question whether there is a unique 'theory of everything' with a unique solution—the only possible Universe— far from settled. I argue below (3.2.3) that the assumption of 'many worlds' is separate, and not in itself a consequence of anthropic reasoning.

5. Rozental uses as definition that the physical laws governing the observable portion of the Universe, a region which he calls the Metagalaxy, are necessary for the emergence of complex forms of matter (Rozental 1988, 118). This is a somewhat stronger expression than the definition followed here, which does not introduce the notion of necessity. However, Rozental still applies it as a selection rule on many possible metagalaxies which are, according to him, realized.

6. Hallberg (1988, 145) argues that both weak anthropic reasoning and the 'transcendental' deductions of Kant deal with presuppositions. Weak anthropic arguments deal with causal presuppositions of our existence; Kant with the presuppositions of (re)cognition. Hence, according to Hallberg, the weak anthropic principle is not tautological.

My argument in the text is not that WAP is tautological but trivial, as it merely leads to a repetition of one of the factual claims (Hallberg's causal presuppositions) of the argument. There is also the naturalistic issue: are such presuppositions beyond further analysis? I am not dealing with the discussion concerning conceptual presuppositions and, for example, their possible origin in the evolutionary process. But it seems to me that the naturalistic case against untraceable causal presuppositions is much stronger than against the Kantian type of presuppositions.

7. Hacking (1987a, b) gives a clear exposition of the use of probabilities as frequencies in discussions about design. He points out that most arguments of this kind suffer from the inverse gambler's fallacy. Assume that one enters a room. A pair of dice is thrown. An improbable event, double six, happens. The question is whether this was the first roll this evening or one in a sequence. Other information, about the way people look and the time of the day, might provide clues. However, it is a fallacy to assume that

the improbable outcome itself provides a clue. According to Hacking, this fallacy is committed in arguments for a sequence of universes, ours being the last. There might be independent arguments for such a sequence, but the improbability of the present universe does not provide information about our location in such a sequence, nor about the existence of the sequence. A sequence does not explain our universe. "Our present orderly universe is not made more probable on the assumption of many previous universes spontaneously formed by chance" (Hacking 1987b, 338). The other position, the co-existence of all possible universes, explains our universe. The two, a sequence or a co-existent plenitude, are not equivalent, according to Hacking.

The argument is well-defended. Plenitude is indeed what makes the argument with many co-existent worlds work. However, the version with a sequence of universes, say like bubbles in Linde's cosmology, might introduce plenitude as well. The argument shows, in my opinion, that we cannot use a finite sequence. Rather, to make the argument cogent, we need to assume an actual infinite (past and future) series of universes. The explanation of our order would not suffer from the inverse gambler's fallacy, as it would not be based upon the observation and infer to a past sequence, but rather assume the plenitude and the weak anthropic principle.

Hacking refers to such a series as "Wheeler Universes." Wheeler has in the past defended this idea (Misner, Thorne, Wheeler, 1973, Chapter 44), but has changed his mind (for his most recent position see below, 3.2.4). Tipler (1979) therefore refers to more recent writings when he uses "Wheeler Universe" for a single closed universe. The sequence idea could today be more properly seen in relation to Linde's cosmology. Hacking's inverse gambler's fallacy is contested by McGrath (1988) and Leslie (1988b).

8. Page (1987) introduced a weak version of the strong anthropic principle, SWAP. It states that in at least one world of the many-worlds universe life must develop. However, this is essentially the same as the SAP itself. SAP does not require life everywhere, say on all planets. According to SAP any universe must have the properties necessary for life, though not necessarily in all its sub-systems, the many worlds.

9. Kirschenmann (1987, 78) and Plomp (1987, 97) come to similar conclusions.

10. The theistic option is defended by, among others, Polkinghorne, Leslie (1982, 1983a, 1983b, 1985), Jaki (1978, 1982), Montefiore, Köhler (1982), Green, Newbigin (1987, 72), Clark, and Carr. [Added in proof: John Leslie's book *Universes* (1989) offers the most extensive philosophical discussion of this topic so far.] Ford interprets the anthropic coincidences as suggesting "a universe made to make man" (Ford 1986, 42). Highlighting the absence of a widely shared vocabulary, he calls "a weak version of the anthropic principle" one which argues with an infinite number of universes in which all possibilities are explored (Ford 1986, 60). McLaren (1987) rejects the possibility of 'many universes' as equally metaphysical as the idea, used by 'creationists', that God created a 'developed' universe with evidence of a past which never existed.

A weak anthropic selection and many quantum universes as sufficient explanation, and hence the superfluous character of a 'god-hypothesis', is the position taken by, again among others, Haynes (1987). A similar dichotomy of 'many worlds' and 'contingency, hence creation' was made by Russell (1988a, 29f), though more open-minded with respect to the conclusion. Russell suggests, in a response to Pannenberg's emphasis on contingency as a topic for conversation between science and theology, a number of categories of contingency (see below, 3.4.1, and note 14). If the anthropic coincidences remained without explanation, we would have a remarkable model of global empirical contingency: the specific properties of the world could have been different. And the connection between the existence of a universe and the properties for life, as suggested by the strong anthropic principles, conjoins the global ontological and empirical contingencies. However, Russell takes seriously the many worlds argument and therefore considers the relation between the anthropic coincidences and design an open issue, though with fruitful possibilities for relating a doctrine of creation to contemporary cosmology.

11. Davies suggests the same possibility, a God as explanation of the 'superlaw', at the end of Chapter 16 of his popular *God and the New Physics* (1983a). However, Davies also considers the possibility that there would be only one unique set of possible consistent laws. The laws would be self-sufficient (Chapter 17). That would, according to him, only leave the possibility of a natural God as the highest level of organization within the Universe.

12. For a popular introduction, see Gleick 1987.

13. The distinctions were introduced during a symposium with the theologian Wolfhart Pannenberg at the Lutheran School of Theology at Chicago in April 1985. Pannenberg had in a preceding lecture (Pannenberg 1988c) emphasized contingency as one of the most important issues for the conversation between theology and the natural sciences. He especially asked for a revision of the concept of inertia, understood as the automatic continuation in existence and in movement of an object, because it seemed to deny God's creative role in the conservation of everything, not only in change but also in constancy (also in Pannenberg 1981).

Russell's concept of ontological local contingency (1988a) caught this kind of contingency nicely, and clarified it as one of a number of contingencies under consideration. The other forms of contingency are ontological global contingency (corresponding to the contingency of existence), empirical local contingency and empirical global contingency (the latter corresponding to the contingency of the features of the Universe, for example its initial conditions), and nomological contingency, the contingency of the theories (or laws) valid in the Universe. Of the latter Russell mentions five varieties, but that is more specifically related to Pannenberg's use of contingency.

14. Russell agrees that contingency faces, as an alternative at any level, a 'many worlds' option. However, he presents an argument which uses many levels:

i. The lowest level would be the set of possible universes with different initial conditions, but the same laws of physics. We can now opt for contingency: we could have had another universe from this set. Hence, there is something like a choice or design aimed at life. Or we can opt for necessity: all the possible universes of this set are actual; there is no choice. ii. The first higher level is the set of all possible laws of physics. Again there is the possibility of opting for contingency, one actual choice out of many possible ones, or necessity because all the possibilities are actual—a many worlds view. iii. The next higher level is the set of all possible formal logical systems.

And so on. Russell envisages an infinite ladder of levels. If the series ends at a specific level, the contingency of that end-point serves as a basis for a design argument. The alternative is that one accepts the existence of all possibilities at that level, a kind of 'many worlds' view. That removes the contingency at that level. But the same options return at the next level. "Even if the series of levels never ends, the series itself suggests its own form of design argument" (Russell 1989). He concludes that i. "no matter how strong the explanation science can give of 'the way things are', an element of the unexplained always remains; hence science will never eliminate the meaningfulness of contingency in the creation tradition," and ii. "the kind of contingency which exists in each particular scientific theory provides a special context of meaning for our understanding of divine creativity" (Russell 1989). The second point is a fruitful methodological principle, the intent to express theological concerns anew in relation to particular scientific theories. However, I doubt whether the argument itself supports an understanding of contingency outside of the specific levels. I have four concerns: a. Russell assumes that there is a multitude of options at every level. Would it not be possible that there would be only one consistent theory, or only one logic, on the level under consideration? That would mean that the necessity option would not be a many-worlds view and that there would be no contingency at that level. b. The meaning of the levels beyond the third level is unclear. Could it not be that formal logic takes reasoning as far apart as possible? c. Russell says that the whole series might be the starting point for an argument for design, aside from the arguments which take off from a specific level. However, he also admits that the organization of the levels is our construction. If it is a consequence of our way of organizing our ideas, how can the series also serve as premiss in an argument about contingency in reality? d. One could make a similar presentation of levels of necessity.

15. Both the mathematical existence of a solution (a wave-function), and its uniqueness given the boundary condition, have not been established in full generality.

16. Isham (1988, 401) mentions as assumptions: i. the possibility of applying ideas from quantum physics to the Universe at large; ii. the representation of space and/or spacetime by a mathematical continuum; iii. the correctness of general relativity as description of the large-scale properties of the Universe; and iv. the possibility of describing the material content of the Universe with local, interacting quantum fields.

17. A further question is the status of mathematics itself. Is a proof or a new theorem a discovery or an invention? Barrow (1988, 247–253) gives an intriguing dialogue between a 'Platonist' with respect to mathematics and someone who regards mathematics as a human invention (see also Barrow 1989b). According to Michael Heller, "the metaphysical miracle is not that certain mathematical structures break down at the beginning of time, but that they so perfectly work during the entire world's evolution, allowing the universe to exist" (Heller 1987, 424).

18. John Hick, who titled one part of his *An Interpretation of Religion* (1989) 'The Religious Ambiguity of the Universe', argues for a similar conclusion along somewhat more general lines.

4.   ESCHATOLOGY AND THE COSMIC FUTURE

1. Russell has pointed to the theological significance of the contributions by Dyson (Russell 1985 and 1986a) and Tipler (Russell 1988c). These new

developments in physical cosmology re-open, according to Russell, the possibility of a fruitful interaction between theological and physical eschatology.

2. It is not clear that an increasing number of significant digits of a given fact, like the angle between two stars—from the observer's point of view—is memory which can be used to *store* information. It already contains information, but not ours. Would the ability to manipulate the positions not be necessary if we wanted to store our information? Or, if not manipulable, should the positions not be supplemented with an explanation of the meaning of all those digits, a code book—which would have to use more memory capacity than it decodes? And is it possible to determine an infinite amount of digits with a finite amount of energy? The discussion in the texts was about the energy needed to maintain a metabolism, not the energy needed to obtain information about the external world and to store such information in the significant digits of the angle between stars.

3. This deviates from most process philosophers and theologians, who defend an objective immortality, as contributions remain present in God, but deny subjective immortality. See for instance the exchange by Ogden (1975) and Suchocki (1977). Suchocki's primary reason for this emphasis is the assertion that God is the overcomer of evil, which she holds to be basic to Christian faith.

4. Barrow and Tipler argue that there will be an infinite amount of information stored (1986, 677). However, that does not seem to warrant the knowledge of everything knowable. If the latter is infinite, half of it would also require an infinite amount of information. And if this knowledge is related to the property of the Omega Point of having all events in its causal past, what about knowledge of counterfactuals, events which could have happened but didn't? Tipler seems to allow those to exist in his Many Worlds Interpretation of quantum theories, and all those Many Worlds converge upon the same Omega Point (Barrow and Tipler 1986, 676). Nonetheless, one can think of counterfactuals, say a universe which does not have an Omega Point but rather has the Hartle-Hawking boundary condition.

5. They need to assume that the bit-processing rate for every living being increases in the same way when counted in physical proper time (Barrow and Tipler 1986, 661). Otherwise one might have an infinite number of thoughts, but among this infinity also thoughts about one's neighbor, who will continue to live in cosmic time even after one's own infinity is finished after a finite proper time. That would be life forever according to the original definition of Barrow and Tipler, but with the peculiar feature of having a neighbor with a life continuing even after one's own forever is over.

6. Unidirectional time implies the prediction that Hawking's proposal must be wrong (Barrow and Tipler 1986, 674; Tipler 1988, n4). This surely applies to Hawking's original idea that the thermodynamic arrow of time would reverse in the contracting phase, leading to a final phase which is identical with the initial state played in reverse (Hawking 1985). However, as I pointed out earlier (2.3.2), Hawking gave up this idea, and now maintains that the thermodynamic arrow need not reverse when the Universe contracts. As I see it, the disagreement still remains, as for Hawking the directionality of time is only a feature of our description, and not well definable close to singularities.

7. This seems to underlie Hallberg's criticisms of the Final Anthropic Principle as unsatisfactory in its anthropology and theology. The indefinite survival and expansion presents a technological route to salvation which

expresses the values of a vigorous youth, unable to face limitations and failures (Hallberg 1988). This criticism is directed against the first approach taken by Tipler (1988), in which life is the agent which brings about the Omega Point. Tipler's second approach, to be discussed in 4.3.3, seems less vulnerable, because of the more intricate relation between the future and the Omega Point, with the latter taking the shape of a *non-temporal* 'ultimate'. However, Tipler is still expressing the 'values of a vigorous youth', and denying the ultimacy of limitations and failures. Which is not unlike many theologies.

8. Tipler acknowledges that opacity and loss of coherence complicate the issue, but he maintains that sufficient information from the past remains ontologically present and available for analysis in times close to the Omega Point, or else that the Omega Point, the universal system at such moments still in time, is able to resurrect *by brute force* everything that could have existed, because of the increase in total information processing capacity in time:

> Thus the computer capacity will be there to preserve even drunken porters (and perfected drunken porters), provided only that the Omega Point waits long enough before resurrecting them. Even though the computer capacity required to simulate perfectly is exponentially related to the complexity of (the, W.B.D.) entity simulated, it is physically possible to resurrect an actual infinity of individuals between now and the Omega Point—even assuming the complexity of the average individual diverges as the Omega Point is approached—and guide them *all* into perfection. Total perfection of all would be achieved at the instant of the Omega Point. (Tipler 1989, 249)

Russell (1988c) emphasizes the loss of coherence as a serious problem of Tipler's theory as a scientific theory. What about absorption by walls and what about the interior of solids? The energy still comes out, but in a degraded form—say as infrared radiation. Does not the degradation pose problems for the reconstruction of the information? It seems to me that this is a valid objection. To develop another example: does light scattered by a wall provide information about the wall and the source? It seems that the information about the source is lost if the wall is rough. It might seem that a perfect mirror fares better: reception of an undistorted image provides information about the source (like the image) and the mirror (perfect, since the image was undistorted). However, even such a case is problematic: how do we find out about the quality of the mirror unless we have independent information which makes it possible to compare the original and the source, and hence to establish that the image is undistorted?

9. The identity of a simulation with the process itself appears to be somewhat more complicated in this case, because we have two levels together. There is life as it has been growing all along—and this life collects all the information and does construct the simulation. Hence, for those beings the simulations might seem different from real living beings like themselves. The 'real living beings' still have the power switch for the computer on which the simulation is done.

10. They need to make some changes in any case, because the resurrected beings will live in a different environment. Their program will run

on a different kind of substrate, instead of Carbon, Oxygen, and the stuff we use. Unless, as Tipler holds, we assume that the simulated resurrected beings will run on simulated carbon, simulated oxygen, and simulations of whatever other atoms are needed (private communication).

11. This is, slightly modified, an expression from Frank Tipler in a letter to Pannenberg, dated June 16, 1989.

12. Aside from the four reasons discussed in the text he has given, in a letter to Pannenberg, June 16, 1989, two closely related technical arguments: In regular quantum physics, the probability for a certain situation is set to 1 by integrating (summing) the probabilities at a certain instant for all places, ranging from minus infinity to plus infinity. This implies that the probabilities have to drop sufficiently fast to 0 towards plus and minus infinity. This is equivalent to a boundary condition at infinity, which states that no influence can come from infinity. The conservation of probability, which constrains the operator in the basic equation of quantum physics, implies that this 'no influence' condition holds for all times. In quantum cosmology the integration might range over the radius of the Universe, and hence from 0 to infinity instead of ranging from minus infinity to plus infinity. This implies that there might be unpredictable influences pouring in at 0 at the instant for which the normalization integral is calculated. This boundary might be a singularity.

Furthermore the corresponding condition for the operator, and hence the conservation of probability, are disputed in quantum cosmology. Thus, unpredictable influences might perhaps flow in from the singularity and from infinity.

13. Private communication; to be published in the revised edition of Tipler's 1989 article, now titled 'Physics Near the Final State: God and the Resurrection of the Dead to Eternal Life', in proceedings of the Second Pannenberg Symposium, 15–17 November 1988, at the Chicago Center for Religion and Science (Lutheran School of Theology, Chicago).

14. The infinity of extensions excluded is of a higher order than the infinity of points ( ); rather, it is equivalent to the infinity of the ways in which subsets of points can be picked out of the spacetime ( ).

15. The same feature makes the Omega Point theory a supreme example of the view that scientific theories aren't open to verification, but should be falsifiable. Imagine that it would be possible to calculate the complete description of the Universe on the basis of the Teilhard Boundary Condition and the other assumptions of the Omega Point theory. The 'empirical' question would be whether the Universe as observed agrees with the outcome of these calculations. Two conclusions follow: Against verification: there never will be sufficient information, from all points, until the end of times. But strongly falsifiable: every point has to fit the calculated wavefunction; the data at every point can, in principle, falsify the Omega Point theory, though, of course, it would still be open to discussion whether the Teilhard Boundary Condition would have been falsified, as opposed to the calculations, or the mathematics, or the quantum formalism used.

16. Questions about the flow of time have often been mixed up with issues of order, a linear order relation, and asymmetry between the past direction and the future direction. However: i. An order relation seems necessary, but is not sufficient—we do not perceive anything flowing along the line representing the real numbers; a present is necessary for the notion of a flow of time. ii. Time asymmetry is neither sufficient nor necessary. In an asymmetric process all moments qualify as potential presents. There is

no way to single out, on the basis of a time-asymmetric description, a present as our present. And even in purely symmetric reversible systems, say a frictionless pendulum or a planet orbiting a star, we still have the impression that there is a present position, which is immediately superseded by another 'present' position, and so forth.

Events in the past seem necessary and fixed in memories, while events in the future seem contingent. It has been attempted to use this modal difference to formulate a distinction between the past of the present moment and its future and hence an objective notion of 'the present'. However, this cannot "be reformulated into a physical discourse so as to allow a physically significant distinction between past, present and future" (Kroes 1985, 200). Reichenbach (1971 [1956]) appealed to quantum mechanics, where the present is the moment processes become determined. However, Grünbaum (1971) showed that every moment of time satisfies Reichenbach's definition.

17. It seems as if the more 'holistic' picture of theories about whole histories implies determinism—one can only sell complete films once they are complete. However, selling is an action in time, and hence leads to the other type of description. The timeless approach, without claiming to have the final perspective on our world at a certain moment of time, does not imply determinism. This can be explained with the notion of 'universe pictures'. A universe picture is, according to McCall (1976), a complete description of the history of a universe, including past, present, and future. Assuming that the past is fixed and the future is a set of possibilities, a universe picture at a certain moment is like a tree: one stem (fixed past) and many branches (future possibilities). The present of a universe picture is the point where the branching begins. McCall hopes to formulate an objective flow of time in terms of such trees, as later trees are subtrees of earlier trees. That, however, does not single out a unique tree as corresponding to the present (Kroes 1985, 203f). We can talk about the whole set of trees, hence possible universe pictures, without implying that the future is determined or even already should have happened, as is necessary for having the complete film. Having the 'last' tree of a series—which would consist of only a stem without branches—would mean that everything was fixed relative to the present defined by that tree, but then everything is in the past. Talking about systems in terms of such trees provides a language for talking about complete histories without implying determinism. Determinism is a feature of some physical theories which can be formulated in this 'complete history' way, like classical mechanics and general relativity. But that does not warrant the inverse argument, that such a timeless description is necessarily tied up with determinism.

18. The theory has been presented as a theory about individual states, three-dimensional geometries representing the world at a moment (Isham 1989). Hartle, Hawking's collaborator on this topic, has proposed to take spacetime as basic, and not just individual spaces (Hartle 1988a,b,c,; see below in 4.4.2).

19. Isham, in his contribution to a conference at the Vatican, made similar remarks, related both to the flow of time and the notion of complete histories. He sees phrases like 'evolution in time', 'beginning', and 'end' "as a psychological hangover from the peculiar human experience of time, not as positing any sense in which a point actually 'moves' along the path in S," the abstract space of possible states (Isham 1988).

20. Hartle (1988c) mentions as other proponents of such a view Wheeler (1988), Page and Wootters (1983), Wootters (1984, 1986), Banks (1985) and

Ashtekar, Barbour, and Smolin, Horowitz and Rovelli (contributions which will be published in the *Proceedings of the Osgood Hill Conference on the Conceptual Problems of Quantum Gravity, May 16–19, 1988*, ed. by J. Stachel). The way I interpret it, Hawking's cosmology too abandons time and spacetime in favor of a formalism which deals essentially only with spaces. For a similar, though more technical, discussion see Heller (1987).

21. Hartle defends, as fundamental methods for calculations of probabilities, path-integrals (Appendix 4) or sums-over-histories.

22. Penrose's twistor program, which has not been very successful so far, intends to describe both spacetime and particles in terms of the same more fundamental entities, twistors.

23. Barth seems to have defended a similar distinction between ordinary time and God's time when he understood Jesus as the lord of time and distinguished between an uncreated time which is one of the perfections of the divine being and created time, with its succession of past, present, and future (K. D. III/2, par. 47).

24. This criticism of natural theology has been put forward by the German theologian Eberhard Jüngel. For an introduction to this theme, see J. B. Webster, *Eberhard Jüngel: An Introduction to his Theology*, especially Chapter 10. Possibilities for transformation are, of course, a quite pervasive theme in theology, for instance Tracy 1975, 135f.

25. For another example from process theology one could consider John Cobb's *Process Theology as Political Theology*, especially the third part of Chapter 4.

26. Papers read at a recent 'science and religion' conference on determinism in relation to physics and biology have been published as *Free Will and Determinism* (Mortensen and Sorensen 1987).

5. METHOD IN RELATING THEOLOGY TO SCIENCE

1. Almost everybody would like to be critical and realistic; the terms have many uses. However, in this book the term is restricted to a specific approach to the relation between theology and science.

2. Peacocke and Soskice especially oppose the anti-realistic accounts represented on the British scene by Don Cupit and Dewi Z. Phillips.

I am indebted to discussions with R.J. Russell for my thinking on 'critical realism' (Russell 1986b). Similar questions concerning Peacocke's realism, and especially his use of a continuous linguistic community, have been raised by others (Murphy 1985b; Barbour 1986). My criticism of 'critical realism' concerns the intellectual justification of the position; certainly not the personal intentions and integrity of those that defend it. Ian Barbour and Arthur Peacocke, among others, have given major initiating and innovating contributions to the academic study of the relations between science and theology.

The interest in continuity is, perhaps, to be understood as a response to arguments against scientific realism based upon the history of science. If past theories have been succeeded and discarded, why should one trust the present theories as better representations of reality? Hence, to defend the position that terms in present theories refer to reality, we might argue that preceding theories have not been discarded but modified in a more continuous way, preserving reference while improving on the details of the depiction.

3. For a similar criticism, Gerhart and Russell 1984, 8.

4. The dependence of Peacocke's program on specific philosophical positions on critical realism and on hierarchical non-reductionism in epistemology in combination with a reductionistic ontology has also been pointed out as a weakness by Robert J. Russell (1986b).

5. (Gilkey 1987b). Gilkey speaks of "cosmologists", but that seems inadequate. Some of the authors he considers, like Dawkins, present a worldview in relation to other sciences, in his case, biology.

6. What Gilkey suggests seems similar to the need for a 'second naiveté' as formulated by Paul Ricoeur (1967, 355).

7. The example comes from Hanson (1958) who asks whether Brahe, whom Hanson takes to believe that the Sun circles the Earth, and Kepler, who held the Earth to orbit the Sun, saw the same thing. Hanson's conclusion is that they saw different things. Gerhart and Russell argue that they did see, at the level of direct experience, the same thing: the Sun rising. However, at a more reflective level they intepreted their experiences differently.

8. An excellent study on different responses to Darwinian biology among German theologians has been written by Jürgen Hübner (1966). The same categories could have been applied to the responses to cosmology as well; I only learned of Hübner's work after the completion of this study.

An Overview of Dutch Contributions

One liberal wing of Dutch Protestantism has emphasized the vastness of the Universe in relation to human proportions. One could briefly distinguish between two responses. Some, such as De Wilde and Smits, have argued for a non-geocentric and open-minded faith in which the Universe is our home. The vastness of the Universe reflects the grandeur of God: "heaven and earth, all planets of the immense cosmos, are full of God's glory" (De Wilde, 1955a, 60). Smits sees the process of becoming more fully human as a widening of horizons (Smits 1972, 82). Others within the liberal tradition, such as Van Holk and Hensen, have defended a less optimistic view. Hensen distinguishes between philosophies which see life as advance, crossing boundaries, and philosophies which see life as a walk on a tightrope. Upon this second view, humans are not at home in the cosmos, but thrown into a rough existence, into a world of brute factuality (Hensen 1955, 123–24). Humans are eccentric in a Universe which is indifferent to their presence. Religion might well be needed to save us from nihilism in a Universe in which we are not comfortably at home. We have to face the challenges of freedom and loneliness in a responsible way (Van Holk 1960, 101). The emphasis on God's absence or elusive presence (see 6.1.2) is not completely unrelated to this line in Dutch liberal theology; Hensen was actively involved as thesis advisor in the development of my position as presented here.

Some other Dutch contributions to theology and science have been marked by a significant influence from the Swiss theologian Karl Barth (1886–1968), and from the Dutch dialectical theologian K. H. Miskotte. This is especially true for the two volumes on faith and the natural sciences (De Jong and Dippel 1965, 1967). In his theological dissertation De Jong criticized Bultmann's understanding of reality, and Bultmann's separation of theology and science, each within its own domain, existence and physical reality. Dippel was a chemist, who received an honorary degree in theology. Typical is his emphasis on the distinction between 'unique information', religious knowledge, and 'public information', scientific knowledge. The theologian should positively affirm the methodological atheism of the sciences. Dialogue is neither a quest for support nor for an encompassing system. Rather, the encounter is primarily about the ethos of humans in a culture dominated by science and technology. Conceptual clarification is in the service of proper acting (Van Dijk 1985, 178 & 237 ff).

Dingemans's dissertation (1974) on causality and miracles is a hermeneutical inquiry into the meaning of faith if we take the sciences seriously. Nature is granted a relative independence from God. Dingemans uses a cybernetical model when he proposes to think of the world as a probabilistic self-regulating process. The configuration the process aims at can be approached analytically with the help of the sciences, but can also be considered programmatically, in relation to a view of the whole. "Gott hat die Welt geschaffen in der Form eines sich selbst entwickelden Prozesses, der von Anfang an einen Sollwert mitbekommen hat, um den die Entwicklung stattfinden kann. Dieser Sollwert ist die Berührungsebene von Glaube und Naturwissenschaft, weil man dem Sollwert sowohl 'programmatisch' von einer Gesamtschau aus näherkommen kann als auch 'analytisch' von den Naturwissenschaften her" (Dingemans 1974, 233). In more recent work Dingemans has found the process theology of John Cobb a scheme which is at least as fruitful as the cybernetics he used previously (Dingemans 1983).

Others influenced by process theology are Plomp and the Catholic Belgian authors Wildiers (1982, 1985, 1988) and Van der Veken (Fennema and Paul 1990). A more neo-thomistic Catholic approach is followed by Van Melsen (1977, 1983, 1989).

The Free University (Amsterdam) has been involved over the years in many disputes concerning evolution. More recent activities through their Center for the Interdisciplinary Study of Science, Society, and Religion (Bezinningscentrum) include a book against 'creationism' (Houtman et al 1986) and a symposium on cosmology (Hovenier et al 1987). A specific strand of philosophical thought within the orthodox reformed tradition has been developed by D. H. T. Vollenhoven and H. Dooyeweerd. The Dutch astronomer Spoelstra has written a study on cosmology from this perspective (Spoelstra 1984).

9. Torrance 1969; 1971; 1976; 1984 Chapter 8; 1985a; 1985b.

10. The use of 'kinds' was an explicit issue in a trial in Arkansas in December 1981 on a law which required equal consideration of 'evolution science' and 'creation science' in science classes in public schools. It was mentioned in the opinion written by Judge Overton in his ruling against the law. The identification of species (contemporary biology) with 'kinds' (Genesis 1) was among the weaknesses of the law according to the decision of the court (*Judgement by the Federal Court in the United States District Court Eastern District of Arkansas Western Division, No. LR C 81 322, d.d. January 5, 1982;* See Gilkey 1985, 282).

11. Another example of the anthropocentrism, even in the way Moltmann incorporates nature in the theological framework, is Moltmann's view of the task of Christianity. Christianity was understood by some in medieval Judaism to be a useful preparation of the peoples of the Earth for the coming messiah, a *praeparatio messianica*. Moltmann extends this idea; Christianity is also there for the preparation of nature for the messianic time to come, for the Kingdom (Moltmann 1985, 22f). He thus crosses easily the

boundary from socio-systems to eco-systems. It is a grand vision; too grand it seems. Besides, it neglects the differences between these types of systems.

Moltmann's expectations about the overcoming of death appear to be a similar extension from human desires to a vision for nature. He refers to finite creatures which do not die: stones and angels (Moltmann 1987a, 208; cf. 1985, 221). Mortality is understood as only a consequence of sexual reproduction. The vision of death as the relevant form of decay, which will be overcome, is transferred from the human realm (and the wider realm of living beings) to the whole of nature.

Manenschijn (1988, 159–167) positively relates his ecological ethics from a Christian perspective to Moltmann's theology. However he implicitly deviates significantly from Moltmann, precisely because Manenschijn strongly emphasizes the distinction (with consequences for ethical reflection) between sociosystems and ecosystems (101–07).

12. But Pannenberg too has instances of naive identification of biblical and scientific accounts, for instance when he points to the similarity between Genesis 1 and evolutionary theory in the order of appearance of different kinds of beings (Pannenberg 1988c).

13. "Die chronische Bedürftigkeit, die unendliche Angewiesenheit des Menschen setzt ein Gegenüber jenseits aller Welterfahrung voraus. Der Mensch *schafft* sich nicht erst unter dem Druck seines Antriebsüberschusses einen phantastischen Gegenstand seiner Sehnsucht und Ehrfurcht über alle in der Welt möglichen Dinge heraus, vielmehr setzt er in seiner unendlichen Angewiesenheit ein entsprechend unendliches, nicht endliches, jenseitiges Gegenüber immer schon voraus, mit jedem seiner Atemzüge, auch wenn er es nicht zu nennen weiss. . . . Für dieses Gegenüber, auf das der Mensch in seinem unendlichen Streben angewiesen ist, hat die Sprache den Ausdruck Gott." (Pannenberg 1962, 11). And his aim with his extensive book on anthropology: "Ihr get es darum, die von den anthropologischen Disziplinen beschriebenen Phänomene des Menschseins theologisch in Anspruch zu nehmen. Das geschieht, indem ihre säkulare Beschreibung als eine nur vorläufige Auffassung der Sachverhalte angenommen wird, die dadurch zu vertiefen ist, dass an den anthropologischen Befunden selbst eine weitere, theologisch relevante Dimension aufgewiesen wird" (Pannenberg 1983, 19).

14. Pannenberg was severely criticized for his neglect of genetics at a conference held at the Lutheran School of Theology in November 1988. Pannenberg seemed to take cultural anthropology as the relevant science for his anthropological thinking, while the general issue of life could be discussed in dialogue with recent thermodynamics. The geneticist Lindon Eaves argued at length for his science. In the concluding session, Pannenberg explicitly stated that he was planning to pay more attention to genetic aspects in anthropology.

15. Barrow and Tipler suggest simulating the Universe by a computer program. If the simulation is perfect, the program would be sufficient to explain what we, as subprograms of the Universe-program, experience. The 'real' Universe can be dismissed. However, even upon this view there is a reality external to human subprograms.

16. Harré distinguishes in his *Varieties of Realism* between three levels, the realm of common perception, that of possible objects of experience, and the realm beyond possible experience. 'Black holes', at least their external appearances, or Nemesis, a postulated companion star to our Sun, fit in the second realm, as did once the planet Pluto, the continent Australia, atoms,

genes, microbes and the like. The policy of realism implies that one assumes
these entities to exist, and hence searches for them, if one considers the
theory in which the terms arise to be a good theory. There is, of course,
something provisional and tentative about the assumption that they exist.
The policy itself is justified inductively, by past successes.

The third realm, beyond possible experience, is the most relevant to this
study. Harré takes together in this realm unobservable entities of the same
kind as observed entities, like galaxies receding at superluminal velocities,
and more abstract notions, like energy. Is there 'metaphysical anarchy' at
this level? Harré (1986, 243) argues that the conservation laws at this level
suggest the existence of 'substances' as referred to by the theory. Conservation laws themselves are rooted in certain formal properties of theories,
like symmetries (invariances under certain transformations). This approach
builds upon a modified metaphysical notion of substance. It would be somewhat circular to derive the metaphysics from the 'level 3' properties of reality.
It is rather a form of mutual support than a one-way process.

6.   GOD

1. There exists a diverse theological literature which refers to God's
absence or presence in one way or another, for example H. K. Miskotte's
Als de goden zwijgen (Amsterdam: Holland, 1956) or Samuel Terrien's *The
Elusive Presence: Toward a New Biblical Theology*. It is related to many fundamental and contemporary themes, ranging from suffering (of which what
happened in Auschwitz is a prime example) to secularization. This study
does not deal with this 'presence/absence' in its full intensity, but rather
gives it its own provisional and limited meaning in relation to the line of
thought developed here.

2. A hypothesis is in science a conjecture, held tentatively, which intends
to be explanatory with respect to phenomena. Such a hypothesis should be
accompanied by ideas about ways it could be falsified. The word 'hypothesis'
as used in the present study has a slightly different meaning, especially with
respect to falsification. It is a tentative proposal for ordering and integrating
experiences and ideas. Such a hypothesis is fruitful if it opens new perspectives.

Opting for a hypothesis requires consideration of the evidence in favor
of it. "One must also be concerned with evaluating the consequences of
accepting it as a true belief and acting on it in the event that it is correct
and *in the event that it is not*" (King-Farlow, Christensen 1971, 123). They
side with William James *(The Will to Believe)*. There is some similarity with
an argument of Pascal *(Pensées*, nr. 233). Pascal defends present belief in
God with a game-theoretical argument about present stake and future gain
or loss: if God exists you win posthumously infinitely; if God does not exist
you have only lost a finite stake. However, William James evaluates on the
basis of "a desire to live wisely and in harmony *now* with 'eternal things' as
they truly are" (King-Farlow, Christensen 1971, 124). That is the kind of
evaluation which fits the use of hypothesis in the context of this chapter.

3. That seems to characterize the strict logical approach in philosophy
of religion followed by Plantinga. For example, he argues in *God, Freedom,
and Evil* (1974b) for the logical compatibility of moral evil with God's goodness. He then reduces natural evil to moral evil by ascribing it to personal

powers, say fallen angels. Plantinga sets up a defense, an argument for the logical possibility, while explicitly acknowledging that the defender need not assert that this is true (Plantinga 1974a, 192). It is only a defense against the charge of inconsistency, not against implausibility. A Dutch representative of such an approach is Luco van den Brom (1982, 1984), who defends God's omnipresence by invoking at least two additional dimensions beyond the physical dimensions of space and time. Such approaches may easily neglect the plausibility of the proposal. They are therefore of rather limited value in a dialogue with science which goes beyond the strictly logical quest for compatibility.

4. Eduardo Rodrigues Da Cruz's dissertation on 'The Ambivalence of Science: a theological study informed by the thought of Paul Tillich and the Latin American Experience' deals with the ambivalence of science in a very intriguing way, though in a different context.

5. Not because the truth is often found in the middle, as Polkinghorne argues in favor of critical realism in the preface to his *One World* (1986). It has become the middle position in my description because I contrast it with different positions, one on each side.

6. If, as some physical theories do, reality is understood to be higher-dimensional, that does not change the nature of the position. God should at least have additional dimensions aside from those incorporated in physical theories.

7. I owe the play with these words no-where and now-here to R. Hensen, who brought to my notice their use by Jürgen Ebach in *Ursprung und Ziel: Erinnerte Zukunft und erhoffte Vergangenheit* (Neukirchener Verlag 1986, 152).

8. The is/ought distinction is discussed in almost any major textbook on ethics. It is, of course, not without its critics, but it seems nonetheless a reasonable assumption for my argument.

9. Sociobiology is the battlefield for such issues. Burhoe, the founder of *Zygon*, is one of the major theological thinkers on such issues (Burhoe 1981, and many articles in *Zygon*).

10. Pannenberg has asked questions about the notion of inertia (mass) precisely because it seems to make the continuity necessary, independent of God's conserving activities (Pannenberg 1981; 1988).

11. An interesting discussion of God and chance has been given by Bartholomew (1984).

12. The approach fits in with at least two of the major contributions to the World Council of Churches reflections. Process theologians like Charles Birch (two papers in WCC 1987a) and Jay McDaniel (two papers in WCC 1987a), are likely to introduce the emphasis on God's immanence. They are also 'critical realists' (McDaniel in WCC 1987a, 105f), as is Arthur Peacocke who participated in the drafting of the theological report (WCC 1987a). 'Critical realists' are likely to emphasize the reality of God's presence in the world, and hence the objective, though somewhat hidden, integrity of creation. However not everybody within the World Council of Churches seems happy with this emphasis, as has become explicit in a report on a combined meeting of two subunits of the WCC, Church and Society (which we considered so far) and Faith and Order. In one report there is an explicit warning against 'panentheism', the technical term which many process theologians prefer for their view. "Despite the extent to which it is used by some, as in the Church and Society documents for example, panentheism should not be accepted uncritically" (WCC 1988b, 55). Process theology is seen as "a 'mediation philosophy' which may displace more specifically Christian understanding of God's activity in creation" (WCC 1988b, 55).

BIBLIOGRAPHY

Adam, A.	1965.	*Lehrbuch der Dogmengeschichte.* Bd 1. Gütersloh: Mohn.
Adams, D.	1985.	*The Restaurant at the End of the Universe.* New York: Pocket Books. (Orig. 1980, New York: Crown Publishers.)
Albrecht, A., P. J. Steinhardt.	1982.	Cosmology for Grand Unified Theories with Radiatively Induced Symmetry Breaking. *Physical Review Letters* 48: 1220–23.
Alfvén, H. O.	1966.	*Worlds-Antiworlds: Antimatter in Cosmology.* San Francisco: Freeman.
	1977.	Cosmology: Myth or Science? In *Cosmology, History and Theology,* eds. W. Yourgrau, A. D. Breck. New York: Plenum Press.
Allen, F.	1958.	The Origin of the World—by Chance or Design? In *The Evidence of God in an Expanding Universe,* ed. J. C. Monsma. New York: Putnam's Sons.
Alpher, R. A.	1983.	Theology of the Big Bang. *Religious Humanism* 17:2–13.
Alpher, R. A., R. C. Herman.	1948.	Evolution of the Universe. *Nature* 162: 774.
Andersen, S., A. Peacocke, eds.	1987.	*Evolution and Creation: a European Perspective.* Aarhus: Aarhus University Press.
Anderson, B. W.	1987.	*Creation versus Chaos: The Reinterpretation of the Mythical Symbolism in the Bible.* Philadelphia: Fortress. (Orig. 1967, New York: Association Press; repr. with new foreword and postscript.)
Arp, H.	1987.	*Quasars, Redshifts and Controversies.* Berkeley: Interstellar Media.
Atkatz, D., H. R. Pagels.	1982.	Origin of the Universe as a Quantum Tunneling Event. *Physical Review* D 25: 2065–073.
Atkins, P. W.	1981.	*The Creation.* Oxford, San Francisco: Freeman.
Audouze, J., J. Tran Thanh Van, eds.	1982.	*The Birth of the Universe.* Gif sur Yvette: Ed. Frontières.
Bahcall, J. N.	1990.	The Solar-Neutrino Problem. *Scientific American* 262 (May): 26–33.
Banks, T.	1985.	TCP, Quantum gravity, the Cosmological Constant and All That . . . . *Nuclear Physics* B 249: 332–360.
Barbour, I. G.	1966.	*Issues in Science and Religion.* Englewood Cliffs, N. J.: Prentice-Hall.
	1968.	Science and Religion Today. In *Science and Religion: New Perspectives on the Dialogue,* ed. I. G. Barbour. London: SCM.
	1974.	*Myths, Models, and Paradigms.* New York: Harper and Row.
	1986.	Response: For Further Exploration. *Religion and Intellectual Life* 5 (Spring): 59–63.
	1988.	Ways of Relating Science and Theology. In *Physics, Philosophy, and Theology,* eds. R. J. Russell, W. R. Stoeger,

		G. V. Coyne. Vatican: Vatican Observatory (distr. by University of Notre Dame Press).
	1989.	Creation and Cosmology. In *Cosmos as Creation*, ed. T. Peters. Nashville: Abingdon.
	1990.	*Religion in an Age of Science*. San Francisco: Harper and Row.
Barnes, B.	1974.	*Scientific Knowledge and Sociological Theory*. London: Routledge & Kegan Paul.
Barrow, J. D.	1983a.	Anthropic Definitions. *Quarterly Journal of the Royal Astronomical Society* 24: 146–153.
	1983b.	Dimensionality. *Philosophical Transactions of the Royal Society of London* A 310: 337–346.
	1988.	*The World within the World*. Oxford: Clarendon Press.
	1988a.	The Inflationary Universe: Modern Developments. *Quarterly Journal of the Royal Astronomical Society* 29: 101–117.
	1989a.	What is the Principal Evidence for the Cosmological Principle? *Quarterly Journal of the Royal Astronomical Society* 30: 163–167.
	1989b.	The Mathematical Universe. *The World and I* (May) 306–311.
	1989c.	Patterns of Explanation in Cosmology. In *The Anthropic Principle*, ed. U. Curi. Cambridge: Cambridge University Press.
Barrow, J. D., F. J. Tipler.	1978.	Eternity is Unstable. *Nature* 276: 453–459.
	1986.	*The Anthropic Cosmological Principle*. Oxford: Clarendon Press.
	1988.	Action Principles in Nature. *Nature* 331: 31–34.
Barth, K.	1945.	*Die Kirchliche Dogmatik III/1. Die Lehre von der Schöpfung, erster Teil*. Zollikon-Zürich: Evangelischer Verlag.
	1948.	*Die Kirchliche Dogmatik III/2. Die Lehre von der Schöpfung, zweiter Teil*. Zollikon-Zürich: Evangelischer Verlag.
Bartholomew, D. J.	1984.	*God of Chance*. London: SCM.
Batten, A. H.	1984.	Astronomers and Creationism. *Journal of the Royal Astronomical Society of Canada* 78: 32–38.
Bell, J. S.	1981.	Quantum Mechanics for Cosmologists. In *Quantum Gravity 2*, eds. C. J. Isham, R. Penrose, D. W. Sciama. Oxford: Clarendon Press.
	1987.	Are There Quantum Jumps? In *Schrödinger: Centenary Celebration of a Polymath*, ed. C. W. Kilmister. Cambridge: Cambridge University Press. (Repr. in J. S. Bell, *Speakable and Unspeakable in Quantum Mechanics*. Cambridge: Cambridge University Press, 1987.)
Benatti, F., G. C. Ghirardi, A. Rimini, T. Weber.	1987.	Quantum Mechanics with Spontaneous Localization and the Quantum Theory of Measurement. *Il Nuovo Cimento* B 100: 27–41.
Berman, M.	1981.	*The Re-enchantment of the World*. Ithaca: Cornell University Press.
Berry, R. W.	1983.	The Beginning. In *Is God a Creationist?*, ed. R. M. Frye. New York: Scribner's Sons. (Also in *Theology Today* 39: 249–259.)
Bertola, F., J. W. Sulentic, B. F. Madore.	1988.	*New Ideas in Astronomy: Proceedings of a Conference Held in Honor of the 60th Birthday of Halton C. Arp, Venice Italy May 5–7 1987*. Cambridge: Cambridge University Press.

Birch, C., J. B. Cobb, Jr.	1981.	*The Liberation of Life*. Cambridge: Cambridge University Press.
Birtel, F. T., ed.	1987.	*Religion, Science, and Public Policy*. New York: Crossroad.
Blau, S. K., A. Guth.	1987.	Inflationary Cosmology. In *Three Hundred Years of Gravitation*, eds. S. W. Hawking, W. Israel. Cambridge: Cambridge University Press.
Bloor, D.	1976.	*Knowledge and Social Imagery*. London: Routledge & Kegan Paul.
Bludman, S. A.	1984.	Thermodynamics and the End of a Closed Universe. *Nature* 308: 319–322.
Bondi, H., T. Gold.	1948.	The Steady-State Theory of the Expanding Universe. *Mon. Not. Roy. Astr. Soc.* 108:252–270.
Boslaugh, J.	1985.	*Stephen Hawking's Universe*. New York: Quill/William Morrow.
Bosshard, S. N.	1985.	*Erschafft die Welt sich selbst?* (Quaestiones Disputatae 103) Freiburg: Herder.
Bouhuijs, K., K. A. Deurloo.	1967.	*Dichter bij Genesis*. Baarn: Ten Have.
Braaten, C. E.	1972.	*Christ and Counter-Christ*. Philadelphia: Fortress.
	1974.	*Eschatology and Ethics*. Minneapolis: Augsburg.
Braaten, C.E., P. Clayton, eds.	1988.	*The Theology of Wolfhart Pannenberg*. Minneapolis: Augsburg Publishing House.
Brauer, O. L.	1958.	The Most Vital Question Confronting Us. In *The Evidence of God in an Expanding Universe*, ed. J. C. Monsma. New York: Putnam's Sons.
Breuer, R.	1981.	*Das anthropische Prinzip*. München: Meyster. (Reprinted in 1984, Frankfurt am M., etc.: Ullstein.)
Brom, L. J. van den	1982.	*God Alomtegenwoordig*. Kampen: Kok.
	1984.	God's Omnipresent Agency. *Religious Studies* 20: 637–655.
Brongers, H. A.	1945.	*De scheppingstradities bij de profeten*. Amsterdam: H. J. Paris.
Brout, R., F. Englert, E. Gunzig.	1978.	The Creation of the Universe as a Quantum Phenomenon. *Annals of Physics* 115: 78–106.
Brout, R., F. Englert, P. Spindel.	1979.	Cosmological Origins of the Grand Unification Mass Scale. *Physical Review Letters* 43: 417–420.
Brout, R., et al.	1980.	Cosmogenesis and the Origin of the Fundamental Length Scale. *Nuclear Physics* B 170: 228–264.
Brown, D.	1987.	*Continental Philosophy and Modern Theology*. Oxford: Basil Blackwell.
Brugger, H. R.	1982.	Die Geschichte der Schöpfung: Ist die Erde ein junger Planet? *Reformatio* 31 (March): 160–175.
Brush, S. G.	1978.	*The Temperature of History*. New York: Franklin.
Bultmann, R.	1958.	*Jesus Christ and Mythology*. New York: Scribner's Sons.
Burhoe, R. W.	1981.	*Towards a Scientific Theology*. Belfast: Christian Journals Limited.
Cameron, N. M. de S.	1983.	*Evolution and the Authority of the Bible*. Exeter: Paternoster Press.
Capra, F.	1982.	*The Turning Point*. New York: Simon and Schuster.
	1984.	*The Tao of Physics*. New York: Bantam Books. (Orig. 1976.)
Carr, B. J.	1982.	On the Origin, Evolution, and Purpose of the Physical Universe. *The Irish Astronomical Journal* 15 (3, March): 237–253.

Carr, B. J.,   1979.   The Anthropic Principle and the Structure of the Phys-
  M. J. Rees.   ical World. *Nature* 278 (12 April): 605–612.
Carter, B.   1974.   Large Number Coincidences and the Anthropic Prin-
                               ciple in Cosmology. In *Confrontation of Cosmological The-
                               ory with Observational Data*, ed. M. S. Longair. Dordrecht:
                               Reidel.
Carvin, W. P.   1983.   Creation and Scientific Explanation. *Scottish Journal of
                               Theology* 36: 289–307.
                      1988.   *Creation and Scientific Explanation*. Edinburgh: Scottish
                               Academic Press.
Cassuto, U.   1961.   *A Commentary on the Book of Genesis, Part 1*. Jerusalem:
                               Magnes Press, Hebrew University.
Clark, R. E. D.   1982.   *God Beyond Nature*. 2d. ed. Exeter: Paternoster Press.
                               (1st. Ed. 1978).
Clarke, C. J. S.   1974.   Quantum Theory and Cosmology. *Philosophy of Science*
                               41:317–332.
Clarke, W. N.   1988.   Is a Natural Theology Still Possible Today? In *Physics,
                               Philosophy, and Theology*, eds. R. J. Russell, W. R. Stoeger,
                               G. V. Coyne. Vatican: Vatican Observatory. (Distr. by
                               University of Notre Dame Press.)
Clayton, P.   1988.   Anticipation and Theological Method. In *The Theology
                               of Wolfhart Pannenberg*, eds. C. E. Braaten and P. Clay-
                               ton. Minneapolis: Augsburg Publishing House.
Clifford, R. J.   1988.   Creation in the Hebrew Bible. In *Physics, Philosophy, and
                               Theology*, eds. R. J. Russell, W. R. Stoeger, G. V. Coyne.
                               Vatican: Vatican Observatory. (Distr. by University of
                               Notre Dame Press.)
Close, F.   1988.   *End: Cosmic Catastrophe and the Fate of the Universe*. Lon-
                               don: Simon and Schuster.
Cobb, J. B.   1969.   *God and the World*. Philadelphia: Westminster.
                      1972.   What is the Future? In *Hope and the Future of Man*, ed.
                               E. H. Cousins. Philadelphia: Fortress.
                      1982.   *Process Theology as Political Theology*. Manchester:
                               Manchester University Press & Philadelphia: West-
                               minster Press.
                      1988.   Pannenberg and Process Theology. In *The Theology of
                               Wolfhart Pannenberg*, eds. C. E. Braaten, P. Clayton.
                               Minneapolis: Augsburg.
Cobb, J. B.,   1976.   *Process Theology: An Introductory Exposition*. Philadelphia:
  D. R. Griffin.   Westminster Press.
Coleman, S.,   1980.   Gravitational Effects on and of Vacuum Decay. *Physical
  F. de Luccia.   Review* D 21: 3305–315.
Cook, A. H.   1987.   Experiments on Gravitation. In *Three Hundred Years of
                               Gravitation*, eds. S. W. Hawking, W. Israel. Cambridge:
                               Cambridge University Press.
Craig, W. L.   1979.   *The Kalām Cosmological Argument*. London: Macmillan.
Crick, F.   1981.   *Life Itself*. New York: Simon and Schuster.
Da Cruz, E. R.   1987.   *The Ambivalence of Science: A Theological Study Informed
                               by the Thought of Paul Tillich and the Latin American Ex-
                               perience*. Doctoral dissertation defended at the Lutheran
                               School of Theology at Chicago.
Däppen, W.,   1986.   Weakly Interacting Massive Particles, Solar Neutrinos,
  R. Gilliland,   and Solar Oscillations. *Nature* 321: 229–231.
  J. Christensen-
  Dalsgaard.
Davies, P. C. W.   1973.   The Thermal Future of the Universe. *Monthly Notices
                               of the Royal Astronomical Society* 161: 1–5.
                      1974.   *The Physics of Time Asymmetry*. London: Surrey Univer-
                               sity Press; Berkeley and Los Angeles: University of
                               Calif. Press.

	1978.	*The Runaway Universe*. London: Dent.
	1981.	*The Edge of Infinity*. London: Dent; New York: Simon and Schuster.
	1982.	*The Accidental Universe*. Cambridge: Cambridge University Press.
	1983a.	*God and the New Physics*. London: Dent.
	1983b.	God and the New Physics. *The New Scientist* 98 (1363, June 23): 872–73.
	1984.	*Superforce: The Search for a Grand Unified Theory of Nature*. New York: Simon and Schuster.
	1988.	*The Cosmic Blueprint*. New York: Simon and Schuster.
Demaret, J., C. Barbier.	1981.	Le principe anthropique en cosmologie. *Revue des Questions Scientifiques* 152:181–222, 461–509.
Deprit, A.	1984.	Monsignor Georges Lemaître. In *The Big Bang and George Lemaître*, ed. A. Berger. Dordrecht: Reidel.
Deutsch, D.	1986.	Three Connections Between Everett's Interpretation and Experiment. In *Quantum Concepts in Space and Time*, eds. R. Penrose, C. J. Isham. Oxford: Clarendon Press.
DeWitt, B. S.	1967a.	Quantum Theory of Gravity: I. The canonical theory. *Physical Review* 160: 1113–148.
	1967b.	Quantum theory of Gravity: II. The manifestly Covariant Theory. *Physical Review* 162: 1195–1239.
DeWitt, B. S. N. Graham, eds.	1973.	*The Many-Worlds Interpretation of Quantum Mechanics. A Fundamental Exposition by Hugh Everett III with papers by J. A. Wheeler, B. S. DeWitt, L. N. Cooper and D. Van Vechten, and N. Graham*. Princeton: Princeton University Press.
DeYoung, D. B., J. C. Whitcomb.	1980.	The Origin of the Universe. *Grace Theological Journal* (Winona Lake, Ind.) 1: 149–161.
Dicke, R. H.	1961.	Dirac's Cosmology and Mach's Principle. *Nature* 192: 440–41.
Dicke, R. H., P. J. E. Peebles.	1979.	The Big Bang Cosmology—Enigmas and Nostrums. In *General Relativity: an Einstein Centenary Review*, eds. S. W. Hawking, W. Israel. Cambridge University Press.
Dicus, D. A., J. R. Letaw, D. C. Teplitz, V. L. Teplitz.	1982.	Effects of Proton Decay on the Cosmological Future. *Astrophysical Journal* 252: 1–9.
	1983.	The Future of the Universe. *Scientific American* 248 (3): 74–85.
Dijk, P. van.	1985.	*Op de grens van twee werelden: een onderzoek naar het ethische denken van de natuurwetenschapper C. J. Dippel*. 's-Gravenhage: Boekencentrum.
	1986.	Eine neue Runde im Gespräch zwischen Naturwiisenschaft und Theologie. *Zeitschrift für dialektische Theologie* 2: 149–162 & 283–308.
	1987.	Eine neue Runde im Gespräch zwischen Naturwiisenschaft und Theologie III. *Zeitschrift für dialektische Theologie* 3: 17–28.
Dingemans, G. D. J.	1974.	*Wetmatigheid en wonder*. 's-Gravenhage: Boekencentrum.
	1983.	Schepping in eschatologisch perspectief. *Kerk en Theologie* 34: 293–309.
Dippel, C. J., J. M. de Jong	1965.	*Geloof en natuurwetenschap I: scheppingsgeloof, natuur, en natuurwetenschap*. 's-Gravenhage: Boekencentrum.
Dippel, C. J., H. C. van de Hulst, J. M. de Jong, *et al.*	1967.	*Geloof en natuurwetenschap II: wijsgerige en ethische aspecten der natuurwetenschappen*. 's-Gravenhage: Boekencentrum.
Ditfurth, H. von	1984.	*Wir sind nicht nur von dieser Welt: Naturwissenschaft, Religion und die Zukunft des Menschen*. München: Deutsche

Taschenbuch Verlag. (Orig. 1981, Hamburg: Hoffmann und Campe Verlag.)

Drees, W. B.   1987.   The Interpretation of 'the Wave Function of the Universe.' *International Journal of Theoretical Physics* 26: 939–942.

1988.   Beyond the Limitations of Big Bang theory: Cosmology and Theological Reflection. *CTNS Bulletin* (Berkeley) 8 (1, Winter): 1–15.

1990.   Theology and Cosmology Beyond the Big Bang theory. In *Science and Religion: One World–Changing Perspectives*, eds. J. Fennema, I. Paul. Dordrecht: Kluwer Academic Publishers.

Duff, M. J.,   1982.   *Quantum Structure of Space and Time*. Cambridge: Cambridge University Press.
C. J. Isham,
eds.

Duhem, P.   1954.   *The Aim and Structure of Physical Theory*. Princeton, N. J.: Princeton University Press. (partly in Harding, ed., 1976.; transl. from *La theorie physique: son objet, sa structure*. Paris, 1906.)

Dyson, F. J.   1979a.   *Disturbing the Universe*. New York: Harper and Row.
1979b.   Time Without End: physics and biology in an open universe. *Reviews of Modern Physics* 51: 447–460.

1982.   Comment on the Topic of 'Beyond the Black Hole'. In *Some Strangeness in the Proportion: a Centennial Symposium to Celebrate the Achievements of Albert Einstein*, ed. H. Woolf. Reading, Mass.: Addison-Wesley.

1988.   *Infinite in All Directions*. New York: Harper and Row.

Earman, J.   1986.   *A Primer on Determinism*. Dordrecht: Reidel.

Eaves, L.   1989.   Spirit, Method, and Content in Science and Religion: the Theological Perspective of a Geneticist. *Zygon* 24: 185–215.

Eccles, J. C.   1979.   *The Human Mystery*. New York: Springer.

Einstein, A.   1917.   Kosmologische Betrachtungen zur allgmeinen Relativitätstheorie. *Sitzungsberichte der königl. Preuss. Akad. Wiss.* 142–152.

Ellis, G. F. R.   1984.   Alternatives to the Big Bang. *Annual Reviews in Astronomy and Astrophysics* 22: 157–184.

Evans, D. D.   1963.   *The Logic of Self-Involvement*. London: SCM.

Everett, H.   1957.   'Relative state' Formulation of Quantum Mechanics. *Reviews of Modern Physics* 29: 454–465.

Farhi, E.,   1987.   An Obstacle to Creating a Universe in the Laboratory. *Physics Letters* B 183: 149–155.
A. H. Guth.

Faulkner, J.,   1985.   Weakly Interacting, Massive Particles and the Solar Neutrino Flux. *Astrophysical Journal* 299: 994–1000.
R. L. Gilliland.

Faulkner, J.,   1986.   Weakly Interacting Particles and Solar Oscillations. *Nature* 321: 226–29.
D. O. Gough,
M. N. Vahia.

Fennema, J.,   1990.   *Science and Religion: One World–Changing Perspectives*, Dordrecht: Kluwer Academic Publishers.
I. Paul, eds.

Feinberg, G.   1981.   The Coldest Neutron Star. *Physical Review* D 23: 3075.

Feinberg, G.,   1980.   *Life Beyond Earth*. New York: Morrow.
R. Shapiro.

Field, G. B.,   1973.   *The Redshift Controversy*. Reading, Mass.: Benjamin.
H. Arp,
J. N. Bahcall.

Ford, A.   1986.   *Universe: God, Man and Science*. London: Hodder and Stoughton.

Ford, L.   1988.   The Nature of the Power of the Future. In *The Theology of Wolfhart Pannenberg,* eds. C. E. Braaten, P. Clayton. Minneapolis: Augsburg.

Fowles, J.   1980.   *The Aristos.* (Rev. ed.). Falmouth (Cornwall): Triad/Granada.

Frankena, W. K.   1963.   *Ethics.* Englewood Cliffs, N. J.: Prentice-Hall.

Frautschi, S.   1982.   Entropy in an Expanding Universe. *Science* 217: 593–599.

Frye, R. M., ed.   1983.   *Is God a Creationist?* New York: Scribner's Sons.

Gal-Or, B.   1981.   *Cosmology, Physics, and Philosophy.* New York: Springer Verlag.

Gale, G.   1981.   The Anthropic Principle. *Scientific American* 245 (6):114–122.

Gardner, M.   1986.   WAP, SAP, PAP & FAP. *The New York Review* 33 (May 8): 22–25.

Gerhart, M.,   1984.   *Metaphoric Process: The Creation of Scientific and Religious Understanding.* Fort Worth: Texas Christian Univ. Press.
A. Russell.
                    1987.   A Generalized Conception of Text Applied to Both Scientific and Religious Objects. *Zygon* 22: 299–316.

Geroch, R.   1984.   The Everett Interpretation. *Noûs* 18: 617–633.

Ghirardi, G. C.,   1988.   Spontaneous Localization of a System of Identical Particles. *Il Nuovo Cimento* B 102: 383–396.
et al.

Ghirardi, G. C.,   1986.   Unified Dynamics for Microscopic and Macroscopic Systems. *Physical Review D* 34: 470–491.
A. Rimini,
T. Weber.   1987.   Disentanglement of Quantum Wave Functions: Answer to 'Comment on "Unified dynamics for Microscopic and Macroscopic systems"'. *Physical Review D* 36: 3287–89.

Gibbons, G. W.,   1983.   *The Very Early Universe.* Cambridge: Cambridge University Press.
S. W. Hawking,
S. T. C. Siklos,
eds.

Gibbons, G. W.,   1987.   A Natural Measure on the Set of All Universes. *Nuclear Physics* B 281: 736–751.
S. W. Hawking,
J. M. Stewart.

Gilkey, L.   1959.   *Maker of Heaven and Earth: The Christian Doctrine of Creation in the Light of Modern Knowledge.* Garden City, N. Y. : Doubleday. (Repr. 1985, Lanham: University Press of America.)
                    1969.   *Naming the Whirlwind: The Renewal of God-Language.* Indianapolis: Bobbs-Merrill.
                    1970.   *Religion and the Scientific Future.* London: SCM.
                    1976.   *Reaping the Whirlwind: A Christian Interpretation of History.* New York: Seabury Press.
                    1979.   *Message and Existence.* San Francisco: Harper and Row.
                    1985.   *Creationism on Trial: Evolution and God at Little Rock.* San Francisco: Harper and Row.
                    1987.   Is Religious Faith Possible in an Age of Science? In *Religion, Science, and Public Policy,* ed. F. T. Birtel. New York: Crossroad.
                    1987b.   Whatever Happened to Immanuel Kant? A Study of Selected Cosmologies. In *The Church and Contemporary Cosmology,* eds. J.B. Miller and K.E. McCall. Pittsburgh: Carnegie-Mellon University.

Gingerich, O.   1983.   Let There Be Light: Modern Cosmogony and Biblical Creation. In *Is God a Creationist?,* ed. R. M. Frye. New York: Scribner's Sons.

Gish, D. T.   1982.   It is Either 'In the Beginning, God'—or '. . . Hydrogen'. *Christianity Today* (Caroll Stream, Illinois) 26 (Oct. 8): 28–33.

	1985.	A Consistent Biblical and Scientific View of Origins. In *Creation and Evolution*, ed. D. Burke. Leicester: Inter-Varsity Press.
Gleick, J.	1987.	*Chaos: Making a New Science.* New York: Viking Penguin.
Godart, O., M. Heller.	1985.	*Cosmology of Lemaître.* Tucson: Pachart Publishing House.
Gödel, K.	1949.	A Remark about the Relationship between Relativity Theory and Idealistic Philosophy. In *Albert Einstein: Philosopher-Scientist.* (Library of Living philosophers, vol. 7), ed. P. A. Schilpp. La Salle, Illinois: Open Court.
Gott, J. R.	1982.	Creation of Open Universes from De Sitter Space. *Nature* 295: 304–07.
	1986.	The Very Early Universe. In *Creation and the End of Days*, eds. D. Novak, N. Samuelson. Lanham: University Press of America.
Gott, J. R., J. E. Gunn, D. N. Schramm, B. M. Tinsley.	1976.	Will the Universe Expand For Ever? *Scientific American* 234 (3): 62–79.
Green, L.	1985.	God and the Big Bang. *Journal of the Royal Astronomical Society of Canada* 79: 160–66.
Green, M. B.	1986.	Superstrings. *Scientific American* 252(3):46–56.
Gribbin, J.	1982.	*Genesis.* Oxford: Oxford University Press.
	1986.	*In Search of the Big Bang.* New York: Bantam Books.
	1988.	*The Omega Point.* Toronto: Bantam Books.
Gribbin, J., M. Rees.	1989.	*Cosmic Coincidences: Dark Matter, Mankind, and Anthropic Cosmology.* New York: Bantam Books.
Griffin, D. R., ed.	1986.	*Physics and the Ultimate Significance of Time.* Albany: SUNY Press.
Grishchuk, L. P., Ya. B. Zel'dovich.	1982.	Complete Cosmological Theories. In *Quantum Structure of Space and Time*, eds. M. J. Duff, C. J. Isham. Cambridge: Cambridge University Press.
Grünbaum, A.	1971.	The Meaning of Time. In *Basic Issues in the Philosophy of Time*, eds. E. Freeman, W. Sellars. La Salle: Open Court.
Guth, A. H.	1981.	Inflationary Universe: A Possible Solution to the Horizon and Flatness Problems. *Physical Review* D 23: 347–356.
	1982.	10^{-35} Seconds after the Big Bang. In *The Birth of the Universe*, eds. J. Audouze, J. Tran Thanh Van. Gif sur Yvette: Ed. Frontières.
	1983.	Phase Transitions in the Very Early Universe. In *The Very Early Universe*, eds. G. W. Gibbons, S. W. Hawking, S. T. C. Siklos. Cambridge: Cambridge University Press.
Guth, A. H., P. J. Steinhardt.	1984.	The Inflationary Universe. *Scientific American* 250 (5):116–128.
Guth, A. H., M. Sher.	1983.	The Impossibility of a Bouncing Universe. *Nature* 302:505–06.
Hacking, I.	1983.	*Representing and Intervening*, Cambridge: Cambridge University Press.
	1987a.	Coincidences: Mundane and Cosmological. In *Origin and Evolution of the Universe: Evidence for Design?* ed. J. M. Robson. Kingston and Montreal: McGill-Queen's University Press.
	1987b.	The Inverse Gambler's Fallacy: The Argument from Design. The anthropic principle applied to Wheeler universes. *Mind* 96: 331–340.
Hall, D. J.	1987.	The Integrity of Creation: Biblical and Theological

		Background of the term. In *Reintegrating God's Creation.* Geneva: World Council of Churches.
Hallberg, F. W.	1988.	Barrow and Tipler's Anthropic Cosmological Principle. *Zygon* 23: 139–157.
Hanson, N. R.	1958.	*Patterns of Discovery.* Cambridge: Cambridge University Press.
Harding, S. G., ed.	1976.	*Can Theories be Refuted? Essays on the Duhem-Quine Thesis.* Dordrecht: Reidel.
Harré, R.	1986.	*Varieties of Realism.* Oxford: Basil Blackwell.
Harrison, E.	1985.	*Masks of the Universe.* New York: Macmillan.
	1987.	*Darkness at Night.* Cambridge, Mass.: Harvard University Press.
Hartle, J. B.	1988a.	Quantum Kinematics of Spacetime. I. Nonrelativistic theory. *Physical Review* D 37: 2818–832.
	1988b.	Quantum Kinematics of Spacetime. II. A Model Quantum Cosmology with Real Clocks. *Physical Review* D 38: 2985–999.
	1988c.	Time and Prediction in Quantum Cosmology. Talk delivered at the Osgood Hill Conference on Conceptual Problems in Quantum Gravity May 16–19 1988 (proceedings to be published, ed. J. Stachel) and the 5th Marcel Grossman Conference, Perth, Australia, August 8–12 1988. Preprint UCSBTH-88-03.
Hartle, J. B., S. W. Hawking.	1983.	Wave Function of the Universe. *Physical Review* D 28:2960–975.
Hartshorne, Ch.	1948.	*The Divine Relativity.* New Haven and London: Yale University Press.
	1967.	*A Natural Theology for Our Time.* La Salle, Illinois: Open Court.
Harvey, V. A.	1964.	*A Handbook of Theological Terms.* New York: Collier Books, Macmillan.
Hawking, S. W.	1978.	Spacetime Foam. *Nuclear Physics* B 144:349–362.
	1979.	The Path-Integral Approach to Quantum Gravity. In *General Relativity: An Einstein Centenary Survey,* eds. S. W. Hawking, W. Israel. Cambridge: Cambridge University Press.
	1980.	*Is the End in Sight for Theoretical Physics?* Cambridge: Cambridge University Press. (Repr. in J. Boslaugh, *Stephen Hawking's Universe.* New York: Quill/William Morrow, 1985.)
	1982.	The Boundary Conditions of the Universe. In *Astrophysical Cosmology: Proceedings of the Study Week on Cosmology and Fundamental Physics,* eds. H. A. Brück, G. V. Coyne, M. S. Longair. Vatican: Pontifica Academia Scientiarum.
	1984a.	Quantum Cosmology. In *Relativity, Groups and Topology II,* eds. B. S. DeWitt, R. Stora. Amsterdam: North Holland Physics Publishing.
	1984b.	The Quantum State of the Universe. *Nuclear Physics* B 239: 257–276.
	1984c.	The Edge of Spacetime. *New Scientist* 103 (16 August): 10–14.
	1984d.	The Edge of Spacetime. *American Scientist* 72: 355–59.
	1985.	Arrow of Time in Cosmology. *Physical Review* D 32: 2489–495.
	1987.	Quantum Cosmology. In *Three Hundred Years of Gravitation,* eds. S. W. Hawking, W. Israel. Cambridge: Cambridge University Press.
	1988.	*A Brief History of Time.* New York: Bantam Books.

Hawking, S. W., 1979. *General Relativity: An Einstein Centenary Survey.* Cam-
W. Israel, eds.   bridge: Cambridge University Press.
               1987. *Three Hundred Years of Gravitation.* Cambridge: Cam-
                      bridge University Press.
Hawking, S. W., 1986. Operator Ordering and the Flatness of the Universe.
D. N. Page.   *Nuclear Physics* B 264: 185–196.
Hawking, S. W., 1970. The Singularities of Gravitational Collapse and Cos-
R. Penrose.   mology. *Proceedings of the Royal Society of London* A 314:
                      529–548.
Haynes, R. H.   1987. The 'Purpose' of Chance in Light of the Physical Basis
                      of Evolution. In *Origin and Evolution of the Universe:
                      Evidence for Design?*, ed. J. M. Robson. Kingston and
                      Montreal: McGill-Queen's University Press.
Healey, R. A.   1984. How Many Worlds? *Noûs* 18: 591–616.
Hefner, P. J.   1970. The Relocation of the God-Question. *Zygon* 5: 5–17.
               1984a. The Creation. In *Christian Dogmatics, Vol. 1*, eds. C. E.
                      Braaten, R. W. Jenson. Philadelphia: Fortress.
               1984b. Creation: Viewed by Science, Affirmed by Faith. In *Cry
                      of the Environment*, eds. P. N. Joranson, K. Butigan.
                      Santa Fe, New Mexico: Bear and Co.
               1984c. God and Chaos: the Demiurge versus the *Ungrund.*
                      Zygon 19: 469–486.
               1988. Theology's Truth and Scientific Formulation. *Zygon* 23:
                      263–279.
Heidel, A.   1942. *The Babylonian Genesis.* Chicago. (2d. Edition 1951).
Heller, M.   1986a. *Questions to the Universe: Ten Lectures on the Foundations
                      of Physics and Cosmology.* Tucson: Pachart Publishing
                      House.
               1986b. *The Word and the World.* Tucson: Pachart Publishing
                      House.
               1986c. On the Cosmological Problem. *Acta Cosmologica* 14:
                      57–72.
               1987. Big Bang on Ultimate Questions. In *Origin and Early
                      History of the Universe: Proceedings of the 26th Liège Inter-
                      national Astrophysics Colloquium, July 1–4 1986.* Cointe-
                      Ougree (Belgique).
               1988a. Scientific Rationality and Christian Logos. In *Physics,
                      Philosophy, and Theology*, eds. R. J. Russell, W. R. Stoeger,
                      and G. V. Coyne. Vatican: Vatican Observatory (distr.
                      by University of Notre Dame Press.)
               1988b. Experience of Limits: New Physics and New Theology.
                      Paper presented at the Second European Conference
                      on Science and Religion, March 10–13 1988, Enschede,
                      Netherlands.
Hendry, G. S.   1980. *Theology of Nature.* Philadelphia: Westminster Press.
Hensen, R.   1953. Theologie en wijsbegeerte. In *Uitzichten: vrijzinnig prot-
                      estantse bijdragen*, by H. Faber, J. de Graaf, H. J. Heering,
                      et al. Delft: Gaade.
               1955. Opmars, grens, en koorddans. In *Leven op aarde*, ed. R.
                      Hensen. Delft: Gaade.
               1967. *Paul Tillich.* Baarn: Het Wereldvenster.
Hesse, M.   1970. Duhem, Quine, and a New Empiricism. In *Knowledge
                      and Necessity*, ed. G. Vesey. Harvester: Hassocks. (Repr.
                      in Harding, ed., 1976.)
               1975. Criteria of Truth in Science and Theology. *Religious
                      Studies* 11: 385–400. (Repr. in Hesse 1980).
               1980. *Revolutions and Reconstructions in the Philosophy of Science.*
                      Brighton (Sussex): Harvester Press.
               1981. Retrospect. In *The Sciences and Theology in the Twentieth*

Century, ed. A. R. Peacocke. Notre Dame: University of Notre Dame Press.

1983. Cosmology as Myth. *Concilium* 1983 (6):49–54 (also as *Cosmology and Theology*, eds. D. Tracy, N. Lash. Edinburgh: Clark, New York: Seabury Press).

1988. Physics, Philosophy, and Myth. In *Physics, Philosophy, and Theology*, eds. R. J. Russell, W. R. Stoeger, and G. V. Coyne. Vatican: Vatican Observatory (distr. by University of Notre Dame Press.)

Heyward, I. Carter. 1982. *The Redemption of God*. Lanham: University Press of America.

Hick, J. 1966. *Evil and the God of Love*. London: Macmillan. (Rev. ed. 1977, San Francisco: Harper & Row.)

1968. *Christianity at the Centre*. London: Macmillan.

1989. *An Interpretation of Religion*. Houndmills & London: Macmillan.

Hiebert, E. 1966. The Uses and Abuses of Thermodynamics in Religion. *Daedalus* 95: 1046–080.

1967. Thermodynamics and Religion a Historical Appraisal. In *Science and Contemporary Society*, ed. F. J. Crosson. Notre Dame: University of Notre Dame Press.

Hilhorst, M. T. 1987. *Verantwoordelijk voor toekomstige generaties?* Kampen: Kok.

Holk, L. J. 1960. *De rebellerende mens*. 's-Gravenhage: Boucher.

Hooykaas, R. 1972. *Religion and the Rise of Modern Science*. Edinburgh: Scottish Academic Press.

Houtman, C. J., et al. 1986. *Schepping of evolutie: het creationisme een alternatief?* Kampen: Kok.

Hovenier, J. W., et al. 1987. *De plaats van aarde en mens in het heelal*. Kampen: Kok.

Hoyle, F. 1948. A New Model for the Expanding Universe. *Monthly Notices of the Royal Astronomical Society* 108:372-382.

1980. *Steady-State Cosmology Re-visited*. Cardiff: University College Cardiff Press.

1982. *Facts and Dogmas in Cosmology and Elsewhere*. Cambridge: Cambridge University Press.

Hoyle, F., C. Wickramasinghe. 1980. *The Origin of Life*. Cardiff: University College Cardiff Press.

Hubbeling, H. G. 1963. *Is the Christian God-Conception Philosophically Inferior?* Assen: Van Gorcum.

1987. *Principles of the Philosophy of Religion*. Assen: Van Gorcum.

Hübner, J. 1966. *Theologie und biologische Entwicklungslehre*. München: Beck.

Hut, P., M. J. Rees. 1983. How Stable is Our Vacuum? *Nature* 302: 508–09.

Isham, C. J. 1988. Creation of the Universe as a Quantum Process. In *Physics, Philosophy, and Theology*, eds. R. J. Russell, W. R. Stoeger, and G. V. Coyne. Vatican: Vatican Observatory (distr. by University of Notre Dame Press).

Isham, C. J. R. Penrose, D. W. Sciama, eds. 1975. *Quantum Gravity*. Oxford: Oxford University Press.

1981. *Quantum Gravity 2*. Oxford: Clarendon Press.

Islam, J. N. 1977. Possible Ultimate Fate of the Universe. *Quarterly Journal of the Royal Astronomical Society* 18:3–8.

1979a. The Long-Term Future of the Universe. *Vistas in Astronomy* 23: 265–277.

	1979b.	The Ultimate Fate of the Universe. *Sky and Telescope* 57: 13–18.
	1983.	*The Ultimate Fate of the Universe.* Cambridge: Cambridge University Press.
Jaki, S. L.	1969.	*The Paradox of Olbers' Paradox.* New York: Herder.
	1974.	*Science and Creation: From Eternal Cycles to an Oscillating Universe.* Edinburgh: Scottish Academic Press.
	1978.	*The Road of Science and the Ways to God.* Chicago: University of Chicago Press.
	1980.	*Cosmos and Creator.* Edinburgh: Scottish Academic Press.
	1982.	From Scientific Cosmology to a Created Universe. *Irish Astronomical Journal* 15: 253–262.
James, E. O.	1969.	The Conception of Creation in Cosmology. In *Liber Amicorum. Studies in honour of professor dr. C. J. Bleeker.* Studies in the history of religions (supplements to Numen) XVII. Leiden: Brill.
Jantsch, E.	1980.	*The Self-Organizing Universe.* Oxford: Pergamon Press.
Jastrow, R.	1980.	*God and the Astronomers.* New York: Warner Books. (1st. ed. 1978, Reader's Libr. Inc.).
Jeffner, A.	1976.	*Kriterien christlicher Glaubenslehre.* Acta Universitatis Upsaliensis, Studia Doctrinae Christianae Upsaliensia 15. Distributed by Almquist & Wicksell International, Stockholm, and by Vandenhoeck und Ruprecht, Göttingen.
John Paul II.	1982.	Allocution of His Holiness John Paul II. In *Astrophysical Cosmology*, eds. H. A. Brück, G. V. Coyne, M. S. Longair. Vatican: Pontifical Academium Scientiarum. (In French; transl. in *Origins, the weekly Magazine of the National Catholic News Service* 11 (1981): 277–280, and partly in *Is God a Creationist?*, ed. R. M. Frye. New York: Scribner's Sons, 1983.)
	1988.	Message of His Holiness John Paul II. In *Physics, Philosophy, and Theology*, eds. R. J. Russell, W. R. Stoeger, G. V. Coyne. Vatican: Vatican Observatory (distr. by University of Notre Dame Press.)
Jong, J. M. de	1958.	*Kerygma.* Assen: Van Gorcum.
Jüngel, E.	1975a.	Das Dilemma der natürlichen Theologie und die Wahrheit ihres Problems. In *Denken im Schatten des Nihilismus. Festschrift für Wilhelm Weischedel zum 70. Geburtstag am 11. April 1975*, ed. A. Schwan. Darmstadt: Wissenschaftliche Buchgesellschaft. (Repr. in Jüngel 1980; references to that edition.)
	1975b.	Gott—um seiner selbst willen interessant. Plädoyer für eine natürlichere Theologie. *Neue Züricher Zeitung* 218 (20/21 September 1975): 57f. (Repr. in Jüngel 1980; references to that edition.)
	1980.	*Entsprechungen: Gott—Wahrheit—Mensch.* München: Kaiser Verlag.
	1983.	*God as the Mystery of the World.* Grand Rapids, Mich.: Eerdmans. (Transl. of *Gott als Geheimniss der Welt*, third ed., Tübingen: J. C. B. Mohr, 1977.)
Juengst, E. T.	1986.	Response: Carving Nature at its Joints. *Religion and Intellectual Life* 5 (Spring): 70–78.
Kanitschneider, B.	1989.	The Anthropic Principle—Physical Constraints for the Evolution of Intelligent Life: An Epistemological Assessment. *International Journal on the Unity of the Sciences* 2: 273–297.
Károlyházy, F.,	1982.	On the Possibility of Observing the Eventual Break-

A. Frenkel, B. Lukács.		down of the Superposition Principle. In *Physics as Natural Philosophy*, eds. A. Shimony, H. Feshbach. Cambridge, Mass.: M. I. T. Press.
	1986.	On the Possible Role of Gravity in the Reduction of the Wave Function. In *Quantum Concepts in Space and Time*, eds. R. Penrose, C. J. Isham. Oxford: Clarendon Press.
Kelsey, D.	1985.	The Doctrine of Creation from Nothing. In *Evolution and Creation*, ed. E. McMullin. Notre Dame, Ind.: University of Notre Dame Press.
King-Farlow, J., W. N. Christensen.	1971.	Faith—and Faith in Hypotheses. *Religious Studies* 7:113–124.
Kirschenmann, P. P.	1987.	Leven: een toeval in de kosmos? In *De Plaats van Aarde en Mens in het Heelal*, J. W. Hovenier, H. J. Boersma, P. P. Kirschenmann, H. R. Plomp, and M. A. Maurice. Kampen: Kok.
Kitcher, Ph.	1982.	*Abusing Science: The Case Against Creationism*. Cambridge, Mass.: M. I. T. Press.
Knight, D. A.	1985.	Cosmogony and Order in the Hebrew Tradition. In *Cosmogony and Ethical Order*, eds. R. W. Lovin, F. E. Reynolds. Chicago: University of Chicago Press.
Köhler, U.	1982.	*Allein im All—doch seine Mitte*. Stuttgart: Quell Verlag.
	1983.	*Sündenfall und Urknall*. Stuttgart: Quell Verlag.
Kragh, H.	1987.	The Beginning of the World: George Lemaître and the Expanding Universe. *Centaurus* 30: 114–139.
Kroes, P.	1985.	*Time: Its Structure and Role in Physical Theories*. Dordrecht: Reidel.
Küng, H.	1978.	*Existiert Gott?* München: Piper Verlag.
Kuhn, T. S.	1962.	*The Structure of Scientific Revolutions*. Chicago: University of Chicago Press.
Lakatos, I.	1970.	Falsification and the Methodology of Scientific Research Programmes. In *Criticism and the Growth of Knowledge*, ed. I. Lakatos, A. Musgrave. Cambridge: Cambridge University Press. (Reprinted in Harding, ed. 1976, and in I. Lakatos, *Philosophical papers, Vol. 1*, eds. J. Worrall, G. Currie. Cambridge: Cambridge University Press, 1978.)
Langerbeck, H.	1967.	*Aufsätze zur Gnosis*. (Abhandlungen der Akademie der Wissenschaften in Göttingen, Philologisch-historische Klasse. Dritte Folge, Nr. 69.) Göttingen: Vandenhoeck & Ruprecht.
Lash, N.	1988.	Observation, Revelation, and the Posteriority of Noach. In *Physics, Philosophy, and Theology*, eds. R. J. Russell, W. R. Stoeger, and G. V. Coyne. Vatican: Vatican Observatory. (Distr. by University of Notre Dame Press.)
Layzer, D.	1975.	The Arrow of Time. *Scientific American* 233 (6): 56–69.
Leplin, J.	1984.	Introduction. In *Scientific Realism*, ed. J. Leplin. Berkeley and Los Angeles: University of California Press.
Leslie, J.	1970.	The Theory that the World Exists Because it Should. *American Philosophical Quarterly* 7: 286–298.
	1972.	Ethically Related Existence. *American Philosophical Quarterly* 9: 215–224.
	1976a.	The Value of Time. *American Philosophical Quarterly* 13: 109–121.
	1976b.	The Best World Possible. In *The Challenge of Religion Today*, ed. J. King-Farlow. New York: Neale Watson.
	1978a.	God and Scientific Verifiability. *Philosophy* 53: 71–78.
	1978b.	Efforts to Explain All Existence. *Mind* 87: 181–194.
	1979.	*Value and Existence*. Oxford: Basil Blackwell.

	1980.	The World's Necessary Existence. *International Journal for Philosophy of Religion* 11: 207–240.
	1982.	Anthropic Principle, World Ensemble, Design. *American Philosophical Quarterly* 19: 141–151.
	1983a.	Cosmology, Probability, and the Need to Explain All Existence. In *Scientific Explanation and Understanding: Essays on Reasoning and Rationality in Science,* ed. N. Rescher. Lanham: University Press of America.
	1983b.	Observership in Cosmology: the Anthropic Principle. *Mind* 42: 573–79.
	1985.	Modern Cosmology and the Creation of Life. In *Evolution and Creation,* ed. E. McMullin. Notre Dame: University of Notre Dame Press.
	1988a.	How to Draw Conclusions from a Fine-tuned Universe. In *Physics, Philosophy, and Theology,* eds. R. J. Russell, W. R. Stoeger, G. V. Coyne. Vatican: Vatican Observatory. (Distr. by University of Notre Dame Press.)
	1988b.	No Inverse Gambler's Fallacy in Cosmology. *Mind* 97: 269–272.
	1989.	*Universes.* London: Routledge.
Levenson, J. D.	1988.	*Creation and the Persistence of Evil.* San Francisco: Harper and Row.
Liedke, G.	1979.	*Im Bauch des Fisches.* Stuttgart, Berlin: Kreuz Verlag.
Linde, A. D.	1982a.	A New Inflationary Universe Scenario: A Possible Solution of the Horizon, Flatness, Homogeneity, Isotropy and Primordial Monopole Problems. *Physics Letters* 108B: 389–393.
	1982b.	Coleman-Weinberg Theory and the New Inflationary Universe Scenario. *Physics Letters* 114B: 431–35.
	1983a.	The New Inflationary Universe Scenario. In *The Very Early Universe,* eds. G. W. Gibbons, S. W. Hawking, S. T. C. Siklos. Cambridge: Cambridge University Press.
	1983b.	Chaotic Inflation. *Physics Letters* 129B: 177–181.
	1984.	Quantum Creation of the Inflationary Universe. *Lettere al Nuovo Cimento* 39: 401–05.
	1985a.	Initial Conditions for Inflation. *Physics Letters* 162B: 281–85.
	1985b.	Particle Physics and Cosmology. *Progress of Theoretical Physics, Supp.* 85: 279–291.
	1987a.	Inflation and Quantum Cosmology. In *Three Hundred Years of Gravitation,* eds. S. W. Hawking, W. Israel. Cambridge: Cambridge University Press.
	1987b.	Particle Physics and Inflationary Cosmology. *Physics Today* 40 (9): 61–68.
	1988.	Life After Inflation. *Physics Letters* 211B: 29–31.
	1989.	Life after Inflation and the Cosmological Constant Problem. *Physics Letters* 227B: 352–58.
Link, C.	1982.	*Die Welt als Gleichniss: Studien zum Problem der natürlichen Theologie,* Second ed. (First ed. 1976.) München: Kaiser Verlag.
	1987.	Theologische Aussage und geschichtlicher Ort der Schöpfungslehre Karl Barths. *Zeitschrift für dialektische Theologie* 3: 171–190.
Long, C. H.	1963.	*Alpha: The Myths of Creation.* New York: Braziller.
	1987.	Cosmogony. In *The Encyclopedia of Religion,* Vol. 4, ed. M. Eliade. New York: Macmillan.
Lovell, B.	1980.	Creation. *Theology* 83: 359–364.
Lovin, R. W., F. E. Reynolds, eds.	1985.	*Cosmogony and Ethical Order.* Chicago: University of Chicago Press.

Mackie, J. L.   1982.   *The Miracle of Theism.* Oxford: Clarendon Press.
Manenschijn, G.   1988.   *Geplunderde aarde, getergde hemel: ontwerp voor een chris-*
                             telijke milieu-ethiek. Baarn: Ten Have.
Markov, M. A.   1983a.   Some Remarks on the Problem of the Very Early Uni-
                             verse. In *The Very Early Universe,* eds. G. W. Gibbons,
                             S. W. Hawking, S. T. C. Siklos. Cambridge: Cambridge
                             University Press.
                    1983b.   Asymptotic Freedom and Entropy in a Perpetually Os-
                             cillating Universe. *Physics Letters* 94 A: 427–29.
                    1984.   Problems of a Perpetually Oscillating Universe. *Annals*
                             of Physics 155: 333–357.
Mascall, E. L.   1956.   *Christian Theology and Natural Science.* London: Long-
                             mans, Green and Co.
May, G.   1978.   *Schöpfung aus dem Nichts: Die Entstehung der Lehre von der*
                             creatio ex nihilo. Berlin, New York: Walter de Gruyter.
McCall, S.   1976.   Objective Time Flow. *Philosophy of Science* 43: 337–362.
McGrath, P. J.   1988.   The Inverse Gambler's Fallacy and Cosmology—A Re-
                             ply to Hacking. *Mind* 97: 265–68.
McLaren, D. J.   1987.   An Anthropocentric View of the Universe: Evidence
                             from Geology. In *Origin and Evolution of the Universe:*
                             Evidence for Design?, ed. J. M. Robson. Kingston and
                             Montreal: McGill-Queen's University Press.
McMullin, E.   1981.   How should Cosmology Relate to Theology? In *The*
                             Sciences and Theology in the Twentieth Century, ed. A. R.
                             Peacocke. Notre Dame: University of Notre Dame
                             Press.
                    1984.   The Case for Scientific Realism. In *Scientific Realism,* ed.
                             J. Leplin. Berkeley and Los Angeles: University of
                             Calif. Press.
                    1988a.   The Shaping of Scientific Rationality: Construction and
                             Constraint. In *Construction and Constraint,* ed. E. Mc-
                             Mullin. Notre Dame: University of Notre Dame Press.
                    1988b.   Natural Science and Belief in a Creator: Historical
                             Notes. In *Physics, Philosophy, and Theology,* eds. R. J. Rus-
                             sell, W. R. Stoeger, G. V. Coyne. Vatican: Vatican Ob-
                             servatory (distr. by University of Notre Dame Press.)
Melsen, A. G. M.   1977.   *Geloof, wetenschap, en maatschappelijke omwentelingen.*
                             Baarn: Ambo & Nijmegen: Katholiek Studiecentrum.
                    1983.   *Natuurwetenschap en natuur.* Baarn: Ambo & Nijmegen:
                             Katholiek Studiecentrum.
                    1989.   *Geloof, rede, en ervaring.* Kampen: Kok & Nijmegen:
                             Katholiek Studiecentrum.
Meynell, H.   1982.   *The Intelligible Universe: A Cosmological Argument.* Lon-
                             don: Macmillan.
                    1987.   More Gaps for God? In *Origin and Evolution of the Uni-*
                             verse: Evidence for Design?, ed. J. M. Robson. Kingston
                             and Montreal: McGill-Queen's University Press.
Miskotte, K. H.   1960.   Natürliche Religion und Theologie. In *Die Religion in*
                             Geschichte und Gegenwart, Drite Auflage. Band IV, 1322–
                             1326.
Misner, Ch. W.   1969.   Absolute Zero of Time. *Physical Review* 186: 1328–333.
                    1977.   Cosmology and Theology. In *Cosmology, History and The-*
                             ology, eds. W. Yourgrau, A. D. Breck. New York: Plenum
                             Press.
Misner, C. W.,   1973.   *Gravitation.* San Francisco: Freeman.
   K. S. Thorne,
   J. A. Wheeler.
Moltmann, J.   1967.   *Theology of Hope.* New York: Harper and Row.
                    1985.   *Gott in der Schöpfung: Ökologische Schöpfungslehre.*

		München: Kaiser Verlag. (Also *God in Creation: an Ecological Doctrine of Creation*, London: SCM, 1985.)
	1987a.	Schöpfung, Bund und Herrlichkeit. *Zeitschrift für dialektische Theologie* 3: 191–214. (Slightly changed, with same title, in *Evangelische Theologie* 48 [1988]: 108–126.)
	1987b.	Zum Gespräch mit Christian Link. *Evangelische Theologie* 47: 93–95.
Monsma, J. C., ed.	1958.	*The Evidence of God in an Expanding Universe. Forty American Scientists declare their affirmative views on religion.* New York: Putnam's Sons.
Montagu, A., ed.	1984.	*Science and Creationism.* Oxford: Oxford University Press.
Montefiore, H.	1985.	*The Probability of God.* London: SCM.
Morris, H.	1974.	*Scientific Creationism.* San Diego: Inst. of Creation Research.
Mortensen, V., R. C. Sorensen.	1987.	*Free Will and Determinism.* Aarhus (Denmark): Aarhus University Press.
Moss, I. G., W. A. Wright.	1984.	Wave Function of the Inflationary Universe. *Physical Review* D 29: 1067–075.
Munitz, M. K.	1974.	*The Mystery of Existence.* New York: New York University Press.
	1981.	*Space, Time, and Creation.* Rev. Ed. New York: Dover Publ. Inc. (Orig. 1957, Glencoe, Illinois: Free Press.)
	1986.	*Cosmic Understanding.* Princeton: Princeton University Press.
Murphy, N.	1985a.	Theology the Transformer of Science? A Niebuhrian Typology for the Relation of Theology to Science. *Pacific Theological Review* 18 (3): 16–23. (Also in *CTNS Bulletin* [Berkeley] 5 [4, Autumn 1985]: 1–8.)
	1985b.	Review of A. R. Peacocke's *Intimations of Reality. Zygon* 20: 464–66. (Also *CTNS Bulletin* 5 [2, Spring 1985]: 12–14.)
	1987.	Acceptability Criteria for Work in Theology and Science. *Zygon* 22: 279–297. (Also *CTNS Bulletin* [Berkeley] 7 [4, Autumn 1987]: 1–10.)
	1989.	Truth, Relativism, and Crossword Puzzles. *Zygon* 24: 299–314.
Narlikar, J. V.	1988.	*The Primeval Universe.* Oxford: Oxford University Press.
Neville, R. C.	1968.	*God the Creator.* Chicago: University of Chicago Press.
	1981.	*Reconstruction of Thinking.* Albany: SUNY.
	1982.	*The Tao and the Daimon.* Albany: SUNY.
Newbigin, L.	1986.	*Foolishness to the Greeks: The Gospel and Western Culture.* London: SPCK.
North, J.	1965.	*The Measure of the Universe.* Oxford: Oxford University Press.
Novak, D., N. Samuelson, eds.	1986.	*Creation and the End of Days: Judaism and Scientific Cosmology.* Lanham: University Press of America.
Ogden, S.	1975.	The Meaning of Christian Hope. *Union Seminary Quarterly Review* 30: 153–164.
O'Keefe, J. A.	1980.	The Theological Impact of the New Cosmology. Afterword in R. Jastrow, *God and the Astronomers.* New York: Warner Books.
Ovenden, M. W.	1987.	Of Stars, Planets, and Life. In *Origin and Evolution of the Universe: Evidence for Design?*, ed. J. M. Robson. Kingston and Montreal: McGill-Queen's University Press.
Pacholczyk, A. G.	1984.	*The Catastrophic Universe: An Essay in the Philosophy of Cosmology.* Tucson: Pachart Publishing House.

Page, D. N.	1984.	Can Inflation Explain Thermodynamics? *International Journal of Theoretical Physics* 23: 725–733.
	1985.	Will Entropy Decrease if the Universe Recollapses? *Physical Review* D 32: 2496–99.
	1987.	The Importance of the Anthropic principle. *The World and I* 2 (August): 392.
Page, D. N., M. R. McKee.	1981.	Eternity Matters. *Nature* 291: 44–45.
Page, D. N., W. K. Wootters.	1983.	Evolution Without Evolution: Dynamics Described by Stationary Observables. *Physical Review* D27: 2885–892.
Pagels, H. R.	1985a.	*Perfect Symmetry: The Search for the Beginning of Time*. New York: Simon and Schuster.
	1985b.	A Cozy Cosmology. *The Sciences* 25 (2): 34–38.
	1988.	*The Dreams of Reason: The Computer and the Rise of the Sciences of Complexity*. New York: Simon and Schuster.
Pannenberg, W.	1962.	*Was ist der Mensch?* Göttingen: Vandenhoeck und Ruprecht. (Transl. *What is Man?*, Fortress, Philadelphia, 1970.)
	1969.	*Theology and the Kingdom of God*, ed. Richard John Neuhaus. Philadelphia: Westminster Press.
	1970.	Kontingenz und Naturgesetz. In *Erwägungen zu einer Theologie der Natur*, A. M. Klaus Müller und W. Pannenberg. Gütersloh: Gerd Mohn.
	1971a.	*Basic Questions in Theology. Vol. 1*. Philadelphia: Fortress. (Transl. of *Grundfragen Systematischer Theologie*, 1–201, Vandenhoeck und Ruprecht, Göttingen, 1967.)
	1971b.	*Basic Questions in Theology. Vol. 2*. Philadelphia: Fortress. (Transl. of *Grundfragen Systematischer Theologie*, 202–398, Vandenhoeck und Ruprecht, Göttingen, 1967.)
	1973.	*Theology and the Philosophy of Science*. London: Darton, Longman and Todd / Philadelphia: Westminster (orig. *Wissenschaftstheorie und Theologie*, Suhrkamp Verlag, Frankfurt, 1973).
	1981.	Theological Questions to Scientists. In *The Sciences and Theology in the Twentieth Century*, ed. A. R. Peacocke, Notre Dame: University of Notre Dame Press. (Also in *Zygon* 16: 65–77.)
	1983.	*Anthropologie in theologischer Perspektive*. Göttingen: Vandenhoeck und Ruprecht.
	1988a.	*Systematische Theologie, Band 1*. Göttingen: Vandenhoeck und Ruprecht.
	1988b.	*Metaphysik und Gottesgedanke*. Göttingen: Vandenhoeck und Ruprecht.
	1988c.	The Doctrine of Creation and Modern Science. *Zygon* 23: 3–21.
	1988d.	A Response to my American Friends. In *The Theology of Wolfhart Pannenberg*, eds. C. E. Braaten, P. Clayton. Minneapolis: Augsburg Publ. House.
	1989.	Theological Appropriation of Scientific Understandings: Response to Hefner, Wicken, Eaves, and Tipler. *Zygon* 24: 255–271.
Patton, G. M., J. A. Wheeler.	1975.	Is Physics Legislated by Cosmogony? In *Quantum Gravity*, eds. C. J. Isham, R. Penrose, D. W. Sciama. Oxford: Oxford University Press.
Peacocke, A. R.	1979.	*Creation and the World of Science*. Oxford: Clarendon Press.
	1981.	Introduction. In *The Sciences and Theology in the Twentieth Century*, ed. A. R. Peacocke. Notre Dame: University of Notre Dame Press.

1984a.   *Intimations of Reality*. Notre Dame: University of Notre Dame Press.

1984b.   Thermodynamics and Life. *Zygon* 19: 395–432 (repr. in 1986a).

1985.   Biological Evolution and Christian Theology—Yesterday and Today. In *Darwinism and Divinity*, ed. J. Durant. Oxford: Basil Blackwell.

1986a.   *God and the New Biology*. London: Dent and Sons.

1986b.   Science and Theology Today: A Critical Realist Perspective. *Religion and Intellectual Life* 5 (Spring): 45–58.

1986c.   Science and Theology Today: A Critical Realist Perspective. *CTNS Bulletin* (Berkeley) 6 (2, Spring): 1–16.

1987a.   Rethinking Religious Faith in a World of Science. In *Religion, Science, and Public Policy*, ed. F. T. Birtel. New York: Crossroad. (Expanded and modified version of Chapter 1 of 1984a.)

1987b.   The Disguised Friend: Biological Evolution and Belief in God. In *Religion, Science, and Public Policy*, ed. F. T. Birtel. New York: Crossroad. (Almost unchanged reprint of 1985.)

Penelhum, T.   1987.   Science, Design, and Ambiguity: Concluding Reflections. In *Origin and Evolution of the Universe: Evidence for Design?*, ed. J. M. Robson. Kingston and Montreal: McGill-Queen's University Press.

Penrose, R.   1972.   On the Nature of Quantum Geometry. In *Magic Without Magic: John Archibald Wheeler*, ed. J. R. Klauder. San Francisco: Freeman.

1975.   Twistor Theory: its Aims and Achievements. In *Quantum Gravity*, ed. C. J. Isham, R. Penrose, D. W. Sciama. Oxford: Oxford University Press.

1978.   Singularities of Space-Time. In *Theoretical Principles in Astrophysics and Relativity*, ed. N. R. Lebovitz, W. H. Reid, P. O. Vandervoort. Chicago: Chicago University Press.

1979.   Singularities and Time-Asymmetry. In *General Relativity: an Einstein Centenary Survey*, eds. S. W. Hawking, W. Israel. Cambridge: Cambridge University Press.

1980.   A Brief Outline of Twistor Theory. In *Cosmology and Gravitation: Spin, Torsion, Rotation, and Supergravity*, eds. P. G. Bergmann, V. De Sabatta. New York: Plenum Press.

1981a.   Time Asymmetry and Quantum Gravity. In *Quantum Gravity 2*, eds. C. J. Isham, R. Penrose, D. W. Sciama. Oxford: Clarendon.

1981b.   Some Remarks on Twistors and Curved-Space Quantization. In *Quantum Gravity 2*, eds. C. J. Isham, R. Penrose, D. W. Sciama. Oxford: Clarendon.

1982a.   Some Remarks on Gravity and Quantum Mechanics. In *Quantum Structure of Space and Time*, eds. M. J. Duff, C. J. Isham. Cambridge: Cambridge University Press.

1982b.   Quasilocal Mass and Angular Momentum. *Proc. Roy. Soc. Lond.* A 381: 53–63.

1986a.   Gravity and State Vector Reduction. In *Quantum Concepts in Space and Time*, eds. R. Penrose, C. J. Isham. Oxford: Clarendon.

1986b.   Herman Weyl, Space-Time and Conformal Geometry. In *Herman Weyl 1885–1985*, ed. K. Chandrasekharan. Berlin: Springer Verlag.

1986c.   Big Bangs, Black Holes, and 'Time's Arrow'. In *The Nature of Time*, eds. R. Flood, M. Lockwood. Oxford: Basil Blackwell.

	1987a.	Newton, Quantum Theory, and Reality. In *Three Hundred Years of Gravitation*, eds. S. W. Hawking, W. Israel. Cambridge: Cambridge University Press.
	1987b.	Quantum Physics and Conscious Thought. In *Quantum Implications: Essays in Honour of David Bohm*, ed. B. J. Hiley, F. D. Peat. London: Routledge and Kegan Paul.
	1989.	*The Emperor's New Mind: Concerning Computers, Minds, and the Laws of Physics*. Oxford: Oxford University Press.
Penrose, R., C. J. Isham.	1986.	*Quantum Concepts in Space and Time*. Oxford: Clarendon Press.
Penrose, R., W. Rindler.	1984.	*Spinors and Space-time. Volume 1: Two-spinor Calculus and Relativistic Fields*. Cambridge: Cambridge University Press.
	1986.	*Spinors and Space-time. Volume 2: Spinor and Twistor Methods in Space-time Geometry*. Cambridge: Cambridge University Press.
Peters, K. E.	1987.	Toward a Physics, Metaphysics, and Theology of Creation: A Trinitarian View. In *Religion, Science, and Public Policy*, ed. Frank T. Birtel. New York: Crossroad.
Peters, T.	1984.	Cosmos and Creation. *Word and World* 4: 372–390. (Also *CTNS Bulletin* 5 [1, Winter 1985]: 1–12; expanded version in *Cosmos as Creation*, ed. T. Peters, 1989.)
	1988.	On Creating the Cosmos. In *Physics, Philosophy, and Theology*, eds. R. J. Russell, W. R. Stoeger, G. V. Coyne. Vatican: Vatican Observatory. (Distr. by University of Notre Dame Press.)
Peters, T., ed.	1989.	*Cosmos as Creation*. Nashville: Abingdon.
Petrosian, V.	1982.	Phase Transitions and Dynamics of the Universe. *Nature* 298: 805–08.
Pettazzoni, R.	1954.	*Essays on the History of Religions*. (Studies in the history of religions. Supplements to Numen. I.) Leiden: Brill.
Pike, N.	1970.	*God and Timelessness*. London: Routledge and Kegan Paul.
Pius XII.	1952.	Le prove della esistenza de dio alla luce della scienza naturale moderna. *Acta Apostolicae Sedis. Commentarium Officiale*, 44: 31–43. (Partial transl. as 'Theology and Modern Science. Pope Pius XII on the Harmony of the Work of God', *Bulletin of the Atomic Scientists* 8 [5, June]: 143–46, 165.)
Plantinga, A. C.	1974a.	*The Nature of Necessity*. Oxford: Oxford University Press.
	1974b.	*God, Freedom, and Evil*. New York: Harper and Row.
Plomp, H. R.	1987.	Het heelal als hemel en aarde? Kosmologie en theologie. In *De plaats van aarde en mens in het heelal*, J. W. Hovenier et al., Kampen: Kok.
	1987b.	John Cobb und Karl Barth. *Zeitschrift für dialektische Theologie* 3: 45–64.
Polk, D. P.	1988.	The All-Determining God and the Peril of Determinism. In *The Theology of Wolfhart Pannenberg*, eds. C. E. Braaten, P. Clayton. Minneapolis: Augsburg.
Polkinghorne, J.	1985.	*The Quantum World*. Princeton: Princeton University Press.
	1986.	*One World: The Interaction of Science and Theology*. Princeton: Princeton University Press.
	1987.	Creation and the Structure of the Physical World. *Theology Today* 44: 53–68.
	1988a.	The Unity of Truth in Science and Theology. In *Science and the Theology of Creation* (Church and Society Documents No. 4). Geneva: World Council of Churches.
	1988b.	The Quantum World. In *Physics, Philosophy, and Theol-*

ogy, eds. R. J. Russell, W. R. Stoeger, G. V. Coyne. Vatican: Vatican Observatory. (Distr. by University of Notre Dame Press.)

| | 1988c. | *Science and Creation: The Search for Understanding.* London: SCM & Boston: New Science Library/Shambala. |

Prigogine, I., 1984. *Order Out of Chaos.* New York: Bantam. (Transl. and
I. Stengers. revision of *La nouvelle alliance,* Paris: Gallimard. 1972).

Quine, W. V. O. 1951. Two Dogmas of Empiricism. *The Philosophical Review* 60: 20–43. (Repr. in *From a Logical Point of View,* Cambridge: Harvard University Press, 1961, and in Harding, ed., 1976.)

1970. On the reasons for Indeterminacy of Translation. *Journal of Philosophy* 67: 178–183.

Quine, W. V. O., 1978. *The Web of Belief.* Second Edition. New York: Random
J. S. Ullian. House.

Rad, G. von. 1964. *Das erste Buch Mose. Genesis.* (Das Alte Testament Deutsch 2/4.) Göttingen: Vandenhoeck und Ruprecht. (First ed. 1949).

Rahner, K. 1988. *Theological Investigations XXI: Science and Christian Faith.* New York: Crossroad. (Translation of *Schriften zur Theologie, Band XV: Wissenschaft und Theologie,* Zürich: Benzinger Verlag, 1983.)

Raingard, P. 1934. *Le peri tou prosopou de Plutarque.* Chartres.

Raschke, C. 1980. The New Cosmology and the Overcoming of Metaphysics. *Philosophy Today* 24: 375–387.

Rawer, K., 1981. Weltall—Erde—Mensch. In *Christlicher Glaube in mod-
K. Rahner. erner Gesellschaft,* Teilband 3, eds. F. Böckle, F. X. Kaufmann, K. Rahner, B. Welte. Freiburg: Herder.

Rees, M. J. 1969. The Collapse of the Universe: An Eschatological Study. *Observatory* 89: 193–98.

1981. Our Universe and Others. *Quarterly Journal of the Royal Astronomical Society* 22: 109–124.

Reeves, H. 1981. *Patience dans l'azur: l'Evolution cosmique.* Paris: Ed. du Seuil. (Transl. as *Atoms of Silence,* Cambridge, Mass.: M. I. T. Press, 1985).

1986. *L'Heure de s'enivrer, L'Univers a-t-il un sens?* Paris: Éditions du Seuil.

Reichenbach, H. 1957. *The Philosophy of Space and Time.* New York: Dover Publ. (First ed. 1927.)

1971. *The Direction of Time.* Berkeley and Los Angeles: University of Calif. Press. (1st. ed. 1956).

Rescher, N. 1973. *The Coherence Theory of Truth.* Oxford: Clarendon Press.
1985. *Pascal's Wager.* Notre Dame: University of Notre Dame Press.

Restivo, S. 1984. *The Social Relations of Physics, Mysticism and Mathematics.* Dordrecht/Boston: Reidel.

Reumann, J. 1975. Creatio, Continua and Nova. In *The Gospel as History,* ed. V. Vajta. Philadelphia: Fortress.

Ricoeur, P. 1967. *The Symbolism of Evil.* New York: Harper and Row.

Robbins, J. W. 1988. Seriously but not Literally: Pragmatism and Realism in Religion and Science. *Zygon* 23: 229–245.

Robson, J. M., 1987. *Origin and Evolution of the Universe: Evidence for Design?*
ed. Kingston and Montreal: McGill-Queen's University Press.

Rolston III, H. 1987. *Science and Religion: A Critical Survey.* Philadelphia: Temple University Press and New York: Random House.

Rosen, J. 1985. The Anthropic Principle. *American Journal of Physics* 53: 335–39.

Rozental, I. L.   1988.   *Big Bang Big Bounce*. Berlin: Springer Verlag. (Transl. from Russian, *Elementarnye chastitsy i struktura bselennoj*, Moscow: Nauka, 1984 and *Problemy nachala i kontsa metagalaktiki*, Moscow: Znanie, 1985.)

Ruse, M.   1982.   *Darwinism Defended*. Reading, Mass.: Addison Wesley.

Russell, B.   1931.   *The Scientific Outlook*. London: Allen and Unwin.

Russell, R. J.   1984.   Entropy and Evil. *Zygon* 19: 449–468.

                    1985.   How Does Modern Physical Cosmology Affect Creation Theology? *Pacific Theological Review* 18 (3, Spring): 33–42.

                    1986a.   How Does Scientific Cosmology Shape a Theology of Nature? *CTNS Bulletin* (Berkeley) 6 (1, Winter 1986): 1–12.

                    1986b.   Response: A Fresh Appraisal. *Religion and Intellectual Life* 5 (Spring): 64–69.

                    1988a.   Contingency in Physics and Cosmology: A Critique of the Theology of W. Pannenberg. *Zygon* 23: 23–43.

                    1988b.   Quantum Physics in Philosophical and Theological Perspective. In *Physics, Philosophy, and Theology*, eds. R. J. Russell, W. R. Stoeger, G. V. Coyne. Vatican: Vatican Observatory (distr. University of Notre Dame Press).

                    1988c.   Cosmology and Eschatology: A New Reason to Hope. A response to Tipler's 'Evolving God' Hypothesis in Light of Pannenberg's Theological Program. Paper presented at the Pannenberg Symposium II, held at the Lutheran School of Theology at Chicago, November 15–17 1988. (Partly also presented as response at session on eschatology and science at the American Academy of Religion, November 19–22 1988.)

                    1988d.   Christian Discipleship and the Challenge of Physics: Formation, Flux, and Focus. *CTNS Bulletin* 8 (4, Autumn): 1–16.

                    1989.   Cosmology, Creation, and Contingency. In *Cosmos as Creation*, ed. T. Peters. Nashville: Abingdon.

                    1990.   Theological Implications of Physics and Cosmology. In *The Church and Contemporary Cosmology*, eds. J. B. Miller and K. E. McCall. Pittsburgh: Carnegie-Mellon University Press.

Russell, R. J.,   1988.   *Physics, Philosophy, and Theology: A Common Quest for Understanding*. Vatican: Vatican Observatory. (Distr. by University of Notre Dame Press.)
W. R. Stoeger,
G. V. Coyne.

Sagan, C.   1980.   *Cosmos*. New York: Random House.

                    1988.   Introduction. In S. W. Hawking, *A Brief History of Time*. New York: Bantam Books.

Sato, K.,   1982.   Multi-production of Universes by First Order Phase Transition of a Vacuum. *Physics Letters* 108B: 103–07.
H. Kodama,
M. Sasaki,
K. Maeda.

Schipper, F.   1986.   Het contingentiebegrip in de dialoog tussen natuurwetenschap en theologie. *Algemeen Nederlands Tijdschrift voor Wijsbegeerte* 78: 81–96.

Schmidt, W. H.   1967.   *Die Schöpfungsgeschichte der Priesterschrift*. Zweite überarbeitete und erweiterte Auflage. Neukirchen-Vluyn: Neukirchener Verlag.

Schwarz, H.   1972.   *On the Way to the Future: A Christian View of Eschatology in the Light of Current Trends in Religion, Philosophy, and Science*. Minneapolis: Augsburg.

Schwarz, J. H.   1987.   Superstring Unification. In *Three Hundred Years of Gravitation*, eds. S. W. Hawking, W. Israel. Cambridge: Cambridge University Press.

Selms, A. van.   1967.   *Genesis Deel I.* (De prediking van het Oude Testament) Nijkerk: Callenbach.

Sharpe, K. J.   1982.   Stanley L. Jaki's Critique of Physics. *Religious Studies* 18: 55–75.

                     1984.   *From Science to an Adequate Mythology.* Auckland (New Zealand): Interface Press.

Shimony, A.   1986.   Events and Processes in the Quantum World. In *Quantum Concepts in Space and Time,* eds. R. Penrose, C. J. Isham. Oxford: Clarendon Press.

Shipman, H. L.   1986.   The Creation of Order from Chaos: Making Galaxies, Stars, Planets, and People from Uniformly Expanding Matter. In *Creation and the End of Days,* eds. D. Novak and N. Samuelson. Lanham: University Press of America.

Shu, F. H.   1982.   *The Physical Universe.* Mill Valley, CA: University Science Books.

Silk, J.   1980.   *The Big Bang.* San Francisco: Freeman.

Slusher, H. S.   1977.   Een astronoom over ontstaan en geschiedenis van het heelal. In *Schepping of evolutie? Argumenten voor en tegen de evolutieleer,* ed. A. van Delden. Goes: Oosterbaan & LeCointre.

                     1978.   *The Origin of the Universe.* San Diego: Institute of Creation Research.

Slusher, H. S., S. J. Duursma.   1978.   *The Age of the Solar System.* San Diego: Institute of Creation Research.

Slusher, H. S., T. P. Gamwell.   1978.   *The Age of the Earth.* San Diego: Institute of Creation Research.

Smits, P.   1969.   Napraten over God. *Theologie en Practijk* 29: 76–89.

                     1972.   *Anders geloven: de erosie van het kerkelijk christendom.* Assen: Van Gorcum.

                     1981.   *Veranderend wereldbeeld, mensbeeld, godsbeeld.* Assen: Van Gorcum.

Soskice, J. M.   1985.   *Metaphor and Religious Language.* Oxford: Clarendon Press.

                     1988.   Knowledge and Experience in Science and Religion: Can We Be Realists? In *Physics, Philosophy, and Theology,* eds. R. J. Russell, W. R. Stoeger, G. V. Coyne. Vatican: Vatican Observatory. (Distr. by University of Notre Dame Press.)

Spoelstra, T. A. Th.   1984.   *Het sterrenkundig wereldbeeld—een wijsgerige analyse.* (Thesis, Universiteit van die Oranje Vrystaat, Bloemfontein, South Africa).

Sproul, B. C.   1979.   *Primal Myths: Creating the World.* San Francisco: Harper and Row.

Stachel, J. ed.   1989.   *Proceedings of the Osgood Hill Conference on the Conceptual Problems of Quantum Mechanics.* (Conference held May 16–19 1988; proceedings to be published)

Starobinsky, A. A.   1980.   A New Type of Isotropic Cosmological Models Without Singularity. *Physics Letters* 91B: 99–102.

Steck, O. H.   1975.   *Der Schöpfungsbericht der Priesterschrift.* Göttingen: Vandenhoeck & Ruprecht.

Stein, H.   1984.   The Everett Interpretation of Quantum Mechanics: Many Worlds or None? *Noûs* 18: 635–652.

Stoeger, W. R.   1988.   Contemporary Cosmology and its Implications for the Science-Religion Dialogue. In *Physics, Philosophy, and Theology,* eds. R. J. Russell, W. R. Stoeger, G. V. Coyne. Vatican: Vatican Observatory. (Distr. by University of Notre Dame Press.)

Stoner, P. W.   1958.   Genesis I in the Light of Modern Astronomy. In *The*

		Evidence of God in an Expanding Universe, ed. J. C. Monsma. New York: Putnam's Sons.
Stuhr, C.	1986.	Speaking of God and the Universe. *Journal of the Royal Astronomical Society of Canada* 80: 87–90.
Suchocki, M. H.	1977.	The Question of Immortality. *Journal of Religion* 57: 288–306.
	1982.	*God, Christ, Church*. New York: Crossroad.
	1988.	*The End of Evil: Process Eschatology in Historical Context*. Albany, N.Y.: SUNY Press.
Sutherland, S. R.	1984.	*God, Jesus and Belief: the Legacy of Theism*. Oxford: Basil Blackwell.
Swinburne, R.	1979.	*The Existence of God*. Oxford: Oxford University Press.
Taylor, J. H., J. M. Weisberg.	1989.	Further Experimental Tests of Relativistic Gravity Using the Binary Pulsar PSR 1913 + 16. *Astrophysical Journal* 345: 436–450.
Terrien, S.	1978.	*The Elusive Presence: Toward a New Biblical Theology*. San Francisco: Harper and Row.
Theissen, G.	1985.	*Biblical Faith: an Evolutionary Approach*. Philadelphia: Fortress. (Transl. of *Biblischer Glaube in evolutionärer Sicht*, München: Kaiser Verlag, 1984.)
Tillich, P.	1963.	*Systematic Theology, Volume III*. Chicago: University of Chicago Press.
Tipler, F. J.	1978.	Energy Conditions and Spacetime Singularities. *Physical Review* D 17: 2521–28.
	1979.	General Relativity, Thermodynamics, and the Poincaré Cycle. *Nature* 280: 203–05.
	1980.	General Relativity and the Eternal Return. In *Essays in General Relativity: a Festschrift for Abraham H. Taub*, ed. F. J. Tipler. New York: Academic Press.
	1986a.	The Many-Worlds Interpretation of Quantum Mechanics in Quantum Cosmology. In *Quantum Concepts in Space and Time*, eds. R. Penrose, C. J. Isham. Oxford: Clarendon Press.
	1986b.	Interpreting the Wave Function of the Universe. *Physics Reports* 137: 231–275.
	1988.	The Omega Point Theory: A Model of an Evolving God. In *Physics, Philosophy, and Theology*, eds. R. J. Russell, W. R. Stoeger, and G. V. Coyne. Vatican: Vatican Observatory. (Distr. by University of Notre Dame Press.)
	1989.	The Omega Point as *Eschaton*: Answers to Pannenberg's Questions for Scientists. *Zygon* 24: 217–253.
Tolman, R. C.	1934.	*Relativity, Thermodynamics, and Cosmology*. Oxford: Clarendon.
Torrance, T. F.	1969.	*Theological Science*. London: Oxford University Press.
	1971.	*God and Rationality*. London: Oxford University Press.
	1976.	*Space, Time and Resurrection*. Edinburgh: Handsel Press.
	1981a.	*Divine and Contingent Order*. Oxford: Oxford University Press.
	1981b.	Divine and Contingent Order. Oxford: Oxford University Press.
	1981b.	Divine and Contingent Order. In *The Sciences and Theology in the Twentieth Century*, ed. A. R. Peacocke. Notre Dame: University of Notre Dame Press.
	1984.	*Transformation and Convergence in the Frame of Knowledge*. Belfast: Christian Journals & Grand Rapids: Eerdmans.
	1985a.	*Reality and Scientific Theology*. Edinburgh: Scottish Academic Press.
	1985b.	*The Christian Frame of Mind*. Edinburgh: Handsel Press.

	1988.	Realism and openness in scientific inquiry. *Zygon* 23: 159–169.

Toulmin, S. E.   1957.   Contemporary scientific mythology. In *Metaphysical Beliefs*, ed. A. MacIntyre. London: SCM. (Reprinted in *The Return to Cosmology*. Berkeley and Los Angeles: University of California Press, 1982.)

Tracy, D.   1975.   *Blessed Rage for Order*. Minneapolis: Seabury.

Trefil, J. S.   1983.   *The Moment of Creation: Big Bang Physics from Before the First Millisecond to the Present Universe*. New York: Scribner's.

Tresmontant, C.   1966.   *Comment se pose aujourd'hui le problème de l'existence de Dieu*. Paris: Éditions du Seuil.

Tryon, E. P.   1973.   Is the Universe a Vacuum Fluctuation? *Nature* 246: 396–97.

1984.   What Made the World? *New Scientist* 101 (1400, 8 March): 14–16.

Turner, M.   1985.   The Inflationary Paradigm. In *Fundamental Interactions and Cosmology*, eds. J. Audouze, J. Tran Than Thanh Van. Gif sur Yvette: éditions Frontières.

Turner, M., F. Wilczek.   1982.   Is Our Vacuum Metastable? *Nature* 298: 633–34.

Van Till, H. J.   1986a.   *The Fourth Day: What the Bible and the Heavens Are Telling Us About the Creation*. Grand Rapids: Eerdmans.

1986b.   The Legend of the Shrinking Sun: A Case Study Comparing Professional Science and 'Creation-Science' in Action. *Journal of the American Scientific Affiliation* 38: 164–174.

Vawter, B.   1977.   *On Genesis: A New Reading*. London: Geoffrey Chapman.

Vilenkin, A.   1982.   Creation of Universes from Nothing. *Physics Letters* 117B: 25–28.

1983.   Birth of Inflationary Universes. *Physical Review* D 27: 2848–855.

1984.   Quantum Creation of Universes. *Physical Review* D 30:509–511.

1985a.   Classical and Quantum Cosmology of the Starobinsky Inflationary Model. *Physical Review* D 32: 2511–2521.

1985b.   Quantum Origin of the Universe. *Nuclear Physics* B 252: 141–151.

1986.   Boundary Conditions in Quantum Cosmology. *Physical Review* D 33: 3560–69.

1988.   Quantum Cosmology and the Initial State of the Universe. *Physical Review* D 37: 888–897.

Wald, R. M.   1984.   *General Relativity*. Chicago: University of Chicago Press.

WCC (References to publications by the World Council of Churches in Geneva)   1986.   *Church and Society: Report and Background Papers of the Meeting of the Working Group Potsdam, GDR, July 1986.*

1987a.   *Church and Society: Report and Background Papers of the Meeting of the Working Group Glion, Switzerland, September 1987.*

1987b.   *Reintegrating God's Creation*. Church and Society Documents No. 3 (September 1987).

1988a.   *Science and the Theology of Creation: Bossey Seminar*. Church and Society Documents No. 4 (August 1988).

1988b.   *Creation and the Kingdom of God: Consultation with Faith and Order*. Church and Society Documents No. 5 (August 1988).

Webster, J. B.   1986.   *Eberhard Jüngel: An Introduction to his Theology*. Cambridge: Cambridge University Press.

Weinberg, S.	1972.	*Gravitation and Cosmology*. New York: Wiley & Sons.
	1977.	*The First Three Minutes*. New York: Basic Books.
Westermann, C.	1974.	*Genesis 1–11*. (Biblischer Kommentar Altes Testament BandI/1) Neukirchen-Vluyn: Neukirchener Verlag. (Transl. *Genesis 1–11: a Commentary*. Minneapolis: Augsburg, 1984.)
Wheeler, J. A.	1964.	Geometrodynamics and the Issue of the Final State. In *Relativity, Groups and Topology*, eds. C. and B. S. DeWitt. New York: Gordon and Breach, London: Blackie and Son.
	1968.	Superspace and the Nature of Quantum Geometrodynamics. In *Batelle Rencontres*, ed. C. M. DeWitt, J. A. Wheeler. New York: Benjamin.
	1974.	From Mendeléev's Atom to the Collapsing Star. In *Philosophical Foundations of Science. Proceedings of section L, 1969, American Association for the Advancement of Science*, eds. R. J. Seeger, R. S. Cohen. (Boston Studies in the Philosophy of Science Vol. XI, Synthese Library, Vol. 58). Dordrecht: Reidel.
	1977.	Genesis and Observership. In *Foundational Problems in the Special Sciences. Part Two of the Proceedings of the Fifth International Congress of Logic, Methodology and Philosophy of Science, London, Ontario, Canada 1975*, eds. R. E. Butts, J. Hintikka. (The University of Western Ontario Series in Philosophy of Science Vol. 10.) Dordrecht: Reidel.
	1978.	The 'Past' and the 'Delayed Choice' Double Slit Experiment. In *Mathematical Foundations of Quantum Theory*, ed. A. R. Marlow. New York: Academic Press.
	1980.	Pregeometry: Motivations and Prospects. In *Quantum Theory and Gravitation*, ed. A. R. Marlow. New York: Academic Press.
	1982a.	Beyond the Black Hole. In *Some Strangeness in the Proportion*, ed. H. Woolfe. Reading, Mass.: Addison-Wesley.
	1982b.	The Computer and the Universe. *International Journal of Theoretical Physics* 21:557–572.
	1988.	World as System Self-Synthesized by Quantum Networking. *IBM Journal of Research and Development* 32: 4–15.
Whitehead, A. N.	1926.	*Science and the Modern World*. London: Cambridge University Press.
	1978.	*Process and Reality: an Essay in Cosmology*. Corrected ed. by D. R. Griffin, D. W. Sherburne. (1st. ed. 1929) New York: Macmillan.
Wilczek, F.	1983.	Foundations and Working Pictures in Microphysical Cosmology. In *The Very Early Universe*, eds. G. W. Gibbins, S. W. Hawking, S. T. C. Siklos. Cambridge: Cambridge University Press.
Wilde, A. de	1955a.	De kerkleer en het wereldbeeld. In *Leven op Aarde*, ed. R. Hensen. Delft: Gaade.
	1955b.	De Christelijke kerk en de toekomst. In *Leven op Aarde*, ed. R. Hensen. Delft: Gaade.
	1957.	Vrijzinnigheid en rechtzinnigheid. *Woord en Dienst* 6: 289–292, 306–310, 325–28, 338–344, 354–58. (An exchange of letters with J. J. Buskes).
Wildiers, N. M.	1982.	*The Theologian and His Universe: Theology and Cosmology from the Middle Ages to the Present*. New York: Seabury Press.
	1985.	*Theologie op nieuwe wegen*. Antwerpen: De Nederlandsche Boekhandel & Kampen: Kok.

316   BIBLIOGRAPHY

	1988.	*Kosmologie in de westerse cultuur*. Kapellen: DNB/Pelck-mans & Kampen: Kok. (revised version of Wildiers 1982).
Will, C. M.	1979.	The Confrontation between Gravitation Theory and Experiment. In *General Relativity: an Einstein Centenary Survey*, eds. S. W. Hawking, W. Israel. Cambridge: Cambridge University Press.
	1981.	*Theory and Experiment in Gravitational Physics*. Cambridge: Cambridge University Press.
	1986.	*Was Einstein Right?* New York: Basic Books.
	1988.	Experimental Gravitation from Newton's *Principia* to Einstein's General Relativity. In *Three Hundred Years of Gravitation*, eds. S. W. Hawking, W. Israel. Cambridge: Cambridge University Press.
Wölfel, E.	1981.	*Welt als Schöpfung.* (Theol. Existenz heute Nr. 212.) München: Kaiser.
Wootters, W. K.	1984.	'Time' Replaced by Quantum Correlations. *International Journal of Theoretical Physics* 23: 701–711.
	1986.	Is Spacetime a Book-Keeping Device for Quantum Correlations? In *Fundamental Questions in Quantum Mechanics*, eds. L. M. Roth, A. Inomata. New York: Gordon and Breach.
Young, D. A.	1982.	*Christianity and the Age of the Earth*. Grand Rapids: Zondervan.
Yourgrau, W., A. D. Breck, eds.	1977.	*Cosmology, History, and Theology*. New York: Plenum Press.
Zanstra, H.	1968.	Is Religion Refuted by Astronomy? *Vistas in Astronomy* 10: 1–21.
Zel'dovich, Y. B.	1981.	The Birth of a Closed Universe and the Anthropogenetic Principle. *Soviet Astronomy Letters* 7: 322–23.
	1982.	Spontaneous Birth of the Closed Universe and the Anthropic Principle. In *Astrophysical Cosmology: Proceedings of the study week on cosmology and fundamental physics*, eds. H. A. Brück, G. V. Coyne, M. S. Longair. Vatican: Pontificia Academia Scientiarum.
Zel'dovich, Y. B., L. P. Grishchuk.	1984.	Structure and Future of the 'New' Universe. *Monthly Notices of the Royal Astronomical Society* 207: 23P–28P.
Zel'dovich, Y. B., A. A. Starobinsky.	1984.	Quantum Creation of a Universe with Nontrivial Topology. *Soviet Astronomy Letters* 10: 135–37.

INDEX